institute of
financial services

D1477003

Bank Treasury Management

Vincent Baritsch

Institute of Financial Services
IFS House
4-9 Burgate Lane
Canterbury
Kent
CT1 2XJ

T   01227 818649
F   01227 479641
E   editorial@ifslearning.com

Institute of Financial Services publications are published by The Chartered Institute of Bankers, a non-profit making registered educational charity.

Typeset by Kevin O'Connor
Printed by Antony Rowe Ltd, Wiltshire

ISBN 0-85297-697-6

ifs **institute of financial services**

Bank Treasury Management

Contents

One

The functions of a bank's treasury

Objectives

This chapter will cover the following topics:

- ◆ function of bank's treasury;
- ◆ front-office;
- ◆ back-office.

1.1   Introduction

The underlying activity of bank treasury functions is best understood by looking at non-financial companies, where the distinction between the activities of the corporate treasury function and the rest of the company is relatively straightforward. Admittedly this is a simplification, but one that is helpful to look at the scope of treasury activities.

A corporate treasury function will deal with the management of the company's funds, be it the raising of equity capital, working capital or investing surplus funds. It also has to ensure that funds are available when they are needed to support the main business. Its role is therefore a key head office function that enables the business managers to focus on their own areas of expertise, be it, for example, the sales department or the manufacturing plants. Whether such a company has a separate treasury function or whether this is incorporated into their finance department does not change the nature of the underlying activity. The key is that it is a function that supports the main business activity. It thus attempts to improve the net worth of the company by managing its funds in the most appropriate manner.

The same applies to a bank's treasury function. The only difference is that most banking activities directly deal with money and thus the grey area between what is clearly a treasury activity and what is not, will remain large. It is this grey area which explains why there is such variety between the roles that treasury functions are given in different banks. Nevertheless the underlying objective remains to improve business performance and increase the net worth of each bank.

Increasing the net worth will require detailed knowledge of a variety of areas. Of prime importance will be the overall business strategy, which will set the framework that drives the treasury function. The framework will be unique to every bank. The syllabus for Bank Treasury Management covers the more general matters that bank treasury managers will need to have detailed knowledge of:

- ◆ Controls over dealing operations: middle office, internal audit and compliance;
- ◆ How to manage balance-sheet exposures (funding, liquidity and cash management);
- ◆ Risk management principles for market, operational and credit risks;
- ◆ Regulatory requirement and capital adequacy;
- ◆ Functions and characteristics of financial markets, including offshore financial centres;
- ◆ Financial products, practice and procedures (products reviewed are money, foreign exchange and money market instruments, bonds and derivatives).

The study text begins with a review of the risk management structures that are common to banks and how these relate to the management of bank's own balance-sheet exposures. This is followed by a review of the risks faced by banks and how these are managed in practice. The risks covered will fall under the headings of liquidity, interest rate, foreign exchange and settlement risk. It will also consider market risk, credit risk and operational risk. The text will then turn to the domestic and international regulatory structures that complement risk management standards. In the UK the Financial Services Authority (FSA) deals with domestic practice. It has to take account of international developments, such as those driven by the Basel Committee on Banking Supervision. Directives agreed by the European Union also increasingly influence financial regulation. Although supervision and regulation are often seen as being slightly different, the concept of a unified regulator, such as the FSA, has blurred the distinction. Originally the term regulation referred more to a set of rules, with the regulatory body ensuring compliance with these rules. In contrast, supervision tends to refer to ongoing supervision based on high-level principles. This textbook will use the terms synonymously. Readers should be aware that regulation is a rapidly developing field internationally, especially within the EU, where attempts at harmonizing standards are constantly progressing. Readers should therefore pay particular attention to the journals and web sites on the recommended reading list to ensure that their knowledge is up to date. A general review of the functions and characteristics of financial markets, including the use of offshore financial centres, follows the chapters on regulation.

The textbook will then turn to products that are available to treasury staff for their risk management activities. Particular areas of interest for this course are money and foreign exchange markets. The practices and procedures relating to the various types of financial instruments will be reviewed. Finally, the use of derivatives will be described, as these have taken on an increasing importance in the risk management activities of banks. Candidates should be aware that they are expected to be able to undertake and explain basic calculations concerning bonds, interest rates, spot and forward foreign exchange contracts and the derivative products covered by the syllabus.

1.2 Development of treasury function

Increasing net worth initially meant that treasury function had to ensure effective cash and liquidity management. They needed to ensure sufficient cash was available for business transactions and that available funds were invested to ensure that the bank remained liquid. To meet these goals of managing firm's liquidity, treasury functions need the ability to determine what the actual exposures are. This in turn requires the ability to monitor changes on an on-going basis and to some extent the need to control the activities of other business areas to ensure these do not endanger the treasury functions remit. For example, a treasury function will need to know when, and in what currency, large payments are due to avoid a potential default when a payment demand is made.

The emergence of more complex bank treasury management and new approaches to risk management were driven by changes in the competitive environment faced by banks. The nature of international banking changed significantly during the early 1970s. Previously interest rates and exchange rates were very much influenced by governments, leaving little room for competition between banks. The ensuing increase in volatility of stock markets, interest rates and exchange rates meant new vulnerabilities and increased scope for real competition. Exchange rates became more volatile after the breakdown in the early 1970s of the Bretton Woods system of fixed exchange rates. During its existence, the European Exchange Rate Mechanism (ERM) also saw significant changes in exchange rates, often as a result of devaluations. Significant falls in the value of sterling and the Italian lira in September 1992 were good examples.

Interest rates also fluctuated significantly over the period. The inflationary period following the oil shocks in the 1970s and inflationary monetary policy drove interest rates to very high levels in most developed countries in the mid-1970s. They then tended to drop, only to rise again subsequently. UK interest rates increased significantly after sterling's ejection from the ERM and still remain higher than in the Eurozone. The US has seen several interest rate cycles. In a number of cases, inappropriate management of this interest rate risk has lead to bank defaults.

Stock market volatility was also a feature of the new environment faced by banks. High inflation in the 1970s lead to stock prices increasing significantly, only to fall again subsequently. Another rise was followed by the stock market crash in 1987. The long period of stock market growth in the 1990s ended with a slow decline from 2000 onwards. This volatility affected banks with proprietary trading units, as well as indirectly via the damage the volatility created for their borrowers.

Detailed laws setting out what banks were allowed to do reduced the scope for competition prior to the 1970s. This began to change when governments relaxed their close control. Similarly, the slow relaxation of previously tight regulation of banking activities led to growth opportunities and created more competition. At the same time, this created new risks that needed managing. The UK small banks crisis in the early 1990s was an example of the effects of liberalization. Many other countries, such as Sweden and Norway, have had similar examples, where poorly managed market liberalization subsequently lead to banking crisis.

The development of the banks' internal treasury functions as key departments was a response to these developments. Their increased importance was made possible by two concurrent developments. On one side, risk management techniques began to be developed to provide competitive advantages to those banks embracing them. At the same time, new products evolved to facilitate active risk management. Currently we are seeing the development of credit derivatives to manage credit risk. The 1990s saw increased levels of securitizations, while the rise of options and futures during the 1980s was another example of products that significantly enhanced treasurers' ability to actively manage their bank's books.

These developments were of course helped by the changes in technology. The first PCs only appeared in the early 1980s and processing power and memory capacity has increased beyond what was foreseeable at the time. This in turn improved the ability to communicate; the evolution of the Internet is just one of the examples of this revolution. For treasury functions, the facilitation in terms of both communication and the ability to calculate the risks of complex products means that treasury functions are unrecognizable from what they used to be.

1.3   The remit of treasury functions

Finance theory suggests that high returns can only be achieved at the expense of taking higher risks. Thus, a bank with a high-risk appetite also faces potentially higher levels of losses. Such a high-risk appetite would be exhibited if a bank invested spare cash in high-yield bonds, rather than UK gilts. Assuming that an institution has decided in favour of a low-risk appetite, then it will be up to the treasury function to buy low-risk investment products. This is the dealing and settlement role of a treasury function. Clearly, in large institutions, the governing body will only be able to give broad guidance, with the instruments that best fit the broad guidance being decided at the level of the treasury function. The function will thus require an excellent knowledge of the financial instruments available in the market.

A treasury function can thus be seen as the function that implements and executes the decisions taken by the company's governing body, most often the Board of Directors or an Executive Committee of a bank. This senior committee will have set the general business strategy of the bank, the mix of activities and risk parameters for the execution of these activities. In larger organizations, the more detailed formulation of these will have been delegated to sub-committees, such as an Asset and Liability Management Committee that exists in many financial institutions. At the same time, the high-level committee will also need assurances that its decisions are implemented correctly and that they are appropriate given the constraints of external market developments. It will also need to advise on the trade-offs between various business activities.

This last role sees bank treasury management as being an exercise of portfolio management. A bank's balance-sheet can be seen as a large portfolio of investments. To determine how such a portfolio is invested, the bank's governing body will not only need underlying research, but also detailed information on the positions within this portfolio. This monitoring function, and its extension to risk management, forms an increasingly important part of bank treasury management. In practice, however, such portfolio management requires the involvement of a variety of functions, which will be located differently within each bank. Irrespective of specific arrangements, the competitive environment banks face means that each bank needs a function that can ensure the general risk appetite relating to balance-sheet exposure expressed by its governing board is implemented and adequately controlled.

Thus, the execution function of a treasury area, ie its dealing and settlement role, cannot be undertaken in isolation of the risk management functions that banks require. Although risk management and treasury activities are often split into different areas for the sake of systems and controls, the two should always be considered together to ensure the bank's net worth is maximized.

Let us leave aside the wider risk management issues for the time being and look at the dealing and settlement role of a treasury unit. For the avoidance of doubt, it should be pointed out that treasury activities are conceptually very different from proprietary trading functions. Proprietary trading units are departments that utilize the bank's funds to trade actively in such areas as bond and equity markets. While a treasury function supports and facilitates the running of the bank in general, proprietary trading is more akin to other business units, such as retail banking or international trade finance. Business units will have been given a specific capital allocation to achieve a given profit target. Thus, a proprietary trading unit is more comparable to a hedge fund, only interested in absolute returns, without having to have regard to wider strategic issues.

Despite these conceptual differences, the trading activities of both treasury functions and proprietary trading units share many similarities. For example, both require dealing desks and settlement departments. Indeed, in many banks, the two utilize the same systems, as the instruments traded are often similar. Furthermore, systems and controls that apply to trading operations are often the same, particularly as it does make business sense to combine similar back-office activities. It is thus not surprising that in many banks proprietary trading and treasury management are undertaken within the same department. This does, however, raise control issues, which we will look at later in this text.

In practice, many banks only treat their equity and bond trading as proprietary trading units. These activities tend to be less driven by risk management aspects and therefore can be separated more easily into clearly defined business units. In contrast, it is almost impossible to distinguish between those money market or currency dealings that are related to risk management and those own account trades that are not related to risk management. Indeed, one could argue that they are almost always related to risk management. This results in the common practice of incorporating all currency and money market dealing into the treasury function, independent of the conceptual differences between those activities driven by risk management and those that are not. Such arrangements make sense where a treasury function is mainly seen as having to ensure asset and liability management. This in short requires the management of liquidity by ensuring that sufficient funds are available for other business activities, and ensuring those funds that are not required immediately are utilized to maximize returns. On that basis, the dealing activities of treasury functions will deal with ensuring the liquidity and cash management, both in domestic currency, foreign and potentially eurocurrency markets, support and improve the bank's net worth.

We have already seen that international banking has experienced a marked increase in the level of competition. The response to these pressures has necessitated the examination of the ways of conducting business in order to optimize returns. As the raw material of banking is money, this money must be generated at the lowest funding cost. Operational effectiveness at the lending and investment front can become incidental if the cost of funds is too high to create an acceptable margin, particularly in the modern competitive environment.

Different subsidiaries may have completely different treasury operations, which may be a matter of well thought out policy or may hide an underlying structural defect in the parent's overall operations. It takes a considerable skill to make the best judgment on how the banking operations are structured and managed. Consideration must be given to the legal and tax situations in overseas operations, the need to meet local regulations with some level of flexibility, and the need to meet local service requirements. Opportunities to rationalize operations require a great deal of short-term investment for a long-term payback, and this may not always be a feasible or popular proposition.

1.4   Front-office activities

Dealers, as dealmakers, will seek to conclude transactions, but products must be priced in order to generate the necessary level of margin. Often the ultimate level of profit will be unknown until the deal has run its course, defaulted, or realized any of the risks underlying the transaction. For example, depending on interest rate and foreign exchange risk, the final profit could be higher or lower than priced initially.

Throughout the dealing day the bank needs to optimize its cashflows in order to ensure that shortfalls are fully funded, and any surpluses are invested in order to maximize its returns. These activities can be placed under the heading 'cash management'. Doing the deal is classed as ' front-office', whereas the reconciliation of payments is 'back-office'. Dealers and back-office managers have to forecast activity in order to ensure prudence is being applied in its trading activities and that all liabilities can be met in the course of the trading day or week.

A dealer will input the deal to be electronically transferred to the back-office for processing. Historically, the dealer wrote the details of the deal on a slip of paper, which was later input into the system by the back-office. In either case, the transactions delivered from the dealing room will be processed alongside all the other different forms of balance-sheet activity taking place.

We have already noted that an important treasury function is to manage the cashflows effectively by forecasting future cashflows, taking into account, for example, loan commitments, the maturity of these loans, the maturity of deposits and currency dealing, plus the likely withdrawals on the retail deposits side of the bank's business. The bank will normally use liquidity maturity ladders based on information related to projected movements on all of the above, in order to assess their liquidity position.

A good treasury function will be expected to be innovative in its approach to maximizing profitability by loan types and in various geographical markets and across client bases. In order to fund these activities more profitably, the bank's senior management will expect the treasury team to develop new ways of attracting the cheapest funds. In the competitive markets in which the banks now operate, these funding costs are key, as is the need to maximize the flow of income. More recently there has been a trend towards charging fees for various services around loan advances and credit lines, securities, and new financial instruments. This off-balance-sheet income is very attractive for treasury managers who will often be the party to encourage their use.

In the same way that banks must take care not to concentrate their loan book geographically or by client or industrial sector, similar considerations arise when looking at deposits. If the source of funds is equally concentrated, then the bank is vulnerable to the removal of these funds, and will need to seek out new funds in the future. Overconcentration on short-term interbank funding was one of the reasons for the difficulties experienced by Continental Illinois in the US in the 1980s, precipitating its collapse. By maintaining a portfolio of deposit sources the bank reduces the 'concentration risk' that could sit alongside the other risks banks face.

In order to have the ability to make loans for periods in excess of one year, extending into the medium and long term, it is necessary for the bank to attract deposits on a longer-term basis. A bank will need to exercise a great deal of prudence in matching assets and liabilities, while, at the same time, taking the necessary steps to maintain confidence in the bank. In turn this will help to promote stability in deposit levels. But by definition, the short-term funds sought and attracted are not in themselves matched to the bank's asset portfolio.

The same situation arises in investment portfolios as well as in loan portfolios. Inevitably, investment portfolio lifespans will exceed the funding that lies behind them, whereas at the other end of the spectrum trading portfolios do require short-term funds for short-term transactions. Three-month money would normally be the maximum funding requirement for engaging in short-term trading.

One of the bank's objectives therefore will be to have depositors roll over their money held on deposit, so that short-term deposits effectively become medium-term funds for the bank. The higher the proportion of the funds being rolled over, the more likely it is that the banks can respond to changes in market conditions. The extent to which the bank is prepared to mismatch its assets and liabilities is another consideration for senior management on a day-by-day, period-by-period basis, but inevitably maturity transformation will form part of that policy. Ensuring that a bank can cope with this maturity transformation role is a key area of treasury functions.

1.5   Back-office activities

Once a deal has been done in the front-office, it will need to be cleared and settled. This is generally seen as the role of the back-office.

Clearing covers all the activities prior to settlement such as trade comparison and matching, trade netting, securities messages and numbering and, if applicable, securities lending. The first part of the clearing process is trade comparison and matching. This involves confirmation between the counterparties that a deal has been done and that the details of the deal are the same on both sides. A next step may involve netting of trades. During the course of a trading day, a bank may deposit $50 million in the interbank market with a specific counterparty. Later in the day, it may borrow $30 million from the same counterparty, for example if it had an unexpected outflow of funds. This means that at the end of the day the treasury function may, depending on contract, only have to transfer the difference of $20 million, rather than transferring the full $50 million and having to await receipt of the second deal.

Settlement deals with the actual transfer of ownership in exchange for cash or security and the subsequent confirmation that the transfer has taken place. Although back-office activities are sometimes seen as less glamorous than front-office activities, this crucial area needs robust systems and controls. Otherwise, a bank may face the potential risk of being unable to settle its respective outstandings, a situation that can arise for reasons of fraud, poor management, exceptional circumstances and systems failure.

Poor management can create the inability to process payments and reconcile transactions on time. On days of heavy dealing, this can present management with a real problem, but under normal circumstances contingencies will be built in. There are very extreme examples where it can be near impossible to keep up the sheer volumes, as demonstrated by the London Big Bang in 1986, when the shortage of experienced settlement staff in London was exposed by the frenzied trading activity taking place. Backlogs were then in need of funding, often involving very large amounts of money.

A fraud that was nearly perpetrated on Hill Samuel demonstrates the type of settlement risk. Prior to detection, the bank risked the loss of millions through the attempt to access the EUCLID system for transferring Eurobonds. Another example was when the Bank of New York had to borrow $24 billion from the Federal Reserve in overnight funds in 1985 in order to overcome the problems of being unable to settle outstandings due to the inadequate testing of a new system, which subsequently broke down.

Two

Prudential controls

Objectives

This chapter will cover the following topics:

- ◆ risk management;
- ◆ internal audit;
- ◆ compliance.

2.1   Risk management

Risk management always has been at the heart of treasury management, and its scope has increased significantly in recent years. Liquidity could never be appropriately managed without clear knowledge about the underlying business to which it had to provide liquidity. In addition to this strategic knowledge, a treasurer always needed to have the ability to identify the underlying position of the business and to assess the risks this posed to the ability to manage liquidity. Furthermore, treasuries needed the ability to monitor and control to ensure that the information on which dealing decisions were based was accurate. Operational controls to ensure that the treasury function did not inadvertently threaten the rest of the organization were part of this control function.

Yet, risk management standards have become more sophisticated as a result of the environmental challenges already mentioned. It has increasingly become clear that risk management works most effectively when it takes a firm-wide approach. This in turn means that all risks across a bank have to be managed together, for example requiring similar reporting structures. As a result, risk management has increasingly become a function in its own right, and in many cases is no longer located within treasury areas.

The need to look at risks in a holistic manner became evident as a result of a number of bank failures. The management of credit risk has always been at the core of banking. Consequently, most banks already had sophisticated approaches to assess borrower's ability to repay loans. Readers may already have reviewed lending practices in other parts of their studies, for example International Trade Finance or Business Lending. What did, however, change was that banks began to realize that even good credit risk management was not sufficient to ensure survival. We have already seen that market risk grew as a result of the increased volatility in interest rates, exchange rates and asset prices. The increased awareness of operational risk as a risk that needed managing, rather than only controlling, reinforced this trend.

Bankhaus Herstatt provides a good example of these risk interdependencies. This German bank is widely known for having shown that settlement risk, a form of credit risk, needed to be taken seriously. Indeed settlement risk is sometimes known as Herstatt risk. Bankhaus Herstatt was closed by German regulators before it could deliver the US dollar transactions it was committed to pay under its foreign exchange dealings. Other banks had, however, delivered on their side of the bargain on the European currencies, thus leaving them with large losses. But which risk brought Bankhaus Herstatt down? The answer must be several. Market risk, ie the adverse movement of exchange rates, certainly played a key role. At the same time, operational risk mismanagement, which allowed the bank's chief dealer to take positions far in excess of what it could manage played just as important a role.

Effective risk management will need to have a high level committee, such as a board of directors, to determine the strategic business plan of the organization. This in turn ought to clarify the risk appetite of the organization, which will set the framework for the risk management approach. In this context, it is important to realize that risk management is not about eliminating all risk. It is about choosing which risks can be undertaken, what trade-offs should be accepted between different risks and what losses the organization will be willing to incur. Controls are important to ensure that only those risks are taken on that fit in with the approved strategy.

In order to implement its strategy an organization will require a monitoring and control system to provide relevant management information. The information will be needed to provide the inputs necessary to take the right decisions. It will also be needed as a feedback mechanism to ensure decisions have been implemented correctly, and, assuming that they have been implemented correctly, to monitor that the decisions taken were the right ones. This is the control and monitoring role of risk management. Treasury functions, being so close to the heart of a bank's activities, will have an important role to play. It is therefore not uncommon that such a monitoring and control function is often included directly within a treasury function itself, where it is often known as the middle office. A recent trend within banks is, however, to have a separate risk management function to fulfil this role across the organization, with a middle office within a treasury area having a dual reporting line.

Independently of where risk management is located within a bank, it will have to report on the risks facing the institution and the potential options available to the high level committee that decided upon the risk management framework. As such, risk management will have to quantify the liquidity, interest rate and other risks facing the bank. To do so it will have to obtain input from other business units of the risks being run. For example, branches may create different exposures by selling mortgages or by selling overdrafts. The former will require long-term funding, while overdrafts may mean a different liquidity management policy. To provide an analysis of the risks being run will also require economic forecasts, be it the likely movement of interest rates, or the likely probability of borrowers defaulting on their obligations.

There is a further dimension to this. Let us assume that a strategic position has been taken. There is then also a need to ensure that business units will not run counter to that decision, or, if the market environment forces change, to bring this to the attention of the relevant internal decision makers and particularly the board. Risk management thus has a role of channelling information between the board and business units. The communication will need to flow upwards when reporting back on risk exposures and downwards when enforcing strategic decisions.

It is clear that such a role is a key central function of an institution, which requires cross-functional awareness of all the activities undertaken by banks. Especially if such a risk management role is organized as a separate unit, it will require particular close liaison with the treasury, finance and compliance functions.

2.1.1   Risk management principles

Risk management has many meanings and implementation of it differs significantly between banks, but there are some broad principles on which most can agree. The principles described here are mainly derived from those promulgated by the Basel Committee of Banking Supervision. Generally referred to as the Basel Committee, it has developed risk management standards for several of the key risks faced by banks. The Basel Committee is a forum enabling supervisors to discuss and set standards for internationally active banks. They are then incorporated into local supervision by supervisors around the globe. The role and the function of the Basel Committee will be looked at in more detail in later units. The main risk management principles are briefly introduced below.

Establishing an appropriate risk management environment

Principles under this heading state that the board of directors should have the responsibility of approving the strategy appropriate for the risks undertaken by the institution. Senior management should have responsibility for implementation of the strategy and develop the systems needed for implementation. The strategy should be applied across the whole of the organization and needs to be reviewed on a regular basis.

Identification, assessment, monitoring and control

Banks should develop appropriate systems that allow them to identify, assess, monitor and control the risks they run. In relation to credit risk management, this means that banks should, for example, establish overall credit limits at the level of individual borrowers and counterparties. There should be clear processes for new business and existing business. Again, in relation to credit risk, there should be systems in place ensuring the ongoing administration of bank's portfolios, including the trading book and off-balance-sheet activities.

Ensuring adequate controls

Banks should establish a system of independent reviews of how the strategy decided upon by the board has been implemented. Such reviews should be communicated directly to the board of directors and senior management to reduce conflicts of interests.

Business continuity

Banks should have in place contingency and business continuity plans to ensure their ability to operate on an ongoing basis and limit losses in the event of severe business disruption.

Readers interested in the subject may wish to look at the website of the Basel Committee at www.bis.org. The site contains the various risk management papers issued by the Basel Committee, the key ones being:

- ♦ Sound Practices for the Management and Supervision of Operational Risk
- ♦ Principles for the Management of Credit Risk
- ♦ Sound Practices for Managing Liquidity in Banking Organizations
- ♦ Principles for the Management of Interest-rate risk

Many of these principles are directly relevant to the UK financial services sector, as they have been incorporated into the FSA Handbook. The FSA Handbook is the set of rules and guidance issued by the UK banking regulator, the Financial Services Authority (FSA). In particular, Principle 3 of the FSA's principles for businesses is of relevance, as it states that an authorized firm must 'take reasonable care to organize and control its affairs responsibly and effectively, with adequate risk management systems'. The principle is amplified in several other parts of the Handbook and especially in the Systems and Controls Chapter of the FSA Handbook.

2.1.2   Risk management committees

In order to meet the above principles, various committees have evolved within banks that deal with different aspects of risk management. The same committees often also serve to ensure that the banks meet generally accepted corporate governance principles by, for example, providing audit trails of how decisions have been agreed. Meetings of these committees are thus usually minuted.

Board of directors

We have already seen the key role of the board of directors in determining strategy. Technically only companies with limited liability will have boards of directors. In practice, however, every organization will have a committee fulfilling the role of a board of directors. With the increasing complexity in companies' business, many boards have felt the need to delegate some of their responsibilities and the following committees are common in many banking organizations. Nevertheless, one should bear in mind that the terms of reference of these sub-committees will be determined by the full board and that these sub-committees remain responsible to the board.

The Executive Committee is such a sub-committee, which tends to exclude non-executive directors. The aim is that day-to-day decisions can be taken at the highest level of the organization, without creating the difficulty of involving non-executive directors, who almost by definition do not work full-time within the organization.

Another board sub-committee that has gained increased importance in risk management is the Audit Committee. It tends to be chaired by a non-executive director with a financial background. Its role tends to focus on financial and compliance issues. It tends to review internal audit reports and track corrective actions. It will also discuss external audits in detail. In many organizations, it will also look at compliance reports and report on these to the board. In particular, its role relating to internal audit and compliance means that risk management issues will be a key are of concern to audit committees.

Asset and liability management committee

Often boards have delegated the setting of the general risk appetite relating to balance-sheet exposure to a specially formed Asset Liability Management Committee, generally referred to as ALCO. A mission statement for an ALCO could read as follows:

'The asset/liability management function involves, planning, direction and controlling the flow, level, mix, cost and yield of the consolidated funds of the corporation. These responsibilities are interwoven with the overall objectives of achieving the corporation's financial goals and controlling financial risks.'

Thus ALCO will set the framework for treasury activities, in line with the principles determined by the board of directors. Members are likely to be senior risk management officers, the bank's treasurer and representatives of other key business areas. Depending on the size of the organization, it is usual to have the director responsible for the treasury function participate in its deliberations.

Credit committee

Credit committees are not directly relevant to this syllabus, but they perform an essential risk management role. As indicated previously credit risk is a key risk to banks, which needs careful management. It is the credit committee's role to ensure that credit strategies are adhered to. It will also have the role of ensuring that individual loans meet with the individual limits that have been set to manage credit risk. Similar committees exist for other risks such as operational risk.

2.1.3 Internal controls over dealing operations

The dealing function can potentially create very large risk exposures, yet it is an area that requires a great deal of initiative and delegated authority on the part of the dealer. It is therefore important to control the function without suppressing the talent of the profit-generating traders. The initiative levels shown by the typical dealer can lead to them crossing the line where the rules are not enforced rigorously. Similarly, overbearing controls can affect the individual's ability to optimize the use of their skills, while the temptation to take an extreme arm's length approach can result in regret. The senior managers involved in overseeing Barings Singapore office have shown great regret for their inability to control the dealings of this overseas operation. The same is true for Allfirst Bank, at that time a US subsidiary of Allied Irish Bank. In 2002, a dealer was found to have incurred a $691 million loss as a result of lax controls. Senior management was not found to have any involvement in the fraud, but their failure to act in the interests of the bank and their trust in the dealing operations of one trader, in particular, clearly demonstrates the laxity of controls that enabled the trader to accumulate these losses.

Those treasury staff involved in controlling dealing tend to be from a trading background themselves, this being an almost essential prerequisite given the complexities of international finance. It is unlikely that this level of technical expertise could be acquired without some form of involvement with dealing operations. Commonly employed approaches to the control of dealing operations are surprise visits by representatives of Head Office treasury in order to assess the maintenance of adequate control levels and audits, and review by internal auditors and inspection teams. The issue of prudential control is examined further in later chapters.

Controls need to operate at a number of levels. We have already seen some of the risk management controls that must be established to ensure that treasury functions meet the strategic role delegated to them. Central treasury function will also need to control local treasury functions for the sake of implementing the same systems and procedures. Another set of direct controls will exist over dealing activities, and will depend on the level of delegated authority. Delegated authority refers to dealing limits by product or by trader. Another level of controls will ensure separation between front and back-office functions. Let us now look at these types of controls separately.

The centralized treasury function, where there is a local treasury located in the local market, will have a major role revolving around the control of each of its business units, and the issue of risk exposure management. It will formulate policy and develop the procedures to be followed by each of the dealing operations. It is very common for centralized treasury functions to put their own man in at the local level in order to exercise a measure of control in an environment of trust in the integrity and ability of those in the driving seat. This was the case at Allfirst Bank, where the treasurer was sent over by the central function in Dublin. Ultimately he was not able to maintain the high standards that the central function had set. At the same time, the head office was never aware, until the losses came to light, that their representative did not meet the expectations head office had of him.

More generally, the relationship with a centralized function revolves around the arm's length management of risk and the control of group liabilities and dealing operations. Policy directives also come from the centre on general strategy and on such matters as the treatment of profits. Profits may be subject to local regulations, which can impact on their retention and their distribution. This can provide an incentive to locate capital in foreign subsidiaries. In other countries, capital injections from Head Office may also be subject to local rules, relating to the scale of operations in the local market. In the case of a branch, we are referring to quasi capital under the control of the local treasury or the centralized treasury. There will also be a high degree of contact with the internal auditor and with local and central management relating to the controls, some of which are required in law and others that are part of prudent management. In order to develop a compromise between centralization and the benefits of dealing locally one common practice is to operate an internal system of transfer pricing which sets the price of money to the business unit, while the local operation continues to retain a high degree of freedom to act.

Controls also exist at the dealer or desk level. It is common to set hard limits to the size of deals that individual dealers can undertake. They may also be restricted in terms of types of products they can trade. Other limits will relate to intra-day exposures and the size of open positions. In particular, the trading of complex products, such as options, should only be allowed after a dealer has proven their skills on more standard products. Other banks will introduce stop-loss limits, which, when broken, will force the dealer to close out his or her books. Another way of controlling positions will be to look at the Value at Risk (VaR) of each position, dealing desk or dealing room. We will look in more detail at VaR as a risk management tool when reviewing market risk in a later chapter. Credit risk, and, in particular, settlement risk, will also restrict dealing activities, as banks will not want to be over-exposed to any one counterparty. This is not only an issue in money market dealing, but also applies to foreign exchange transactions. These types of controls will often be enforced by a function known as middle office, whose role is to ensure adherence to the systems and controls put in place within the treasury organization.

Another level of controls will ensure separation between front-office and back-office functions. For example, dealers should not be allowed to initiate wire transfers. The same control concepts, such as separating duties and requiring dual approvals in order to reduce the opportunities for collusion, apply with both manual and electronic fund transfers. Back-offices also have an important role in checking dealing slips against the details provided by the counterparties to ensure that deals have in fact been agreed. Another key control exerted by back-office functions will be to obtain independent prices to ensure that the valuations used to determine dealers' daily profit and loss accounts accurately reflect current prices. It should also be their role to ensure that new products cannot be traded until the appropriate settlement channels have been set up. It should be a requirement, based on common sense, that no new product be approved until the back-office function has said that it can handle them. Back-offices will also be the physical location where records are kept and processed. Again, this is a control to minimize the opportunities for collusion between individuals to harm an institution.

In addition to these detailed controls, treasury functions should also be regularly reviewed by internal audit and, where appropriate, other compliance functions. Apart from adherence to internal procedures, these reviews should look at wider issues. They can often spot issues that are missed in the daily buzz of dealing activities. A good example is the need to check that a bank has deleted the signatures of employees who no longer have signing authority. PCs are often used by dealers to monitor their positions. Such reviews need to check that it is appropriate for the details to be held at that level, rather than a more central level, which may be more appropriate.

2.2   Internal audit

Internal audit functions have important control functions. Its role is generally to monitor the appropriateness and effectiveness of a firm's systems and controls. Internal audit will tend to review how other departments have delivered on their specific roles. Therefore it is important that internal audit functions have a reporting line directly to the board of directors or the audit committee in order to minimize the possibility of findings being suppressed or areas excluded from a review. It is therefore common for internal audit to report to an audit committee or an appropriate senior manager where the bank has no audit committee in place. In smaller banks, audit functions may sometimes be outsourced to an accountancy firm, but the bank would have to ensure that this is appropriate given the nature, scale and complexity of its business. In practice, it would be only the very smallest institutions that would be able to convince banking supervisors that their systems and controls are not undermined by the absence of an internal audit function.

This is reflected in The Institute of Internal Auditors definition of internal auditing:

> 'Internal auditing is an independent, objective assurance and consulting activity designed to add value and improve an organization's operations. It helps an organization accomplish its objectives by bringing a systematic, disciplined approach to evaluate and improve the effectiveness of risk management, control, and governance processes.'

As such, the output of internal auditing is mainly addressed to those that hold ultimate responsibility for the company, such as the board of directors or its equivalent.

Internal auditors provide this function by examining and evaluating the adequacy and effectiveness of the internal control systems. This tends to be done by reviewing the application and effectiveness of risk management procedures and risk assessment methodologies. As these rely on management and financial information systems, these will be included in reviews. Thus, the role extends to ensuring the accuracy and reliability of the accounting records and financial reports. Nevertheless, such reviews would not extend to the auditing of the bank's financial statements. This would be the sole responsibility of the bank's external auditors, the role of internal audit in this area being limited to supporting the external auditors.

Other areas of concern to internal auditors will be the systems used to safeguarding assets. This would involve checking the reconciliations process and controls established over cash. As an extension of this, internal auditors also review the systems established to ensure compliance with legal and regulatory requirements, codes of conduct and the implementation of policies and procedures. This often involves the testing of both transactions and the functioning of specific internal control procedures. It would also involve the testing of the reliability and timeliness of the regulatory reporting. In banks where such activities fall under the remit of compliance functions, the role of internal audit will be restricted to auditing how the compliance function delivers on its objectives.

At a strategic level, internal auditors sometimes appraise the economy and efficiency of operations. In some banks, they are also used to review the allocation of capital in relation to the riskiness of operations. Similarly, it is common for internal auditors to carry out special reviews of areas that are of particular concern to senior managers. It is thus clear that the scope of internal audit is broad and includes such major areas as internal control systems, risk management procedures, financial information systems, testing of transactions and procedures, adherence to legal and regulatory requirements, testing of regulatory returns, and special investigations.

In order to meet such a broad scope, internal audit functions are increasingly using a risk-based approach. Thus, rather than having a rolling programme of examinations, the timetable for work would be a model which takes account of the riskiness of the underlying activity. The model itself, the input and output will be reviewed and agreed by the Audit Committee to ensure the independence of the internal audit function from other business units.

For treasury functions, the risk-based approach means that internal auditor's reviews have changed. Rather than utilizing a tick-box approach, reviews now focus on systems and controls, including adherence to procedures manuals. This development has been helped by the emergence of middle office functions, which tend to analyse trading data on a more frequent basis than internal auditors could ever do on a continuous basis. In combination with middle offices, compliance functions now focus on the adherence to rules. This again frees time for internal audit functions to take a more strategic approach to their work.

2.3   Compliance function

Banks increasingly use compliance functions to evaluate adherence to legal and regulatory requirements. In the UK, compliance functions are viewed by the FSA as a key internal control, which it would expect to be in place to ensure compliance with the FSA Handbook. Given its scope, compliance functions would monitor areas such as market abuse and money laundering, to name just a few areas.

As with audit functions, the FSA expects compliance functions to have clear reporting lines to senior management. This will require compliance staff to have adequate status within the firm. They will need to be given access to all files and records (even corporate finance where confidentiality is vital). Indeed a firm's management will be expected to prove that it has sufficiently resourced its compliance function to meet its objectives.

The FSA requires each authorized firm to appoint a compliance officer to act as the primary point of contact between the firm and the regulator. The compliance officer must derive sufficient status in the organization by being a partner or a director, or by reporting directly to one of the partners or directors. The FSA and its predecessor organizations have found that if compliance officers are at middle management level or below, they will not have access to sufficient information, nor can they command adequate resources to fulfil their duties effectively and advise a board member if there is a compliance risk to the business.

The compliance officer in a large organization may have a team of compliance staff to whom he delegates responsibility for specific sections of the rules, and which constitutes the compliance department or compliance function. The size and structure of this department or function varies with the size and complexity of the firm. Historically compliance functions tended to be fairly small. However, as the effects of regulation began to be felt through disciplinary procedures, adverse publicity and fines, compliance functions grew, sometimes out of all proportion to the size of the organization. Today many firms have delegated the responsibility for compliance to as many individuals as possible throughout the organization, so that the central compliance function is reduced to a minimum.

In larger organizations a compliance officer would head a department responsible for:

- interpreting the FSA rules for the company in line with the company's business strategy, goals and attitude to risk;
- using the interpreted rules to develop the company's compliance policy and plans;
- developing the company's compliance manuals and procedures;
- implementing the company's compliance monitoring plan;
- monitoring compliance with the company's plan;
- reporting on the findings of the compliance monitoring and remedying any weaknesses;
- measuring compliance effectiveness in the company;
- re-planning the company's compliance approach.

Like internal auditors, compliance officers are increasingly using risk-based approaches to focus their compliance work. To help planning, this is often recorded in a document known as a compliance plan. It will specify the action to be taken in the succeeding year to secure compliance with FSA rules, and will need to be reviewed regularly to take account of changes within the firm itself. This compliance plan should include the following:

- the compliance work to be undertaken by the firm in visiting its offices and branches;
- the individuals who will be responsible for it and carry it out;
- a detailed monitoring programme;
- details of the member's system for reporting and taking remedial action.

In general, companies tend to follow set procedures when conducting compliance visits to offices and branches by using standard working papers which set out the tasks of the annual monitoring programme. These are designed to identify and record rule breaches. Written reports are compiled from working papers completed on site and copied to the branch or office visited and to the head of monitoring who compiles summary reports for the compliance officer. Reports usually set out the evidence of each rule breached and the action that must be taken to comply in the future. Where resources allow, a follow-up visit is undertaken to the branch or office to check that remedial action has been implemented to ensure on-going compliance with the rules.

Three

Funding issues

Objectives

This chapter will cover the following topics:

- ◆ funding considerations;
- ◆ types of shares;
- ◆ retail funding;
- ◆ wholesale funding.

3.1   Introduction

In the previous chapter we saw that funding a bank's activities, and ensuring sufficient liquidity, is a, if not the, key aim of treasury functions. This chapter will revisit funding in more detail.

Funding relates to the liability side of a balance-sheet and the role of the treasury function will be to obtain the right mix between various types of deposits given to a bank by its customers and other market participants. Bringing the appropriate mix between equity and debt into the operation will be part of the difficulties of funding a banking business. Effective balance-sheet management will have to take a joint view of bank's assets and liabilities, funding being only one side of it. This chapter will not, however, look at the asset side, ie how these funds are re-invested. We will look at re-investment issues, such as credit and market risk, in later chapters.

The balance-sheet make up will determine the level of liquidity in the business. Managing liquidity is focused on maintaining the ability to fund increases in assets and meet obligations as they become due. This goes very much to the core of banking. Not only do banks need to be able to repay deposits on demand; liquidity problems in one bank can also create contagion. This is the technical term for the system-wide repercussions that one bank failure, or simple liquidity problem, can cause to the rest of the banking system. Such systemic risk, if it arises, could have a significant impact on the economic performance of countries and is thus seen as one of the rationales for banking supervision.

As a result of the risk of contagion treasury functions take liquidity management very seriously. The details of how liquidity is managed will depend on the size and complexity of a bank's activities but certain areas of importance are universally acknowledged. Monitoring and analysis of net funding requirements, diversification of funding sources, contingency planning and scenario testing are just some of these principles. Cash management is part of liquidity management, but given the importance of cash this chapter will also look at some specific issues relating to cash management.

Many of the exposures driving balance-sheet management may not be overtly obvious or revealed in any statutory accounts, which by their nature are historical and based on a fixed period. Instead they may exist on a daily basis due to the need to reconcile accounts on a continuous basis. The latent risks for banks lie as much in the short term as in the long term. A day is a long time in the trading activities of an international bank. Managing the assets and liabilities is about keeping the operation both solvent and sufficiently liquid to meet its commitments today, this week and beyond. The treasury function will in effect manage the bank's finances to achieve this. On a day-to-day basis, cash management is a priority and dealers have to account for the surpluses and shortfalls. They also need to ensure that surpluses are invested and shortfalls funded. Equally, liquidity has to be monitored and managed through a set of policies played out through daily practices and based on clearly defined procedures.

3.2 Funding considerations

The economic function of a bank is to intermediate between those that have funds available and those that require them for consumption or production. This generally tends to imply a maturity transformation, as most depositors will lend funds to banks on a short-term basis. However, for firms to invest funds effectively they will want to borrow on a much longer basis. Banks can achieve this transformation by managing how they fund their liabilities and ensuring that this is compatible with how they lend them out as assets. There are several ways to categorize funding: long-term funding versus short-term funding, wholesale versus retail funding. Determining the mix between these will be one of the key functions of the treasurer. The business strategy will to a large extent determine the size of funding required, as well as its maturity. However, once the overall strategy is agreed, the treasurer and his dealers will have some latitude in determining the details.

How a strategy will be implemented will depend on current market conditions. Market conditions, at least in relation to funding, are driven by the level of interest rates. The term structure of interest rates, otherwise known as the yield curve, is a graphical illustration of the cost of funds in relation to their maturity.

Figure 3.1: Normal yield curve

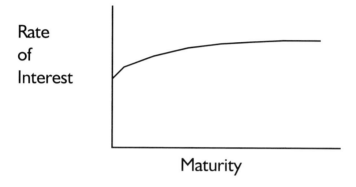

Under the conditions of a normal yield curve, as shown above, short-term interest rates will be lower than long-term interest rates. This is because, generally, lending long-term will require a higher risk premium than lending short-term. However, under certain market conditions a yield curve can also be inverted, meaning that it will be cheaper to fund activities long term. This can occur for example if a tight monetary policy is being run by the authorities to reduce inflation. The shape of the yield curve, and the interest cost this implies for funding at a given maturity, will thus have a significant impact on the decisions of dealers. Indeed they may trade the yield curve, which means taking positions that are expected to become profitable once the yield curve changes in line with the dealer's predictions.

Nevertheless the yield curve will not be the only driver for funding issues. The process of raising funds will also create costs, which will need to be taken into account. This cost will often depend on the type of products used to raise funds, be it the cost of consultants or the cost of marketing particular rates on retail deposits. Then there are the characteristics of the various funding methods, which will also strongly influence the decision-making process. For example, retail deposits may be less volatile than wholesale funding. On the other hand increasing retail deposits may be quite expensive if there is no appropriate branch network in existence. Other things the treasurer will have to take account of are the currency of the funding and the flexibility needed should markets or business strategy change. There is for example no need to issue 15-year bonds when the average mortgage maturity is only five years. Other determinants will be the capital requirements, both from a regulatory point of view and from a reputational/ratings point of view.

The future funding needs of the business will largely depend on the business strategy set by the board. The treasurer will implement this strategy. Another consideration will be how the strategy may change as a result of market development and what in-built flexibility this will require. Decisions on long-term funding and, in particular, equity issues will often involve areas outside of treasury functions, but the treasurer will be expected to be very much involved in the decision-making process given the impact it will have on the treasury function. The following subsections will look more closely at some of the main product-related issues, which will impinge on funding decisions.

3.2.1 Ordinary shares

Equity capital is finance raised through shareholders and although there may be a secondary market, or stock market, in the trading of its shares, ordinary share capital is not normally repayable. For the purpose of raising equity capital, banks are little different from other limited liability commercial organizations. Interest is not paid on this finance although shareholders expect a return on their money through either dividends based on the profits of the bank or through the increase in share prices as a result of retained earnings and future expectations of profit. Because ordinary shares are not repayable and shareholders are the last ones to be repaid in case of insolvency (if at all), equity is generally viewed as being a relatively expensive form of finance.

However, the level of equity will also determine the credit rating of the bank itself and therefore the interest cost that the bank will face on its other sources of funding. This means that the reduced funding cost gained from low equity levels would instead have to be spent on higher interest cost of debt financing. Most practitioners believe that there is an ideal debt/equity mix and the treasurer will be expected to input into the determination of where it lies.

It is in the nature of the industry that banks are more highly geared than other commercial companies, making the prudential control, supported by supervisory authorities, even more important. This is because traditional banking is based on taking deposits and these deposits should be viewed as debts that a bank owes to its depositors. The term that is used to describe the equity base required is 'capital adequacy', with the capital ratio (ratio of the bank's primary capital to a weighted value of assets) being one of the bank's most important prudential ratios. The term 'capital adequacy' is also used to describe the capital requirements that banking supervisors impose on the banks under their respective jurisdiction. We will look at the capital adequacy requirements in more detail in a later chapter.

But over and above the regulatory requirements the bank will decide how much shareholders' money it requires to support its operations, including its potential losses. This is generally referred to as the economic capital a bank needs. As with all companies, the gearing ratio, or proportion of debt to equity, is important because debt is repayable and a number of loss-making periods will result in the institution being unable to sustain its operations. This will be a key factor in the credit rating each bank will be given.

It is also worth noting that the process of issuing equity is itself quite expensive, especially for banks that are listed on a stock exchange. For banks that are not listed on stock markets issuing new equity capital may not even be an option, existing shareholders may not be able to fund an increase in capital and issuing it to others may involve an unwanted change in ownership structure. Although this syllabus does not look at the detailed process of issuing shares, suffice it to say that the cost of compliance, advisers, publicity, management time and other connected costs ensures that equity issuance is not undertaken very lightly. Instead many banks prefer to bolster their equity base by retaining earned profits, rather than returning it to shareholders via dividends.

3.2.2 Other forms of capital

There are other types of shares that are somewhat in between ordinary shares and debt financing. Preference shares, for example, rank above ordinary shares and often provide fixed dividends. In return holders may not be able to vote at AGMs and are therefore not technically owners of the company. Some years ago perpetual bonds were a common way of raising finance. Because these were not repayable they had many features in common with ordinary shares, even though they paid either fixed or variable interest to holders.

Subordinated debt – loans that rank for repayment and interest behind other loans – are also more akin to equity than to loans. Up to limits provided by supervisors subordinated loans may therefore be treated as capital for capital adequacy purposes. They exist in a variety of maturities, although they will need to have a maturity of at least five years to be treated as capital for regulatory purposes. Large issues are often intended for the wholesale markets, but other subordinated debt may be issued directly to retail clients. Although this is rare within the UK market, subordinated debt sales to retail investors is more common in many other countries. Many of the large issues are actively traded on secondary markets, while many smaller issues are not rated and have no active secondary market.

From a treasurer's point of view, subordinated loans are a very efficient way of influencing capital ratios, both from an economic and regulatory perspective. In practice a more important role of subordinated term debt may be to raise additional working capital. Subordinated loans can be relatively straightforward to issue and do not involve the costs generally associated with shares. Furthermore, given that the generic term subordinated loans covers such a wide range of instruments from complex bond issues to simple loan agreements, a treasurer ought to be able to find the appropriate instrument for each objective. Some of these instruments, which depending on structure may or may not fall under the categorization of subordinated debt, will be considered in more detail in the later chapters.

3.2.3 Asset sales and securitization

Other ways of raising funds may be to sell assets, such as loans, to other market participants. Asset sales may occur as a result of a risk management decision to change the asset mix or to raise cash in difficult trading conditions. However, the market for securitization shows that it is often part of the larger business strategy to accumulate assets only to repackage them subsequently for sale to other market participants.

Securitizations are broadly the bundling of types of assets into special purpose vehicles. The special purpose vehicle will then refinance its assets by selling securities into the market. Common securitizations are for credit card debts and mortgages, but bounds in this market are only set by the imagination of the treasury involved. Benefits for the original lender will mainly be to remove the asset from its balance-sheet, thus freeing resources for new business activities. This is an attractive option to manage both liquidity and risk exposures. Moreover assets can often be sold off at a higher value than they had when they were first taken on the bank's book. Other benefits of securitization may be that the bank can increase its access to market funding, while reducing reliance on retail funding. By enabling risky assets to be taken completely off the balance-sheet and thus reduce its gearing ratio, securitizations can also be used by a bank's management to improve its credit rating and thus reduce its cost of funds.

3.2.4 Retail deposits

Most traditional banks will be involved in taking deposits in their domestic market and some in their branches and subsidiaries in other countries. A proportion of these deposits will be held in cash, or in other very liquid instruments to cover the withdrawal of funds at a moment's notice. A further portion of the depositor funds is held in investments that are less liquid. The rest can be used to fund banking operations. Confidence is again a key factor in being able to maintain the minimum amounts of money on call and short notice, in the event of depositor requests for withdrawal. If confidence is shaken by events or rumour, this may lead to a crisis for the bank as it experiences a massive net outflow of funds as a run on the bank develops. This renders it unable to sustain its own operations based on customer deposits and makes it reliant on raising money in the wholesale markets. These are all elements that need to be taken into account for the purpose of liquidity management.

The bank's ability to raise funds from the retail market is dependent upon the attractiveness of the rates and the population's propensity to save. In an era of consumer choice there has been a tendency to place savings in more sophisticated vehicles with more promising returns. In the UK, for example, schemes based on additional voluntary contributions (AVCs) in company pension schemes, unit trusts, PEPs, ISA schemes and holding shares directly have become popular. The tax breaks existing for the AVC and ISA schemes and the advantageous terms on which the privatized utilities have issued their shares have resulted in further funds moving away from traditional bank and building society accounts.

The issue of confidence is clearly a vital one for banks' operation in the retail market, as it is in the wholesale markets. A bank must always maintain that the bank is a safe and secure place for customers to place their money in order to avoid a run on the bank's deposit holdings. In order to avoid any crisis of confidence it is unlikely, whatever the circumstances, that the senior management of a bank would openly admit to any funding problems.

From a treasurer's point of view retail funding can have a number of advantages. Generally it is relatively sticky. This means that once funds are received they tend to remain with a bank for a while. This is a particular advantage for large banks that can rely on these funds for a large part of their working capital.

3.2.5 Wholesale funds

The potential for a crisis of confidence in the wholesale funding market can have even more devastating results in a market where the well-informed operator and depositor/lender will be even more discerning. Wholesale funds are borrowed in the money markets, adding to the money banks have available to lend or invest. The funds are made available by banks, large companies and other financial institutions. When a bank considers which source of funds it wishes to pursue it will need to consider which funding vehicle to use.

Interbank lending and borrowing that takes place from one bank to another. In the financial press there is a series of rates published for deposits made between the banks based on overnight money, money deposited at seven days notice, one-month money, three-month money, six-month money and one-year money. Published rates in London are known as LIBOR – the London Interbank Offered Rate – charged by one bank to another for lending. The LIBID – London Interbank Bid Rate – is the rate paid by one bank to another for a deposit. Other currency will have their own benchmark rates, such as EONIA – Euro Overnight Index Average interest rate – or EURIBOR for the Euro.

Certificates of deposit may be used where a bank has amounts of cash it wishes to put on deposit for a set period at the best rate of interest it can obtain. In return it receives a certificate for the amount deposited and receives a rate of interest on it.

If it wishes to retrieve its cash before the certificate has matured, the certificate of deposit can be sold on the money markets. In fact there is a very active market in the buying and selling of this type of instrument in the US and Europe. Yield rates tend to be a little lower for certificates of deposit compared with other forms of investment because of the relative liquidity they offer through the availability and access to the secondary market.

Bankers' acceptances are otherwise known as bank bills. The bank accepts the bills up to a certain value which represents a maximum ceiling known as 'acceptance certificates'. The bill of exchange is a signed promise to pay by the receiver of goods, usually in trade transactions, and kept by the supplier. They are written for fixed periods (or sight). The bill is drawn on a bank in order to generate finance that is marketable in the secondary market. The bank may choose to accept the bill, discount it, and then sell it on to attract liquid funds for its own operations.

Commercial paper is a short-term IOU that is usually issued at a discount rather than bearing interest. The average life of commercial paper in the UK has been close to 40 days since the market got under way in 1986. When the bank wishes to raise this form of short-term cash, it alerts dealers who find a paper issue of the maturity required. The paper is then sold at a discount to its face value, equivalent to a rate of interest. By rolling over this type of finance, replacing the maturing issues with new issues, this essentially short-term financing vehicle can become a medium-term vehicle for raising funds.

Overall banks have a number of alternative sources of funding, divided principally into two main categories: retail deposits attracted normally through a branch network or other distribution channels, and wholesale moneys sourced, often on a daily basis, to match lending and investment activity. The latter source of funds has become increasingly more important as traditional depositors have become more sophisticated in their approach to saving. Many banks now use the money markets, ie wholesale funding, as their primary source of funds. In any case, the movement of funds and the assets and liabilities of the banks have to be managed very carefully and very efficiently. The downside to not doing so is potential losses and cashflow problems.

Four

Liquidity

Objectives

This chapter will cover the following topics:

- ◆ liquidity risk;
- ◆ liquidity management;
- ◆ cash management;
- ◆ associated regulatory requirements.

4.1 Liquidity risk

Liquidity risk is the risk that a bank is unable to meet its commitments due to a lack of sufficiently liquid assets to pay for them. The underlying assumption when looking at liquidity risk is that the institution is solvent in itself. Liquidity risk is a key risk for banks, which historically has brought down numerous institutions that did not have enough cash to meet their immediate commitments. This can occur despite the business remaining profitable. A comparison can be drawn between Bank of America and Continental Bank of Illinois in the 1980s. The latter went out of business due to its reliance on the wholesale markets and the market's unwillingness to provide it with sufficient credit lines following the bank's heavy losses on its energy lending portfolio. Bank of America, on the other hand, experienced heavy losses, but was able to maintain its operation due to its retail deposit-taking activities, which generally tend to be less volatile as a funding source.

Many bank portfolios contain assets and liabilities that are matched in terms of interest rate but not matched in terms of their maturity dates. Maturity matching, although on the face of it representing the right approach, can bring with it its own structural problems, resulting in a lack of flexibility and overuse of the markets that allow matching in the wrong market conditions. Therefore it is expedient to allow mismatching to take place in certain circumstances and within certain limits. These limits will be in terms of currency amount and usually in terms of time and will require careful risk management.

The Asset and Liability Management Committee plays a key role in liquidity risk management. It will decide on strategy, review implementation, approve limits and look at all aspects of these activities.

4.2 Definition

In practice, liquidity exposure arises when a bank is lending long and borrowing short, ie when there is a mismatch in final maturity dates. Banking activities are inherently about such a maturity transformation. Retail customers for example provide their deposits on the condition that they retain almost immediate access to their funds, while banks lend these deposits out at much longer maturities, such as mortgages. A bank's commercial products are often related to medium- and long-term financing, whereas the instrument for raising those funds will tend to be fairly short-term. If, for example, a bank lends money over a period of one year, but funds this advance with three-month money, there will be a liquidity exposure for nine months. The exposure arises because it may not be able to find the advance after the initial three months. If this pattern is repeated across the portfolio of business and the funds cannot be replaced, the bank's operations can become unsustainable and the bank may have to close. There are certain contingency plans that can be put into place should other banks or central banks feel the bank can survive in the longer term. This could be via special liquidity facilities, often based on repos.

The subject of liquidity management is critical to the point of being fundamental to the very survival of the bank. A treasury's reason d'être can be traced to this responsibility. In order to control these risks, banks will normally monitor the maturity of liabilities against the maturity of assets – tracking their funding profiles. Treasurers will also track the lines of credit available to them for the purposes of maintaining their short-term funding position.

The concept of liquidity risk revolves around the ability of banks to maintain sufficient funds to meet their commitments, which may, in turn, be related to their ability to attract deposits or maintain sufficient committed lines of credit with various other banking groups. It will also involve matching the maturity of assets and liabilities daily and coping with any short-term pressures that may arise in the process of ensuring the assets are fully funded. Day-to-day matching is an exercise in detailed monitoring and control, which then generates the need to access the money markets to find the most appropriate funding vehicle.

In a wider context it should be noted that bank's published accounts can never tell the whole story in a fast-moving trading environment against a background of volatile interest rates and exchange rates. The bank may be profitable, but if it is unable to meet its short-term commitments then it is still in danger of ceasing to trade. It is clear therefore why the confidence issue arises yet again, as banks look to call on facilities to help them overcome their short-term problems. In a market of scarce resources there will always be a natural tendency, however unfair in the final analysis, to direct those resources where there is little known risk involved.

Thus an important treasury function is to effectively manage the cash by forecasting future cashflows taking into account, for example, loan commitments, the maturity of these loans and the maturity of deposits, currency dealing, plus the probabilities involved in relating to the levels of withdrawal on the retail deposits side of the bank's business. The bank will normally use liquidity maturity ladders based on information related to projected movements on all of the above, in order to assess their liquidity position.

4.3   Measurement of liquidity risk

To manage risk it first needs to be measured. The measurement can then be used to set internal limits to ensure adequate liquidity is maintained. There are two main approaches that banks use to measure their liquidity exposure. One looks at the cumulative cashflow mismatches over particular periods – next day, next five days, next month, etc. These mismatches can either be expressed in absolute terms or as a percentage of total liabilities. It is important that these mismatches be calculated using prudent assumptions of marketability. For example, to take account of price volatility, it may be appropriate to apply a discount factor on the value of relevant assets. Any drops in price in the event of a forced sale and likely outflows as a result of drawdown of commitments should also be included. The second, related, methodology looks at liquid assets as a percentage of short-term liabilities. Again, this should be based on prudent assumptions; otherwise the results of the measurement will be misleading. Thus the assets included in this category should only be those which are highly liquid – ie only those in which there is a ready market, even in periods of stress.

In the UK the FSA mandates a version of the first methodology, which is commonly known as the liquidity maturity ladder. Only large UK retail banks, once they have received supervisory approval, can move onto the sterling stock liquidity approach, which is more akin to the second methodology.

4.3.1   Liquidity maturity ladders

The liquidity maturity ladder is best understood by looking at a tabular representation of the underlying liquidity data. Such a table will show the maturity time bands together with the asset and liability amounts relating to these time bands. An example is provided below.

Table 4.1: Liquidity maturity ladders

	Assets	Liabilities	Mismatch
Local Currency ($m)			
Overnight	100	115	(15)
1-8 days	35	25	10
9 days- 1 month	45	45	0
1-3 months	70	60	10
3-6 months	45	20	25
6-9 months	55	50	5
9-12 months	45	55	(10)
Over 1 year	100	120	(20)
Total	495	490	5
Foreign Currency ($m)			
Overnight	55	75	(20)
1-8 days	45	40	5
9 days- 1 month	60	35	25
1-3 months	25	35	(10)
3-6 months	45	30	15
6-9 months	70	55	15
9-12 months	50	60	(10)
Over 1 year	200	180	20
Total	550	510	40
Total Mismatch			45

In this example, assets in foreign currency exceed liabilities for 1-8 day money by $5m. For local currency, assets exceed liabilities by $10m. In local currency assets exceed liabilities by $10m for 1-3 month transactions, and in foreign currency liabilities exceed assets by the same amount.

The tables are normally split into domestic and foreign currency assets and liabilities, although banks that are very active in foreign currencies may calculate separate liquidity maturity ladder for each of their currency exposures. Depending on complexity of their operations banks may extend such analysis to separate tables showing the contractual situation alongside the forecasted or expected situation.

A further complexity would arise if, for example, domestic liquidity was funded in a different currency. This could be dealt with by, for example, making several exchange rate assumptions or by applying discounts to such liabilities based on historic volatility. The above shows that measuring liquidity is far from simple and one of the roles of the treasurer will be to make the right assumptions for interpreting the data available. This will be even more of a skill for those treasurers working under the sterling stock liquidity approach.

4.3.2   Sterling stock liquidity

The prudent approach of the cumulative cashflow mismatch may not be appropriate for banks whose liquidity profile is dominated by retail deposits at call or short notice. The reason is that such funding would lead to extreme mismatches in the overnight or 1-8 days time band, when in reality retail funding is relatively sticky. This means that it is highly unlikely that liquidity problems would arise despite the large mismatches that the maturity ladder would suggest. Therefore it is more important that such banks hold an appropriate stock of sterling liquid assets against an unexpected loss of funding.

Accordingly the UK banking supervisor, the FSA, states that 'a bank covered by the Sterling Stock Liquidity policy should hold a reserve of high quality sterling liquid assets large enough for it to survive for at least five working days without renewal of its maturing sterling wholesale funding (on a net basis) and after the leakage of a small proportion (5%) of its gross retail deposits'. Even banks that are not covered by the sterling stock liquidity policy may use variations of this approach as one of their liquidity management tools.

The objective is that this stock should enable the bank to continue business for a period of five working days. Five working days was chosen because it is deemed to be a critical period for a bank in crisis, and in which remedial action is most needed and most effective. In reality it is difficult to predict accurately how the various classes of depositors will behave if a bank gets into difficulties. For internal purposes banks could make assumptions on how various types of retail depositors will react and thus make predictions of their 'stickiness of deposits' to incorporate into their own models. Similarly it may be the safest working assumption that wholesale depositors will be the quickest to react by withdrawing funds almost as soon as they can in time of crisis.

4.4 Liquidity management

Liquidity management cannot be undertaken effectively without measuring the extent of liquidity risk inherent in a bank's books. Given that this may change significantly during each trading day the on-going monitoring and measurement of the liquidity risk is a key part of liquidity measurement. At the same time there are a number of additional requirements that banks need to follow to manage their liquidity in line with best practice. Readers wishing to research this topic further may wish to begin with the 'Sound Practices for Managing Liquidity in Banking Organisations' that was published by the Basel Committee of Banking Supervision in February 2000.

As with other types of risk, good liquidity risk management needs appropriate structures. Senior management must set the strategic framework for liquidity management and ensure this is communicated across the organization. Policies and procedures need to be established and implemented to control and limit liquidity risk. We have already seen how the measuring and monitoring of the net funding requirements has a key role to play. This will involve scenario testing to ensure that adverse scenarios do not threaten the survival of the institution. Maintaining a diversified spread of liabilities, and aiming to ensure its capacity to sell assets will give further protection. We have already alluded to the need to include foreign currency liquidity management into the framework. A particularity of liquidity management is the need to take public disclosure into account. As indicated previously, liquidity risk is self-realizing when the perception of liquidity problems has reached the markets. It is therefore essential to have procedures in place to manage such events that could lead to significant unpredictable cash outflows. This could for example arise as a result of a downgrade in the credit rating of an institution or other events threatening its reputation.

4.4.1 Liquidity policy

It is common for banks to review the issues raised in the previous paragraph in the form of a liquidity policy. Indeed, under the current supervisory rules in the UK it is a requirement to have such a policy in place. More generally the bank's liquidity policy is concerned with assessing when it might need cash, and how claims may be made on liquid assets by depositors. It is also concerned about liquidity levels that may be developed through the use of the secondary markets. Secondary markets in financial instruments have become an important consideration with the increased reliance other banks have on money markets to fund their activities. For example, London, New York and other European countries provide large markets for the availability of funds, and most day-to-day shortfalls can be addressed often by simply borrowing overnight money. This gives banks considerable flexibility. Nevertheless a bank will want to use these facilities sparingly in order not to create the impression that it is experiencing any kind of difficulties in generating liquidity. In addition, if there is a general liquidity shortage in the market, then it is quite likely that competitor banks will want to hold on to what funds they have, just in case they themselves have to call upon them. A more secure way of maintaining sufficient levels of liquidity is to establish a policy of retaining sufficient levels of marketable assets or retaining access to the secondary markets.

4.4.2   Crisis situations

The bank will need to have a contingency plan in place which takes a view on the requirements needed should there be a crisis in the banking system, or in its own business. For such situations each bank will need to have some form of safety net, although it has to be mindful that the depth and scope of any crisis is unpredictable until it actually happens. Even the relative safety of government securities can no longer be taken for granted, neither can prime certificates of deposit with first class banks. But these represent the best possible safety net and should prove effective in most situations. In a crisis situation, the bank will normally be in a position where it has to sell these assets and realize the liquidity in the asset.

Banks are fully aware of how interdependent they are, so the level of competitiveness they encounter from each other, on a day-to-day basis, does not mean they would wish their banking sector competitors out of business. Therefore there are contingencies in place which involve certain banks joining together in a commitment to provide short-term assistance in any liquidity crisis. Each bank, as party to such an arrangement, would provide stand-by arrangements by way of counterparty loans or provide deposits.

The Basel Concordat of 1975 provided guidance on how a host country's central bank should respond to the severe liquidity problems suffered by banks operating in its country. It was issued by the Basel Committee, which until 1999 was known as the Basle Committee. Following the recommendations of the Basel Concordat, the measures were loosely in place for the central bank to act as 'lenders of last resort'. This acceptance of the principle does not necessarily mean that the central bank will come to the rescue in all situations, as witnessed by Barings in 1995.

In practical terms, banks should have a contingency plan in place should there be a liquidity crisis, making quite clear who has management responsibility in these circumstances and what the sequence of events should be. Yet again the issue of confidence arises when trying to assess the most appropriate time to sell assets, in the process running the risk of advertising the bank's liquidity problems. Ideally the bank maintains its position with short-term borrowing while the position rights itself.

It is up to the treasury function to ensure that assets and liabilities are matched in terms of maturity taking into account the entire portfolio in the domestic market and in the foreign currency market. Where there are mismatches' treasury management will seek to engage in raising the appropriate funds to avoid liquidity problems.

We already saw that maturity matching, although on the face of it representing the right approach, can bring with it its own structural problems, resulting in a lack of flexibility. Overuse of the markets could also lead to matching in the wrong market conditions. Therefore banks accept that mismatches will take place in certain circumstances and within certain limits. These limits will be in terms of currency amount and usually in terms of time. This situation also arises in the spot and forward exchange dealings, where mismatching is allowed but carefully managed within established limits. Once limits are established care needs to be taken to ensure they are reviewed on a periodic basis and adjusted when necessary.

4.5   Regulatory requirements

Although the FSA, the UK regulator, sets some rules governing liquidity, it makes clear that the responsibility for ensuring a bank can meet its obligations as they fall due rests with the bank's own management. It is thus up to each and every individual bank to ensure it takes account of its own characteristics and position when determining a prudent liquidity policy. The FSA thus states that 'A bank should be able to satisfy the FSA on an on-going basis that it has a prudent liquidity policy, and adequate management systems in place to ensure that the policy is adhered to'. The FSA has numerous tools available to check the prudent application of a bank's liquidity policy. Primary reliance will be taken from the regular reporting requirements and any ensuing prudential discussions. Additionally supervisors will review the bank's policy statement. Focused visits, sometime by treasury experts, or reports by independent professionals are other tools available. The latter are known as skilled persons reports, which the FSA has the legal power to require.

The FSA lists four overarching principles as the main prudential policies applying to banks:

◆ A bank must maintain adequate liquidity at all times.
◆ A bank must formulate a statement of its liquidity management policy. It should agree with the FSA standards for adherence to this policy, ie mismatch guidelines and the procedures for the notification of breaches of those guidelines.
◆ A bank should have adequate systems for monitoring liquidity on a daily basis.
◆ A bank should notify the FSA of any breaches of its liquidity mismatch guidelines as soon as they occur.

4.5.1   Limits

Earlier in the chapter we saw how the maturity mismatch ladder and the stock liquidity approaches function. As indicated, most banks in the UK are required by the FSA to use the maturity mismatch approach for reporting purposes. Supervisors will agree mismatch limits with banks, particularly in the sight to eight days and sight to one month time bands. Banks that breach these mismatch limits need to report the event to the FSA immediately.

In setting mismatch guidelines the FSA will take account of a number of factors. The volatility, diversity and source of deposits will be a key consideration. Volatility, for example, may be driven more by perceived creditworthiness or financial conditions, than the precise terms and conditions attached to the deposits. Certain deposits may also have reputational impact, while reliance on single counterparties also needs to be considered. Other factors will include the degree of reliance on marketable assets, the depth of market in such assets, the price volatility of such assets and the degree of diversification in a bank's portfolio of marketable assets. For example, large holdings of single assets may not be sufficiently liquid to be relied upon. As a safety net the availability and reliability of undrawn standby lines will also determine the liquidity risk faced by the institution, as will off-balance-sheet obligations. The FSA may also take into account some qualitative factors, such as the quality of management information systems and the expertise held in the treasury function. Although these are areas that supervisors will take into account, good management will already have taken them into account for their own internal liquidity risk management.

To facilitate bank's liquidity management the FSA allows two adjustments. The first one is a materiality concession, which is intended to facilitate reporting. Once given it enables a bank to exclude certain cashflows from its liquidity reporting where they are not material in relation to the total. This is given where the cost of including them exceeds the impact on the total cashflows.

A second adjustment allows a bank to introduce behavioural adjustments subject to FSA approval. Normally a bank's liquidity position should be looked at on a 'worst case' basis. This would, however, imply that those banks that have significant retail deposits would have to count these into the 1-8 days timeband, when in fact retail deposits are unlikely to disappear that quickly. The same rationale is used for the stock liquidity approach.

Given that such adjustment may make it significantly easier for a bank to meet its mismatch guidelines, the FSA will only allow such an adjustment after careful consideration. In particular it will want to see that any proposed adjustment is based on sound evidence, such as historic data, and that the implications of granting such an adjustment have been clearly identified.

4.5.2   Policy statements

The FSA requires each bank to provide a statement of its liquidity management policy. Although the policy should be given to the supervisor, it remains a document whose primary role is for internal consumption, as it should be used to manage liquidity internally. One would expect a liquidity policy to cover at least the following areas:

◆ Policy on how liquidity positions are controlled and monitored. This should cover each individual currency in which a bank has exposures. This is particularly important for those currencies that are not quickly and easily convertible.
◆ Management of liquidity in both normal times and circumstances of severe funding difficulties.
◆ Agreed guidelines, its retail/wholesale split and any behavioural or materiality adjustments.

The following details should certainly be included in a liquidity policy:

◆ who is responsible for liquidity management on a day-to-day basis, and
◆ who is responsible for crisis management in the event of a liquidity crisis;
◆ what are likely to be the most reliable sources of funds in normal and crisis circumstances;
◆ what warning indicators are used as signs of an approaching crisis; and
◆ what action is planned to pre-empt it?

4.5.3   Sterling stock liquidity approach

We have already seen that the sterling stock liquidity approach is only available to those banks with large retail deposits in the form of short-term deposits. Other banks may wish to use some features of this for internal purposes, but, unless approved by the FSA, it cannot be used to replace the mismatch approach described previously.

A sterling stock liquidity bank should include in its liquidity management policy notified to the FSA its intention to:

◆ maintain an internal limit for its maximum wholesale sterling net outflow over the next five working days, as agreed with the FSA;
◆ hold, as a minimum requirement, a stock of sterling liquid assets sufficient to cover the 'floor', as agreed with the FSA;
◆ ensure that its sterling stock liquidity ratio is at least 100%; and
◆ notify the FSA of any breaches.

4.5.4   Future developments

In March 2002 the FSA issued a consultation paper on revised liquidity management and, in particular, systems and controls areas. The changes are designed to give banks more latitude on how to manage their liquidity. This is in line with the FSA policy of putting responsibility for risk management back to the banks themselves. The new rules are to be published in summer 2003 to give banks time to prepare for implementation by summer 2004. At the same time the FSA intends to publish a consultation paper on the revised rules for the more quantitative aspects of liquidity risk management. Near final text for these rules is expected in Q2 2004. Implementation is intended for summer 2005. Given the above, readers are advised to read relevant newspapers, websites and other material to keep abreast of developments.

4.6   Cash management

While liquidity management deals with ensuring that a bank has sufficient financial resources available to enable it to meet its obligations as they fall due without excessive cost, cash management deals more with ensuring that shortfalls are fully funded and surpluses are invested in order to maximize returns. Clearly the two have large areas of overlap, as cashflow problems may threaten a bank's liquidity. Similarly, when funds are invested, the effect this will have on the liquidity of the bank is one of the key items for consideration by dealers. Conceptually the main difference between cash management and liquidity management is that cash management is more concerned with returns than liquidity management, which is only concerned with the absolute level of liquidity. However, in practice the two need to be managed on an integrated basis to ensure efficient use of resources.

It should be noted that the management of notes and coins throughout a bank is not undertaken by treasury functions and therefore not part of this syllabus. Instead this syllabus is concerned with the dealing operations that will be undertaken to maximize returns on a bank's money market book. To achieve this aim a bank needs to optimize its cashflows throughout the dealing day. In order to manage cash effectively the treasury function will have to continuously monitor its cashflows:

Receipts	*Outflows*
◆ Deposits	◆ Fees
◆ Repayments of loans	◆ Commissions
◆ Repayments or part repayments of overdrafts	◆ Interest payments
◆ Current account credits	◆ Drawdowns on loans and overdrafts
◆ Fees	◆ Drawings on current accounts
◆ Interest	◆ Repayment of deposits
◆ Commission	◆ Operating expenses
◆ Dividend income	◆ Taxation
	◆ Payment of dividends

Cashflow is generated from two broad sources, and the balance of these sources depends on where the bank sees its core business. These two sources are retail and wholesale funds as previously described. Retail funds are an invaluable source of liquidity and can put a bank in a stronger position than its competitors who lend and borrow entirely in the money markets.

There is a downside though, characterized by the uncertainty involved in attempting to predict balances on any particular day. For example, overdrafts can fluctuate widely and forecasting their behaviour is an inexact science. The bank normally states that overdrafts can be recalled at a moment's notice, but this is clearly impractical as well as, most probably, causing a bad debt to occur rather than substantially improving the liquidity situation. Generally, retail deposits require access at short notice but there will be inflows and outflows on a daily basis. So, from the bank's perspective, it should expend effort in drawing some conclusions on how it expects retail depositors to act in a particular period, so that it can adjust its plans and match its assets and liabilities. Several patterns are likely to emerge, for example in seasonal variations, which can then be used to improve management.

We have already noted the potential importance of attracting deposits as a stable source of funding. The ability to attract deposits will depend on many factors. One will be the standing of the institution, probably reflected by the rating given by the rating agencies. In case of poor ratings it may be that even if funds can be attracted, the cost of attracting deposits becomes prohibitive. In order to attract the necessary funds it is imperative that the bank is seen to maintain a good balance-sheet profile, that its ratios are healthy, its capital adequacy is being maintained and that it is involved in prudent practices where risks are minimized or at least actively managed.

Wholesale money on the other hand does tend to be more predictable, revolving around set maturity and value dates. A bank would expect that their final reconciliations will relate closely to the predetermined contract dates. It will therefore be able to better predict its liquidity situation. However, in the case of changes of credit worthiness, for example, wholesale funding may also be very difficult to renew, as such funding is not as sticky as retail deposits.

Liquidity problems can exist for a number of reasons, which may make it difficult for the bank to balance its commitments. For example, retail and wholesale overdrafts require little or no notice and can therefore place a burden on the bank's liquidity. Although this facility usually exists in return for a higher rate of interest, which compensates the bank for its inability to make an alternative use of the capital, the bank cannot normally optimize its profit potential as a result. Again, where there is a shortage of retail funds, the bank has to go to the market. It will tend to go for fairly short-term money in order to minimize the risk of interest rate volatility and liquidity problems.

Although fixed-rate funding would appear to be more predictable and therefore more reliable for funding purposes, the various bases of interest rates from Prime-related rates to interbank rates make even this form of funding difficult to match. The degree of matched funding required will depend on the structure of the bank's liabilities, and the funds matched will depend on the funds and hedging available in the market at that point in time.

The interest-rate swap market has been instrumental in providing banks with the means to fund longer-term commitments in terms of the provision of loans, for example those in the medium-term financing market. Short-term funding, backed up by a long-term interest-rate swap, provides the means to match the loan requirement more closely.

In foreign exchange commitments, the bank must ensure it has the cash resources to settle foreign exchange transactions once they have been committed, and this can prove difficult where dollar deposits are reaching maturity and where these have to be replaced.

In situations where facilities have been committed but not yet fulfilled, the bank will need to take account of how many of the commitments may be called upon at any one time, making allowances at the margin for higher than normal drawings.

4.6.1   Nostro accounts

Managing nostro accounts from a cashflow point of view also tends to fall under the remit of treasury functions. Nostro accounts are the accounts between the domestic bank and the foreign bank in cross-border trading – they represent 'our balances with you'. For example, Barclays Bank would think of its dollar balances with Citibank as its nostro account. It considers Citibank's sterling account with Barclays Bank as the vostro account or 'your account with us'. Both are collectively referred to as nostro accounts and the department involved in settlement and reconciliation is the nostro department.

After every day of trading, the treasury function will review the amounts held in each currency account. It will aim to achieve the lowest possible balances such that the funds are being employed to the maximum advantage, while ensuring all liabilities have been covered. It should, however, be noted that the use of nostro accounts has declined in recent years. This is partly due to the creation of the Eurozone, which has led many banks to rationalize their correspondence banking network. At the same time the emergence of improved payment and settlement systems has also reduced the need for nostro accounts. Nevertheless, for those banks that use them, they form an integral part of cash management.

4.6.2 Exposures created by nostro accounts

The charging regime for the use of nostro accounts and the interest-bearing nature of them varies. Most tend not to pay interest on credit balances, while they tend to charge interest, sometimes at a penal rate, when debit balances occur. It is the responsibility of the bank's treasury to keep balances as low as possible, but avoid unnecessary charges as well as liquidity problems from not having sufficient funds to cover liabilities. Some institutions also charge fees for processing transactions.

Those accounts permitting overdrafts where there are debit balances at the end of the trading period tend to be charged at the highest overnight money rate. Banks generally discourage this form of loan as a source of short-term finance and see it as a day-to-day facility only.

Managing foreign currency nostro accounts is not as straightforward as handling ordinary domestic accounts. The additional challenges faced include:

◆ international time differences;
◆ differing bank practices;
◆ different computer systems.

However, banks are becoming more and more sophisticated in managing the daily movements in the volatile money markets, including the use of specialist management information and communications systems to monitor the situation.

Although transactions will have a 'value date' on which transactions should be settled, it is near impossible for a bank to predict its end-of-day position. Even with agreed value dates and good faith on both sides; a situation still often arises where payments are not received on time. Although payment of interest is usual practice, this can still make the job of the reconciliation department very difficult.

Such is the importance of the end-of-day positions that one bank's position can impact on another bank's end-of-day position. Therefore, management from each bank will, where necessary, keep each other informed of the current situation so that each can get the best possible idea of their end-of-day exposure.

Five

Market risk

Objectives

This chapter will cover the following topics:

◆ market risk;
◆ interest-rate risk;
◆ foreign exchange risk.

5.1   Introduction

Market risk deals with the risks stemming from adverse movements in market prices or market rates affecting both on and off-balance-sheet activities. Market risk, in turn, can be subdivided into a series of other risks: interest rate risks, equity price risks, exchange rate risks and commodity price risks, to name just a few. Interest rate risk and foreign exchange rate risk on on-balance and off-balance-sheet assets that are not intended for trading are, however, managed differently and will thus be looked at separately in this chapter. Although market risk theoretically exists on every asset, from a risk management point of view it is only sensible to look at it for those products which have liquid and deep markets and where prices are readily available. In practice it is therefore common to calculate market risk only for those instruments that are revalued at frequent intervals, particularly for those that are revalued on a daily basis.

Unlike credit risk, market risk is not directly driven by probability of default. Instruments representing indebtedness, such as bonds, clearly contain credit risk and their market price will reflect changes in it. But this is indirect, as changes in credit risk will change supply and demand, and therefore the price of the instrument. It is therefore appropriate to manage those instruments involving risks mainly driven by price changes separately as part of market risk management.

Market risk has risen dramatically in importance over the last 30 years and risk management techniques have become significantly more sophisticated as a result. As with risk management in general, this has been very much driven by the high level of instability in the environment within which banks operate. We have already touched upon the exchange rate instability that followed the breakdown of the Bretton Woods system of fixed exchange rates. Indeed the creation of the Euro was driven by the significant volatility of the legacy currencies over the years prior to its creation. The strains of the European exchange rate mechanism in September 1992, when both the Italian lira (temporarily) and pound sterling (permanently) were forced to exit the mechanism, was a symptom of the underlying problems. Similarly interest rate instability, caused by very high interest rates, had significant impact on asset prices.

Another development was technological change, which in turn led to the growth of debt and equity markets as access to them become global, rather than being restricted to domestic players. At the same time this has lead to increased correlation between markets around the world, posing new risk management challenges to treasurers. Independently of whether this was driven by technological changes, reduced regulation or increased interconnection between financial markets worldwide, the result was that banks took on board many more risks than had previously been the case. Price volatility, whether in stock markets or commodities, only reinforced the need for improved market risk management.

It should also be noted that the 1996 'Amendment to the Capital Accord to Incorporate Market Risk', issued by the Basel Committee on Banking Supervision has given significant impetus to the management of market risk. It is sometimes also referred to as the market risk amendment. To some extent it has distilled best practice and this helped its implementation by banks that previously had not considered market risk as being that important. The amendment is, however, mostly concerned with ensuring sufficient capital is held by banks for market risk. As a result we will look at the market risk management separately from the market risk amendment.

5.2   Market risk measurement

Measuring and monitoring market risk mainly involves two techniques. 'Marking to market' refers to valuing (and revaluing) positions in marketable instruments on the basis of current market prices. 'Value at risk' methodologies take price changes to compute how much value is at risk on a normal or average trading day. Value at risk has become an important management tool, but one that should only be used with knowledge of its limitations. Both techniques are closely linked to bank's trading books, although the techniques are beginning to be used in other areas. The term trading book is generally referred to as those assets that are managed with an intention of active trading, as opposed to holding an asset till maturity. The Basel Committee defines the trading book as a 'bank's proprietary positions in financial instruments (including positions in derivative products and off-balance-sheet instruments) which are intentionally held for short-term resale and/or which are taken on by the bank with the intention of benefiting in the short-term from actual and/or expected differences between their buying and selling process, or from other price or interest rate variations, and positions in financial instrument arising from matched principal brokering and market marking, or positions taken in order to hedge other elements of the trading book'.

Holding securities, or other assets, for trading purposes increases the need to constantly monitor price developments. This soon began to mean marking to market and it is reasonable to say that almost all assets in a trading book would now be expected to be marked to market from a risk management perspective.

5.2.1　Marking to market

Marking to market is based on the idea that the value of assets in a bank's trading book should reflect their current market value. The valuation tends to be done on a daily basis for most instruments, although for instruments whose prices are not so readily available some longer periods are used. Marking to market has a number of advantages over other valuation methods, such as historic cost accounting. To briefly recap, historic cost accounting is the method most commonly used in accounting, where assets remain on the books at the value at which they were originally purchased.

Marking to market, which can be linked to fair value accounting, provides relative objective and reliable means of valuing positions, as it is based on current prices. More importantly it facilitates accountability by making it harder for managers to hide profits and losses by applying subjective adjustments. At the same time it can be used to reveal profit and losses very quickly, which will again increase accountability of those managing portfolios. It can thus be used very effectively to give managers and dealers feedback on their investment strategies. For example, a failing strategy will make losses that highlight its failure, and this loss signal should enable managers to change strategy before their losses grow much further.

One of the consequences of marking to market is that it will increase the volatility of profit and loss reporting. This does, however, create better risk awareness and should therefore lead to improved risk management. Better risk management will not work, however, if it is not combined with certain controls to ensure the accuracy of the marking to market process. A key requirement here is that prices are checked independently from the dealers and that dealers can have no input into the calculations. There have been several high profile instances where this simple control had not been implemented and where dealers were thus able to provide inaccurate prices with devastating effects for their organizations. This is particularly important as valuations are usually undertaken in the back-office, which in many organizational cultures means that it has less power to resist strong-arm tactics by dealers. A good example of this was again provided by Allfirst, which we have already mentioned.

5.2.2 Value at risk

Value at risk methodologies, generally referred to as VaR methodologies, attempt to measure losses due to normal market movements. It is calculated on the basis of statistical analysis at a given confidence level. Confidence levels used in practice are generally either 95% or 99%. The value at risk is thus the upper limit of price changes that would only be breached in either 5% or 1% of cases. In other words, a 95% confidence level would mean that one out of every 20 trading days would see market movements in excess of the limits suggested by VaR.

Figure 5.1: Confidence levels and variability of returns

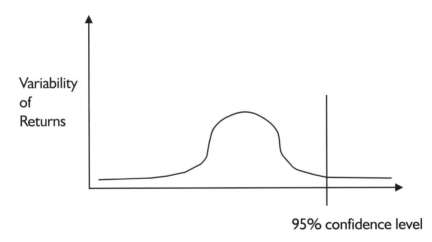

95% confidence level

Figure 5.1 shows the concept behind VaR. The bell shaped curve shows the distribution of the value at risk, bunched around the average. The 95% confidence level means that only in 5% of cases will the variability of returns be to the right of the 95% confidence line.

Particularly since the Market Risk Amendment it has become common to use a 99% confidence level. Similarly the amendment prescribes a one year minimal data set. It also requires that VaR calculations should be based on an instantaneous shock equivalent to a 10-day move in prices. It should be noted that these parameters are only required to be used for the calculation of regulatory capital, and banks may therefore use different requirements for their own internal purposes. Different requirements are often used to be even more prudent.

Benefits

An advantage of VaR is that it can be calculated for a variety of risks. These can then be aggregated, while still taking account of portfolio effects by incorporating correlations between different risk factors. Thus it helps to take account of portfolio risk. By providing a single number it is also suitable for reporting purposes, be it for senior management, regulatory reporting or disclosure in annual reports. As such it is simply a way to describe the magnitude of the likely losses on the portfolio, without taking extremes into account. It provides a common risk yardstick, and this yardstick makes it possible for institutions to manage their risks in a variety of new ways that were not possible before VaR was introduced.

Going into the detailed calculations aspects of VaR is beyond the scope of this text. Instead we can focus on the benefits of VaR approaches to senior management. A key benefit is that it allows senior management to quantify and therefore set their overall risk appetite or risk target. It tells them how risky, or in other words how volatile, the bank's portfolio is. At the same time such a figure can be used to manage the risk figure either up or down, depending on the strategic decision taken. This is where it can be used to set risk targets. A further advantage is that VaR can be used to determine risk targets and position limits at various intermediate levels, from a portfolio level down to the individual dealing desk.

VaR has another potential use in relation to internal capital allocation. The riskier an activity, the more capital there should be to support it. By providing a measure of riskiness, VaR models provide a yardstick to determine internal capital allocation. At another level VaR can be helpful to assess the risks of different investment opportunities before decisions are made. It can be used for that purpose because it is mathematically based and results can therefore be easily simulated. In the same vein it can be used to evaluate the performance of business units after the event.

The availability of VaR models has had a significant effect on risk management. It certainly has given senior management in banks a much better handle on risks than they could otherwise have. This has lead to more informed and therefore better risk management. It enables senior management to understand the risks their organizations are facing and they can use this to set their own risk targets. It does so by providing a consistent and integrated treatment of risks across banks. This paragraph has been discussing risk management in general, as VaR methodologies can also be used to measure other risks, such as credit, liquidity and cashflow risks. This in turn can lead to a more integrated approach to the management of different kinds of risks, improved budget planning, and better strategic management.

Particularly useful from a treasurer's point of view is that VaR models provide operational decision rules to guide investment, hedging and trading decisions. These rules take full account of the risk implications of alternative choices and substantially improve the quality of decision making.

From an operational point of view VaR models have lead to more robust control systems. These in return make it much harder for fraud and human error to go undetected. It generates greater risk transparency and a more consistent treatment of risks across a bank. Another operational benefit is that it can be used to provide incentives that are better aligned with risk than would otherwise be possible. By taking risk into account VaR models can be used for remuneration rules for traders, managers and other employees to take account of the risks they take. This discourages excessive risk-taking, unlike reward structures that are based purely on profits. Given that high returns are correlated to high risk, profit-based incentive structures generally reward high risk-taking, and are therefore unlikely to be incentives compatible with the risk appetite set by senior management.

Limitations

Despite all the benefits that VaR can provide, its limitations need to be well understood. Otherwise it could easily lead to the VaR number itself providing a comfort, while it in reality distracts from the underlying risks that may or may not be addressed. One of the main deficiencies of VaR models is that they are backward looking. The notion is that historic data can be used to forecast likely future losses, based on the assumption that any relationship that drove historic data will hold in the future. While this is a reasonable assumption given that there is no better alternative, it reinforces the need to treat VaR as one out of a list of complementary management tools. This helps to ensure that should the underlying assumption break down and the model lose its value, there are still other management tools in place. A useful tool in such an instance is stress testing, which will allow senior management to assess how a portfolio will react to events not incorporated into the model's design. Sometimes stress tests can be based on historic scenarios, such as the events after 11 September 2001, or the slow decline in share prices since the peak of 2000.

Like all models, VaR calculations are based on assumptions, particularly when aggregating risks to analyse portfolios. Risk managers and senior management need to remain aware of these assumptions and how they affect the model. It is therefore important that any existing model is compared with other models to ensure it is up to date. Back testing should also be a key tool for validating a system on a continuous basis. Back testing is the term used for running historic data through the model. Risk managers can then compare the actual outcome with the outcomes predicted by the model.

Finally it needs to be remembered that no system is foolproof and, as we have already said, VaR models are only one tool among many others. Nevertheless there are certain things management can do to ensure that the value of the model is maximized. It is essential to employ staff that have the appropriate skills to oversee and maintain a VaR model. They need to understand the implications of what is done with the model and still remain aware of the overall aim of risk management. This requires specialized skills that do not come cheaply, and senior management needs to accept this as part of running the business. There are other simple controls that can be put in place to enhance the value of a VaR model. Access controls to the model, procedures on how to validate the model and changes to it, separation between front-office and risk management, defining the role of internal audit in reviewing process are all controls that can help protect the integrity of the model.

Statistical issues

Although we said earlier that technical details of such models were beyond the scope of this textbook, readers may nevertheless find a quick introduction to the key statistical issues of use, even if this will not be tested. In particular it may be helpful to describe the two generic approaches that VaR models can take and which form part of the key assumptions on which models will be built.

One type of VaR methodology is based on historical simulation. This approach uses the historical distributions of returns to the assets in the portfolio to simulate the portfolio's VaR. It is thus based on the hypothetical assumption that a bank held the constituent items of the historical data set and held it for the same period of time as covered by the historical data set. This makes it conceptually simple and easy to report, as the model does not depend on assumptions about distribution of returns or their interdependencies. However, this dependency on a particular historical data set, may in itself distort the results. This is particularly the case if the estimation period was unusual, for example too quiet or too volatile. It could also be that the period included unusual events that are unlikely to re-occur. This methodology is also not appropriate if there have been permanent changes in risk factors that did not yet exist at the time of the data set. This also means that the methodology cannot be used to forecast future events as plausible as they may be. An example of this would be currency devaluations, which could not be factored in unless they were already incorporated into the initial data set.

The second methodology is to estimate VaR on the basis of simulation results derived from statistical or mathematical models. The idea is to simulate repeatedly the random processes governing the prices of financial instruments that the model is designed to capture. Based on statistical theory, the more simulations the more likely the distribution of the portfolio is to equal the portfolio's true, or real, distribution. The advantage of this model is that it can cope with unusual returns. At the same time it also significantly increases model risk. Model risk is the risk that the model itself provides the wrong results. Model risk is often checked for via back testing. As we saw earlier back testing checks how a model would have compared with the real outcome of historic occurrence.

5.3 Other market risk management tools

In addition to VaR models, a number of other controls that provide useful input into risk management exist. Indeed those banks that do not use VaR models will have to rely entirely on these risk management tools. All dealing operations for example will put in place dealing limits as a risk management tool. These limits help control the trading environment, but more importantly, if they are set on a holistic basis they will increase the transparency of risk-taking. The setting of limits itself therefore provides a key tool to determine the risk appetite that a bank is willing to take on to its books.

Limits can be based on absolute exposure, VaR numbers, profit and loss limits or other risk-adjusted limits. Limits can be applied, for example, to individual dealers, to dealing desks, to portfolios, to divisions or even a bank as a whole. The aim is to provide management with some confidence that its risk parameters are not exceeded or, if they are, that they are made aware of them so as to enable them to take appropriate corrective actions. Should limits be exceeded this generally means that positions need to be closed, which either means selling them off or taking positions onto the books that countervail the existing one.

Historically limits began with absolute limits. Thus a dealing desk would have a limit in terms of the number or size of open positions. Limits would also exist in order to restrict dealers from dealing in products they were not yet sufficiently experienced in. It would also protect dealers from dealing in instruments that the back-office could not settle. Foreign exchange dealers for example would be given a set type of instruments they would be allowed to undertake, such as only G-10 currencies in terms of forwards. Other dealers would be allowed to trade foreign currencies via options or future contracts. Swaps may also have limits attached to them. Many of these instruments will also have limits imposed to control other risks, such as credit or settlement risk that is inherent in many products dealt in by treasury functions.

Stop-loss limits are another common type of limit that can be applied to most instruments. Rather than looking at the absolute or risk-adjusted level, stop-loss limits work on the profit and loss account. Instead of incurring the risk of further losses it will make sense from a risk management point of view to crystallize losses at a specified level. The rationale behind this type of limit is to protect the resources of an organization, so that ultimately they can be used for another activity with hopefully better results. Stop-loss limits can exist in a variety of forms. They can be dynamic or fixed. Dynamic limits are those that keep being adjusted to take account of developments. An example are stop-loss limits that are reduced as a financial year progresses. This will ensure that profits already achieved are not put at risk and do not undermine the financial performance of the bank. By their very nature limits expressed in VaR numbers are dynamic, as they take account of market developments. Although not strictly speaking stop-loss limits they can have similar results. This is because after a breach of a VaR limit the only way to return to a position within the agreed trading limits may be to cut the losses and start again. In contrast fixed stop-loss limits would be those that remain unchanged until a general review is undertaken of the limit structure.

In relation to VaR models stress testing and scenario analysis are key management tools. They are in effect procedures to gauge the vulnerability of portfolio to hypothetical or real scenarios, such as 11 September 2001. Although they say nothing about how likely scenarios are, the results of stress tests help identify hidden assumptions or the results of large market movements. The difficulty for risk managers will be to determine what are appropriate scenarios. They can also be used to run simulations on potential investment opportunities or what the effects of hedging versus open positions might be. They are thus a necessary complement to VaR models. Regular back testing is of similar importance, in as much as it can be necessary to validate the model and therefore its appropriateness as a risk management tool.

An important risk management issue for treasury functions is whether to hedge or not. Whether to hedge will often be determined by corporate policies. Some banks have clear guidelines, for example that all interest rate risk or foreign exchange rate risk is hedged, while openly taking on other risks such as credit risk. The danger of hedging all transactions are that this can easily lead to overhedging, particularly if there are correlations between various instruments. This is the case because many risks are offset by other risks; thus aggregation is an inappropriate treatment. It may also be the case that natural hedges already exist and anything additional would therefore lead to overhedging as well. This arises because hedging on an individual basis would be based on gross exposures, rather than net exposures. This has financial implications, as hedging is generally an expensive activity. Banks may therefore not wish to hedge where they feel that they have a skills advantage compared to competitors. VaR models are therefore again an important risk management tool, as they make it possible to factor in net positions and correlation effects between types of risk.

Risk management also needs to incorporate the general principles of risk management. Issues like independence of the risk management function, robust procedures and separation between front and back-offices have already been mentioned. Detailed procedures on how activities are due to be undertaken are key, and adherence to these procedures is essential. In addition to procedures it is common for banks to have a Trading Book Policy statement which will outline the high level principles governing trading and risk management activities.

Readers wishing to take the topic of controls in trading rooms further are recommended to read the 'Report to the Boards of Directors of Allied Irish Banks, Plc., Allfirst Financial Inc. and Allfirst Bank Concerning Currency Trading Losses' published in March 2002. This report, also known as the Ludwig Report, provides practical details of how controls over trading can break down and what impact this has on risk management.

Six

Interest rate risk

Objectives

This chapter will cover the following topics:

- ◆ sources of interest rate risk;
- ◆ interest rate risk management.

6.1   Introduction

Interest rate risk is, simply put, the exposure a bank has to adverse movement in interest rates. For the trading book interest rate risk is incorporated into market risk, which we discussed previously. But interest rate risk also applies more widely to those parts of a bank that fall in the banking book, as opposed to the trading book. Given that banking is the activity of borrowing and lending money based on interest rates, interest rate risk is one of the main risks that banks face. We have already seen that the last 30 years have seen considerable volatility in interest rates, which has ensured that bankers remain very well aware of this risk. This is because changes in interest rates will affect the underlying value of bank's assets and liabilities, both on- and off-balance-sheet. It will also affect cashflows.

From an earning perspective changes in interest rates will change the income figures. In the case of an adverse change, it may lead to a bank incurring losses rather than remaining profitable. This in turn could ultimately threaten the financial stability of the bank. From a risk management point of view changes in interest rates will not only affect the bank via the interest it earns on loans. It also needs to consider fee income, which in many instances is directly affected by changes in interest rates. For example, administration fees based on the value of the interest earning funds can fall significantly as rates increase, given that the value of existing bonds will fall as a result.

Interest-rates not only affect future cashflows, they also affect the net worth of organizations. This is because the value of individual assets in the portfolio is in reality the value of the present value of the future income streams. In economic terms the present value is calculated by discounting the value of the future income streams by the current market rate. An increase in interest rates will thus reduce the value of existing assets, while interest rate falls will increase their value. Aggregated over a whole bank's portfolio the net effect will be of considerable concern to shareholders and management.

6.2   Sources of interest rate risk

Those banks that manage their portfolio with specific regard to interest rate risk will be able to use this to enhance their profitability, by taking on risk they deem appropriate. At the same time they will minimize excessive risk exposure, for example via hedging.

Misjudging interest development can lead to large losses as the cost of funding loans may exceed the income obtained from such loans. This can happen if income is fixed, or can only be adjusted slowly, as may be the case for fixed or capped loans. If the funding of such loans is on variable rates with a shorter term, losses can arise quite quickly. The role of the treasury function will be to understand the interest rate exposure and to develop adequate contingency plans. Part of this will be to ensure an appropriate mix of funding with different maturities to provide diversity of funding.

There are several sources of interest rate risk, which a treasury function needs to be aware of to ensure it can manage its exposures. The most common one follows from the maturity transformation role of banks. We already saw the effect a maturity mismatch had on liquidity, but it will also have an effect on interest rates. For floating-rate exposures this is also known as repricing risk, as each time the rate is changed it in effect reprices the loan. The effect on a bank will be significant, as it may affect both future income, as well as the underlying value of its assets, liabilities and off-balance-sheet positions. This will happen because, in economic terms, the value of assets will be the discounted value of the future income streams.

Table 6.1: Risk associated with providing loans

	Jan	Feb	Mar	April	May	June	July	Aug	Sep	Oct	Nov	Dec
Loan	—									—		
Borrowing	—					—						
Interest-rate risk							—				—	

The diagrammatic representation above illustrates, in simple terms, the risk associated with providing loans at fixed rates and funding those loans out of step. Here the bank faces an interest rate risk from July onwards, when it needs to fund the remaining six months of the one year loan.

A different source of interest rate risk is yield curve risk. As we have already seen the yield curve is the relationship between the rate of interest and time till maturity. The yield curve is upward sloping and positive if longer-term lending rates are higher than for short-term lending. Although a positive yield curve is considered the norm, in reality the slope can be downward or negative. Short-term interest rates may be increased, for example on the basis of government intervention designed to control variables in the economy, particularly inflation. This was the case in the UK in 1989-90. With inflation of about 10%, the Chancellor of the Exchequer felt it necessary to raise short-term rates to 15%, while at the same time ten-year government bonds were yielding only just 11%.

Yield curve risk comes in two forms. There can be a parallel shift of the curve, which would mean that all interest rates change by the same magnitude. At other times only the shape of the curve will change, leaving certain maturities changed by less than others. Treasurers will have to be prepared for both types of yield curve risk.

Basis risk is another source of interest rate risk. It refers to changes in the pattern of interest rates and the relationship between two different costs of money – ie the basis on which the money is borrowed and the way it is lent, such that at roll-over time the relationship between the levels of the respective interest rates can change. For example, suppose that LIBOR deposit rates fall by $\frac{1}{2}$% and interest payable on the loan falls by only $\frac{1}{8}$% – this creates a mismatch of interest rates due to the different rates of change in the individual benchmark rates (LIBOR, New York Prime Lending Rate, etc). This differential in the rates following a general interest rate movement creates an exposure, which in turn involves a risk to margins. Equally the differential can work in the bank's favour.

The use of embedded options also creates interest rate exposures. Embedded options are put or call options that are incorporated into other, more traditional instruments. Embedded options are becoming increasingly common in instruments such as bonds. Callable bonds for example allow the issuer to repay them at any time, while those including put options allow owners to demand repayment. They tend to be more prevalent in non-trading environments, because exchange-traded and over-the-counter (OTC) markets tend to need more homogeneity among products.

6.3   Interest rate risk measurement

Interest rate risk measurement ranges from simple mismatch ladders of the current positions to the use of very complex dynamic modelling techniques. In between there are various other alternatives from static modelling to including changes in future business opportunities.

6.3.1   Interest rate mismatch ladders

An interest rate mismatch ladder shows balances by the time they are fixed or, in other words, the time remaining before repricing. The interest rate mismatch ladder is also known as a gap report. Whereas the maturity mismatch ladder shows the full length of the contract until maturity, which could be, say, one year, the interest rate mismatch ladder might show a time period of three months as the loan is rolled over and fixed on a three-month basis. Some ladders might show the rate at which the original deal was done, but for the purpose of illustration a simple example is used in Table 6.2.

Table 6.2: Mismatch ladder

Interest rate period	Liabilities	Assets	Net mismatch
Under one month	700	600	(100)
Up to three months	200	130	(70)
Three to six months	50	40	(10)
Six to nine months	20	40	20

The report informs management about the general interest rate sensitivity position of the bank that arises from a mismatch in the repricing of assets and liabilities during any specific period. The report indicates whether the bank is positioned to benefit from rising interest rates by having a positive gap position or whether it is positioned to benefit from declining interest rates by its negative gap position. In this example, there is a net mismatch of interest rates for all but the six-to-nine-months category. For under one month, up to three months and three to six months the position is 'over borrowed' – when the bank has more liabilities repricing than assets. In the six-to-nine-month category, the position is 'over lent'. If the position is mainly over borrowed an increase in interest rates on the bank's liabilities will not be fully compensated for by the receipt of increased interest payments on the loan book, or on its other assets.

Such tables provide an overview of the situation and are useful in understanding where a bank's interest rate risk is occurring and provides insight as to how the risk position can be changed. In reality, trading positions can become quite complex, with overlapping transactions and rapidly changing positions between being over lent and over borrowed. The use of floating versus fixed rates will further increase the complexity of such tables. As a result they have limited use and the meaning behind the figures is not always obvious. In particular they fail to provide all the information necessary to measure bank's total interest rate risk exposure as it fails to measure the impact of basis risk and embedded options. Therefore it cannot measure the impact a change in interest income will have on a bank's net interest income or an effect on the market value of an institution's assets and liabilities.

The mismatch ladder approach can be further extended to take account of the effects of changing interest rates on the economic value by applying sensitivity weights to each time band. These could be derived from estimates of duration. Duration is calculated by the weighted average maturity of a bond using the relative discounted cashflows in each period as weights. What this provides is a single figure indicating the sensitivity of individual transactions or whole portfolios to changes in interest rates. It does that because changes in interest rates will change the discounts used for the calculation.

In the duration approach the difference between the duration of the asset structure and the duration of the liability structure is the bank's net duration. A positive net duration means that the duration of the assets is longer than the duration of the liabilities. A decrease in interest rates will increase the net value of the institution. Net duration analysis has the advantage that it does not rely in interest rate forecasts because it is based on parallel shifts in the yield curve. For this reason, it fails to account for basis risk. It also fails to adjust for accelerated prepayment of loans or early withdrawals of time deposits. The change in duration due to the activating of embedded options, which is often referred to as convexity, causes similar problems. However, convexity factors can be computed and duration can be adjusted accordingly to take account of the exercising of embedded options. Such adjustments improve the ability of duration analysis to more accurately measure the impact on the value of an institution's equity when interest rates change.

Another measurement methodology estimates the impact of an interest rate change by conducting a net present value analysis. This analysis determines the net present value of all the cashflows included in the model. This can be developed so as to take account of embedded options and basis risk. Such models have the advantage that they can be used to simulate a number of scenarios based on changes in the shape of the yield curve. Models can also be used to conduct dynamic simulations analysis that estimates the impact on interest rate risk on an institution's earnings. It can for example be used to provide a worst case, a best case and a likely scenario to senior management as a help for decision making.

6.4   Management of interest rate risk

The management of interest rate risk has become simpler. There has been a proliferation of hedging instruments that have enabled risk to be more easily assessed and mitigated. Approaches to managing interest rate risk can be divided into passive approaches and active approaches. Passive approaches involve monitoring the mismatches and taking a fairly cautious approach to matching assets and liabilities, whereas an active approach involves embracing the risk and introducing instruments to hedge the risks. To what extent these more complex tools will be used will depend on the complexity of the bank's activities and the sophistication of its risk management. After all, banks with simple operations may have less need for active management. They know that interest rate risk is inherent in banking and as long as it is kept within prudent bounds there is no need for active management. Other banks, however, see active interest rate risk management as a key tool for enhancing the net worth of the organization by improving profitability and minimizing losses.

Gap reports are useful to both the active and passive risk managers, although it is likely that active risk managers will use it in combination with other tools. Gap reports help to isolate areas of the balance-sheet that constitute large portions of a bank's interest rate risk position caused by timing differences either due to positions reaching maturity or simply being repriced. The information contained in the gap report often suggests various strategies for managing interest rate risk. Thus it can provide information on where the asset/liability mix of the balance-sheet needs to be adjusted to reduce exposure.

In contrast, net duration, particularly if adjusted for convexity, results in a single figure indicating the degree to which the value of the bank can change for a given change in interest rates. Duration of individual instruments is also useful when deciding on how to hedge individual positions. Finally, full-scale models can be used for simulations and will enable the testing of the effects of specific risk management decisions on the bank's portfolio. The cost of running these models makes it likely that they will be of particular benefit to active risk managers as they will reap more benefit from the models.

There are various strategies that banks can use to manage their interest rate risk. These range from simply using the bank's investment portfolio to using derivatives to achieve the desired exposure.

Often the simplest way to manage the risk is to sell off fixed-income securities from the bank's investment portfolio and to re-invest at a different maturity. This will be reflected in the gap report and reduce or increase the risk exposure accordingly. Whether this is an option will depend on the availability of marketable securities for resale and the effect on other risks this may have. Particularly the sale of short-term paper, while being sensible from an interest rate risk management point of view, may have significant implications for the liquidity risk the bank faces. In addition the way the funds are re-invested will result in new credit risk exposure and may also affect the net income margin of the bank.

Extensions of this tool would include securitizing certain exposures so as to get them off the bank's balance-sheet. This would free cash that can be invested in either new products or to achieve a specified desired risk exposure. To continue on the asset side it may be possible to utilize reverse repurchase agreements to change the balance sheet mix. Reverse repos represent the sale of a security with a simultaneous agreement to repurchase them at a fixed price on a specific date. This can be done at various maturities, allowing very accurate targeting of specific exposure. On the liability side banks may be able to issue certificates of deposit, known as CDs.

A longer term risk management tool may be the introduction of new products. New products may introduce new repricing periods or may include new embedded options into instruments or products. For such a strategy to work, it will need very effective communication between the risk managers and those marketing various products to the end-user. Examples are the repricing of deposit or loan rates to have the desired shift in interest rate risk. This is not a straightforward management tool and is therefore only used in conjunction with other tools.

Finally there are the more complex instruments that can be used for both hedging and interest rate risk management purposes:

♦ Financial futures – contracts to sell a financial instrument on or before a specified date at an agreed price. In banking as opposed to commodities this would normally be an interest-bearing contract such as a Treasury bond or perhaps a three-month Eurodollar interest rate contract.

♦ Forward rate agreement (FRA)– contracts where there is no commitment to make a loan or take a deposit, only an interest rate and a nominal principal amount are agreed. The amount that then becomes payable is determined by the difference between the prevailing and the actual rate in the transactions (if any). The banks are thus insuring themselves against rate movements in exchange for a risk premium.

♦ Interest rate swap – for the purpose of long-term interest rate management the interest-rate swap is the most popular instrument, allowing the parties involved to exchange cashflows. The underlying principal positions are unchanged, but the idea is that the two parties are able to find a better solution to their own particular funding requirement.

♦ Financial options – contracts that give to its holder the right but not the obligation to buy or sell an underlying security at a fixed price at or before a specific date. They are particularly useful for interest rate risk management when combined with caps and/or floors. These would be options structured so that they would limit the holder's risks up to a pre-determined level.

Banks should have an overall strategy for the management of interest rate risk. The day-to-day techniques would depend upon:

- the structure of its loans and investments;
- information on borrowing;
- information on interest-bearing investments and loans;
- total amount borrowed and invested;
- the mix in the portfolio between fixed-rate and variable or floating-rate contracts; and
- the currencies in which the transactions have taken place.

In addition there are several questions that risk managers need to ask themselves to determine which strategy to follow:

- How will it affect the gap report?
- Will it increase or decrease the bank's basis risk?
- What is the effect on the net interest margin?
- How will it affect the liquidity exposure?
- Will it expand the balance-sheet?
- How quickly can it be implemented?
- What are transaction costs?

As ever, there are a number of key controls that banks need to introduce to ensure that their interest rate risk management is appropriate and that they can rely on the reports that are produced internally. Strategies and policies should be approved at the highest level of the organization. Reporting lines should be clear and individual responsibility assigned. The larger and more complex an organization, the more important the independence of the interest rate risk management unit will become. Procedures should be clearly defined and, often forgotten, adhered to! Especially new products need to be reviewed to ensure the interest rate risk inherent in them are caught by the risk management processes.

We have seen some of the issues relevant to the monitoring and measurement of interest rate risk. Any systems should capture all material sources of interest rate risk. It is particularly important in this context that those making decisions on the interest rate structure of the books clearly understand the assumptions underpinning their systems. Limits and delegated authorities, ie what is the maximum exposure and who can (or needs to) take actions to remedy them, need to be clearly established. Adherence to them and the adequacy of the whole interest rate risk management framework should be independently assessed. Particularly the accuracy of any reporting should be verified. It is also good practice to ensure that each bank is aware of how its books will cope under stressful market conditions. Only the simplest operations should be able to do without such strict processes, and even then the reasons for that ought to be reviewed on a regular basis to ensure that the policies in place remain appropriate to the level of operations.

Seven

Foreign exchange risk

Objectives

This chapter will cover the following topics:

- ◆ translation exposure;
- ◆ transaction exposure.

7.1   Introduction

Foreign exchange risk, or FX risk, is the risk stemming from the movement of the value of one currency against the value of another. Movements in the exchange rate can result in significant increases or decreases in bank profits – a trading risk known as transaction exposure. A bank operating from its domestic market may encounter fluctuations in the effective value of its international portfolio through exchange rate movements, and for the foreign subsidiary there is the issue of how the operation will be funded and in which currency, taking into account the likely movements in exchange rates. This is known as translation exposure.

Like other risks, foreign exchange rate risk needs to be adequately controlled and managed. This is especially the case for internationally active banks that have large investments in foreign currency. The translation of currency assets into domestic currency can have a drastic effect on the performance of an institution as such book losses can have a significant impact on the published accounts. Such exposures need to be analysed in order to take the necessary steps to avoid or at least minimize the effects of adverse currency movements. At a different level FX exposures also arise from simple banking transactions, especially if a bank is heavily involved as proprietary trader in foreign currency transactions. To minimize losses a bank will require its treasury function to implement strong controls.

The whole issue of exchange rate exposure has increased in importance, as exchange rates have become more volatile, increasing the need for effective controls. Foreign exchange risk relates to structural balance-sheet exposures, which come from decisions made on currency mix in both international currency dealings and from operating subsidiaries in other countries. Here we are not concerned solely with foreign exchange (FOREX or FX) dealing but with all the lending, investment and borrowing that takes place as a natural part of the wholesale money markets. These activities will try to take advantage of exchange rate volatility and mitigate negative risk outcome but will not trade solely on the movements in exchange rates as is the case in the FX markets.

The world economy now exists within a world of mainly floating exchange rates. We have already seen that this developed subsequent to the collapse of the Bretton Woods agreement which had set up a framework of exchange stability. The floating exchange rate system has become even more prevalent since the introduction of the Euro, which reduced the number of currencies trading within agreed bands. Although intervention by central banks has become less important as a result of the Euro, intervention still exists as central banks strive to maintain a stable regime of interest rates, exchange rates and inflation. Indeed, as more countries join the Euro, these countries are likely to increase interventions to bring about the convergence of their currency to the Euro, as required by the Euro entry criteria.

7.2   Translation exposures

Translation exposure relates to the foreign-currency financial statements being translated into the reporting currency of the parent company. As the exchange rate changes the parent currency value of the exposed asset or liability changes. The assets and liabilities would be translated for a number of reasons:

- ◆ consolidation of accounts;
- ◆ performance evaluation;
- ◆ creditworthiness reviews;
- ◆ assessment of taxation liabilities.

The effects of changes in exchange rates on the translated accounts do not affect the cashflow of the trading subsidiary because the figures are only being translated rather than converted into the currency of the parent book. Nevertheless the effects matter because of their impact on the accounts and thus the perception the company has in the market place.

Take the example of a UK bank with a subsidiary in Spain. The UK bank has an asset whose value is dependent on movements in the Euro. However, if the UK bank decides to fund the Spanish subsidiary in sterling there is a different risk again. The assets are valued in Euros and the liabilities are denominated in sterling. If sterling then strengthens against the Euro, there will be a shortfall in the subsidiary in sterling terms. This would then require the parent bank to write off the shortfall from reserves. But this approach may have been taken for good reason, in the anticipation that the Euro was to strengthen against sterling.

7.3   Transaction exposures

A bank's transaction risk relates to its foreign exchange exposures in its trading and banking positions. The receivable or the payable change in value as the exchange rate changes. For example, take a British bank faced with repaying funding it procured from an American bank on a three-month basis and that will reach maturity on a date in the future. If sterling weakens against the dollar, then repayment of the maturity value would cost more.

If an investment was made in the US by a British bank, the real return on that investment has to take account of movements in the exchange rate – from the point at which investment was initiated to the point at which it is realized. Equally, if a deposit is made with a US bank, the value of that deposit can go down in line with the exchange or, alternatively, go up, generating a greater than expected profit.

International banks in fact thrive on this risk by marketing forward and options instruments on behalf of trading companies. These instruments, to be covered in depth later in this text, are designed so that import-export risks for commercial companies are shared in return for a margin. The risk is taken from the trading company and the bank profits or losses based on the actual exchange of goods and money that takes place in, say, three months' time. For example, a French pharmaceutical company agrees to sell an assignment of drugs to an American company in three months' time. In order to fix the interest rate so that profit margins can be assessed and fixed, the American company gets a quote from the bank for a forward exchange rate which largely respects the margin negotiated on the imported goods. If the bank's calculations are correct, it too will receive a profit from the transaction. But there is an inherent risk of losing on the deal and this will be reflected in the spread the bank will use to quote for payment in three months' time. However, the larger the bank's book is, the more the bank will be diversified. It will thus have a natural hedge against the risk contained in each individual trade and it will therefore be able to live off the margins that it is making on individual deals.

Taking the example back into the financial sector, let us look at an American bank with USD50m on deposit with another bank in the USA, earning 3%. Seeing UK interest rates move to 5%, the bank moves its USD50m deposit to a UK bank for nine months. The transaction risk to the US depositor bank is that sterling could then fall by, say, 10% in relation to the US dollar, thus reducing the value of the investment to USD45m. The net effect would have been to cancel out the gain from moving the funds to attract the higher rate of interest.

7.4   Managing foreign exchange risk

7.4.1   Managing translation risk

The attitude a bank takes to translation exposure – the risk from designating the fund currency for subsidiaries – will vary from bank to bank. Rather than see it as a loss in real terms, some banks will see it merely as an accounting imbalance that reaches an equilibrium over a period of time. Under this interpretation the bank might automatically elect to fund in the parent company's domestic currency. But, in spite of the fact that the bank may not have chosen to employ the hedging tactic, it may choose to ensure that it has a diversified currency portfolio in order to control the level of risk exposure.

7.4.2   Managing transaction exposure

The management of transaction exposure is likely to be treated as a separate issue to managing translation exposure. The transaction exposure will result in an actual cashflow, whereas the translation exposure would normally involve a reporting currency exposure. It will be the general strategy of the bank which will determine to what extent transaction exposure ought to be hedged.

7.4.3   Foreign exchange exposure policy

The management at all levels has to decide which risks are important and then establish reporting and policy-making structures to establish at what level exposure-related decisions will be made. Policy decisions will need to be made on such issues as under what circumstances hedging would take place and how exposures on translation risks are considered – in other words, how they should be managed or indeed whether they should be managed.

The issue of whether or not to hedge is a subject of some debate. Hedging can be very costly. Therefore, if one considers translation risk to net itself out over the long run there appears to be limited justification for the practice. If, on the other hand, the desire is not to distort asset values and earnings per share, then hedging provides a means of showing a less volatile picture. Other strategies, which would be less concerned with hedging all foreign exchange risk, would use hedging only when it was necessary to keep risk exposures within predetermined bands.

In determining the liability structure, the bank would normally consider the bank's natural business to determine its funding approach. Depending upon the type of trading it is engaged in, it might have no hesitation in dealing in the subsidiary country's domestic currency, which may or may not involve an element of hedging of the exposure. If the subsidiary is heavily involved with further currencies, other than that of the subsidiary and its parent, then Head Office would have to consider the risks involved in dealings in that third currency.

7.4.4 Forecasting foreign exchange rate movements

Economists are often maligned for their inability to forecast accurately. The complexity of macroeconomics makes the proposition of successfully forecasting movements in economic variables difficult. But, with varying degrees of success, bank treasury economists use a combination of gut feeling and sophisticated forecasting and scenario planning techniques in an attempt to forecast the direction, magnitude, and timing of exchange rate changes with varying degrees of success. This will then be used, in combination with dealers' gut feeling to decide on the future positions that should be taken.

7.4.5 Measurement and reporting

A first step for bank management will be to define its foreign exchange exposures. Only then will it be able to manage them. It needs to be able to forecast its degree of exposure for each major currency in which it operates. This involves forecasting worst-case and probable exposure scenarios, not attempting to forecast exchange rate movements themselves, which is a more speculative endeavour.

Once a bank has decided how it wishes to measure foreign exchange exposure, it then needs to establish a reporting system which calls on the centralized control functions and the local personnel in the subsidiaries or branches. The foreign input is required in order to utilize the most relevant and best quality information, given that those located in the foreign country will have a better 'feel' for the local economy.

The centralized reporting and control is necessary to take account of the overall exposure within the parent corporation. By setting out uniform reporting requirements for branches, affiliates and subsidiaries it can then get a complete picture, and employ its strategy for dealing with the exposures. There are usually different levels of review. First of all reviews would take place at a local level, then it is likely that the reported exposure would be reported at a regional level – eg Europe, Asia – or that determined by the organizational structure. The region might consolidate its data by account and by currency for each time period, with final reporting at corporate level where broad-based strategies are developed.

To some extent the more transactions a bank undertakes the lower its effective exposures. This is because the more transactions are on its book, the more the various individual exposures are likely to net out. The result is that the bank, despite increased risk taking, will increase its profitability from the margins it earns on each single trade, as a diversified portfolio will provide it with a natural hedge.

Eight

Credit risk

Objectives

This chapter will cover the following topics:

- ◆ definition of credit risk;
- ◆ rating systems, rating agencies and rating methodologies;
- ◆ credit risk management;
- ◆ country risk;
- ◆ settlement risk.

8.1   Introduction

The previous chapters looked at the key risks with which treasury units are generally associated. Although credit risk is not foremost associated with treasury functions, it remains an underlying risk that drives both treasury operations directly and indirectly via its impact on the business units that a treasury function supports.

Although banks often try to organize their activities around different risks, such as market risk in dealing rooms, one should always remain aware that many risks are interrelated and that it would be self-defeating to manage them in isolation. Credit risk, for example, is prevalent in the corporate lending areas, but it will also exist in a trading environment. Country risk, as a particular type of credit risk, is similar. It will underlie all exposures to foreign counterparties, but it is unlikely to be foremost in the mind of traders, who will be looking at their internal limits to ensure that they do not threaten the risk management approach of their institutions. The same can be said for settlement risk, which is the risk that the counterparty does not deliver on their part of the deal as a result of problems with settlement.

Credit risk is defined as the risk of loss arising from the failure of a counterparty to make a contractual payment. Given that traditional banking is about lending of money, credit risk is one of the more pervasive banking risks. Credit risk not only arises from loans but also in the wider banking book, be it guarantees and other on- and off-balance-sheet activities. It also exists in the trading book, where bonds for example can default. Credit risk, which is often referred to as counterparty risk, is all pervasive: it exists within acceptances, interbank transactions, trade financing, foreign exchange transactions, financial futures, swaps, bonds, equities, options, commitments and guarantees. Settlement risk is also a type of credit risk. It will thus be discussed separately at the end of this chapter.

In the UK the small banks crisis was a good example of credit risk affecting a banking sector. In the early 1990s, the small and medium-sized banks consisted of over one hundred institutions, many of which specialized in lending to particular geographical regions, industrial sectors or ethnic/religious groups. Many of these small (and medium-size) banks were heavily exposed to property lending and, to a lesser extent, to instalment credit and hire purchase lending. On the liabilities side, most of the banks were heavily reliant on wholesale funding. Many of the small banks that subsequently went on to fail enjoyed particularly rapid loan growth in the second half of the 1980s. With the benefit of hindsight, this marked increase in lending was an indicator of excessive credit risk taking. During the economic downturn of the early 1990s, many of these small banks experienced pressure on both sides of their balance-sheets. The impact of the recession was particularly severe on the property market and this resulted in a marked decline in banks' asset quality and collateral values. At the end three small banks – Chancery, Edington and Authority – were allowed to fail in early 1991. As the Bank of England did not consider such failures a threat to the financial system, no emergency support was provided.

Credit risk continues to plague banking systems. Poor credit risk management led to the problems in two German banks in 2001, Delbrück & Co. and Schmidt Bank. Both banks had been unable to make sufficient profit margins to compensate for the level of default inherent in their portfolio, which consisted mainly of loans to small and medium-sized enterprises. In short they did not manage their credit risk appropriately.

Improving credit risk management is one of the main goals of the new Basel Capital Accord. One of the difficulties of credit risk management is its cyclical nature. Banks tend to lend when the economic outlook is positive and corporates expect significant profits to cover their financing cost. This is often driven by what has become known as the herd instinct, where banks begin bto lend because their competitors do, rather than because the deals make economic sense. At the same time every economic downturn leads to an increase in default rates of corporates and retail customers, which tends to significantly affect the profitability of banks.

Credit risk is of both direct and indirect importance to treasurers. It is directly relevant because funds placed by treasury departments will incur a credit risk. This needs to be controlled and taken into account when pricing any transactions. Similarly the bank itself will be a credit risk to other institutions and the treasurer will need to know what this is in order to maximize returns. Dealing activities undertaken by the treasury function will also incur settlement risk for which controls need to be in place. Credit risk will also affect the treasury function indirectly as a result of its impact on other business units. Defaults of counterparties of other business units may have a significant impact on cashflows and the treasurer needs to be able to adapt to these in order to maintain the liquidity of the institution.

8.2   Measurement of credit risk and rating agencies

The aim of credit risk measurement is to find some methodology that will enable banks to categorize their exposures in terms of bands of riskiness. Conceptually this should be aimed at assigning a probability of default to each counterparty or issue, but in practice many banks use a less complex framework. For the sake of simplicity most banks, even those that work off probability of defaults, transpose their assessments into rating categories. The complexity of banks' credit risks will determine what type of methodology is sufficient for management. The main issue is that the system can be used to assess the probability of a particular issue not being repaid in full when it falls due for redemption, or give an indication of the likelihood of future problems at a counterparty.

The simplest rating methodology would only use four categories:

◆ low risk;
◆ medium risk;
◆ high risk; and
◆ in default.

A more common approach is to reflect the rating system introduced by Standard's & Poors or Moody's, the largest rating agencies. Their long-term ratings follow the following structure:

Table 7.1: Long-term ratings

S & P	Moody's	Interpretation	Moody's average default rates for a one year holding period
AAA	Aaa	Extremely strong	0.00%
AA	Aa	Very strong	0.08%
A	A	Very strong but susceptible to changes in circumstances	0.08%
BBB	Baa	Adequate – minimum to be considered investment grade	0.3%
BB	Ba	Has some speculative elements	1.43%
B	B	Assurance of interest and principal payment may be small	4.48%
CCC	Caa	Poor standing – may be in default	
CC	Ca	Highly speculative – may be in default	19.09%
C	C	Very poor prospects	
D	D	In default	

These grades may be modified by adding +/- or 1/2/3 suffixes.

Although there may be significant differences between rating agencies and bank internal approaches there are certain quantitative and qualitative factors that are invariably taken into account for a credit assessment of each individual credit or credit proposal.

The main quantitative factors are likely to be:

◆ Capital, including its composition and quality, an assessment of capital adequacy, access to additional capital in a crisis and, if relevant, how it will be repaid.
◆ Asset quality, including concentration of portfolio, overall credit quality and approach to provisioning.
◆ Market risk inherent in the portfolio, including an assessment of the key products and markets, as well as how market risk, interest rate risk and foreign exchange risk are measured.
◆ Earnings, including stability of earnings and future prospects.
◆ Liquidity, ie the ability to meet payments as they fall due, which will depend on the liquidity of assets, their composition and concentrations.

Qualitative factors, although more subjective, also need to be included into a credit rating/assessment:

- Business franchise, ie the scope of business activities and its value – it would also include group issues, customer base, competitive differentiation, external drivers, staff issues, etc.
- Internal controls, such as effectiveness of internal audit and compliance functions.
- Organization, ie its ownership structure and other organizational issues, such as any government ownership, or large single shareholders. Country of origin would also be relevant.
- Management quality, ie culture, experience, board composition, non-executive directors, approach to planning and strategy.

Other aspects that would be included are any hidden strength and reserves, or hidden weaknesses and overvalued assets. A company's underlying country risk would also have to be factored in when the counterparty in question comes from overseas. How economic conditions are taken into account will depend on the methodology used. Some banks use a through-the-cycle approach, meaning that the final rating should already have factored in any changes due to economic conditions. Other banks use a point in time methodology, which will only hold under the economic conditions at the time the rating was given.

In practice banks often use both their internal ratings as well as the ratings given by credit rating agencies to help in their decision making process. Credit ratings from independent bodies have advantages in terms of being already available and being widely recognized. Thus where speed is essential, such as in a dealing environment, they can provide a useful input. Furthermore they provide a useful reference against which to compare internal ratings. Nevertheless many banks feel they have additional knowledge and expertise that is not available to rating agencies and that they can get a competitive advantage by utilizing their own ratings. Some banks have invested significant amounts to come up with automated rating systems. Although credit scoring is more common for retail transactions, variations of it may also be used for some parts of the corporate lending portfolio. Credit scoring is based on assigning values to various factors that are likely to determine probability of default. To qualify for a positive lending decision the credit scoring has to pass a given hurdle. At the other extreme are credit assessments that are only based on expert judgement without a qualitative framework underpinning it. In reality most methodologies used by banks are some form of hybrid between the extremes of expert judgement or pure credit scoring approaches. Like other credit risk management tools internal ratings need to be effectively controlled. This is particularly important since internal ratings methodologies are likely to become increasingly important as part of the future capital adequacy rules.

Credit risk cannot be managed without a clear definition of what is defined as 'default'. A default is generally considered to have occurred with regard to a particular obligor when a bank considers that the obligor is unlikely to pay its credit obligations to the banking group in full. For the assessment of default, the possibility of realizing a collateral to obtain payment would be discounted. Definition of default is, however, very subjective. Thus many institutions have come up with some additional, objective measures. Certainly if an obligor is past due more than, say, 90 days on any material credit obligation then it ought to be treated as being in default. The period is, however, variable with some banks waiting until up to 180 days, or more depending on product, before treating an obligor as being in default. For other areas, such as overdrafts, a simple limit breach may be treated as being an event of default.

Symptoms of default may include:

◆ The bank makes a charge-off or account-specific provision to take account of the significant perceived decline in credit quality subsequent to the bank taking on the exposure.
◆ The bank sells the credit obligation at a material credit-related economic loss.
◆ The bank consents to a distressed restructuring of the credit obligation where this is likely to result in a diminished financial obligation caused by the material forgiveness, or postponement, of principal, interest or (where relevant) fees.
◆ The bank has filed for the obligor's bankruptcy or a similar order in respect of the obligor's credit obligation or indeed the obligor itself may have sought or been placed in bankruptcy or similar protection. This in turn is likely to avoid or delay repayment of the credit obligation to the bank.

Moody's, the rating agency, describes its own definition of default for long-term debt securities as: 'Default usually involves missed or delayed payments of interest or principal or bankruptcy and is therefore clearly identifiable. However, Moody's definition of default also includes a category called "distressed exchange" which, while less prevalent, is more difficult to define and apply.'

8.3   Credit risk management

Credit risk management processes will differ from bank to bank, but over time sound practices have developed. These were codified by the Basel Committee on Banking Supervision in September 2000 in its 'Principles for the Management of Credit Risk' paper.

8.3.1   Establish appropriate credit risk environment

The credit risk environment should be driven by the highest authority of an institution. Thus the board of directors or its counterpart should approve and review credit risk strategy on a regular basis. The strategy needs to reflect the bank's tolerance for risk and the level of profitability the bank expects to achieve from its credit risk exposures. The strategy should be consistent with other processes within the bank, for example remuneration, and, in particular, bonuses, should reflect risk taking instead of only rewarding volumes. Senior management should be accountable for implementing the credit risk strategy. This will involve the development of policies and procedures for identifying, measuring, monitoring and controlling credit risk, at both individual credit and portfolio levels. Particular care should be taken to identify and manage credit risk inherent in all products and activities, especially with new products, instead of only managing the obvious credit exposures from, for example, the retail and corporate loan book.

8.3.2   Operating under a sound credit-granting process

It is essential that banks operate with sound, well-defined credit-granting criteria. These criteria must be communicated and understood throughout the organization. To ensure adherence internal procedures should give a clear indication of the bank's target markets. Credits should only be granted following a thorough understanding of the borrower or counterparty. This should be combined with an understanding of the purpose and structure of the credit and source of repayment. In practice this is the role of credit officers to assess and credit committees to approve. It certainly should not be delegated to outsiders, such as lead underwriters or credit rating agencies.

It is common practice to get credit proposals over certain limits (or exceeding delegated authorities) to be approved by a credit committee. For the largest transactions the credit committee may be the board itself. It is generally the credit committee which fulfils the requirement to have a clearly-established process in place for approving new credits as well as the amendment, renewal and re-financing of existing credits. Moreover extensions of credit to connected parties, such as subsidiaries or other group companies, must be made on an arm's length basis. The more obvious the potential conflict of interest for providing the loan, the more important it becomes to adhere to the arm's length principle.

A sound credit-granting process will also include overall credit limits at the level of individual borrowers and counterparties. To be effective these limits will include exposures to other parts of a group, should the transaction be with a group company. Furthermore it is essential to consider all existing credit exposures, including those in the trading book, banking book and on- and off-balance-sheet items. Only that way can a bank ensure that it does not unwittingly open itself to large exposures that it could not cope with if a default was to occur. This is where treasury functions will need to be integrated into the overall credit risk strategy of the bank.

8.3.3   Maintain an appropriate credit administration, measurement and monitoring process

It may sound facetious, but lending money is the easy part. The real banking skill lies in ensuring that borrowers repay their loans as they are due. This can only be achieved consistently if a bank has in place a system for the ongoing administration of its various credit risk-bearing portfolios. This should include a system for monitoring the condition of each individual loan, including determining the adequacy of provisions and reserves. Information systems and analytical techniques should enable management to measure the credit risk inherent in all on- and off-balance-sheet activities. Reporting credit exposures is also fundamental to enable pro-active credit risk management. This in turn requires appropriate management information systems to provide adequate information on the composition of the whole bank's credit portfolio, including identification of any concentrations of risk. It should enable ongoing monitoring of the overall composition and quality of the credit portfolio. Furthermore banks should consider potential future changes in economic conditions when assessing individual credit and portfolio, particularly under stressful conditions. The processes also need to be clearly linked to the definition of default and the actions that a bank needs to take once it becomes aware of a default.

8.3.4 Ensure adequate controls over credit risks

The importance of controls over credit risk management cannot be overestimated. It will be the responsibility of senior management to ensure that the credit-granting function is being properly managed and that credit exposures are within levels consistent with prudential standards, such as large exposure requirements, and internal limits. Internal limits should reflect the overall credit risk strategy of the bank, including concentration levels and large exposures. Furthermore banks should establish and enforce internal controls and practices to ensure that exceptions to policies, procedures and limits are reported in a timely manner to the appropriate level of management for action. Early remedial action needs to be taken on deteriorating credits, problem credits need to be managed and particularly default situations need to be actively pursued. Additionally a system of independent, ongoing assessment of the bank's credit risk management process must be in place. The results of such reviews should be communicated directly to the board. In practice such reviews can be undertaken by internal audit functions, be outsourced or be undertaken by specialized risk management units.

8.4 Credit risk management in practice

As ever in risk management it is important that the strategy is agreed at the highest level of the organization, such as a board of directors. It is the board's role to establish an appropriate credit risk environment by, for instance, deciding on the target market of the institution. The level of desired riskiness is both an input into the decision and also an outcome of the same strategic decision. Similarly the level of concentration of the credit risk will be part of that decision. The decision will in turn impact on how procedures are implemented, responsibility assigned and limits set.

High concentration of exposures to specific industries will also affect the credit risk faced by an institution. The small banks crisis in the early 1990s was an example where concentration in the real-estate sector was so high that a number of institutions were not able to survive. Although concentration risk is one of the inputs into risk management it should not be seen as an absolute requirement, as diversification for its own sake can create new risks. There is a particular risk that management that diversifies for the sake of it does not have the knowledge required to undertake the new activity successfully. In turn such diversification could create more operational risk, which may ultimately be of a bigger risk to the institution than the concentration risk ever was. This is another example showing that risk management is about finding the right trade-offs between risks, rather than eliminating risks altogether.

In most banks, credit committees form the mainstay of credit risk management, as it is the credit committee that will provide a sound credit-granting process. In practice the board of directors will delegate a certain level of authority to the credit committee, which will approve loans and limits that fall within its delegated authority. For large exposures the board itself may act as the credit committee, while for smaller loans individual bank officers may have sufficient delegated authority to lend without additional input. Treasury functions operate in such a fast moving environment that it will be impractical to have every deal approved by a committee; and given the size of deals, which are generally in the millions rather than lower, it is also not possible to leave the delegated authority with one individual. It is thus common practice to work on the basis of limits for individual counterparties. These will have to be approved by the credit committee and once established give dealers the parameters within which they can create credit risk exposures. The challenge will be to integrate such limits with those exposures created in other parts of the business. Only that way can it be ensured that credit risk is managed on a global basis across the organization, taking into account large exposures and portfolio effects.

Pricing considerations will also have to be taken into account as part of the credit granting process. It is important to ensure that loans get repaid, but interest charged must also include sufficient margin to cover the costs incurred by the bank in providing and administering the loan. From a portfolio management point of view the margin also needs to cover the likely probability of default. Every banker will know that there will be instances when debtors will default on their obligations. This likelihood of default will be determined by the obligor's creditworthiness, which is generally expressed in ratings. Thus every rating will have an explicit or implicit probability of default attached to it. Taking this probability into account a bank should ensure that the interest rate the obligor has to pay covers the risk associated with the loan. Although every banker and particularly treasurer will know of the need to price according to this risk return relationship, it can easily be forgotten. In particular market share considerations, and reputational effects can force banks into accepting returns on loans that are inadequate given the risks undertaken. Syndicated loans are an example, where it has sometimes been the case that participation in a loan was important to remain a player in the market, even if in reality margins were inadequate to cover the risk taken onto the books.

The credit granting process is only the starting point of the whole credit risk management process. In particular within a treasury function, where controls are via limits, it will be important to monitor trading. Segregation will also need to be in place. Dealers should, for example, not be able to initiate payment, as this should be the remit of a separate back-office function. Similarly there need to be controls over who can change limits on the computer system. Other controls need to be in place over settlement procedures. Deal slips should be pro-actively reconciled with the information provided by the counterparty. Finally such back-office procedures need to be as tightly controlled as front-offices to ensure adherence to procedures. Segregation between front-offices and back-offices is a pre-requisite for this. These are the same controls as for the management of market risk.

Not only will it be important to ensure that limits are not breached, the appropriateness of limits needs to be reviewed, especially in light of new financial information that may impact on the creditworthiness of the counterparty. Many loans will also include covenants, breach of which may enable a bank to ask for early repayment. It is thus essential to monitor counterparties to ensure the bank's position is protected. This information will need to be assessed and, in particular, reviewed in order to assess if pro-active management is required. Examples of active management would be the calling for early repayment in case of a breach of contract, such as a breach of a covenant. Another would be the use of credit risk mitigation techniques or, for example, a straight sale of the exposure. When active management is required, for example for resale of a loan to reduce exposure, or taking a decision on whether to call any embedded options, it will be essential to have the original documentation at hand. Good record keeping is thus in each bank's self interest. Collateral and guarantees need to be monitored to ensure they still provide the protection that was originally intended. There also need to be procedures in place to ensure that adequate provisioning for downgrades of creditworthiness is correctly taken into account. The above shows that the process of credit risk management is far from over once a credit has been agreed, indeed active risk management only starts at that point. The appropriateness of procedures is thus important and adherence to them should be monitored continuously. This is generally done via the combination of a risk management unit and internal audit.

8.4.1 Credit risk modelling

The most advanced banks will use credit risk modelling to manage their credit risk. The approach is based on a more rigorous analysis of the bank's credit risk exposure than is common in less sophisticated banks.

Credit risk has three main components:

- ◆ Probability of default is the probability that the counterparty will fail to make a contractual payment.
- ◆ Loss given default is the proportion of claims that cannot be recovered if the counterparty or an exposure defaults.
- ◆ Exposure at default is the credit exposure relating to the amount that the bank will stand to lose in default. This is usually interpreted as the replacement value of the contract in the event of default or, in the case of commitment, the level of usage.

As already indicated there is a strong correlation between credit ratings and default rates. Credit ratings can thus be used to predict default rates. Predictions of default rates can also be improved by referring to other observable factors. Some financial variables can thus be used to discriminate between those firms likely to fail and those that are not. Indeed some banks use these financial variables to directly derive a probability of default for each individual counterparty or issue. Depending on the probability of default they will then assign a rating.

Similarly loss-given default rates can also be modelled. Intuitively there is a link between a rating and the recovery rates. It will vary depending on the seniority ranking of the creditor. Secured debt for example tends to have a recovery rate of up to 90%, while subordinated debt tends to have recovery rates of between 10% and 15%. There are also other differences. Probability of default very much depends on the obligor. In contrast loss given default only becomes an issue once a facility has been put in default. Even then the loss given default will be different for each exposure, even if to the same obligor. Thus a loan secured on a property is likely to have a much lower loss given default, than for example high-yield debt instruments that are treated as subordinated debt.

Any such credit models will have to be validated internally to ensure that results from it are robust. This can be undertaken either by backtesting the model against historic data, or for example by using scenario testing. Here the same issues arise that arise for VaR models. This is particularly the case since credit risk models by definition incorporate diversification effects.

Modelling has certain advantages in terms of risk management. From a business point of view it allows an improved assessment of the underlying capital that is needed for the various lending activities. This ought to help resource allocation within the institution, which in turn should ultimately lead to increased profits. The methodology is also useful from a reporting point of view. It is possible to estimate the maximum credit exposure at some level of confidence. Using a 95% confidence level, the credit at risk figure would show the maximum credit exposure that could be expected for a given holding period. Such a figure is useful to provide a feel for the overall credit risk that the bank is running. As is the case for VaR models, which are used for market risk, such a figure should not be confused with the maximum credit exposure possible. A further advantage of credit risk modelling is that it allows portfolio effects to be taken into account. This means that benefits of having exposures that are not correlated to each other, and therefore reduce the riskiness of the portfolio, could be more clearly identified. It should be noted that the Basel Committee, when proposing a new Capital Accord, has explicitly avoided allowing full scale credit risk modelling for regulatory capital adequacy purposes on the basis that these are as yet insufficiently developed. Some practitioners disagree, and view the half-way step of allowing only internal rating models as insufficient.

8.4.2 Credit risk mitigation techniques

As we have seen, there are three elements of credit risk: default probability, loss given default and exposure at default. Credit risk management can therefore be regarded as a set of techniques for reducing default probability and exposure at default while at the same time increasing recovery rate. There are numerous techniques available to achieve this, some of which will be discussed below.

Netting arrangements

Netting arrangements stipulate that each party should be liable for the net amount, rather than the gross amount they owe to the other party. Netting arrangements protect the non-defaulting party from a situation where its counterparty defaults on one contract and yet simultaneously insists on the payment due on the other. In general, the reduction in credit exposure created by netting will be greater, the greater the number of deals outstanding with a counterparty and the more nearly aligned the individual contracts are in terms of maturities, contract size, etc. Periodic settlement has similar characteristics to netting, although it may be less effective in reducing exposure. Periodic settlement is based on the idea that outstanding obligations are settled at periodic intervals in the value of a contract, rather than aggregating them at the end of the contract. Although periodic settlement can reduce exposure, it can also increase problems under adverse market conditions.

Margin and collateral requirements

Institutions can also reduce their exposure by means of margin or collateral requirements. This means that a counterparty makes available some particular asset that it would forfeit to a creditor in the event of default. Collateral is usually demanded upfront, and it is common for margin requirements to be demanded by organized exchanges and by many derivative brokers. This margin is usually set to cover a specified large adverse move in the value of the underlying instruments.

Credit guarantees

Credit risk can also be reduced by seeking guarantees from third parties. Such guarantees mean that full loss of the principal can only occur if both the counterparty and its guarantor default before payment can be made. This can sometimes lead to a major reduction in credit risk, as the likelihood of both counterparty and guarantor defaulting at the same time ought to be lower than the probability of default of just the counterparty.

Credit triggers

Credit triggers are clauses that allow a contract to be terminated on pre-agreed terms if the credit rating of a counterparty falls to some trigger level. These clauses are similar to the covenants often used in commercial lending that specify that the debtor must maintain minimum net worth or credit rating. These triggers may in theory reduce credit risk by setting a floor to the loss that will be taken. Whether this works as well in practice remains debatable, as significant use of credit triggers creates additional volatility which may not be in anyone's interest.

Credit derivatives

Firms can also manage their credit risks by using credit derivatives. These are derivatives contracts with payments conditional on credit events of one sort or another. Some of the more common credit derivatives are: credit default swaps, credit spread swaps and total return swaps. With credit default swaps one party makes periodic payments to another party in return for a promise of payment in the event of a default by some other party. With credit spread swaps periodic payments are made in return for the promise of a spread-contingent payment. Finally in total-return swaps parties swap bond payments, where at least one of the bonds involved is credit-risky. Firms that sell their credit risk can benefit by freeing up credit lines to good customers, while at the same time reducing their exposure to key or weak customers, so reducing their vulnerability. At the same time, other firms might benefit from acquiring particular credit risks, either from a diversification point of view or to increase yields.

Securitizations

Securitization has similar benefits to credit derivatives, the main difference being that once obligations have been securitized exposures are deemed to have moved completely off the books, rather than being only hedged, as is the case under the credit derivatives approach. Generally securitization refers to the repackaging of obligations into a special purpose company, which then sells its own instruments into the markets. Sometimes securitizations are also thought to include simple sales of individual loans. Either way there remains a question mark about the extent to which such a resale is permanent. The scale of the problem will depend on the exact nature of the securitization.

8.4.3 Impact on treasury activities

There are a number of ways that credit risk will be of importance to treasury functions. Clearly a treasury function will itself create credit risk by lending or placing money into the markets. This needs to be controlled like any other credit risk within a bank, although procedures are likely to be somewhat different to take account of the specific nature of dealing rooms.

Another element for consideration will be the credit risk the bank itself poses to other banks. This will drive the price at which funds can be obtained from the market and will therefore impact on the cost of funding in general. It will also matter with regard to the products that a bank can offer. A good example is in interest-rate swaps. As we will see in a later chapter, depending on the credit risk the bank itself poses, it may be able to enhance the borrowing capacity of some of its clients.

Finally credit risk, as a source of key risk, can lead to crisis. For example, during the Russian crisis in 1998 the market risk faced by some institutions rose significantly, creating pressure on liquidity. In such situations it is up to treasury management to manage the crisis by calling in commitments and creating liquidity by selling assets, sometimes at prices well below the normal market price. It is in such instances that treasury functions will prove their mettle by having clear procedures, and being able to implement these, to avoid a crisis undermining the institution as a whole.

8.5 Country risk

Country risk is the uncertainty created when funds are to cross international frontiers. It is the risk that a foreign borrower will not satisfactorily service its foreign currency debt obligations for economic or political reasons. Sovereign risk is a variation thereof. It arises when the borrower in question is part of the public sector of another country. Borrowers from the private sector would face an additional transfer risk, ie the risk that they are not allowed to transfer funds.

Country risk became more of an issue during the 1970s and 1980s. The assumption on which lending had been based was that debt could be serviced relatively easily given that export growth was higher in percentage terms than the rate of interest on the debt. This turned out to be a wrong assumption during the early 1980s, particularly when interest rates rose significantly as developing countries increased their domestic interest rates to overcome inflation. In 1982 the six-month Eurodollar interest rate for example rose to over 17%. At the same time, between 1980 and 1983, the debt of developing countries rose by almost USD 200bn but export earnings rose by only 10% of that amount. Debt servicing problems ensued and within a year some 15 countries with liabilities to international banks of over USD 200bn were renegotiated. Since 1979 there have been almost 200 rescheduling agreements between over 40 countries and their creditor banks. Although country risk was less of an issue during the 1990s, the recent economic downturn and falls in asset prices have shown that country risk remains a type of credit risk that should not be ignored.

All cross border lending is subject to country risk, but there has always been some lack of clarity regarding what drives it and how to measure it. Starting from points of principle the assessment of country risk should concentrate on the ability of a country to generate or conserve the foreign exchange earnings which will allow residents of that country to service their foreign currency debt. Where the borrower is a state-owned entity the assessment of the country risk alone represents the credit assessment that a lender undertakes when considering any lending proposition.

As for other credit risk assessment, country risk assessment is based on both quantitative and qualitative factors. Typical quantitative factors are:

- Balance of payments and its structure, as a measure of foreign exchange in- and outflows.
- Size of external debt, particularly as a percentage of GNP or GDP.
- GNP growth, as a measure of a country's entrepreneurial dynamic.
- Inflation, on the basis that high inflation will undermine a country's economic performance and governments will have to take drastic actions, which generally increase country risk.
- Debt servicing burden, including debt servicing ratios and debt maturity.
- Structure of exports, a diversified set of exports being a positive characteristic.
- Foreign currency reserves held by the respective central bank.

Qualitative factors will include:

- A country's likelihood of facing internal unrest (ranging from industrial strife to civil war). The higher the likelihood the higher the country risk.
- The possibility of external conflict, which will take away resources from debt repayment, will also increase country risk.
- Similarly the existence of economic sanctions (or the possibility of them being introduced) is likely to undermine a country's debt servicing capacity.
- Previous rescheduling by the same country is also likely to be viewed as increasing country risk.

8.5.1 Rescheduling of sovereign debt

Given the legal aspects of sovereign debt and the amounts involved in sovereign debt, rescheduling negotiations have often been difficult. Sovereign debtors have tended to have large outstanding debt, which has to be placed widely in order for the financial markets to meet the demand. In a restructuring or rescheduling situation, the number of players does, however, increase the complexity of negotiations, particularly given the strong negotiating positions that a large sovereign borrower has against a collection of lenders, particularly since the threat of ostracizing a country from future loans does not work.

Key parties to rescheduling have almost always been the International Monetary Fund (IMF) and the Paris Club. While the World Bank (IBRD) has large sovereign assets it has not had the same influence in renegotiations as the IMF. The Paris Club is an informal forum in which governments of debtor and creditor countries have renegotiated the terms of intra-government debt since 1956. It generally works in combination with the IMF. Organizationally it has been supported by French Treasury officials, thus the term Paris Club.

To some extent it has almost become a precondition for a rescheduling to have an agreement with the IMF. According to the IMF's charter, its main purposes include assisting countries with balance of payments problems and working for an orderly international monetary system. This includes the promotion of policies aimed at avoiding debt problems. This tends to be done via regular consultations with its members, including an exchange of views on a country's financial position and its policies. It often advises on how imbalances and existing or potential problems could be addressed. An IMF agreement would normally make available new IMF funding. Because of its international set-up, the IMF is almost the sole international entity that can force policy changes, often of a structural nature, as a quid pro quo for providing new funding. As a result countries will try to meet IMF payments, even if they have already defaulted on other loans, particularly since failure to meet IMF targets is invariably classified as an event of default under commercial loan agreements.

Rescheduling of commercial bank debt has tried to imitate the structure of the Paris Club. Commercial debt restructuring is sometimes known as the London Club, although in practice is even more ad hoc than the Paris Club. Each London Club is formed at the initiative of the debtor country and is dissolved when a restructuring agreement is signed. London Club 'Advisory Committees' are chaired by a leading financial firm and include representatives from a cross-section of other exposed firms. Recently, Advisory Committees have included representatives from non-bank creditors (notably fund managers holding sovereign bonds). London Club meetings are not restricted to London and may be held in either London, New York, Paris, or other financial centres.

For commercial banks it is almost more important to have an IMF agreement in place prior to renegotiating the debt. This is because they tend to have even less influence over sovereign countries than the large G10 countries, which are generally at the table for the Paris Club meetings. A key negotiation issue is normally to agree what will be covered by the negotiations and what will not. For example, trade debt, such as documentary credits, tends to be excluded as countries know of the difficult economic situations they would face if such a key area of finance for their economies was undermined by inclusion in a debt rescheduling.

Recently the IMF has proposed the setting up of collective action clauses (CACs) for sovereign debt. The idea is that this would lead to a speedier resolution of sovereign debt crises, which would be positive for market confidence. The IMF holds the view that 'the current process for the restructuring of sovereign debt is more prolonged, more damaging to a debtor and its creditors, and more unpredictable than is desirable'. The IMF proposes that the CAC includes a provision enabling a qualified majority to bind all bondholders within the same issue to the financial terms of a restructuring. The intention is to limit the ability of a minority of bondholders to disrupt the restructuring process by enforcing claims after a default and prior to a restructuring agreement. Additionally there would be a universal statutory framework (the sovereign debt restructuring mechanism, SDRM) which could create 'a legal framework of collective decision making by debtors and a supermajority of creditors'. However, doubts about the proposals within the international financial community remain, and progress is likely to remain slow.

8.6   Settlement and delivery risk

Settlement and delivery risk is also known as Herstatt risk. It is named after Bankhaus Herstatt in Germany, which went bankrupt having received German marks but not having delivered US dollars. After the failure in 1974 it took several weeks to untangle the web of transactions that had been undertaken and caused significant liquidity problems in the markets as well – all because the principle of 'valeur compensée', ie that the deal should be completed on the same day, was not honoured.

Technically settlement risk is a credit risk, but it is of such a special nature that it needs to be reviewed separately. Foreign exchange (FX) settlement risk is of particular concern and this section will focus on this type of settlement risk. Basically FX settlement risk is the risk of loss when a bank in a foreign exchange transaction pays the currency it sold but does not receive the currency it bought. FX settlement failures can arise from counterparty default, operational problems, market liquidity constraints and other factors. Settlement risk exists for any traded product but the size of the foreign exchange market makes FX transactions the greatest source of settlement risk for many market participants, involving daily exposures of tens of billions of dollars for the largest banks. Most significantly, for banks of any size, the amount at risk to even a single counterparty could in some cases exceed their capital. FX settlement risk is a form of counterparty risk involving both credit risk and liquidity risk. As with other forms of risk, banks need to ensure that they have a clear understanding of how settlement risk and particularly FX settlement risk arises.

The whole issue of settlement risk is taken very seriously by central banks and supervisory authorities. For example, the UK's Financial Services Authority discusses with banks what actions are being taken to ensure that this category of risk is being minimized. The crash of October 1987 clearly focused the minds of many banking communities, prompting The Group of Thirty to produce a report called 'Clearance and Settlement Systems in the World's Securities Markets', a report which warned against the dangers of treating settlement risk lightly. A breakdown in the principles and practices that underpin the world's financial dealings may have grave consequences for the global money market, the banks that operate in them, and the world economies. Understanding and recognition of FX settlement risk has increased significantly, not least because of the work of the Committee on Payment and Settlement Systems (CPSS) of the Bank for International Settlements and the various reports and recommendations it has published. All banks are now expected to have a good understanding of FX settlement risk and to have formulated clear and firm plans for how to manage it.

8.6.1 Risk reduction

The risk is not just a daytime one, but extends from the moment a trade is struck to the time receipt of funds has been verified, which, with weekends, can easily extend over five days. It is thus important that all stakeholders actively work at reducing settlement risk.

Individual banks can reduce settlement risk by:

♦ Improving their awareness of FX settlement risk, its measurement and risk control.
♦ Ensuring careful release of payment instructions. Achieving this has been made more difficult by the introduction of straight through processing.
♦ Using electronic confirmation systems such as Crossmar® Matching Service, which is used by over 350 banks and 450 fund managers.
♦ Requiring better services from correspondents in turn-round time for payments to be confirmed using Crossmar® Matching Service or equivalent services.
♦ Requiring better services from correspondents in turn-round time for payments and in monitoring and reporting receipts.
♦ Signing bilateral netting agreements using agreements such as IFEMA, or joining FXNET or the SWIFT Accord.
♦ Using CLS Bank.

IFEMA is the International Foreign Exchange Master Agreement. The agreement includes procedures for foreign exchange dealing, close-out provisions, novation netting and settlement netting. Banks sign bilateral agreements but select which provisions from IFEMA will apply. IFEMA has mostly been used for close-out netting to establish obligations in the event of default by one of the parties. The aim of this is to prevent a liquidator 'cherry-picking' contracts, that is, honouring payments in his favour and ignoring the others. IFEMA has not generally been used for novation netting (to replace and net all current transactions) or settlement (payment) netting, although novation is covered in the agreement.

FXNET Limited, a limited partnership set up in the UK and owned by 12 major banks is a limited partnership of the world's leading foreign exchange market-making banks. The first and largest netting system available to banks today, the FXNET System is firmly established in 33 institutions serving 78 trading floors in 13 cities. It is an automated service for handling the netting of spot and forward contract on a bilateral basis. The process of novation is used. This cancels the initial deals and adds them to the running balances on each value date as part of a single netting agreement. Members are free to choose with which members they wish to net settlement amounts.

Using the SWIFT Accord, counterparties who have entered into binding legal agreements with each other may calculate their bilateral positions for payment netting. SWIFT writes that the 'bilateral netting service allows you to confirm, match, net and settle deals using a single supplier that takes financial liability for all subsequent stages of the value chain. By virtue of its real-time reporting mechanism, SWIFTNet Accord is ideally suited for netting by novation.'

8.6.2 Minimizing settlement and delivery risks

If there is a large need for overnight or short-term balances to cover short-term settlement difficulties, the banks will engage their contingency plan using available lines of credit. An example of an extreme case was when the Bank of New York needed USD 24 billion dollars overnight due to a technical problem.

Settlement risk requires particular emphasis and control in back-office operations. Based on this understanding, policies for managing the risk should be developed at the highest levels within the bank and implemented through a formal and independent process with adequate senior management oversight. As part of this process, a bank has to have measurement systems that provide appropriate and realistic estimates of settlement exposures on a timely basis. The development of counterparty settlement limits and the monitoring of the exposures against these limits are a critical control function. The bank also needs to have procedures for reacting in a prompt and balanced manner to failed transactions or other settlement problems.

Industry groups can help by:

♦ Introducing well-founded netting systems. Netting systems reduce the number and size of payment that are necessary when deals are settled on a trade-by-trade basis.
♦ Support continuous linked settlement systems, such as offered by CLS Bank. CLS Bank goes a step further than the multilateral netting systems provided by its predecessor ECHO.

ECHO, based in London, was a clearing house owned by a group of major international banks to provide multilateral netting of spot and forward contracts between participants on a global basis, as is Multinet, based in North America. ECHO, established in August 1995, provided a multilateral netting facility for FX spot (two days) and forward contracts (up to two years), by becoming the central counterparty to trades between its users. It netted 11 currencies and had 24 users (banks). ECHO was owned by CLS Services Ltd, which also developed CLS Bank. ECHO ceased its service in 1999.

Central banks can help by:

- ◆ Improving national payment systems including Real Time Gross Settlement (RTGS). It should be noted that all European central banks already run RTGS systems.
- ◆ Encouraging banks in their country to recognize the risks and helping them to take action to reduce these risks.

More recently, since September 2002, FX settlement risk can be further reduced by the use of CLS Bank. CLS Bank is a private sector bank based in New York. Its sole purpose is to provide continuous linked settlement. CLS Bank eliminates settlement risk in cross-border payment instruction settlement, substantially reducing risk in the FX markets. The simultaneous exchange of value between settling parties (so-called Payment versus Payment – PvP) introduces a far higher degree of certainty in the settlement process which will benefit the market as a whole. The main benefits are that it eliminates the risk in cross currency payment instructions as settlement occurs on the same day and it enables its members to manage their liquidity better as the system enables them to see which transactions are settling in real time.

None of these initiatives will provide a completely risk-free payment system but together they go a long way to reducing risk.

Nine

Operational risk

Objectives

This chapter will cover the following topics:

- ◆ definition of operational risk;
- ◆ measurement and management;
- ◆ legal, reputational and strategic risk.

9.1 Introduction

Operational risk is, like credit risk, one of those banking risks that is almost all pervasive. Indeed one has to be careful to define operational risk in such a way that not every risk becomes an operational risk. Operational risk is self-evidently not particular to treasury functions. Nevertheless, given the nature of dealing activities, the consequences of poor operational risk management in treasury functions can be drastic. The examples of Bankhaus Herstatt, Barings and Allfirst have already been mentioned, and they are by no means the largest failures of operational risk management.

The following table gives examples of some of the larger operational risk events in recent years:

Table 9.1: Large losses from operational risk 1992 – 2002

Amount (USDm)	Bank	Year (of discovery)	Description
1,330	Barings PLC	1995	Due to unauthorized trading
1,110	Daiwa Bank Ltd.	1995	Due to unauthorized trading
900	JP Morgan Chase	2002	Enron-related litigation and regulatory matters
770	First National Bank of Keystone	2001	Loan fraud by senior managers
691	Allied Irish Bank	2002	Due to unauthorized trading
636	Morgan Grenfell (Deutsche Bank)	1997	Due to trades contravening fund management mandate
611	Republic New York Corp	2001	Restitution and fines for its role as custodian of securities
490	Bank of America	2002	Settlement of US class action lawsuit
440	Standard Chartered Bank PLC	1992	Breach of Indian banking laws
440	Superior Bank FSB	2001	Improper accounting

Increasingly the definition of operational risk is seen as the one given by the Basel Committee: 'The risk of loss resulting from inadequate or failed internal processes, people and system or from external events. The definition includes legal risk but excludes strategic and reputational risk'. Although many banks now work with this definition, some exclude legal risks, while others include reputational risk in their definition of operational risk.

This definition of operational risk is very extensive, but unlike other definitions it does leave room for the other risks. The Basel Committee has given the following examples of what the definition would include:

- ◆ Internal fraud. For example, intentional misreporting of positions, employee theft, and insider trading on an employee's own account.
- ◆ External fraud. For example, robbery, forgery, cheque kiting, and damage from computer hacking.
- ◆ Employment practices and workplace safety. For example, workers' compensation claims, violation of employee health and safety rules, organized labour activities, discrimination claims, and general liability.
- ◆ Clients, products and business practices. For example, fiduciary breaches, misuse of confidential customer information, improper trading activities on the bank's account, money laundering, and sale of unauthorized products.

◆ Damage to physical assets. For example, terrorism, vandalism, earthquakes, fires and floods.
◆ Business disruption and system failures. For example, hardware and software failures, telecommunication problems, and utility outages.
◆ Execution, delivery and process management. For example, data entry errors, collateral management failures, incomplete legal documentation, unapproved access given to client accounts, non-client counterparty misperformance and vendor disputes.

9.2   Background

Although credit and market risk remain the best known banking risks, operational risk is moving up the risk management agenda. The large losses incurred by banking institutions from failures in their systems and controls processes are only the symptoms of an increasingly complex environment in which banks operate. Increasing use of technology is an example, which has created new risks that are not easily managed. This not only relates to model risk, but wider uses of technology, such as straight through processing which reduces human input. Another example is e-Commerce and its associated distribution channels. Corporate activities, such as acquisitions and mergers (or de-mergers) bring their own demands on the skills of management teams, which may not always be able to fully meet the challenges that integration of new business units may bring. Outsourcing itself brings new risks that need to be adequately controlled and managed. Finally the complexity of instruments itself has brought about new risks. For example, when a bank misprices its option book, and thus incurs large losses, this is not caught by credit or market risk. Operational risk is a handy term to talk about a variety of risks that can be managed in a uniform manner.

The management of specific operational risks is not new. Indeed, we have looked at a number of these practices in the previous chapters. Examples are the prevention of fraud, independence of risk management units, segregation of duties and reducing manual input. Operational risk is about codifying these and integrating them into a more general operational risk management approach that can be run alongside market and credit risk management. This is particularly the case since the historic focus on internal control mechanisms within business lines, even if supplemented by the audit function, has not been successful in managing operational risk exposures.

Nevertheless operational risk management is still in its infancy and no best practice has yet emerged. There are even some fundamental questions on which banks cannot yet agree. For example, does operational risk arise purely out of business activities and thus is a consequence of business strategy or is operational risk taken on in its own right? The latter view implies that it can be pro-actively managed in its own right. The debate appears to be shifting to the latter view as specific structures and processes are beginning to emerge that are aimed at a distinct class of risk and are emulating approaches that have worked for the treatment of credit and market risk.

This new approach to operational risk is partly driven by the perceived failings of previous methodologies in stemming the number of operational risk events, as shown in Table 9.1. Examples of such methodologies that were not as successful as had been hoped were self-assessments and devolving operational risk management to local business managers. Self-assessments was a methodology where banking units made regular self-assessments of the operational risks they faced and these were then fed into a central pool for action by either risk management units or internal audit. In contrast the devolution to local business managers often did not include any centralized reporting structure.

9.3 Sound practices for operational risk management

The 'Sound Practices for the Management and Supervision of Operational Risk' paper issued by the Basel Committee in February 2003 is a useful summary of the current approach to operational risk management. The paper acknowledges that operational risk management is currently in the process of being developed and that banks still need to evolve to best find how to implement these sound practices.

9.3.1 Developing an appropriate risk management environment

Like other risks, operational risk management requires the operational risk appetite to be clearly defined by senior management. Each bank should provide a firm-wide definition of operational risk and lay down the principles of how operational risk is to be identified, assessed, monitored, and controlled. This should include having staff with the appropriate skills and regular reviews by audit functions. Organizationally this would also require that a unified approach be developed to reporting operational risk exposures to senior management.

9.3.2 Risk management: identification, assessment, monitoring, and mitigation/control

Each bank should review its operations, and identify and assess the operational risk inherent in all material products, activities, processes and systems. This needs to be reviewed on a regular basis, and particularly when new products, activities, processes and systems are introduced. Once established, processes need to be in place to monitor the risk profile and report this to the relevant internal committees. Only that way can banks ensure that their risk limitation and control strategy is appropriate to their overall risk appetite. A key risk mitigation that all banks should have is effective business continuity planning to be put into motion should there be a severe disruption of business.

Recent developments have focused on identifying and measuring operational risks. Tools that banks are trying out to identify operational risks include:

◆ Scorecards are used by some banks to translate qualitative assessments undertaken by staff into numbers to allow a ranking of different types of operational risk exposures. If appropriate the scorecard approach can be used across business lines. They can also be used to rank controls and other risk mitigation tools. Other self- or risk-assessment methodologies may have similar benefits to the scorecard approach.

◆ Risk mapping allows the categorization of activities into various operational risk types. The information can then be used to reveal areas of weakness and help prioritize subsequent management action.

◆ Monitoring risk indicators can also provide insight into a bank's risk position. These indicators may point to underlying problems. Examples are the number of failed trades, staff turnover rates and the frequency and/or severity of errors and omissions. Clearly such risk indicators will only be useful if they are monitored on a regular basis and used to identify issues for pro-active management.

◆ Other banks have taken an even more statistical approach by collecting historical loss data as a means to obtain meaningful information for assessing the bank's exposure to operational risk and developing a policy to mitigate/control the risk. This may be particularly useful if it is used to systematically track and record the frequency, severity and other relevant information on individual loss events. It can then be used to model operational risk, which in turn will enable scenario analysis and simulations to be run. This is likely to be of particular value if combined with risk indicators and other control factors that could give prior indications.

Particularly the modelling of operational risk could be used to differentiate between expected and unexpected losses. Expected losses could then be more systematically incorporated into pricing decisions. Unexpected losses could also be quantified statistically, which in turn may help a decision on whether the purchase of insurance contracts may be a useful risk mitigant.

In practice, many banks will have to continue to use the more traditional operational risk management tools. This will be based on ensuring compliance with internal processes, which for that purpose need to be well documented. It will require credible audit functions and risk management functions, which can ensure that appropriate risk controls and, where appropriate, limits are in place. As ever staff will need the appropriate skills and particularly senior management will need to understand the business they are in. Particularly when an enterprise-wide approach is implemented, senior management should ensure that incentives provided to staff do not run counter to the risk management processes they are trying to implement. An example of this is that bonuses should not reward pure income, as this could lead to risky operations. Instead reward systems that take into account the riskiness of underlying activities are more likely to achieve the desired outcome of aligning the risk appetite chosen by senior management with the one to which the bank is actually exposed.

9.4   Legal risk

Whether legal risk should be included in the definition of operational risk, as suggested by the Basel Committee, remains an area of debate. It is quite often lawyers who believe that legal risk is sufficiently different to be treated separately. Indeed legal risk can be seen as an environmental risk, which is outside of the control sphere of management. This may be the case when there are legal changes that create a challenge to the business model and business practices of a bank. But even then it should be possible for senior management to find ways of controlling and mitigating legal risk, as it does for other operational risks.

Examples of legal risk that have crystallized because of firms' own actions are the misselling of personal pensions in the UK, or the investigations into the role of analysts in the US. Both of these created large costs, not only in legal fees, but also in regulatory fines. Legal risk thus exists from the activities of banks being challenged by regulators and customers. Retail customers may be able to involve the Financial Ombudsman Service for redress, while other clients could go straight to the courts.

A particular challenge of legal risk management is that the size of losses can be large and uncertain. However, in that it is no different from other operational risks. Indeed the effective management of legal risk can be used to mitigate much of the risk. This can be done by ensuring that documentation is retained to justify a bank's action. Prior to that it is a bank's culture which will drive how serious the legal aspects of documentation is taken. Adherence to legal requirements in general, in addition to supervisory requirements, can go a long way in mitigating legal risk. As ever employing staff with the appropriate skills is an important risk management principle. Having the procedures in place that will allow the identification and reporting of legal risk is no different for legal risk than for other operational risks.

9.5   Reputational risk

Even more so than legal risk, reputational risk often crystallizes rapidly. The danger is that once reputation is lost, a bank's brandname loses its value and the whole business model may become threatened. Reputation is even more difficult to measure than other operational risks. This is particularly the case as it does not create losses (or monetary outflows) in itself. Rather, it stops customers doing business, and thus threatens the income generating capacity of an institution.

Nevertheless there is much that banks can do to control and mitigate their reputational risk. A starting point would be to manage how reputational risk arises in the first place. It may arise as a result of legal risk or regulatory action. In this case it is something that senior management can take action on prior to the event by implementing an appropriate culture that is aware of the potential of reputational risks and has reporting lines available that will ensure senior management is aware of the risks being taken by the business.

Managing reputational risk may be more difficult if the reputation is threatened by differences between internal business culture and the evolving public view of what is ethically acceptable. Discussions about senior management remuneration are an example. Nevertheless if managed correctly institutions may be able to mitigate the risk by better countering any inaccurate information that can sometimes drive public debates. A good example outside of the financial sector was Shell's Brent Spar debacle in 1995. Only after the reputation of Shell had been severely tarnished did Greenpeace acknowledge that the initial proposals by Shell were not as environmentally damaging as its own proposals had been.

Reputational risk management has a significant role to play even after a reputational risk event has occurred. Recent history has shown that companies that acknowledge problems early and are open to the public have a better chance of overcoming their reputational problems. This should almost be part of contingency planning, with clear guidelines on who in the organization will talk to the press and the public. The aim will be to show the public that the organization is in control of the situation and is doing the most it can. This will require clear assignation of responsibility and adherence to it by all staff.

9.6   Strategic risk

Strategic risk deals with the possibility that senior management takes strategic decisions that, with hindsight, prove to be bad decisions. The risk is again similar to reputational risk, in as much as it does not create a monetary loss. Instead it can produce significant loss of income, or threaten the institution's own survival. Examples abound where banks have decided to 're-focus on their core activities'. This generally happens after a decision has been taken to change the business mix, and that decision has not proved as successful as hoped.

In terms of risk management, the approach to strategic risk management does not differ significantly from managing other risks. Senior management should have a clear policy on how much risk it is willing to take. This will depend on its existing line of business. It will then have to ensure that this agreed risk appetite is complied with throughout the organization.

Management should think strategically and review its strategy on a regular basis. This will enable it to anticipate major new developments, either to take advantage of them or at least to be prepared. From a control point of view, processes need to be in place to ensure that certain decisions are only taken at the most senior levels. Particular decisions would be major exposures, major investments and joint ventures. Clearly a change in business strategy should also be authorized at the highest level. This will only work if reporting lines and channels of communication are in place to ensure strategic policies are implemented throughout the organization and that potential issues are being reported up to senior management without being censored by middle management. Thus a board which looks at reports on business opportunities and leads, and the underlying economic value of projects, is more likely to be aware of issues than a board that only looks at financial reports.

Clearly strategic management will benefit shareholders significantly. It will facilitate optimal investment decisions. This in turn will protect cashflows and mediate between the different interests of shareholders and bondholders. If nothing else it ought to increase a company's net worth by ensuring that resources are utilized where they are most needed. This in turn should make earnings less volatile and reduce expected losses generally.

Ten

UK financial services legislation

Objectives

This chapter will cover the following topics:

◆ economic rationale for banking supervision;
◆ history of financial regulation in the UK;
◆ Financial Services and Markets Act 2000.

10.1   Economic rationale for banking supervision

Supervision of banks is generally justified as a result of market failures in the banking industry. Systemic risk is an example of such a market failure. Systemic risk in this context is the risk that failure by one institution creates a domino effect that threatens the banking system as a whole, or at least parts of it. The market failure occurs because banks are unlikely to factor systemic risk into their pricing and capital calculations. Banks will therefore be undercapitalized if left to their own devices. It is thought that only supervision can overcome this deficiency. Although regulation is costly, the costs of such unchecked systemic risk is thought to be even higher. For example, the Norwegian and Swedish banking crises of the early 1990s are estimated to have cost respectively 3.1% and 4% of each country's GDP to resolve.

In economic jargon such systemic costs, which will not be factored into firms' own calculations, are known as externalities. Regulation can mitigate such externalities by, for example, increasing consumer confidence. With increased confidence, consumers will be more willing to use financial services and can therefore benefit from the efficiency increases that the industry provides. Efficiency gains would be improved risk allocation across industry, better diversification and lower transaction costs. This in turn will attract more customers, etc. Consumer confidence in itself thus creates a positive spiral. The difficulty is that consumer confidence can only be increased via regulation, as individual consumers do not have the information needed to know when financial services firms do not act properly. This is known as information asymmetry.

Then there is moral hazard. Moral hazard has increased particularly since governments have introduced safety nets. Examples of safety nets are the lender of last resort facility offered by central banks, deposit insurance, and other types of compensation schemes. Their existence to some extent means that there is no benefit in customers, or the banks themselves, fully taking account of risk. Again regulation can force financial institutions to reflect risk accurately and thus reduce externalities.

Finally there is what has become known as the agency problem. Agency problems arise when one party uses agents to undertake a specific job. Agents will, however, have different objectives from the principals and this can lead to problems. The classic example is in relation to shareholders. As the owners of a business, shareholders have in effect delegated the running of their company to management. Managers are thus the agents and they have different objectives from shareholders. The discussion on 'fat cat salaries' is an extension of the agency problem. The question is whether high salaries of senior executives are justified on the basis of achievements, in which case shareholders will benefit from paying them, or are 'a reward for failure'. If the latter were true then the high salaries would be an example of inadequate controls by shareholders. If this deficiency, once proven to be a market failure, cannot be addressed otherwise, regulation may be required.

Regulation can minimize the likelihood of such events occurring. In order to overcome them two generic types of regulation have developed:

- ◆ prudential supervision, which focuses on the solvency, safety and soundness of financial institutions, including high level systems and controls; and
- ◆ conduct of business regulation, which focuses on how financial firms conduct business with their customers.

Both types of regulation are closely linked to the principle of consumer protection. The consumer may lose his deposits (or investments) as a result of the bank's failure. Alternatively a consumer could suffer from the poor conduct of business of the firm used. The failure of a financial firm may have adverse effects on systemic stability, and also cause loss to individual depositors who are regarded as being unable to look after their own interests. The impact of the failure of financial institutions on systemic stability and the interests of consumers means that regulators are almost inevitably bound to have a prudential concern for the liquidity, solvency and riskiness of financial institutions. Such regulation must necessarily focus on institutions per se.

Conduct of business regulation, on the other hand, focuses upon the functions of financial firms irrespective of the type of firm conducting the business. Nevertheless a consumer knowing that conduct of business rules are enforced is likely to have more confidence in the service. Such increased consumer confidence is itself a strong argument in favour of regulation, particularly given the nature of a financial institution's business, which often deals with the whole of a person's livelihood. Conduct of business rules have historically been used primarily for the regulation of investment firms, although the distinction is blurring.

Treasury activities do not tend to have private customers as clients. Conduct of business regulation is therefore of less direct relevance to them and we will therefore focus more closely on prudential regulation. The case for prudential regulation and supervision of financial firms is that consumers are not in practice in a position to judge the safety and soundness of financial firms. Prudential regulation is thus thought necessary because of:

◆ imperfect consumer information or information asymmetry,
◆ agency problems, and
◆ moral hazard.

Furthermore no amount of information at the time contracts are signed and purchases made, protects against changes in firm's behaviour after that event. This is another example of the information asymmetry that disadvantages consumers. Leaving aside any potential systemic dimension, there is therefore a case for prudential regulation of financial firms when:

◆ the institution manages funds on a trust basis or performs a fiduciary role;
◆ consumers are unable to judge the safety and soundness of institutions at the time purchases or contracts are made;
◆ post-contract behaviour of the institution determines the value of contracts, and when the institution may become more risky because of a change in its behaviour after a long-term contract has been taken out by customers;
◆ there is a potential claim on an insurance fund or compensation scheme because the costs of hazardous behaviour of an individual financial firm can be passed on to others (those who in the end pay the compensation).

If, for instance, other firms in the industry are required to pay the compensation liabilities of failed institutions (as is the case in the UK) it would be reasonable for these firms to demand certain minimum standards of behaviour. However, they will be unable to enforce such conduct of business rules themselves and thus external regulation provides a mechanism for intervention.

10.2   The history and evolution of banking regulation

Since 1 December 2001, banks and other financial services firms are regulated by the Financial Services Authority (FSA) under the Financial Services and Markets Act 2000 (FSMA). Much of the thinking behind how the FSA is operating and how regulation is undertaken comes from the evolution that banking legislation has undergone. Current legislation can therefore only be understood in the light of historic legislation such as the Banking Acts 1979 and 1987, the Financial Services Act 1986 and the Bank of England Act 1998.

The Bank of England, formed in 1694, was a private bank, which evolved over the course of the centuries as the bankers' bank and the government's bank. It eventually functioned as the UK's central bank, being the only institution allowed to print money that has legal tender. The nationalization of the bank in 1946 was achieved with very little change in its influence over the country's banking system.

The early 1970s witnessed a number of serious bank failures, which led to calls for stricter controls over deposit-taking institutions. The Banking Act 1979 (the 1979 Act) was the result. This extended the Bank of England's supervisory functions over the banking system, including the right to designate institutions as either banks or licensed deposit-takers. The 1979 Act first defined banks by their activity of deposit-taking.

Two types of institution could be categorized as banks: those that offered a full range of banking services to the public and those, who, while not offering this full service, were of sufficient size and reputation in the specialist international banking field – the merchant banks come into this category. The 1979 Act also established a fund for the protection of depositors. This division into banks and licensed deposit-takers was not popular and together with the failure of the Johnson Matthey Bank in the early 1980s, led to the Banking Act 1987, which improved some of the earlier statutory measures and repealed others. Among other changes it removed the distinction between banks and licensed deposit-takers.

Debate on the banking industry continued and in March 1990 the government published a White Paper entitled Banking Services: Law and Practice. This proposed a number of minor changes relating, mostly, to cheques, electronic funds transfer and payment cards, and a non-statutory statement of best practice, known as the Code of Practice. The closing down of BCCI (Bank of Credit & Commerce International) by the Bank of England in 1991 and the failure of Barings Bank in 1995 following poor internal control systems led to further questions about regulatory practices. This culminated in the Labour government announcing soon after its election in 1997 that it would set up a single financial services regulator. A first step in this direction came in 1998, when under the Bank of England Act 1998 the regulation of banks was transferred to the Financial Services Authority, which assumed all of the powers and responsibilities under the Banking Act 1987. Then, with the Financial Services and Markets Act 2000 coming fully into force on 1 December 2001, the Banking Act 1987 and the parts of the Bank of England Act 1998 relevant to supervision were effectively repealed and the FSA assumed its full role under the powers granted to it by FSMA.

10.2.1   Banking Act 1987

The Banking Act 1987 (the 1987 Act) extended the Banking Act 1979 and increased the powers of the Bank of England. Similar powers in relation to the supervision of building societies by the Building Societies Commission had already been introduced via the Building Societies Act 1986. The 1987 Act enabled the Bank of England to control institutions carrying on deposit-taking. It also restricted the use of names and descriptions linked with banks and banking. For the first time the Act introduced an express duty on the Bank to supervise authorized institutions. The 1987 Act has now been completely superseded by FSMA.

The Act improved corporate governance of the Bank by establishing a new committee, called the Board of Banking Supervision. The Board was established to monitor financial developments in the UK and to ensure that the Bank of England was aware of, and dealt with, any such developments. The Board had to submit an annual report to the Chancellor about its activities. A similar reporting requirement exists under FSMA for the FSA.

It continued the general restriction on the taking of deposits, except by institutions authorized to do so by the Bank of England or those institutions that were exempt. To overcome the restriction to deposit-taking, banks had to obtain authorization from the Bank of England. An application had to be made to the Bank of England, in the prescribed manner, accompanied by a statement setting out the nature and scale of the proposed business together with its proposed management arrangements. A minimum set of fit and proper criteria had to be met to gain authorization.

The Act introduced a restriction on the use of the word 'bank' in the names of institutions. An institution was required to have a minimum capital of £5m, and had to be authorized as deposit-taker, to be called a bank. Again, a number of institutions were exempt from this requirement, such as central banks of other states, certain international bodies and some small organizations, such as school banks.

Finally the 1987 Act established a Deposit Protection Board to hold, manage and apply the Deposit Protection Fund, which had been introduced by the 1979 Act. Contributions to the Fund were levied on all institutions to a total of £6m. If the total fund fell below £3m at the end of any year, additional levies would be required, and a further levy could be applied if the Board felt it was necessary to protect depositors at any time. Payment from the fund covered up to 75% of any deposits (up to a maximum of £20,000) with an insolvent bank or licensed deposit-taker.

10.2.2   Financial Services Act 1986

The traditional banking principles, based on trust and honesty, were no longer considered to be sufficient following a number of examples of fraud and failure by investment firms during the 1970s and early 1980s. This resulted in individuals and institutions losing out, having invested money in the financial markets that had once enjoyed their confidence. The government tried to overcome this by introducing the Financial Services Act 1986 (FSAct) to address the need for an ethical approach to the selling, marketing and servicing of financial services products, and the need to maintain stable, sound financial markets. The aim was to have a combination of principled players operating competently, efficiently and effectively. It would make for a financial system that is based on confidence and integrity. Under these circumstances, the financial system was to become a great asset, particularly if the temptation to over-regulate was avoided.

The particular emphasis was on protection against fraud or hiding the risk – not on reducing the obvious risks involved in any type of investment. The FSAct drew attention to the need not to stifle enterprise by over-regulating the industry, but saw the need to make transactions transparent by encouraging disclosure of information. The FSAct was built on adherence to conduct of business rules.

Taking the approach from banking legislation the Financial Services Act 1986 essentially prohibited all investment activities unless the firm undertaking the investment activity was authorized under the FSAct. Authorization was provided via a two tier system. The Securities and Investments Board (SIB) was established to oversee the Self-Regulatory Organisations (SRO). The SROs were the organizations that provided front-line supervision of investment firms. They were known as SROs because all investment firms were members of them and financed them and had thus some influence on how they exercised their functions.

Similarly to the Banking Act requirements, members of the SROs had to be fit and proper persons. In addition the SROs had comprehensive Conduct of Business rules which members had to abide by. These generally focused on consumer protection and keeping customers sufficiently informed via disclosures and risk warnings. These rules have now been incorporated into the FSA Handbook.

There were three SROs of significance before their roles were transferred to the FSA on 1 December 2001 as part of the move to the regulatory regime introduced by FSMA. The SROs effectively ceased to exist on that date. The three SROs were the Investment Management Regulatory Organization (IMRO), the Securities and Futures Authority (SFA) and the Personal Investment Authority (PIA). The PIA remit covered mainly retail products, while IMRO covered fund management activities. The SFA tended to regulate corporate finance and brokers. There was, however, significant overlap between activities, which allowed regulatory arbitrage. At the same time some business models required authorization under two or more SROs, which increased the cost of doing business.

10.2.3   Bank of England Act 1998

The Bank of England Act 1998 had two separate aims. On one side it transferred the role that the Bank of England had in relation to banking supervision to the

Financial Services Authority (FSA). Until FSMA came into force in 2001, the FSA undertook banking supervision under the Banking Act 1987.

At the same time the Act clarified the Bank of England's operational responsibility for monetary policy decisions and meeting the government's inflation target. In the first instance the Act clarifies the independence of the Bank of England from government. As part of the general overhaul of financial services regulation the Act also required the Bank to meet new principles of transparency and accountability. Thus it introduces a model where most of the Court, the Bank of England's governing body, are non-executive members. Only the Governor and the two deputy governors can have executive functions. The Act also clarifies that the Court has no function in relation to the setting of monetary policy as this will be done by an independent committee, the Monetary Policy Committee. The Act also sets up the Debt Management Office as an executive agency of the government. Debt management had previously been part of the Bank of England's role. It should also be noted that the independence given to the Bank of England in terms of monetary policy is relative and does not meet the criteria for independence that were set out by the Maastricht Treaty.

As a result of the split between the financial stability role and the banking supervision role to two different entities, a way had to be found to overcome any overlaps or gaps. This was achieved with the 'Memorandum of Understanding between HM Treasury, the Bank of England and the FSA', which is sometimes known as the Tripartite Agreement. It sets out how they will work together towards the common objective of financial stability.

The role of the Bank of England subsequent to the Act can be summarized as having to ensure the:

- ◆ overall stability of the financial system as a whole;
- ◆ stability of the monetary system;
- ◆ functioning of the financial system infrastructure, and, in particular, payment systems;
- ◆ ability to conduct official support operations;
- ◆ efficiency and effectiveness of the financial sector, especially with regard to international competitiveness.

The Memorandum also clarifies that it is HM Treasury which is responsible for the overall institutional structure of regulation, and the legislation which governs it.

10.3   Financial Services and Markets Act 2000

FSMA fundamentally changed the nature of financial regulation in the UK. It created a unified regulator, the Financial Services Authority, which is generally referred to as the FSA. It is the FSA's role to regulate most of the financial service industry, from banking, investment management via insurance to funeral plans.

The Act spells out the general duties of the FSA and its regulatory objectives. The FSA's objectives are to ensure market confidence, public awareness, the protection of consumers, and the reduction of financial crime. These objectives are all linked to each other. Furthermore the Act sets out the principles which the FSA has to bear in mind when exercising its functions. The FSA calls these principles the 'Principles of Good Regulation'. The principles are mainly intended to ensure that the FSA uses its resources effectively and does not unnecessarily restrict the industry. The general functions of the FSA are to:

- make rules under the Act,
- prepare and issue codes under the Act,
- give general guidance, and
- determine the general policy and principles by reference to which the FSA will perform particular functions.

10.3.1   Objectives and structure of the FSA

Maintaining confidence in the financial system

The first objective of the FSA is to maintain confidence in the financial system. The aim here is to achieve a financial system that is fair, efficient and transparent. Economic theory suggests that it is these characteristics which a market, and, in particular, a financial market, must have to provide the most benefit to the public. It is this objective that gives the theoretical underpinning to the authorization of exchanges and the official listing function being undertaken by the FSA.

The FSA has clarified that it does not see a zero-failure regime as meeting this objective. This means that the FSA does not see its role to protect every firm from failure or to review every transaction that would harm consumers. Furthermore failure of badly performing firms is an inherent part of ensuring that the financial markets remain innovative and provide consumers with what they need.

Nevertheless failures of firms can sometimes lead to systemic problems via contagion. As we have seen when looking at liquidity risk, contagion occurs when failure of one financial institution would lead to consumers withdrawing their funds from other financial institutions. This in turn could bring down one financial institution after another, thus creating a system-wide problem. It is in such instances that the FSA will have to work with the Bank of England, which remains the lender of last resort to the financial system and could thus provide the liquidity to the financial markets to overcome the problems.

Promoting public awareness ensuring protection of consumers

The twin objectives of promoting public awareness and ensuring protection of consumers are closely linked. Promoting public awareness is a new objective not implicit in any previous legislation. In practice, it means that the FSA is putting considerable effort into explaining the benefits and risks associated with different kinds of investment or other financial dealings. It is in this light that the FSA issues league tables of financial products and consumer guides. It also undertakes general promotion of financial literacy, for example via its website, which has an extensive consumer section. As such it is an aim which underpins the second objective of 'securing the appropriate degree of protection for consumers'. Appropriate, in this context, means that the FSA has to take account of the differing degrees of risk of various investments, the differing degrees of experience and expertise of different consumers, plus the needs that consumers may have for advice and accurate information. Thus the FSA needs to provide more protection to a private investor, who has a poor knowledge of the financial system, than to large companies that are well versed in the financial products they need.

Both of these objectives refer to the underlying assumption that consumers of financial services can suffer because they have less information available than the firms and are therefore vulnerable. It is therefore no longer the case that the principle of caveat emptor – or buyer beware – applies. Instead firms have to actively provide relevant information to clients. The aim of FSMA is to provide consumers with freedom of choice, while ensuring that they obtain full risk disclosures and, where appropriate, a warning of possible consequences. This means that the FSA does not cover consumers for performance risk, ie that the investment does not give the return that the investor hoped for. The Act thus reiterates that consumers should take responsibility for their own decisions. Nevertheless the FSA does try to protect consumers against prudential risk, bad faith risk, and gives a complexity/unsuitability test.

Reduction of financial crime

The fourth objective is the reduction of financial crime. For the purpose of the Act financial crime is defined as any offence involving fraud and dishonesty, misconduct in a financial market and handling the proceeds of crime. In practical terms this means that the FSA should, for example, protect consumers of financial services from being defrauded, to prevent money laundering and to reduce insider dealing. This objective can also be seen as an extension of the first objective, as the existence of financial crime in the financial system would be likely to undermine people's confidence in the system.

These four objectives are key to understanding how the FSA approaches its regulatory function. As such the FSA has stated that it assesses regulated firms by looking at what risk each firm presents to the FSA achieving these objectives. However, in order to understand how this works in practice it is necessary to look at the principles that are included within FSMA.

10.3.2 Principles of good regulation

The Act sets out how the FSA has to manage itself by setting out seven principles to which the FSA needs to have regard when undertaking its functions. The FSA has called these the 'Principles of Good Regulation'.

The first principle states that the FSA has to allocate resources in the most efficient and economic way. It is this principle which is invoked when explaining how the FSA justifies its thematic and risk-based supervision. Thematic and risk-based supervision means that the FSA does not regulate every firm in the same way. Instead it identifies particular firms, or particular investments or investment activities, that it considers to present the biggest risk. Once these are identified the FSA focuses its resources on these firms or activities.

Secondly the FSA needs 'to have regard to the responsibilities of those who manage the affairs of authorized firms'. This means that the FSA should not interfere in the business of managing firms, unless there are risks to consumers or the wider objectives of the FSA. It is thus up to a firm's management to manage the commercial risk faced by a firm and not up to the regulator. This is another aspect of the FSA public statement that it is not running a zero-failure regime and that the FSA should not be involved in commercial decisions. Instead the FSA will attempt to reduce the moral hazard that may allow firms to take more risk than is justifiable in the mistaken belief that the government will bail them out. The FSA thus places full responsibilities on senior management to ensure a high standard of compliance within firms.

The third principle states that regulation needs to be proportionate to the benefits that the regulation is expected to result in. It is partly to meet this principle that the FSA provides a cost benefit analysis for all new regulation. The introduction of a new category of intermediate customers in the conduct of business rule is an attempt to keep the cost of regulation in proportion to its benefits. The principle is a clear attempt to ensure that regulation will not be used to stifle the financial services industry unnecessarily.

The FSA is also to have regard to the desirability of facilitating innovation in connection with regulated activities. Furthermore it is to have regard to the international character of financial services and markets and the desirability of maintaining the competitive position of the UK. It accepts that too much regulation could stifle innovation, with the ensuing loss of choice to consumers, and threaten the pre-eminence of London as a major financial centre.

Similarly the FSA needs to have regard to the need to minimize the adverse effects on competition that regulatory decisions may have. This refers more to domestic competition then the need to have regard to the competitive position of the UK.

Finally the FSA has to have regard to the desirability of facilitating competition between those who are subject to any form of regulation by the FSA. These last two points clearly indicate the importance of maintaining competition in the financial services industry. While the former point is a general requirement to look at the effects of regulatory decisions on the wider economy, the last principle is more clearly focused on competition within the regulatory perimeter. The government had given some thought to making the protection of competition a full regulatory objective in the Act, rather than just a principle. At the end it was thought to create too much of a conflict of interest for the FSA if competition aspects were enshrined as an objective.

In short the principles and objectives should be seen as an attempt to balance between developing a single set of objectives for banking, securities and insurance regulations versus the demands of consumers for security and protection. They also recognize the need to maintain and promote suitably high industry standards and accept that unnecessarily burdensome regulation can stifle innovation and competition in financial markets. Furthermore regulation should not aim to absolve individuals from the responsibility for making their own financial decisions.

10.3.3 General prohibition and prohibited activities

Echoing the approach taken by the Financial Services Act 1986, FSMA has a very wide scope. Section 19 of FSMA, known as the 'general prohibition', makes it a criminal offence to undertake regulated activities in the UK unless authorized or exempt. It is in order to avoid breaching the general prohibition that businesses seek authorization from the FSA.

A person or firm that has obtained authorization to undertake regulated activities is known as an 'authorised person'. The general prohibition unifies and replaces the authorization requirements that were incorporated in statutes such as Financial Services Act 1986, Banking Act 1987 and Insurance Companies Act 1982.

A breach of the general prohibition can lead to severe consequences:

- ◆ As a criminal offence it can lead to up to two years imprisonment and unlimited fines.
- ◆ Any agreement signed despite one party being in breach of the general prohibition is unenforceable. This does not mean that the agreement is illegal, as the innocent party may still enforce the contract. Nevertheless a court may still enforce an agreement if deemed just and equitable. This would mean that an innocent party may also claim for compensation of sustained losses and recover moneys paid, but the innocent party may not claim the profits made by the other party.
- ◆ It should be noted that the unenforceability of agreements and compensation does not apply to deposit taking. However, if a deposit is not repayable immediately the innocent party may apply to the court for an order directing the return of the deposit.

◆ The FSA is also entitled to seek injunctions to restrain anticipated contravention of the general prohibition and orders to pay out profits and require restitution of losses arising from contraventions of the general prohibition.

By definition an authorised person cannot be in breach of the general prohibition. Without any further restrictions the fact that authorised persons can never be in breach of the general prohibition would, however, give them a right to undertake any regulated activity. This is not in the interest of consumers and the Act therefore prohibits authorised persons from carrying on regulated activities without permission.

10.3.4 Regulated activities

It is clear from the discussion of the general prohibition that the definition of 'regulated activities' is of prime importance. The Act only indicates on a very general level which activities it will cover. The detailed activities are specified in the Regulated Activities Order, which is issued separately by HM Treasury. It is an example of a secondary legislation which provides the details not contained in the Act itself and can be amended without having to go through the full parliamentary legislative process. This contrasts with the Financial Services Act 1986 where extending the scope needed to pass the full parliamentary legislative process.

FSMA also states that regulated activities should be described in terms of a specified activity relating to a specified investment. Specified investments can be any asset, right or interest. Nevertheless HM Treasury can deviate from this and include activities which do not relate to investments. In the context of regulated activities the term 'specified' refers to those activities and investments specified in the Regulated Activities Order.

The current Regulated Activities Order specifies a long list of activities that are deemed to be regulated activities. Because the list is so long, many activities have been grouped together into general activities. Those relevant to this syllabus are as follows.

Deposit taking

This is the same activity that was previously regulated by the Banking Act 1987 and the Building Societies Act 1986.

Insurance

The regulated activity is defined as effecting and carrying out contract of insurance as principal. It specifically excludes community co-insurers and breakdown insurance, such as for cars. This activity broadly reflects the relevant activities contained in the

Insurance Companies Act 1982. The scope of insurance regulation is, however, expected to change in 2005.

Investment activities

These are broadly the same activities as those covered by the Financial Services Act 1986: dealing in investments as principal or agent, arranging deals in investments, managing investments, safeguarding and administering investments, sending dematerialized instructions, establishing, operating or winding up of Collective Investment Schemes, advising on investments and establishing Stakeholder Pension schemes.

◆ Dealing in investments: this covers buying, selling, subscribing for or underwriting investments, offering to deal or arrange deals in investments or offering to give investment advice, or agreeing to deal, arrange or give advice, either as principal or as agent. This will cover activities such as marketing.

◆ Arranging deals in investments: this refers to making, offering or agreeing to make arrangements either with a view to another individual buying, selling or subscribing for or underwriting a particular investment, or with a view to an individual who participates in the arrangements buying, selling, subscribing for or underwriting investments. This covers instances when an intermediary brings together the buyer and seller of an investment but does not enter into the transaction himself, eg if a broker sells a life policy which is issued by a life company and is paid commission by the life company.

◆ Managing investments: this covers managing, offering or agreeing to manage another individual's assets if these include investments or may include investments at the discretion of the manager, eg under a discretionary or advisory portfolio management service which a bank offers to a customer.

◆ Investment advice: this covers giving, offering or agreeing to give investors or potential investors advice on buying, selling, subscribing for or underwriting an investment or exercising a right to buy, sell, subscribe or convert an investment. Giving investment advice is distinguished from providing investment information, eg information on when dividends will become payable. Investment advice is specific and often relates to the advantages of buying a particular product. Investment advice can be given to both corporate and private investors.

◆ Establishing, operating or winding up a collective investment scheme: this covers for example the management of unit trusts or acting as a trustee for an authorized unit trust scheme.

Certain activities do not fall under the definition of investment business. These include the following.

◆ Dealing as principal: the aim of this exception is to exclude investors who deal in investments on their own account from the provisions of the FSMA.

◆ Groups and joint enterprises: this exception covers corporate groups and joint enterprises when dealing, arranging deals, managing investments and giving investment advice if the parties involved are corporate bodies in the same group or participators in a joint enterprise to which the transaction relates. Under this exception, a banking group can be organized so that only one company in the group needs to be authorized and transactions are carried out through this dealing company without the need for the other companies to be authorized.

◆ Sale of goods and supply of services: if a supplier's main business is to supply goods and services and not to engage in investment activities, they may be exempted from the need for authorization. This provision exists so that manufacturing or service companies do not need to be authorized when arranging finance for corporate customers as part of their main activities. Similarly a company taking prepayments will not be deemed to take deposits.

◆ Employees' share schemes: this covers corporate bodies, connected bodies and the scheme trustee when transacting in shares under these schemes.

◆ Sale of body corporate: this exception applies to acquisitions and disposals of shares in a company where the shares carry at least 75% of the voting rights or an acquisition would take a shareholding to at least 75%.

◆ Trustees and personal representatives: this exception covers trust corporation activities and can avoid the need for authorization if certain criteria are met. Separate provisions apply to occupational pension schemes. A trustee of an occupational pension scheme will be classed as managing investments when holding scheme assets and will not fall under the exception. However, if investment decisions for scheme assets are made by a separate person who is authorized, exempt or does not require authorization, the trustee will be covered by the exception.

◆ Dealings in the course of non-investment business: this exception covers anything done by an individual in accordance with permission, which the FSA has granted.

◆ Advice given or arrangements made in the course of profession or non-investment business: this exception covers advice or arrangements made while carrying on a profession or business which does not constitute investment business and the advice or arrangements are a necessary part of other advice or services which are being provided.

◆ Newspapers and other media: if a newspaper, journal, magazine, radio broadcast, television or cable programme contains advice, but the main purpose of the publication is not to persuade people to invest, in particular, products, it will be excluded.

◆ International securities SROs: this exception covers a list of international SROs.

Mortgage contracts and mortgage advice are due to come within the regulatory framework in 2004.

10.3.5 Specified investments

A regulated activity is generally associated with a specified investment. Many of these are directly relevant to treasury activities and the whole list of investments from the Regulated Activities Order is shown below:

- Deposits
- Contracts of insurance
- Stocks and shares in the share capital of a company
- Debentures, including debenture stock, loan stock, bonds and certificates of deposit, government and public securities, including local authority loan stocks and bonds
- Warrants or other instruments which allow the investor to subscribe for the above investments
- Certificates or other instruments which confer rights in the above investments
- Instruments creating or acknowledging indebtedness
- Government and public securities
- Instruments giving entitlement to investments
- Certificates representing certain securities
- Units in Collective Investment Schemes
- Rights under a stakeholder pension scheme
- Options to buy or sell the investments in this list, currency, or gold and silver
- Futures, except when entered into for commercial purposes
- Contracts for differences such as currency and interest-rate swaps, commodity swaps and FTSE-100 traded options
- Lloyd's syndicate capacity and syndicate membership
- Funeral plan contracts
- Regulated mortgage contracts
- Rights to or interests in investments
- Electronic money

In addition to regulated activities, FSMA also restricts the communication of financial promotions by unauthorised persons. Financial promotion is the terminology FSMA uses to describe financial advertising. However, communication has a much wider scope then the advertisement and unsolicited calls under the previous regime. This is because the Act defines financial promotion as communication, in the course of business, which invites or induces someone to engage in investment activity. The restriction of financial promotions is only contravened when a person communicates in the course of business. Thus it excludes communication between private individuals in a personal capacity. However, an employer promoting a group personal pension scheme may be caught. This area of the FSA is not directly relevant to the syllabus and is therefore not explained further.

Eleven

Banking supervision and the FSA

Objectives

This chapter will cover the following topics:

- ◆ powers and duties of the FSA;
- ◆ the authorization regime of the FSA;
- ◆ the FSA Handbook;
- ◆ the supervisory process;
- ◆ the Principles for Business;
- ◆ the market abuse regime;
- ◆ discipline and enforcement powers of the FSA.

11.1   Powers and duties of the FSA

The FSA has an extremely wide range of powers and duties.

11.1.1   Authorization and permission

We have already seen that any person carrying on a regulated activity in the UK will need to be authorized by the FSA (unless they are exempt from authorization). Authorization is given by the FSA upon application. An application will be granted if a firm meets the so-called threshold conditions. As part of assessing that the firm meets the threshold conditions the FSA will look at all aspects of a firm including its integrity, financial standing, management and links with other companies and individuals. Once authorized, a firm has to meet these threshold conditions on a continuous basis to maintain its authorization. Authorized firms are called 'authorised persons' under the Act.

Firms are normally authorized by following the application process outlined in FSMA. There is a single application process for all types of firm, whatever type of activity they intend to do and a single register listing all authorized firms. It will be an offence punishable by up to two years imprisonment or £5,000 fine for failing to gain authorization as required. In addition it is an offence punishable by up to two years imprisonment or £5,000 fine to hold yourself out falsely as an authorised person. Furthermore it is an offence punishable with imprisonment to promote an investment if you are not an authorised person. Some firms will be automatically authorized, for example non-UK firms that take advantage of the passporting rights provided for by European legislation.

11.1.2   Supervision and enforcement

In the normal course of supervision, firms will be monitored depending on the risk the firm poses to the FSA's objectives. Thus a large bank will have almost continuous contact with its supervisor, via informal discussion, inspections and other regulatory information. Smaller firms may have few contacts with the FSA, apart from the reporting requirements, unless the FSA looks at the firm in its thematic research or the FSA has suspicions that call for further examination. The FSA can also delegate some of its monitoring tasks to other organizations. The FSA's monitoring under rules and guidance is backed up with powers of information gathering investigation, professional reports, intervention, redress, injunction, discipline and prosecution. The Act also gives the FSA powers to act against market abuse. The government has also transferred the UK Listing Authority to the FSA.

11.1.3   Information gathering powers

The FSA has powers to investigate an authorised person and to require an authorized firm to provide it with the information and documents the FSA needs to carry out its duties. This power also applies to persons connected with authorised persons and exchanges and clearing houses. The FSA can require verification of any information provided and it will be a criminal offence not to comply with a requirement to provide information or documents. Investigators appointed by the FSA have the power to enter the premises of authorised persons with a warrant.

11.1.4   Investigation powers

If it has a 'good reason', the FSA can investigate the affairs, ownership or control of any authorized firm or the affairs of a firm's representative. This includes the whole of the firm's business, not just the regulated activities. If it is relevant to the main investigation, the FSA will also be able to investigate certain companies related to the firm. The power extends to the past business of formerly authorized firms and representatives.

The FSA can require a person under investigation or connected persons to attend to be questioned by an investigator and can require any person to produce documents relevant to an investigation. It is an offence punishable by three months in prison or £5,000 fine not to co-operate with an investigation. It is also an offence to mislead an accountant or an auditor of an authorized firm.

The FSA can, without going to court, require an authorized firm to hand over profits made from a breach of a rule or any other requirement in the Act (or made under it) or to pay compensation. This power includes authorized firms which have been 'knowingly concerned' in a breach even though they have not committed the breach themselves.

11.1.5 Injunction powers

If a firm or individual is breaking, or is likely to break, a rule or other requirement under FSMA or is about to engage in market abuse, the FSA has the power to seek an injunction from the court to prevent or stop the breach or abuse. The FSA can apply to the court to freeze the assets of an authorized firm or market abuser.

11.1.6 Disciplinary powers

The FSA is able to fine and issue statements of public censure against authorized firms and approved employees. The FSA is allowed to name and shame authorised persons or to impose a prohibition order stopping individuals from working in the regulated environment.

11.1.7 Prosecution powers

The FSA has the power to prosecute persons for offences within its remit. These include prosecuting unauthorized firms doing regulated activities, insider traders and market manipulators and persons who break the Money Laundering Regulations.

11.1.8 Powers to control market abuse

The FSA has the power to impose civil fines, which carry a lower burden of proof than criminal fines, for 'market abuse'. Market abuse is behaviour likely to affect confidence that it is a fair and true market. Courts may also impose fines for 'market abuse'. The FSA or its investigators can compel people to cooperate with an investigation into 'market abuse'. It should be noted that the market abuse powers do not only apply to authorised persons, instead the market abuse regime applies to all individuals and companies.

The FSA has the power to seek a warrant from a magistrate authorizing forcible entry of premises in support of its investigation powers. If an investigated person is convicted, the costs of the investigation can be recovered by the FSA.

11.1.9 Professional reports

In addition to using its own staff to look into firms, the FSA can require a firm to appoint auditors, accountants and other professionals for a one-off investigation and report into a firm's activities. These reports are known as skilled persons report. The FSA can also require a firm to appoint an auditor or actuary on an on-going basis when a firm does not already have one.

11.1.10 Intervention powers

The FSA has general power to intervene by imposing tailored requirements on particular firms. For instance, the FSA could intervene to stop a firm from selling a type of investment or impose higher capital requirements on it. The FSA is thus able to intervene to protect actual or potential consumers or if a firm:

◆ has broken a rule or any other requirement of FSMA;
◆ has misled the FSA;
◆ has had an unapproved change of controller.

The FSA can also use its intervention powers at the request of or to help an overseas regulator.

11.1.11 Redress powers

The FSA can apply to the court to require any person who has broken a rule or other requirement of FSMA to hand over profits made from a breach or to pay compensation to customers. This power also applies to a person who is 'knowingly concerned' in someone else breaking a rule or other requirement. The FSA is also able to apply to the court for an order requiring a firm to put right any breach.

11.2 Threshold condition and authorization process

We have already seen that the threshold conditions are the conditions that firms need to meet in order to maintain authorization. In essence the threshold conditions set out the minimum requirements that a firm must meet at all times. The FSA has issued the threshold conditions in its Threshold Conditions Sourcebook. Threshold conditions are only relevant to firms authorized via the permission regime. The reason is that EEA and Treaty firms have their threshold conditions reviewed under their home-state legislation. EEA firms are those financial firms from outside the UK that take advantage of passporting rights contained in various EU financial services legislation. Treaty firms are firms that do not passport under specific legislation, but do so under the general rights provided by European treaties.

It should also be remembered that the threshold conditions are to some extent only guidelines and that harsher requirements can be imposed if there is a threat to consumers. Furthermore, under section 45 of the Act, the FSA is entitled to vary or cancel permissions if a firm is in breach of a threshold condition.

The required legal status of a firm wanting to become authorized depends on the regulated activity that the firm wants to undertake. For example, deposit-takers must be either bodies corporate or partnerships. They cannot be sole traders.

Another threshold condition is that a UK firm must have its head office in the UK, and, if it has a registered office, this must also be in the UK. Having a head office in the UK generally means that its business decisions must be taken mainly in the UK, and key functions like a board of directors should meet mainly in the UK.

In addition the company must not have any close links, ie parents or sister companies, that make it unsupervisable. The threshold conditions would thus not be met if a firm had close links with another person or company that would prevent its effective supervision. Similarly a close link subject to laws and regulations preventing effective supervision in its home-country would not meet this condition. Both requirements are a direct result of the failure of BCCI. BCCI was registered in Luxembourg, but its operational head office was in London. This meant that there was a regulatory gap, with each supervisor assuming the other would be responsible. This made it more difficult for regulators to detect the fraudulent activities that were being perpetrated by BCCI. Close links are defined in an EU Directive commonly known as the Post BCCI Directive. They exist for example between parent and subsidiary companies or if 20% or more of voting rights are held.

Firms must also have adequate resources available. On one level this means that a firm needs to have sufficient capital available to meet its regulatory capital requirements. For example, banks need to have a minimum capital of Euro 5m. On another level it means a subjective assessment by the FSA of whether the firm has the necessary resources in place in terms of quantity and quality to survive in its chosen business line. Thus a firm must have established effective means to manage its risks before it can meet the adequate resources test. The FSA thus requires firms to establish and maintain a clear and appropriate apportionment of significant responsibilities and appropriate systems and controls.

When assessing whether a firm will satisfy and continue to satisfy this threshold condition, the FSA will have regard to all relevant matters, whether arising in the UK or elsewhere.

Relevant matters may include but are not limited to:

◆ whether a firm is likely to meet its prudential requirements, as defined in the FSA's prudential rules;
◆ whether there are any indications that the firm will not be able to meet its debts as they fall due;
◆ whether there are any implications for the adequacy of the firm's resources arising from the history of the firm; for example, whether the firm, or one of its subsidiaries has been the subject of bankruptcy proceedings or, within the last ten years, failed to satisfy a judgment debt under a court order, whether in the UK or elsewhere;
◆ whether the firm has taken reasonable steps to identify and measure any risks of regulatory concern that it may encounter in conducting its business and has installed appropriate systems and controls and appointed appropriate human resources to measure them prudently at all times. The requirements are set out further in the Senior Management Arrangements, Systems and Controls chapter of the FSA Handbook.
◆ whether the firm has conducted sufficient enquiries into the financial services sector in which it intends to conduct business to satisfy itself that it has access to adequate capital to support the business including any losses expected during its start-up period. It must also ensure that client money, deposits, custody assets and policyholders' rights will not be placed at risk if the business fails.

Finally there is a suitability test. This is often described as the fit and proper test. It means that a person must demonstrate that it will manage its affairs soundly and prudently. For the purpose of determining whether a firm is fit and proper, the regulator will take account of:

◆ the information in the application form,
◆ any business or other activity which an applicant carries on or proposes to carry on, and
◆ any other factors it considers relevant, including:
  ● findings or decisions of courts or other bodies,
  ● any decision by the Take-over Panel, and
  ● findings of investigations carried out under the Companies Acts.

The burden of proof that the applicant is fit and proper to undertake regulated activities lies with the individual firm. The assessment of fitness and properness is made in respect of the applicant as a whole, but the regulator will consider not only information relating to the firm itself but also any relevant evidence about firms associated with the applicant, including appointed representatives, and key individuals within the applicant firm. For banks the treasurer may be one such individual.

The main factors to be taken into account in assessing the honesty of an applicant firm are as follows:

- ◆ Openness and accuracy of dealing with the prospective regulator and any existing or former regulators, including any evidence to the contrary in the way the application form is completed.
- ◆ Any evidence of dishonesty in dealing with clients, including the firm's disciplinary and complaints record.
- ◆ Any previous criminal offences, and any adverse civil court judgments which may have a bearing on honesty and reputation in business life.
- ◆ Any investigation currently being undertaken by any agency, that might lead to a conviction for a criminal offence, an adverse civil court judgment or disciplinary action by a regulatory body.
- ◆ Any adverse information regarding the above, that relates to a connected company.
- ◆ Any other adverse information regarding the above, including bankruptcy and individual voluntary arrangements between the firm and its creditors.

A firm must have taken reasonable care to establish and maintain effective systems and controls for compliance with applicable requirements and standards under the regulatory system that apply to the firm and the regulated activities for which it has, or will have permission. These procedures must:

- ◆ ensure that it has made its employees aware of, and compliant with, those requirements and standards under the regulatory system that apply to the firm and the regulated activities for which it has, or will have, permission;
- ◆ ensure that its approved persons (whether or not employed by the firm) are aware of those requirements and standards under the regulatory systems applicable to them;
- ◆ determine that its employees and approved persons are acting in a way compatible with the firm's requirements and standards.

Furthermore the FSA will need to satisfy itself that management is competent and prudent and will exercise due skill, care and diligence. In assessing this the FSA may take into account whether:

- ◆ the governing body of the firm is made up of individuals with an appropriate range of skills and experience to understand, operate and manage the firm's regulated activities;
- ◆ if appropriate, the governing body of the firm includes non-executive representation, at a level appropriate for the control of the regulated activities proposed. For example, an audit committee should be chaired by non-executives with experience in such issues;
- ◆ the governing body of the firm is organized in a way that enables it to address and control the regulated activities of the firm, including those carried on by

managers to whom particular functions have been delegated. This requirement to apportion responsibilities is a key part of the Senior Management Arrangements, Systems and Controls sourcebook;

◆ those persons who perform controlled functions act with due skill, care and diligence in carrying out their controlled function;

◆ the firm has made adequate arrangements in terms of internal controls to comply with the requirements and standards under the regulatory system;

◆ the firm has approached the control of financial and other risk in a prudent manner and has robust risk assessments and reporting systems in place;

◆ the firm has developed human resources policies and procedures designed to ensure that it employs only individuals who are honest and committed to high standards of integrity in the conduct of their activities;

◆ the firm has reasonable assurance, for example through market research or previous activities of the firm, that it will not be posing unacceptable risks to consumers or the financial system;

◆ the firm has in place the appropriate money laundering prevention systems and training, including identification, record-keeping and internal reporting procedures; and

◆ where appropriate the firm has appointed auditors and actuaries, who have sufficient experience in the areas of business to be conducted.

As part of the application process an applicant will need to determine the precise scope of the permission it wishes to apply for. This should include the regulated activities (the specified activities and the specified investments in respect of which the activities are carried on) and any limitations and requirements the applicant wishes to apply for to refine the scope of the regulated activities. An example includes a limitation on the types of client it wishes to carry on business with or a requirement not to hold or control client money. A bank could also apply for a limitation that it will only use wholesale funding rather than rely on retail deposits. As part of on-going supervisory requirements, firms need to keep their permissions up to date.

The firm will also have to collect any information relevant to those areas the FSA will take into account when deciding on an application. This will include the need for a business plan setting out the planned activities (and related risks), budget and resources (human, systems and capital) and internal controls.

The information required from an applicant will thus include details of:

◆ the regulated activities which the applicant firm proposes to carry on and the services which it intends to provide;

◆ the applicant's address in the UK;

◆ the financial position of the firm, including its capital resources; similarly the position of any associated companies, controllers and directors;

◆ the organizational structure of the firm, including its ownership, and information about associated companies and their business activities;

◆ the firm's compliance procedures;

◆ the expertise, experience and record of the applicant, its controllers, directors and key staff;

◆ the firm's record in relation to any other regulator.

It should be noted that the FSA is financed by fees levied on authorized firms. The fee will be dependent on the permitted activities sought and is payable when the application forms are submitted to the FSA.

11.3 The FSA Handbook (Principles, Prudential, CoBs)

The FSA requirements and guidance, as well as its own manuals with the procedures to follow, are collectively known as the FSA Handbook. It contains everything from broad principles to conduct of business rules and rules governing the design of products. The Handbook exists to give practitioners clear guidelines on how they are expected to behave and describe how the FSA will behave. The aim is to provide business certainty so as to facilitate firm's planning. At the same time the rules have also been written to provide protection to consumers.

The handbook is divided into six blocks. Even the headings on their own give a flavour of the broad scope of the Handbook. The Handbook is organized as follows:

◆ Block 1: High level standards
- Principles for Businesses
- Threshold Conditions, ie the qualifying conditions for authorization
- Statements of Principle and Code of Practice for Approved Persons
- The Fit and Proper Test for Approved Persons
- Senior Management Arrangements, Systems and Controls
- General Provisions

◆ Block 2: Business standards
- Prudential sourcebooks
- Conduct of Business sourcebook
- Market Conduct sourcebook
- Training and Competence sourcebook
- Money Laundering sourcebook

◆ Block 3: Regulatory processes
- Authorization manual
- Supervision manual
- Enforcement manual
- Decision Making manual

◆ Block 4: Redress
- Dispute Resolutions: Complaints
- Compensation
- Complaints against the FSA

- ◆ Block 5: Specialist sourcebooks
  - Collective Investment Schemes
  - Credit Unions
  - Recognized Investment exchanges and Clearing Houses
  - Market service providers
  - Professional Firms
  - Lloyd's
  - UKLA
- ◆ Block 6: Special Guides
  - Energy Market Participants
  - Oil Market Participants
  - The Service Company Regime
  - Small Friendly Societies

11.4   The supervisory process

Given the large scope of regulation, the FSA has introduced a risk-based approach to supervision. It uses a methodology called ARROW to categorize the risk that different firms pose to the FSA's objectives. Those with the highest risks are likely to be large firms that have significant dealings with the retail sector. The process also helps the FSA to organize its on-going work with firms, which is sometimes referred to as the risk mitigation programme.

For high-risk firms the programme is likely to be extensive and require considerable commitment of resources in terms of management time. Contact with FSA staff will be extensive. In practice many large banks have introduced compliance departments to deal with the regulators. They will act as link between FSA staff and the various internal departments that are of interest to supervisors. The high-risk firms will also have a direct contact within the FSA. These contacts will be augmented with more high level prudential discussions between the FSA and senior management.

ARROW reviews, which are undertaken for all firms supervised by the FSA, enable FSA staff to make an in-depth analysis of firms and identify those areas that are of potential concern. The process will identify areas where the FSA has insufficient information available and it will use the process to fill the gap. Treasurers are likely to come into relatively frequent contact with the FSA. This is because dealing activities are generally viewed as being high risk and the FSA will want to satisfy itself that appropriate risks and controls have been put in place. In addition the funding and liquidity role of treasury functions will be of key concern from a supervisory perspective. The FSA can obtain the information through a variety of means, collectively known as the regulatory toolkit. Of particular relevance for on-going supervision of banks will be skilled persons reports, such as those produced by external accountants, or dedicated FSA staff with expertise in treasury activities. The more sophisticated banks will also have model approval for their market risk models, which need to be reviewed by the regulators on a regular basis.

Independently of the risk categorization of a firm, it will have contact with the FSA as part of the requirement to provide financial reports. We have already looked at the permission regime implemented by the FSA. A firm wanting to undertake new business activities, or cease existing ones, would have to obtain a change to its permissions. A further level of on-going supervision is the approved persons regime. It enables the FSA to ensure that people who work for authorised persons for certain purposes are fit and proper to perform the function for which they have been engaged. It is thus a means of ensuring that only fit and proper persons undertake customer and management functions.

The Act requires firms to obtain prior FSA approval of those individuals working in specified functions. Before approving individuals the FSA reviews whether the person meets the fit and proper criteria set by the FSA. It will take into account their:

- honesty, integrity and reputation;
- competence and capability; and
- financial soundness.

Approved persons must comply with these criteria on a continuing basis. To clarify what this means FSA has included in the handbook a statement of principle for approved persons. The statement sets out principles and standards of conduct, which apply to approved persons throughout the financial services industry with respect to the controlled functions they undertake.

An approved person must:

- act with integrity in carrying out his controlled functions;
- act with due skill, care and diligence in carrying out his controlled function;
- observe proper standards of market conduct in carrying out this controlled function;
- deal with the FSA and with other regulators in an open and co-operative way and must disclose appropriately any information of which the FSA would reasonably expect notice.

An approved person performing a significant influence function must:

- take reasonable steps to ensure that the business of the firm for which he is responsible in his controlled function is organized so that it can be controlled effectively;
- exercise due skill, care and diligence in managing the business of the firm for which he is responsible in his controlled function;
- take reasonable steps to ensure that the business of the firm for which he is responsible in his controlled function complies with the relevant requirements and standards of the regulatory system.

In assessing the fit and proper status of an approved person, the FSA will take into account relevant facts. In the case of honesty, integrity and reputation the FSA may take into account any criminal history or previous disciplinary proceedings. In relation to competence and capability the FSA looks at the individual's training and competence, as well as proof that the individual has the necessary expertise to undertake the relevant controlled function. The financial soundness criterion would look, for example, at whether the individual was the subject of any judgment debt or award, or had previously become bankrupt.

The FSA has set out a number of functions that it deems to be 'controlled functions'. Anyone undertaking these functions, whether an employee of an authorized firm or a consultant, needs to be approved. There are broadly two categories of functions that fall under the regime. On one side are the significant influence functions, ie individuals that either direct or are instrumental in managing authorised persons. On the other side are the customer functions.

There are 20 significant influence functions and they are broken down further as follows:

- ◆ Governing functions – These functions encompass sole traders, partners, directors of companies and/or their equivalent in other corporate bodies.
- ◆ Required functions – These are functions that are required for regulatory purposes, for example compliance functions, money laundering reporting officers or appointed actuaries.
- ◆ Systems and controls functions – Risk managers, finance and internal audit functions would fall into this category. This is very much relevant to senior risk managers and other individuals that sit on credit committees or asset liability management committees.
- ◆ Significant management functions – This last category includes managers of areas such as settlements and insurance underwriting. Managers for back-office functions are included in this category.

Senior treasury staff are likely to fall under the approved persons regime, either as part of their systems and controls functions or as part of the significant management function.

In addition to the significant influence functions, there are seven customer functions that are also deemed to be 'controlled functions'. They cover those individuals that either deal with customers directly or deal with the property of customers, such as investment advisers, fund managers or dealers that interface with customers.

The Act provides for a single disciplinary regime for those who have failed to adhere to the principles or specific rules. The FSA has power to fine or censure publicly both firms and approved persons. In addition the FSA can also prohibit an individual from performing functions in relation to regulated activities if it considers the person to be not fit and proper.

The FSA retains information on all approved persons allowing it to track persons who move between firms, perhaps to try and avoid being found in breach of certain rules or practices, and to monitor progress and compliance. It also allows the FSA to regularly assess the continuing fitness and properness of the authorized firm. For example, if a number of individuals were deregistered and it was found that they all work for the same firm or group, the FSA may feel some investigation of the firm is necessary to find out the underlying reasons.

Another level of oversight exists as a result of the need to get changes of controllers approved. Approval is required if a shareholder increases or decreases its holding above or below the following thresholds: 10%, 20%, 33% and 50%. Each time prior approval will have to be obtained from the FSA. This will enable the FSA to meet its obligations under the relevant EU directives, which are aimed at ensuring that controllers are fit and proper and that there are no close links within a group that threaten the ability of supervisors to exercise effective oversight.

11.5 Principles for businesses

Although the FSA Handbook is comprehensive, detailed rules can never cover all events. Thus the FSA includes eleven principles for authorised persons. Its aim is to provide an indication of the spirit of the rules and to capture events not already covered in other parts of the handbook.

The principles apply to all regulated firms, but are not intended to extend to general insurance or deposit taking except for the purposes of prudential supervision. This is because the principles are an extension of the conduct of business rules, which the FSA did not want to extend unnecessarily to activities not subject to them under previous legislation. Despite this they form a useful indication of the standards that authorized firms should adhere to. Where the principles refer to clients this also means potential clients.

The eleven principles are shown below.

- ◆ Integrity – A firm must conduct its business with integrity.
- ◆ Skill, care and diligence – A firm must conduct its business with skill, care and diligence.
- ◆ Management and control – A firm must take reasonable care to organize and control its affairs effectively, with adequate risk management systems.
- ◆ Financial prudence – A firm must maintain adequate financial resources.
- ◆ Market conduct – A firm must observe proper standards of market conduct.
- ◆ Customer interests – A firm must pay due regard to the interests of its customers and treat them fairly.
- ◆ Communication with clients – A firm must pay due regard to the information needs of its clients, and communicate information to them in a way which is clear, fair and not misleading. Furthermore it should keep faith with any customer who is entitled to rely upon its judgement. This will include taking reasonable care to ensure the suitability of its advice and discretionary decisions.
- ◆ Conflicts of interest – A firm must manage conflicts of interest fairly, both between itself and its customers and between a customer and another client.

◆ Customers: relationship of trust – A firm must take reasonable care to ensure the suitability of its advice and discretionary decision for any customer who is entitled to rely upon its judgement.

◆ Clients' assets – A firm must arrange adequate protection for those clients' assets for which it is responsible.

◆ Relations with regulators – A firm must deal with its regulators in an open and co-operative way and must disclose to the FSA appropriately anything relating to the firm of which the FSA would reasonably expect notice.

11.6   The FSA's market abuse regime

The FSA's Market Abuse Sourcebook, and the Code of Market Conduct it contains, are part of the FSA's Handbook. It outlines the approach that the FSA takes towards insider dealing and the sanctions which the FSA can use to combat stock market abuse and the manipulation of share prices. Readers should be aware that the Code of Market Conduct applies to every individual, independently of whether they are an approved person or not.

Market abuse is a new civil offence enshrined in FSMA. The FSA can levy unlimited fines or order persons to disgorge their profits and compensate victims. It can also prosecute anyone suspected of insider dealing to combat stock market abuse and the manipulation of share prices. A finding of market abuse does not impact on the underlying transaction itself. The FSA can either use the courts to enforce penalties, such as seeking an injunction against a person, seeking an order for remedial action or seeking a restitution order. Alternatively the FSA can itself require restitution under its own procedures.

The Code sets out behaviour that would be unacceptable in the markets, and it helps in the interpretation of what constitutes market abuse. The objectives of the FSA include sustaining confidence in the market and assisting in the detection and the prevention of financial crime. The FSA's civil fines will require a lower burden of proof than the criminal charges used against insider trading under the Criminal Justice Act 1993. Although the Code is not enshrined in law, a breach of it will be legal evidence of a breach of law.

11.6.1   Definition of market abuse

The Code sets out behaviour that would be unacceptable in the markets. This is behaviour likely to be regarded by a 'regular user' of the market as a failure to observe the standard of behaviour reasonably expected of a person in the position of the person in question. The regular user is intended to provide an objective test of market abuse and is defined as a reasonable person who regularly deals on that market in investments of the kind in question. Behaviour in this context could be action or inaction by a person (alone, jointly or in concert) meeting one or more of these three conditions:

◆ Misuse of information: The behaviour is based on information not generally available to those using the market but which, if available to a regular user of the market, would or would be likely to be regarded by him as relevant when dealing. Information is deemed to be generally available if it is obtained from research and analysis, from public records, by observation or obtained through accepted market channels.

◆ Misleading impression: The behaviour is likely to give the regular user a false or misleading impression as to the supply of, or demand for, or as to the price, or the value of investments of the kind in question.

◆ Market distortion: The behaviour is likely to be regarded by a regular user as behaviour, which would, or would be likely to, distort the market in the relevant investments.

The behaviour must occur in relation to a qualifying investment that is traded on a prescribed markets, such as a UK Recognized Investment Exchange (RIE). Qualifying investments are defined in an HM Treasury order. They tend to be all those instruments that are publicly traded or other instruments that are related to them. They could be related, for example, as a result of using the price of a qualifying investment as reference price or the qualifying investment being the underlying asset of a derivative.

The definition can be seen as encompassing a variety of behaviours. As a result companies could be committing market abuse if they publish information that is false or misleading. There is no need for intent to be proved. Similarly a delay in the announcement of price sensitive information could be interpreted as market abuse. Attempts to take a position with a view to increasing prices artificially is also market abuse. Requiring or encouraging another person to behave in ways described above also falls under the definition of market abuse.

The Code of Market Conduct also includes a number of safe harbours, which describe behaviour that does not constitute market abuse. The circumstances are:

◆ That the transaction is taking legitimate advantage of tax differences or price differences across markets, or is enabling an underlying commercial demand.

◆ That a report or disclosure of information was made in accordance with the law or legal requirements.

◆ That a transaction was undertaken and full information was not available due to effective Chinese walls within the organization.

◆ That the information on which the deal was based was obtained by research or analysis. Such information is regarded to be generally available.

◆ That the behaviour conformed to the Takeover Code or Significant Acquisition Rules.

- That the behaviour conforms to the price stabilization rules. These are rules setting out how a 'stabilizing manager', such as a lead manager, is entitled to intervene in a market to stabilize prices.
- That a person's possession of relevant information that is not generally available did not influence the decision to engage in the dealing or arranging in question. This would occur if a person had decided or had proposed to deal before the information became available.
- That a deal was not solely based on information as to someone's dealing intention. However, if the information relates to possible take-over bids or primary market activities the safe harbour would not apply.

The Code of Market Conduct also sets out circumstances when the FSA cannot impose penalties if there are reasonable grounds to be satisfied that a person:

- believed on reasonable grounds that the behaviour did not constitute market abuse; or
- had taken all reasonable precautions and exercised all due diligence to avoid behaviour constituting market abuse.

11.7 Discipline and enforcement

The FSA has wide powers available to act against those that breach rules or principles, be they authorised persons or approved persons. We have already seen that the FSA can begin criminal proceedings against those that infringe the money laundering and insider dealing legislation. This section will look at the other sanctions that the FSA has available. How in practice the FSA intends to use these is described in the FSA's Enforcement Manual.

In relation to firms the FSA can impose sanctions if the authorised person has contravened requirement imposed by FSMA. This includes direct breaches, such as undertaking activities without permissions or indirect breaches, such as breaches of FSA rules. The FSA can issue a public censure or impose a financial penalty. It should be noted that even in the case of a financial penalty the FSA will issue a press release to that effect.

The FSA can impose sanctions on approved persons if the individual has been guilty of misconduct and the FSA considers it appropriate to do so. Misconduct would occur on a breach of one of the statements of principles for approved persons. It would also be deemed misconduct if an individual is knowingly implicated in a contravention by the relevant authorised person of a requirement imposed on that authorised person by, or under, FSMA. The Enforcement Manual clarifies that the FSA would only take action against an approved person if action was either deliberate or below the standard which would be reasonable in the circumstances.

The FSA has the legal power to apply to the court for an injunction restraining the relevant contravention, ordering any person in breach to take steps to remedy the breach or ordering the person not to dispose of assets. This enables the FSA to apply for a freezing order pending the outcome of an investigation. The power can also be applied against any other person knowingly concerned in the relevant contravention. Furthermore the FSA can apply to the courts for a restitution order requiring a person to disgorge profits the person (and other persons who were knowingly concerned) has made or compensate investors for losses they have suffered from the relevant breach. The FSA can itself impose a restitution order on authorized firms without the need for a court order.

The FSA has is the power to vary, and even cancel, the permission(s) of an authorised person. If the FSA considers that an approved person is not fit and proper to perform the function to which the approval relates, the FSA can withdraw the approval. It can also, in extreme circumstances, make a prohibition order to stop an individual from performing particular functions.

Section 150 of FSMA allows a private individual who has suffered loss as a result of a contravention of certain rules to take action against an authorised person for a rule breach. The FSA Handbook specifies to which rules such action is applicable.

More generally any firm or approved person that objects to a decision by the FSA can, within a specified period, appeal to the Financial Services and Markets Tribunal. It is an independent tribunal set up to review decisions by the FSA. To ensure independence the Tribunal is part of the Lord Chancellor's department, rather than reporting via HM Treasury or the FSA. As such it has its own staff and secretariat and is funded by the Lord Chancellor's Department.

Twelve

Wholesale markets

Objectives

This chapter will cover the following topics:

- the Interprofessional Code;
- the Bank of England's code for non-investment products;
- the Bank of England's role in the UK money markets including the repo markets;
- the operation of monetary policy.

12.1 The Interprofessional Code

The Interprofessional Code (IPC) is part of the FSA Handbook. Its aim is to reduce the regulatory burden on wholesale market activities. It applies to firms that carry on the following regulated activities:

- dealing in investments as principal; or
- dealing in investments as agent; or
- acting as an arranger; or
- giving transaction-specific advice;

but only if the activity is in respect of an interprofessional investment and is undertaken with or for a market counterparty. It is thus directly relevant to treasury activities and replaces the London Code of Conduct that previously governed these activities.

The Code applies only with respect to a firm's activities carried on from an establishment maintained by the firm in the UK. An interprofessional investment is defined as a(n):

◆ share;
◆ debenture;
◆ government and public security;
◆ warrant;
◆ certificate representing certain securities;
◆ option contract, including commodity options;
◆ future contract, including commodity futures and rolling spot forex contracts;
◆ contract for differences, including spread bets and rolling spot forex contracts; and
◆ right to or interest in investments.

The main objective of the IPC is to maintain confidence in the financial system. Its provisions relate to the conduct of bilateral dealing and it seeks to secure good market practice by firms undertaking interprofessional business. It attempts to do this in three ways:

◆ by increasing certainty by explaining how the principles apply to interprofessional business, while acknowledging that what is required to meet the proper standards of conduct for a firm may differ depending on whether or not the firm is dealing with a market counterparty;
◆ by setting out rules for interprofessional business in cases when it is not appropriate to rely on the principles alone; and
◆ by setting out the FSA's understanding of certain market practices and conventions. This assists in creating certainty, reducing the scope for disputes and making it easier to resolve disputes that do arise.

The Code provides guidance on the interpretation of the principles for business. Particular principles covered are Principle 1 (Integrity), Principle 2 (Skill, care and diligence), Principle 5 (Market conduct) and Principle 7 (Communications with clients). The principles, as they apply to interprofessional business, will be interpreted on the basis that market counterparties do not need, or expect, the level of protection provided to private customers or intermediate customer. In many respects, interprofessional dealings are mutually self-disciplining. Market counterparties have commercial sanctions available if they consider the conduct of someone with whom they conduct business is unacceptable, and are responsible for their own decision. These factors are relevant also to the FSA's interpretation of the provisions of the Code.

The implied standards are as follows:

◆ Responsibilities of principals and brokers are as follows:
  ● Those firms dealing with private individuals must have procedures in place demonstrating how the individual will be treated as a private customer, intermediate customer or market counterparty.
  ● All staff must be familiar with the code.
  ● Staff must be adequately trained.
  ● Firms must take full responsibility for the actions of their staff.

- Management must ensure that staff are kept up to date with any FSA requirements.
- Firms dealing with new counterparties should make them aware of the liabilities involved.
- The limited role of brokers should be explained.
- Conflicts of interest should be identified when transacting deals and measures taken to eliminate them.
- Full assessments should be made of counterparties' abilities to meet their commitments.
- All steps must be taken to prevent money laundering.
- All counterparties must accept full responsibility for the risks of entering into wholesale transaction.
- To follow good practice in taking independent legal advice.
- Management of broking firms must advise employees that any attempt to mislead is not acceptable.

◆ Responsibilities of the employee:
- Misrepresentation of a transaction must not be allowed to happen and identities and roles of firms for whom the employee is acting must be clear, as should the products. The facts relating to the deal must be disclosed.
- Employees of broker firms must not unfairly favour one client in any deal.

◆ Role of principals:
- To assess the creditworthiness of counterparties.
- To consider any information given by the broker.
- Agents for connected or other companies should be clear about their capacity and declare for whom they are acting. All confirmations must be clear when the deal is done on an agency basis.

◆ Role of brokers:
- To act as arrangers of deals between parties on mutually acceptable terms, in return for a fee.
- Brokers are expressly disallowed to act as a principal.
- Brokers must respect confidentiality but can discuss information that is in the public domain.

◆ Suitability and advice
The principles do not require a firm to assess the suitability of a particular transaction for its client once it has established that it is dealing with a market counterparty. For example, a firm is not obliged to ensure that the market counterparty understands the risks involved; nor is it under any duty to provide best execution or other dealing protections.

Similarly, a firm is not obliged to give advice to a market counterparty. The mere passing of information does not mean the firm has assumed responsibility of giving advice. Although Principle 7 (Communications with clients) requires a firm to pay due regard to the information needs of its client, the only requirement of Principle 7 relating to market counterparties is that a firm must communicate information to market counterparties in a way that is not misleading.

◆ Communication of information

If a firm volunteers information to a market counterparty, but no formal advisory arrangement is agreed, the firm need not advise a market counterparty about the reliability, relevance or importance of that information. Silence on the part of a firm does not result in a breach of Principle 7, unless in the circumstances, it results in a communication being misleading.

◆ It is for a firm to decide whether it wishes to provide information to a market counterparty. If it does so the firm is not obliged to keep the market counterparty informed of any changes to the information, unless the firm has agreed to do so.

◆ Because the duties owed by a firm to a market counterparty are limited, it will frequently be the case that there will be no clash between the duties owed by the firm to the market counterparty and the firm's interests. There will in those cases be no requirement on the firm to disclose its interests.

◆ When a firm does have a duty to a market counterparty that arises under the general law of contract it should manage any conflict of interest. This can be achieved, for example, by having internal Chinese walls in place. Otherwise, before it transacts, the firm should disclose the nature and extent of any material conflict to the market counterparty.

The following are examples of where there may be responsibilities that potentially give rise to a duty to disclose material conflicts of interest to the market counterparty:

● the firm is acting as agent for the market counterparty;
● the firm has agreed to advise the market counterparty;
● the firm otherwise owes fiduciary duties to the market counterparty.

Thus, a firm acting as an arranger for a market counterparty, when the firm is an affiliated company of the other principal, should disclose that relationship to the market counterparty.

◆ Clarity of role

A firm should take reasonable steps to ensure that it is clear to the market counterparty whether it is acting on its own account, as agent, or as arranger before it enters into a transaction. If a firm is acting as a wholesale market broker, it should indicate what type of broker it is, for example name-passing broker or matched principal broker.

If a firm has agreed with a market counterparty to act in one capacity in a transaction, it should not then act in any other capacity in that transaction without the consent of that market counterparty. For example, if a firm bids to transact on an agency basis, it should not, without consent, execute any part of the trade against its own book. It is not consistent with acting solely as an arranger (or name-passing broker) to take positions, even fleetingly, or act on a matched principal basis in the course of that transaction.

◆ Marketing incentives, inducements and payments in kind
A firm should take reasonable steps to ensure that it, or any person acting on its behalf, does not offer, give, solicit or accept an inducement if it is likely to conflict to a material extent with any duty that a recipient firm owes to another person. Inducement can include entertainment and soft commissions.
If a firm gives an inducement and the recipient, although a market counterparty, is acting on behalf of customers, the firm may be subject to the provisions of the conduct of business rules on inducements and soft commissions. A firm should make and implement appropriate systems, controls and policies consistent with meeting this requirement.

◆ Transactions at non-market prices
A firm should not enter into a transaction which it knows to be improper, or which it ought reasonably to have realized is improper, whether on its own account or for a third party. Firms often do not have the information to be able to assess the reasons why a market counterparty is entering into a transaction; but, a good indication that the purpose may be improper is if the transaction is undertaken at a price other than at the prevailing market price. Failure to use prevailing rates or prices may result in a firm participating, whether deliberately or unknowingly, in the concealment of a profit or loss, or in the perpetration of a fraud. There may, however, be legitimate reason for entering into transactions at non-market prices, and the firm must take reasonable steps to check this. The requirements upon firms when conducting designated investment business with or for a customer are set out in the conduct of business rules on non-market-price transactions.

◆ Passing of names
Special rules apply to name-passing brokers. They should not prematurely divulge the names of the prospective counterparties to each other, for example before both sides display a serious intention to transact. However, as soon as the material terms of a transaction have been agreed, a firm acting as a name-passing broker should aim to achieve a mutual and immediate exchange of names.

◆ Taping and record keeping
The London Code of Conduct expected institutions to tape transactions. Other firms were not subject to this requirement and upon consultation the FSA found that market practice was moving against taping. The IPC thus confirms that firms have some flexibility in how they make and retain records to meet record-keeping requirements. There are various ways of doing this, one of which may include voice recordings. The primary aim of the Code is thus to ensure that firms meet their record keeping requirements. Nevertheless many firms retain tapes, at least for a short period, for internal control purposes and the resolution of disputes.
The requirements on firms to implement appropriate systems and controls are deemed sufficient to meet regulatory requirements. As long as a firm can

ensure that the material terms of all transactions to which they are party, and other material information about such transactions, are promptly and accurately recorded in its books or records it will meet with the requirements. The manner in which this information may be recorded is thus wider than the previous taping requirement and can include:

- voice recordings of transactions,
- voice recordings or oral confirmations,
- written trading logs or blotters, and
- automated electronic records.

FSA guidance suggests that voice recordings, ie taping, may be helpful to:

'a) provide an immediate record of all transactions and therefore may assist firms in resolving any disputes;

b) may assist a firm to identify whether any personnel of the firm or of its market counterparty are involved in inappropriate behaviour, market counterparties may take comfort in knowing that their transactions are immediately recorded and that this provides evidence that can be relied upon; and

c) can provide evidence of the rationale for a particular trading strategy or other aspects of interprofessional business and thereby provide protection to the firm.'

A firm should make and implement policies on the length of time it keeps tapes. The FSA does not expect tapes to be kept for the full period required by the general record-keeping requirement, except where a firm relies on them to comply with its general record-keeping requirements. In that instance they must be kept significantly longer. One factor in setting the retention policy may be the use of tapes to assist the firm in resolving any disputes with market counterparties. Another factor is likely to be the cost of retaining tapes.

12.2 The Bank of England's Code for Non-Investment Products (NIPs)

The Financial Services Act 1986 exempted wholesale market participants from requiring authorization. These exempted firms were known as Section 43 firms, after the part of the Act that exempted them. The exemption covered the wholesale trading of money and foreign exchange, as well as certain debt and derivatives instruments. Instead of formal authorizations firms undertaking such activities were subject to the Grey Book and the London Code of Conduct.

FSMA broke with this practice and required full authorization for those firms that dealt in those instruments listed in the Regulated Activities Order. Trading of these products now falls under the IPC, which, as we have seen, is part of the FSA Handbook.

However, wholesale deposits and foreign exchange do not fall under the Regulated Activities Order. Thus the wholesale deposits and foreign exchange markets fall under the remit of the Bank of England under its role as guardian of financial stability. The Bank has thus issued the Non-Investment Products (NIPs) Code, which covers many of the products that treasury functions routinely deal in. There are many similarities between the NIPs Code and the IPC. Furthermore NIPs is one of the codes that the FSA expects firms to abide by under its principles for business. Nevertheless the NIPs Code is only intended as guidance on what is currently believed to constitute good practice in the markets it covers. The Code has no statutory underpinning except where it refers to existing legal requirements. The Code is also relevant to the trading of gold and silver bullion, but this is outside of the scope of the syllabus. It is recommended that readers obtain a copy of the Code from the Bank of England website.

The Code has four sections and six annexes. The first section introduces the Code and puts it into context. The second section deals with the respective responsibilities of the firms, employees, principals and brokers. Firms and their employees should abide by the spirit of the Code and the general regulatory and legislative framework in which they are working. Employees should ensure that they do not provide misleading information or misrepresent the nature of transactions and where necessary disclose relevant information. Principals and brokers should also be clear about their respective roles.

The third section deals with the controls that firms should have in place with respect to 'Know your counterparty'. These controls should be put in place and reviewed regularly. The section covers many of the areas that are also covered by the IPC, in particular, taping, dealing at non-current rates, conflicts of interest, marketing and incentives, entertainment and gifts.

The last section deals with confirmation and settlement issues and, in particular, the confirmation process, payment and settlement instructions and the settlement of differences. Confirmations need to be passed promptly, recorded and carefully checked to reduce errors. Instructions should be sent as soon as possible to facilitate prompt settlement. The use of standard settlement instructions is recommended.

The first annex is entitled 'Dealing principles and procedures – Statements of Good Practice'. The standards are designed for the London market. Any different terms should be highlighted. The main features are described below:

- Preliminary negotiations of terms: Firms should state at the outset and before a transaction is executed any qualifying conditions to which it will be subject.
- Firmness of quotation: All firms should make clear whether the prices they are quoting are firm or merely indicative. Unless otherwise stated prices quoted by brokers should be taken as firm in marketable amounts.
- Concluding a deal: Principals are bound to a deal once the price and other key commercial terms have been agreed. Oral agreements are considered binding. However, holding brokers unreasonably to a price is viewed as unprofessional

and should be discouraged by management.

◆ Passing of names by brokers: Brokers should not divulge the names of principals prematurely, and certainly not until satisfied that both sides display a serious intention to transact. Principals and brokers should at all times treat the details of transactions as absolutely confidential to the parties involved.

◆ Use of intermediaries: Brokers should not interpose as intermediaries in any deal that could take place without their introduction.

◆ Fraud: There is a need for vigilance by staff against attempted fraud.

◆ Know your counterparty: Firms should be mindful of any reputational risk that might arise from their dealing relationship. Some of the questions staff need to ask include: Do counterparties have the legal capacity to transact? Is advice required and if so is a legal agreement in place? Are there conflicts of interest between firms and customers?

◆ Confidentiality: Management must take account of confidentiality when setting up internal processes. Brokers for example should only transact business from their own premises.

◆ Dealing mandates: It is a matter for the two parties to agree what a mandate should and should not cover. Mandates should not be used to pass on responsibility to a counterparty. There is a need to review, and changes to mandates should be notified promptly.

◆ Deals with unidentified principals: Banks must decide whether it is appropriate for them to deal with discretionary management companies where the underlying counterparties are unknown. The latest amendment states that when anonymity is required fund managers should only disclose the identity of the underlying client to the credit, compliance, or legal functions of their counterparty.

◆ Terms and documentation: The use of legal documentation, such as signed Master Agreements, is now common.

◆ Commission/brokerage: Broker's charges are freely negotiable brokerage bills should be paid promptly.

◆ Entertainment and gifts: Firms need to ensure that entertainment and gifts do not cause reputational damage, cause conflicts of interest or serve as inducements for doing business. Policies and procedures should be in place to cover any grey areas.

◆ Market conventions: Brokers and dealers should act professionally at all times and, as part of this, use clear, unambiguous terminology.

◆ Market disruption/bank holidays: In the event of general disruption to the wholesale markets the Bank of England will determine the rate of interest to be applied to late payments.

◆ Confirmation procedures: Practitioners may find it helpful to undertake oral deal checks at least once a day, especially when using a broker. Written/electronic confirmations should be dispatched and checked carefully and promptly, even when oral deal checks have been undertaken. The issue and checking of confirmations is a back-office responsibility that should be carried

out independently from those who initiate deals.
- ◆ Payment/settlement instructions: The use of Standard Settlement Instructions (SSIs) is becoming more prevalent and their use is recommended.
- ◆ Settlement of differences: Differences should be paid in cash.

The second annex covers details of the Sterling wholesale deposit market (including interest calculations).

The third annex covers foreign currency wholesale deposits and spot and forward foreign exchange. It provides for an arbitration service by the Foreign Exchange Joint Standing Committee to resolve issues on which counterparties cannot find agreement. The annex also provides guidelines for exchanging standard settlement instructions.

The fourth annex deals with the wholesale bullion spot, forward and deposits in gold and silver. As a result it is not relevant to this syllabus.

The fifth annex provides other general guidance including good practices in obtaining data for mark-to-market purposes. This is particularly relevant to OTC markets were it is not self-evident who can provide accurate price data. We have already seen that it is part of good risk management to obtain independent valuations. It suggests that brokers should provide such valuations when they have adequate systems in place.

The final annex details good practice guidelines for foreign exchange trading. The guidelines have been issued by sixteen leading intermediaries in the foreign exchange markets and have since been endorsed by many other market participants. In periods of high market volatility, market makers have the right to refuse customer transactions that may disrupt the markets. False and misleading information should not be used for trading purposes.

12.3 The Bank of England's role in the UK money markets including the repo markets

Until March 1997, the Bank of England (the Bank) used the discount houses as a means of implementing monetary policy. In essence, the whole system was structured in such a way as to ensure that a significant volume of money market flows passed through the books of the discount houses, who acted as banks to the banks. The Bank did not have to deal with the banks directly, and was able to relate to a narrower group.

However, this type of market structure with its preferential and intransparent link between the Bank and the discount houses, which would always be kept aware of the interest rate policy, was no longer sustainable in the context of a modern international money market. Consequently, in March 1997, in response to the introduction of the open repo market, the Bank altered the way in which it implemented policy and effectively ended the dominant position of the discount houses. In the aftermath of the reform the remaining discount houses converted themselves to more general players in the now more competitive money market.

On 3 March 1997, the Bank of England reformed its daily operations in the sterling money markets:

- ◆ The Bank extended the range of instruments in which it conducts its daily open market operations to include gilt repos.
- ◆ It broadened the range of counterparties able to participate directly in these operations to include market participants active in the gilt repo and bill markets.
- ◆ It made changes to the way it provides liquidity at the end of the trading day.

The Bank's aims in its daily operations are to:

- ◆ Steer short-term interest rates to the levels required by monetary policy.
- ◆ Help the banking system to manage its liquidity effectively. The Bank satisfies the marginal liquidity demand of the banking system on a transparent basis using prime-quality market instruments.
- ◆ Foster the development of efficient and competitive sterling markets.

The market's need for refinancing depends on transactions between three sets of players: the Bank itself, the government (the Bank is banker to the government) and all other players including commercial banks and their customers. There is a steady demand for liquidity from the Bank by the market for the following reasons:

- ◆ The main liability on the Bank's balance-sheet is the note issue. Any increase in notes held by banks or their customers has to be paid for either by running down deposits with the Bank or by seeking refinance from the Bank.
- ◆ The Bank manages its balance-sheet in such a way that the market is normally required to go to it for refinancing. The Bank acquires assets in its money market operations, eg bills of exchange, which must be redeemed by the banks. A proportion matures each day in the Bank's hands and repayment drains money from the system to the Bank.
- ◆ The government's account at the bank reflects inflows, eg tax receipts and the proceeds of borrowing, which drain money from the system and means that the market has additional need of financing from the Bank. To ensure that there is a steady demand for liquidity, the Bank drains liquidity from the market by issuing bills. Government expenditure puts money into the system.
- ◆ The settlement banks, which hold accounts at the Bank, have to maintain positive balances at the end of each day. Final daily settlement within the commercial banking system and between the banking system and the Bank occurs over the settlement accounts of these banks at the Bank.

At the end of 2002 the settlement banks were ABN Amro Bank N.V., Bank of Scotland (HBOS), Barclays Bank, Citibank, Clydesdale Bank, The Cooperative Bank PLC, Deutsche Bank, HSBC Bank PLC, Lloyds-TSB PLC, National Westminster Bank, Royal Bank of Scotland, Standard Chartered Bank.

12.3.1   Daily operations

Each morning at 09.45hrs the Bank publishes the official forecast of the daily shortage on its pages on the wire services. The forecast gives details of the main influences affecting the position of the money market, including:

◆ government transactions;
◆ changes in the note issue;
◆ the amount of maturing finance to be repaid to the Bank; and
◆ the deviation from target of the settlement banks' accounts.

If the size of the shortage warrants it, the Bank will offer assistance at the time.

The forecast is kept up to date throughout the day and, when necessary, updates are published before the Bank's noon and 14.30hrs round of operations, and before the time it makes its late repo facility available at 15.50hrs.

Publication of the daily forecast and updates, together with publication of the amount of liquidity supplied to the market, helps to promote transparency of the markets.

Assistance is provided through open-market operations in short-term money market instruments. These instruments need to fulfil the following criteria. They need to be:

◆ of prime credit quality;
◆ actively traded in a continuous, liquid market;
◆ held widely across the financial system for the management of sterling liquidity;
◆ available in adequate supply.

The Bank undertakes open-market operations through repo of gilts, marketable Government foreign currency debt and eligible bills (Bank of England bills, Treasury bills, eligible local authority bills and eligible bank bills) and through outright purchase of these bills. The normal maturity of the Bank's operations in repo is two weeks, since this allows it to influence short-term interest rates.

12.3.2   Counterparties

The Bank deals with a wide variety of financial institutions in its daily operations. These institutions must satisfy a number of functional criteria to ensure that the daily operations run smoothly. The Bank will sign legal agreements with counterparties (banks, building societies and securities firms) which can satisfy the Bank that they:

◆ are subject to appropriate prudential supervision;
◆ have the technical capability to respond quickly and efficiently to the Bank's operations;
◆ maintain an active presence in the gilt repo and/or bill markets, thus contributing to the distribution of liquidity around the system;

- participate regularly in the bank's operations;
- provide the Bank with useful information on market conditions and developments.

12.3.3 Late repo facility for the settlement banks

In its open-market operations, the Bank aims to supply the net amount of liquidity needed by the market by 14.30hrs. It expects its counterparties to manage their liquidity needs sufficiently closely to enable it to meet this aim. When unforeseen variations in positions arise, the Bank will make a late repo facility available to the settlement banks. This provides overnight liquidity against the same types of paper that are also eligible for use in the Bank's open market operations.

Shortly before 15.50hrs each day the Bank publishes its last forecast of the day's shortage and says whether the settlement bank facility will be made available. If so, the settlement banks may apply for liquidity between 15.50hrs and 15.55hrs, but not for amounts in excess of the shortage identified at 14.30hrs. The Bank publishes the total amount of liquidity provided via this facility. The facility would be withdrawn from any settlement bank that does not use it for its intended purpose.

12.4 The operation of monetary policy through the money markets

12.4.1 The establishment of the interest rate market

In May 1997, the incoming Labour government announced that it intended to pass operational responsibility for monetary policy to the Bank of England. This was formalized as part of the Bank of England Act 1998. From this point on, the Bank would set rates in order to achieve a level of inflation within the target range set by the government. This target has been set at a long-run rate of $2\frac{1}{2}$%. However, the Bank has a degree of leeway on either side of this and will only have to justify itself if inflation falls outside the range $1\frac{1}{2}$ to $3\frac{1}{2}$%. The intention behind this is to ensure that the bias of policy will not be overly deflationary. Without the target range, the temptation for the Bank would be to operate an overly cautious monetary policy and thereby induce a deflationary bias to the economy.

Once the Monetary Policy Committee of the Bank has announced its interest rate, it ensures that three-month money rates remain at or around this target rate. This is achieved through the Bank's daily operations in the money market.

In the previous section, we assumed that the Bank would be operating in order to provide liquidity. While this is likely to be the norm with the participants trying to run the lowest liquidity positions, it may equally be the case that the market has surplus liquidity. In these cases, the Bank will act to absorb the excess, by issuing bills, possibly in combination with the Debt Management Office.

Although our focus has been on changing rates, it should be remembered that for the most part the Bank will be acting in the market in order to maintain rates around their current level. In doing this, it will be basing its operations on base rates.

Base rate is the current target of policy with regard to one-week to three-month rates, ie the Bank will operate in the markets to keep one-week to three-month LIBOR around this rate. Commercial banks will use base rate as the foundation for most of their loans because it will remain stable over time. Other rates such as three-month LIBOR will tend to fluctuate daily, thereby necessitating a repricing of their loan book on a regular basis. Thus base rate is not a single rate, but an average of what commercial banks use as their own base rates. This in turn will be driven by the target policy of the Bank.

The Bank is less concerned about overnight rates, which can vary considerably, reflecting supply and demand in the market, although with the advent of the open repo market, the volatility of the overnight rate has diminished considerably.

Thirteen

EU legislation

Objectives

This chapter will cover the following topics:

- ◆ EU financial services law;
- ◆ EC Banking Directives;
- ◆ EC Capital Adequacy Directives.

13.1 EU financial services law

Unlike UK domestic legislation, which is very much concerned with consumers, the European Union (EU) sees its role as almost solely concerned with ensuring a single market is in place for financial services. This means that its prime objective is to ensure that there is a level playing field between institutions. Please note that from a pure legislative viewpoint EU financial services law is still driven by the European Community (EC), which is technically one of the pillars forming the European Union. Under EU terminology regulations will apply directly in all member states. In contrast directives will have to be transposed into domestic law by each individual member state. In the UK this is often done by statutory insturments. For simplicity's sake we will look at the underlying EC directives, rather than their UK implementation.

To understand the impact of these directives it is important to understand some of the background. Under the European Community directives, banking business is deemed to be conducted by two principal groups – banks and investment firms.

For banks, known as credit institutions under EU terminology, the major changes necessitated in preparation for the single European market were included in the Second Banking Co-ordination Directive, which came into force in 1993. This has now been re-issued as what is commonly known as the Banking Consolidation Directive.

For investment firms the key piece of legislation, which led to the creation of a single market, was the Investment Services Directive, which came into force on 31 December 1995. Since 1999 the European Union has been working on the Financial Services Action Plan, which has the aim of further promoting a single financial market.

The purpose of both the Banking Consolidation Directive and the Investment Services Directive was to create a business environment in which European financial institutions of whatever type may operate throughout the European Economic Area (EEA – it includes all EU states plus Norway, Iceland and Liechtenstein) without the burden of having to be separately authorized in each member state and without being bound by various and different capital adequacy regimes.

A summary of major European Directives for banking activities to date, and the year the directive was passed rather than implemented, is given below:

1989	Undertakings in collective investments in transferable securities (UCITS) has enabled certain collective investment schemes to be sold throughout Europe.
1989	Own Funds Directive – provided a common definition of what is defined as capital.
1989	Second Banking Co-ordination Directive – created a single market for banks throughout the EEA.
1989	Solvency Ratio Directive – implemented the 1988 Basel Capital Accord for banks.
1992	Post-BCCI directive – provided for additional authorization requirements and consolidated supervision.
1992	Large Exposure Directive – required banks to limit their large exposures.
1993	Investment Services Directive (ISD) – created single market for investment firms throughout the EEA.
1993	Capital Adequacy Directive – created uniform set of financial requirements for banks, securities and investment firms.
2000	Banking Consolidation Directive – combines many of the above directives into a single document.
2002	Amended UCITS directive – broadens the type of UCITS that can be sold and allows firms that manage UCITS to provide fund management services without separate authorization under the ISD.

2002   Financial Groups Directive – aims to reduce the opportunities for arbitrage between insurance, banking and investment firm capital adequacy rules. It is often referred to as the Financial Conglomerates Directive.

The EC Banking Directives, Investment Services Directive and Capital Adequacy Directive are based on a mutual recognition of the standards which are imposed in the member states and an agreement on specific minimum criteria to be met. The aim is to create a balance between the different demands of widely varied markets and to create a single European market in which competition is opened up. Once a firm is authorized in one member state, it will be allowed to 'passport' this authorization and provide services into other member states.

The EU has accepted the importance of integrated capital markets for economic growth, job creation, financial stability, lower prices and for enabling consumers to reap the full benefits of the Euro. As a result it adopted the Financial Services Action Plan (FSAP) in May 1999. The FSAP set out a number of internal market directives that should be agreed by 2005. A key aim is to introduce a single European securities and financial market as suggested by the work chaired by Baron Alexander Lamfalussy. Progress has already been made with legislation adopted in areas such as combating money laundering, cross-border payments and insurance solvency. The Financial Groups Directive is also directly relevant to treasury activities, as it prescribes the need for consolidation of financial holding companies that span banking, investment services and insurance.

Further work is progressing on agreeing the International Accounting Standards Regulation and the proposed directives on Collateral, Market Abuse, Insurance Intermediaries and Distance Marketing. Moreover it is planned to renew work on such issue as auditor independence and standards; corporate governance; clearing and settlement; financial stability; reinsurance; more advanced insurance solvency rules; money laundering; the integrity of the financial sector and the development of an integrated market for retail financial services. Remaining proposals under the FSAP include a Take-over Directive, a revision of the Investment Services Directive, and a number of company law related directives. The Commission is also working on a draft directive for the implementation into European law of the proposed new Capital Accord of the Basel Committee on Banking Supervision.

13.2   EC banking directives

Banks were the initial focal point in the attempts at European harmonization because they were providing services to many of the member states at that time.

13.2.1   The First Banking Directive

This was agreed in 1977 and the main aim of it was to harmonize the authorization of credit institutions throughout the member states of the EC. It defines credit institutions as 'an undertaking whose business is to receive deposits or other repayable funds from the public and to grant credits for its own account'. This definition covers banks and building societies. The Banking Act 1987 implemented this definition and also included the licensing criteria, which the directive listed.

13.2.2   The Second Banking Directive

This was adopted in 1989 and member states were required to implement its provisions by January 1993. It contains single passport provisions which allow a credit institution to carry out in the EEA any of the activities which are listed in the directive, providing it is permitted to carry out these activities in its home state. Some of the listed activities were previously covered by host regulation, ie the UK rules. The directive was the first that introduced the passporting facilities. Thus a Spanish bank will only need the authorization of the Spanish competent authority, the home supervisor, to set up a branch in London. While the FSA, as the host supervisor, should be notified that a branch will be opened, it will not supervise that London branch. This is with the exception of liquidity issues which do fall under the remit of host supervisors.

The term competent authority is the European legislative term used for supervisory or regulatory authorities that authorize financial institutions. Authorization is given by the home state competent authority to the credit institution, which can then conduct business in the host state either by cross-border services or by establishing a branch in the host state. The type of business to be conducted must be disclosed. The institution should also abide by the conduct of business rules of the host state. The general authorization requirements under EC law have been incorporated into the FSA's threshold conditions.

The principle of reciprocity applies. This means that a member state must be allowed market access to non-EEA markets to the same extent that the member states allow non-EEA institutions access to their own markets. The same competitive opportunities must be available to EEA institutions in these third countries as to non-EEA institutions when operating in the member states.

In addition, the Second Banking Directive listed the business activities which can be passported into other EU countries. Each member state may have additional types of activity which its institutions can undertake and an activity which one member state allows may not be permitted by another member state.

The Banking Consolidation Directive (BCD) retains the principles of the earlier Banking Co-ordination Directives, being only a consolidation of existing directives.

The key directives incorporated are the First and Second Banking Co-ordination Directives, the Own Funds Directive and Solvency Directive. Other directives incorporated into BCD are the post-BCCI Directive and the Large Exposure Directive. The post-BCCI Directive, as it is often known, requires that bank structures be supervisable. Thus a bank needs to be supervised by the country in which the executive decisions are taken. It also requires that competent authorities vet changes of controllers. They also need to take account of the reputation of close-linked (or connected) companies or individuals when making a decision on authorization. The Solvency Ratio directive implemented the 1988 Basel Capital Accord and the capital adequacy requirement that it introduced for banks. The details of the Basel Capital Accord will be looked at in a separate chapter.

13.3   EC capital adequacy directives

In 1993 the Capital Adequacy Directive was put onto the EC statute books. The directive, as subsequently amended, applies the Basel Accord market risk amendment to investment firms and banks. The market risk amendment is notable because for the first time it allows banks and investment firms to use internal models, such as VaR models, for market risk capital adequacy calculations. Such a use is, however, subject to regulatory approval. The Directive was also the means by which uniform capital adequacy requirements for investment firms were implemented, based on the original 1988 Basel Capital Accord. Sometimes the amended Capital Adequacy Directive is referred to as CAD2, even though in reality it was not a new directive.

13.3.1   Recent developments

The European Commission last issued proposals in July 2003 for a new capital adequacy rules covering banks, building societies and investment firms. The proposed rules would implement the new capital framework now under discussion by the Basel Committee. The new proposals are intended to tie the amount of capital required more closely to the actual risk. A wider range of risk weightings would be used, based partly on ratings from external credit agencies such as Moody's and Standard & Poors or, if certain standards are met, by banks' internal risk assessments. Although it is not intended to move away from the 8% minimum, banks are likely to face significantly different capital requirements as the weightings in the new proposals are very different from those in the current directives.

The European rules, once they take effect, would cover a much broader range of banks and securities firms than the Basel rules, which are aimed only at large, internationally active institutions. The current capital adequacy rules require banks to hold a cushion of capital equivalent to at least 8% of their assets, weighted according to risk. Assets such as government bonds or mortgages require less capital than general loans. We will look at capital adequacy rules in more detail in Chapter 16.

Fourteen

US regulation

Objectives

This chapter will cover the following topics:

- ◆ US regulation;
- ◆ Office of the Comptroller of the Currency (OCC);
- ◆ Federal Reserve System (FRS);
- ◆ Federal Deposit Insurance Corporation (FDIC);
- ◆ Securities and Exchange Commission (SEC);
- ◆ Bank and financial holding companies.

14.1   Introduction

In the previous chapters we reviewed the UK regulatory system and the EC law that has been incorporated into it. However, they do not work in isolation. In particular, US regulation has a far wider reach than just the US. This is partly because of the importance of New York as a financial centre. Very few banks can avoid handling US dollars and these are almost invariably routed via the US. Even Eurodollar transactions will be recorded in the US. This, together with the sheer size of the US financial markets, means that many banks have established branches or subsidiaries in the US. Because of the complexity of US banking regulation and supervisory arrangements this text cannot, however, hope to provide more than a flavour of the system in place.

The US has developed its own style of regulation. It is very much based on rules and intensive supervisory examinations. However, the approach is distributed among various regulatory authorities with each one having a slightly different approach. The main regulatory agencies are the Office of Comptroller of the Currency (OCC), the Federal Reserve System (Fed) and the Federal Deposit Insurance Corporation (FDIC). Not only is the US the largest financial market in the world, it is also one that no internationally active banks can avoid. This means that almost every bank will at some point come into contact with US regulation. The effect is that US regulation has a far wider territorial scope than just the US.

In addition to the federal agencies there are numerous state authorities. All banks fall under the supervision and regulation of their chartering authority, at either state or federal level. Almost all banks also have deposit insurance protection and thus fall under the Federal Deposit Insurance Act, and, in the case of state banks that are not also members of the Fed, to direct FDIC supervision. If a state bank becomes a member of the Federal Reserve System, the Fed becomes its primary federal supervisor. The Fed also supervises bank holding companies and financial holding company. It thus has a role in consolidated supervision. National banks fall under the supervision and examination of the OCC.

In addition banking organizations may further be subject to the oversight of insurance, securities, or other regulators as they take on non-banking activities. In addition to state regulation this includes the Securities and Exchange Commission (SEC). The SEC supervises investment firms, including investment banks. Other agencies include the Office of Thrift Supervision, which looks after savings institutions and the Federal Trade Commission, which looks after unfair practices. To some extent one could even say that the federal Department of Justice has a regulatory role in relation to anti-trust issues. As the New York State Attorney General Eliott Spitzer shows, judiciaries can also have a significant role in influencing bank behaviour. They can do so by enforcing legislation even if regulators have been unable to take action themselves.

14.2   The Office of the Comptroller of the Currency

The Office of the Comptroller of the Currency (OCC) is the oldest of the federal bank regulatory agencies. Established by the National Currency Act of 1863 and strengthened by the National Bank Act of 1864, the Comptroller is the primary supervisory agency for national banks. Today, the OCC regulates and supervises more than 2,200 national banks and 56 federal branches of foreign banks in the US, accounting for more than 55% of the total assets of all US commercial banks.

The OCC is part of the Treasury Department and is headed by a single person appointed by the President to a five-year term. In addition to its headquarters in Washington, DC, the OCC has six district offices. Its role includes the power to charter national banks, review national bank branch and merger applications, implement regulations, and examine and supervise all national banks. This means that the OCC also influences the chartering and expansion of national banks through various policy decisions. To assure compliance with its supervisory policies and regulations, the OCC has wide powers. In addition to its examination function it can issue cease and desist orders, remove or suspend bank officials and other parties affiliated with a national bank, and place national banks into conservatorship or revoke their charters. It can also fine national bank officers, directors, employees, or other affiliated parties for such offences as violating banking laws and regulations and engaging in unsafe or unsound practices.

14.3   Federal Reserve System

The Federal Reserve System (FRS) was established in 1913 by the Federal Reserve Act. It is headed by a seven-member Board of Governors, appointed by the US President to 14-year terms. One governor is designated by the President as chairman with a four-year, renewable term, which for some years has now been Alan Greenspan. The Fed is run by the Board of Governors headquartered in Washington, DC. In addition, the Federal Reserve System consists of 12 Federal Reserve Banks and 25 branches located across the country. Each Federal Reserve Bank is independently managed by its own board of nine directors. Six directors are elected by member banks to represent member banks and the wider business community and three are appointed by the Fed's Board of Governors to represent the public.

The Fed's role is to supervise directly those state-chartered banks that choose to become members. At the end of 2002 there were 949 state member banks falling under Fed supervision. Membership of the Federal Reserve is, however, wider. 2,977 banks are members, and account for 38% of all commercial banks in the US and for 74% of all commercial banking offices. In addition to its bank supervisory responsibilities, the Fed reviews membership applications from state banks and, in conjunction with state authorities, merger and branching proposals from state member banks. It thus performs a very similar role to the OCC, but only for member banks.

The Federal Reserve is also the primary supervisor and regulator of bank holding companies and financial holding companies. For these companies, the Federal Reserve either reviews or receives notification of their formation and expansion proposals. It is also responsible for supervising the overall banking organization. This means that the Fed gains an insight into the operations of many banks not directly under its supervision, as most banks are also part of bank holding companies. It is as a result of this that most OCC supervised banks are indirectly also supervised by the Fed. At year-end 2002, 5,963 bank holding companies were in operation, with control of 6,278 insured subsidiary banks. These banks held over 96% of the total deposits in all US commercial banks. As of 20 October 2000, a total of 632 banking organizations had elected to become financial holding companies, 30 of which are foreign owned.

Similarly to the OCC, the Fed has a number of powers to enforce its supervisory policies and regulations. These powers include the authority to issue cease and desist orders, remove bank and holding company officers and other affiliated parties, levy fines, revoke membership, and order divestiture or termination of financial holding company activities. One should, however, note that supervision is only a small part of the Fed's role. It is almost best known for its public policy responsibilities. It sets US monetary policy through open market operations and adjustments in the discount rate and reserve requirements. It acts as the fiscal agent for the federal government and provides settlement services such as those for cheques and money transfers.

Foreign banks wishing to operate in the US will fall under the International Banking Act, as amended by the Foreign Bank Supervision Enhancement Act of 1991. It requires foreign banks to obtain Fed approval before establishing branches, agencies, commercial lending subsidiaries or representative offices. Approval would not be granted if the foreign bank was not subject to comprehensive supervision or regulation on a consolidated basis by its home country supervisor. The home country supervisor would also have to approve of the US offices. Other requirements would include meeting certain financial conditions and capital adequacy requirements, management abilities, anti-money laundering processes and other requirements of a similar nature.

Another frequently used term refers to Edge Act corporations. The Edge Act is the US banking legislation that allows national banks to perform foreign lending through government-chartered subsidiaries. Thus an Edge Act corporation is chartered by the Federal Reserve to engage in international banking operations. The Federal Reserve Board acts upon applications by US and foreign banking organizations to establish Edge corporations. The Board also examines Edge corporations and their subsidiaries.

14.4 Federal Deposit Insurance Company

The FDIC was established by the Banking Act of 1933 to examine insured state-chartered banks that are not members of the Fed. There were 7,887 insured commercial banks and 1,467 insured savings institutions at year-end 2002. Insured funds in 2002 amounted to USD 2,527 trillion. Although the FDIC supervises a large number of banks, its main function is to insure deposits at commercial banks and thrift (savings) institutions. Only FDIC approved banks can obtain deposit insurance. Furthermore the FDIC insurance responsibilities extend to protecting insured depositors, acting as receiver for failed banks, and administering the deposit insurance funds. The FDIC has introduced a system of deposit insurance that takes account of riskiness of various institutions, an assessment of which is undertaken by the FDIC. The FDIC can undertake examination whenever it relates to deposit insurance, independently of whether the bank is supervised by the FDIC or not.

The FDIC has wide powers and also has a role with regards to US thrift institutions. The FDIC, although very relevant to US institutions, is generally less important for treasurers, unless a bank owns a banking network in the US.

The capital adequacy rules of much of the US banking system is driven by The Federal Deposit Insurance Corporation Improvement Act of 1991. It was passed to improve the supervision of banks and reduce or limit the cost of resolving failing institutions, particularly after the Savings & Loans crisis the US banking system had gone through previously. The Act required deposit insurance premiums to be set at levels sufficient to rebuild the insurance fund and for the FDIC to set insurance premia based on the riskiness of institutions. More importantly the Act instituted a system of prompt corrective action, with mandatory and progressively more severe regulatory restrictions on banks that fail to meet specified capital levels. It is the prompt corrective action requirements, which exceed the requirements of the Basel Capital Accord, that lead to significant capital adquacy levels in much of the US banking sysem.

14.5   State banking agencies

As already indicated there are a large number of state chartered banks. For these every state maintains its own regulatory agency to charter and supervise state banks. In many states the supervisory authority has a wider role for financial institutions as well, but there is a wide variety of differences between the 50 states. Individual banking laws also differ widely between states and may even be less exacting than federal regulations. However, as soon as a bank becomes a member of the Fed or takes out federal deposit insurance it has to abide by the relevant federal regulations. In order to ensure some consistency between state banking agencies, the Conference of State Bank Supervisors provides a forum for discussing issues of common interest to all state regulators.

14.6   Securities regulation

The Securities and Exchange Commission (SEC) was established in 1934 to regulate practices in the securities industry. It is headquartered in Washington, DC, and is run by five presidentially appointed commissioners. Banks and banking organizations are subject to SEC regulations and oversight in a number of areas. All banks and banking organizations that have publicly traded shares have to register and report to the SEC. The SEC has a role in ensuring accounts are accurate and will thus look at the accuracy of bank loan loss reserves and other financial disclosures. The Sarbanes-Oxley Act of 2002 has further extended the remit of the SEC in this area.

The SEC is also the primary regulator for securities activities directly. Since the Gramm-Leach-Bliley Act of 1999 banks can avoid registering with the SEC for some of their brokers or dealer activities, but subsidiaries or holding companies that undertake such activities will need to register with the SEC. Depending on the particular activity, the securities operations of banking organizations may also be regulated by other authorities, including the National Association of Securities Dealers, Commodity Futures Trading Commission, Municipal Securities Rulemaking Board, and various securities exchanges.

14.7 Bank holding companies and financial holding companies

14.7.1 Bank holding companies

Bank holding companies have become very important for the US banking structure, as individual banks were severely restricted in terms of additional activities they could undertake. Bank holding companies allowed these restrictions to be overcome by enabling the acquisition of additional banks, expansion into permissible non-banking activities, better access to funds, and the consolidation of certain functions for more efficient operations. Smaller holding companies, on the other hand, are often formed because of consolidated tax benefits, control or estate planning considerations, or the need to provide additional services to local communities. Bank holding companies fall under the Bank Holding Companies Act 1956 and 1970. This was further amended by the Gramm-Leach-Bliley Act of 1999, which limited the new non-banking activities for holding companies that do not elect to become financial holding companies.

14.7.2 Financial holding companies

A new form of bank holding company – the financial holding company – became possible after passage of the Gramm-Leach-Bliley Act of 1999. It allowed financial holding companies to take advantage of a much broader range of affiliations among banks, securities firms, and insurance companies than was possible for traditional bank holding companies. Financial holding companies are a significant development in US financial markets as their establishment has removed many long-standing barriers to affiliations among banks, securities firms, and insurance companies. The Act clarified the registration process and the regulatory standards that these holding companies have to meet. These include the requirement that deposit-taking institutions in the group are well managed and well capitalized. Well capitalized refers to the capital adequacy regime implemented in the US.

The Act also reviewed the regulatory arrangements for the ongoing supervision of bank holding companies and financial holding companies. This framework relies heavily on the concept of 'functional regulation,' under which similar activities are to be regulated by a single regulator with expertise in that area. The Fed continues to serve as the supervisor of all bank holding companies, including financial holding companies, with general authority to examine and require reports from holding companies and their subsidiaries. However, in relation to subsidiaries that fall under the remit of other authorities the Fed has to rely 'to the fullest extent possible,' on the reports and examinations of other regulators. This includes the appropriate state and federal authorities for banks and thrifts; the Securities and Exchange Commission for registered securities brokers, dealers, or investment advisers; and state insurance commissioners for licensed insurance companies. The Fed can take independent action if it feels there is a wider systemic risk, including management risk, or the subsidiary is believed to be in breach of the Bank Holding Company Act or other laws enforced by the Federal Reserve. The Fed may not set capital requirements for functionally regulated subsidiaries that are already in compliance with the capital standards of their primary supervisor. Neither may the Fed require such subsidiaries to assist affiliated banks if that would materially harm their own condition.

Fifteen

International regulatory framework

Objectives

This chapter will cover the following topics:

- ◆ Basel Committee;
- ◆ IOSCO;
- ◆ Financial Stability Forum;
- ◆ Joint Forum;
- ◆ International Monetary Fund.

15.1   Introduction

In addition to local supervision, the more international committees that discuss and agree global standards fulfil an important role in the supervisory process. The main ones relevant to bankers are the Basel Committee, IOSCO and the Financial Stability Forum. The standards and reports written by these committees provide useful background as to the rationale driving domestic regulation. At the same time these fora consult widely and it may be possible for banks to influence future discussion, either directly or in conjunction with other trade bodies.

Among the most pressing issues confronting financial services regulators is the need to develop practical arrangements to supervise an increasingly global industry. Unsurprisingly, regulators are involved in a game of catch up; trying to impose effective regulation of firms who already have global groups, branches and above all global risks, is not simple.

In 1975 the Basel Committee on Banking Supervision was established by the G10 central banks, all of which were also banking supervisors at the time. Its initial focus was to define the role and responsibilities of home and host supervisors of internationally active banks. Its key success has been the development of capital adequacy rules, which set down minimum requirements for internationally active banks, although one should not underestimate the positive effect of the wider standards agreed by the Basel Committee.

The securities industry has the International Organization of Securities Commissions (IOSCO) of which the regulators of some 70 countries are members. More recently the world's derivatives regulators have agreed to co-operate to share information through the Windsor Declaration and the Boca Raton Agreement. These initiatives are the basis of the beginnings of international information sharing and standards setting, a process being actively supported by G7 nations. In 1999 the Financial Stability Forum was established by regulators and finance ministries to cover global financial stability issues. Reports it has issued cover areas such as offshore financial centres and hedge funds.

Banking has for many years been an international business, not least as a result of its role in financing international trade. But where there have been opportunities for profit, there is always risk. The example of Barings has clearly shown that where subsidiaries have been established, events elsewhere in a group can damage other parts of the group, reinforcing the need for active collaboration between financial regulators to supervise financial businesses at a consolidated level.

On a global scale there can be little doubt that regulators' ability to supervise internationally active firms is deficient. The existence of different accountancy standards, insolvency law and hugely variable standards among many national regulators creates a far from ideal background. Coupled with this, the growth of financial markets in the developing world and the emergence of information systems such as the Internet, means that interdependence, and thus systemic risk, grows daily bigger.

15.2 The Basel Committee on Banking Supervision

The Basel Committee was established by the central bank governors of the G10 countries in 1975, following serious disturbances in international currency and banking markets, including the failure of a Bankhaus Herstatt, part way through the trading day. The Committee usually meets at the Bank for International Settlements (BIS) in Basel, Switzerland, where its permanent Secretariat is located. However, technically the Basel Committee is not part of the BIS. The Committee now comprises representatives of central banks and supervisory authorities from Belgium,

Canada, France, Germany, Italy, Japan, Luxembourg, the Netherlands, Spain, Sweden, Switzerland, the UK and the US. The committee is best known for its work on Capital Adequacy. In 1988 it published the Basel Capital Accord, which established a measurement framework and minimum standards which are followed not only in all member countries, but also in virtually all other countries with internationally active banks.

The Committee is also responsible for the Basel Concordat, which has helped to define the respective roles of home and host country supervisors in the supervision of internationally active banks. This framework was developed into a set of minimum standards in 1992.

While the Concordat itself has no legal force, the 1992 paper stresses that the members of the Basel group expect each other to apply the stated minimum standards, and it urges other countries to do so as well. Four minimum conditions for effective supervision are stated.

- ◆ All international banking groups and international banks should be supervised by a home country authority that capably performs consolidated supervision.
- ◆ The creation of a cross-border banking establishment should receive the prior consent of both the host country supervisor and the home country supervisor of the bank or banking group.
- ◆ Supervisors should possess the right to gather information from the cross-border banking establishments of the banks or banking groups for which they are the home country supervisor.
- ◆ If a host country supervisor determines that one of these standards is not met to its satisfaction, it may apply restrictive measures so as to satisfy its prudential concerns, including the prohibition of the creation of banking establishments.

The Concordat places primary responsibility for the supervision of the solvency of cross-border banking establishments with the home authority and that for liquidity with the host authority. The supervision of foreign exchange exposures is a joint responsibility, this being a vital primary area for cooperation between authorities to ensure a consolidated view.

Collaboration between regulators within a single country is also necessary where banking groups include insurance, investment management or other securities businesses. Without co-operation and consistency of treatment, there is a danger that banks (particularly unscrupulous ones) will structure their business in such a way as to minimize the regulatory impact or even frustrate it altogether.

The key objectives of the Committee are to strengthen international co-operation by improving the quality of banking supervision world-wide, and to ensure that no foreign banking entity escapes supervision.

In addition, the Committee's work on multilateral netting schemes culminated in publication of an interpretation note in April 1996. Since then the work of the Committee has been divided into three main areas:

◆ capital adequacy including both credit and market risk;
◆ risk management including operational risk and internal controls; and
◆ information flows and disclosure, assisted by a task force on accounting issues.

In October 1998 the Basel Committee published a paper entitled Framework for Internal Control Systems in Banking Organisations, which is part of the development of guidance on sound risk management practices. The paper notes that typical control breakdowns can be grouped into five broad categories:

◆ lack of adequate management oversight and accountability, and failure to develop a strong control culture within the bank;
◆ inadequate assessment of the risk of certain banking activities, whether on- or off-balance-sheet;
◆ the absence or failure of key control activities, such as segregation of duties, approvals, verifications, reconciliations, and reviews of operating performance;
◆ inadequate communication of information between levels of management within the bank, especially in the upward communication of problems;
◆ inadequate or ineffective audit programs and other monitoring activities.

The paper notes that many recent problem cases highlight the fact that control systems that function well for traditional or simple products are unable to handle more sophisticated or complex situations. Fourteen principles for the assessment of internal control systems are defined in the paper under the categories: management oversight and the control culture; risk assessment; control activities; information and communication; monitoring; and evaluation of internal control systems by supervisory authorities. Under each principle there is a discussion of key issues. In addition, there is a useful appendix entitled 'Supervisory lessons learned from internal control failures'.

The paper notes that the guidance is based on practices currently in place at many major banks, securities houses, and non-financial companies. Nevertheless, many institutions will find value in looking afresh at their control systems, especially given the pace of change across the financial sector.

We have already looked at some of the documents issued by the Basel Committee that are of direct relevance to treasury functions:

◆ Sound Practices for the Management and Supervision of Operational Risk
◆ Principles for the Management of Credit Risk
◆ Sound Practices for Managing Liquidity in Banking Organisations
◆ Principles for the Management of Interest-rate Risk

Another influential document issued by the Basel Committee in 1999 is the Core Principles paper, setting global standards for prudential regulation and supervision. The aim is to provide the international financial community with a benchmark against which the effectiveness of bank supervisory regimes can be assessed. Indeed the IMF and World Bank have taken it upon themselves to undertake such assessments of how countries have implemented the principles as part of their Financial Stability Assessment Program. The document is likely to change as practices evolve.

The paper includes 25 principles on how supervisors should undertake their roles and how they should be organized. The principles have been implemented in the UK and require banks to:

◆ meet the threshold conditions,
◆ only have controllers approved by supervisors,
◆ be organized to have supervisable structures,
◆ meet capital adequacy requirements,
◆ have implemented adequate system and controls, particularly for transactions with connected parties,
◆ have in place comprehensive risk management processes,
◆ have internal controls that are adequate for the nature and scale of their business, and
◆ ensure that they cannot be utilized for criminal activities.

It also requires banking supervisors to:

◆ undertake both on-site and off-site supervision,
◆ have regular contact with bank management and a thorough understanding of the institution's operations,
◆ have a means of collecting, reviewing and analysing prudential reports and statistical returns from banks on a solo and consolidated basis,
◆ be able to independently validate supervisory information either through on-site examinations or use of external auditors,
◆ supervise banking groups on a consolidated basis,
◆ ensure banks maintain adequate records and publish true and fair financial statements,
◆ take appropriate actions, and have the legal capacity to do so, against banks not meeting regulatory requirements,
◆ share relevant information with the various other supervisors involved, and
◆ be able to apply the same high standards to foreign branches or subsidiaries operating in their jurisdiction.

15.3 International Organization of Securities Commissions (IOSCO)

IOSCO was established in 1974. Its members comprise the chief statutory or governmental competent authorities responsible for the regulation of securities and derivatives markets in more than 70 countries. The key role of IOSCO is to facilitate international communication and co-operation between securities regulators, which is achieved through its various committees and working parties. As with the Basel Committee, the conclusions reached by IOSCO are not legally binding, but represent standards, which should be reflected in the national regimes and practices of individual countries.

The agreed objectives of IOSCO include:

◆ to co-operate together to promote high standards of regulation in order to maintain just, efficient and sound markets;

◆ to exchange information on their respective experiences in order to promote the development of domestic markets;

◆ to unite their efforts to establish standards and an effective surveillance of international securities transactions;

◆ to provide mutual assistance to promote the integrity of the markets by a rigorous application of the standards and by effective enforcement against offences.

The Executive Committee of IOSCO has established two specialized working committees. The objective of the first one, the Technical Committee, is to review major regulatory issues related to international securities and futures transactions and to co-ordinate practical responses to these concerns. The work of the Technical Committee is divided into the following five major functional subject areas:

◆ Multinational Disclosure and Accounting;
◆ Regulation of Secondary Markets;
◆ Regulation of Market Intermediaries;
◆ Enforcement and the Exchange of Information;
◆ Investment Management.

The second specialized committee, the Emerging Markets Committee, has the aim of promoting the development and improvement of efficiency of emerging securities and futures markets. It does so by establishing principles and minimum standards, preparing training programs for the staff of members and facilitating exchange of information and transfer of technology and expertise. It has set up Working Groups to address the following functional areas:

◆ Disclosure and Accounting;
◆ Regulation of Secondary Markets;
◆ Regulation of Market Intermediaries;
◆ Enforcement and the Exchange of Information;
◆ Investment Management.

In the spring of 1998 IOSCO published guidelines on managing and controlling risk, that set out 12 principles for ensuring that investment banks and brokers have installed strong control systems and for checking their effectiveness. IOSCO officials hope the principles will serve as benchmarks which companies and supervisors can use to measure their own approaches to risk management.

The guidelines follow a string of disasters, ranging from the 1995 collapse of Barings in the UK to the $1bn of bond trading losses unearthed the same year at Japan's Daiwa Bank. The guidelines urge securities firms to analyse the risks they are running, and to set up an appropriate control structure to manage this risk. This should include standard precautions such as keeping internal audit independent of the trading and revenue side of the business and segregating front-office and back-office responsibilities. The guidelines closely resemble those that apply to banking activities, but the IOSCO stamp makes it clearer that many banking principles are directly relevant to the securities industry.

15.4 Financial Stability Forum

The Financial Stability Forum (FSF) was convened in April 1999. Its aim is to promote international financial stability through information exchange and international co-operation in financial supervision and surveillance. It attempts to do so by bringing together on a regular basis senior representatives of national financial authorities (eg central banks, supervisory authorities and ministries of finance), international financial institutions, international regulatory and supervisory groupings, committees of central bank experts and the European Central Bank. The FSF is currently chaired by Mr Roger W Ferguson Jr, Vice Chairman of the Board of Governors of the Federal Reserve System, in a personal capacity. Following the precedent of the Basel Committee, the FSF is serviced by a small secretariat housed at the Bank for International Settlements in Basel, Switzerland.

The FSF is part of an initiative of G7 Finance Ministers and Central Bank Governors, in order to promote international financial stability, improve the functioning of financial markets and reduce the tendency for financial shocks to propagate from country to country, thus destabilising the world economy.

The FSF's mandate is:

◆ to assess vulnerabilities affecting the international financial system;
◆ to identify and oversee action needed to address these; and
◆ to improve co-ordination and information exchange among the various authorities responsible for financial stability.

So far the FSF has met in bi-annual plenary meetings with various taskforces doing underlying work. It also holds regional meetings with non-member financial authorities to ensure broader support. This is in line with the FSF aim to 'give momentum to a broad-based multilateral agenda for strengthening financial systems and the stability of international financial markets.' It works on the premise that necessary changes will be enacted by the relevant national and international financial authorities.

Recent work includes a working group on Capital Flows. The resulting report, published in April 2000, made specific recommendations for:

◆ risk management by financial authorities and institutions;
◆ transparency and better disclosure of information; and
◆ improved availability and quality of data.

There are a number of other initiatives that the FSF is working on:

- ◆ possible financial stability issues arising from recent large corporate failures and the possible repercussions for market integrity. Members reviewed initiatives that had been set in train;
- ◆ work on combating the financing of terrorism. including the review of offshore financial centres' (OFCs) efforts to strengthen their supervisory, regulatory, information sharing and cooperation practices. It has looked at a number of OFCs and issued a categorization of many centres;
- ◆ review of highly leveraged institution, also known as hedge funds, and how they may affect stability issues.

15.5   Joint Forum

IOSCO, the Basel Committee and the International Association of Insurance Supervisors (IAIS) announced in June 1996 a joint initiative to strengthen co-operation between the regulators of diversified financial groups. This has now become known as the Joint Forum. Initial work looked at whether additional co-ordinating arrangements to facilitate information exchange, in both normal and emergency situations, should be set out, and the extent to which existing provisions of national law may need to be amended to support this objective. Other issues of common interest to the three parent committees relate to financial conglomerates.

As part of looking at issues of common interest to the three parent committees the Joint Forum develops guidance and principles papers to identify best practice in the following areas:

- ◆ risk assessments and management, internal controls and capital;
- ◆ the use of the audit and actuarial functions in the supervision of regulated entities and corporate groups containing regulated entities;
- ◆ corporate governance, including fit and proper tests;
- ◆ outsourcing by regulated firms of functions and activities;
- ◆ different definitions of banking, insurance and securities activities and the potential that they may lead to regulatory arbitrage; and
- ◆ identifying the core principles of the banking, insurance and securities sectors that are common and understanding the differences, where they arise.

Specific mandates of the Joint Forum are to undertake further work on risk assessments and capital with special focus on the following areas:

- ◆ Risk aggregation – Approaches used by firms to manage and aggregate risks across multiple businesses and risk categories (eg credit, market, insurance, operational risks, etc) and approaches used by supervisors to address the challenges of firms whose activities span multiple businesses and risk categories (eg capital distribution in groups).

◆ Operational risk management – Efforts and approaches that firms are making to address operational risks in all their businesses and globally. Approaches of firms that may take on transferred operational risks.

◆ Credit risk management and transfer – Promote supervisory information sharing on issues relevant to credit risk transfer and aggregation of these risks in the firm as a whole.

◆ Disclosure of Financial Risks – Following up on the recommendations of the April 2001 Multidisciplinary Group on Enhanced Disclosure.

The Joint Forum has issued a number of principles papers that may be of interest to readers researching international financial standards:

◆ The Capital Adequacy Principles paper outlines measurement techniques and principles to facilitate the assessment of capital adequacy on a group-wide basis for financial conglomerates.

◆ The Fit and Proper Principles paper provides guidance to supervisors on how to ensure that financial conglomerates are soundly and prudently managed.

◆ The Intra-Group Transactions and Exposures Principles paper provides principles on how regulators can ensure prudent management and control of intragroup transactions and exposures by financial conglomerates.

◆ The Risk Concentrations Principles paper looks at how risk concentrations in financial conglomerates can be supervised.

15.6   The International Monetary Fund

The International Monetary Fund (IMF) was set up as part of the Bretton Woods Conference of 1944, which also introduced a worldwide fixed exchange rate system. The IMF's role was to promote international monetary cooperation, exchange stability, and orderly exchange arrangements; to foster economic growth and high levels of employment; and to provide temporary financial assistance to countries to help ease balance of payments adjustment. This section will only look at the role of the IMF that is relevant to the syllabus, without touching upon the wider aspects of what the IMF does.

The IMF is now increasingly involved in helping to strengthen financial sectors around the globe and promoting global standards in combination with other bodies, such as the Basel Committee. Following the Basel Committee's Core Principles, the IMF and the World Bank in 1999 began joint assessments of member countries' financial sectors. The aim is to help identify actual and potential weaknesses by assessing the strength of financial systems in a number of member countries. These assessments will then be discussed with the relevant countries as a guide to the measures needed. The reports will look particularly at countries' observance of standards and codes, focusing mainly on areas of direct operational concern to the IMF. The IMF calls this part of its work the Financial Sector Assessment Program, often referred to as

FSAP. The UK was subject to the FSAP during 2002 and the report can be downloaded from the IMF's website.

IMF staff are also working with national governments and other international institutions to:

- ◆ strengthen the legal, regulatory, and supervisory frameworks for banks;
- ◆ review minimum capital requirements for banks and financial institutions;
- ◆ develop a core set of international accounting standards;
- ◆ finalize a set of core principles for good corporate governance;
- ◆ avoid exchange rate regimes that are vulnerable to attack; and
- ◆ ensure a freer flow of timely financial data to markets.

Sixteen

Capital adequacy

Objectives

This chapter will cover the following topics:

- ◆ purpose of capital requirements;
- ◆ 1988 Basel Accord;
- ◆ market risk amendment;
- ◆ Basel II;
- ◆ Banking Consolidation Directive/Capital Adequacy Directive;
- ◆ Risk Based Capital Requirement Directive;
- ◆ Integrated Prudential Sourcebook.

16.1   Purpose of capital

The main benefit of capital is that it provides a buffer to absorb unexpected losses. The risk of insolvency is therefore reduced, even if the behaviour of management does not change. This buffer function is also the economic rationale for the existence of capital. We briefly looked at this when looking at equity as part of the review of funding issues in Chapter 2. Because shareholders are the last ones to get repayment (if any) in case of default, and share issues are permanent, they in effect absorb any losses. From a pure accounting point of view losses reduce capital and thus the net worth of a firm. It is thus in shareholders' interest to retain a tight control over management as it is their money that is being invested.

When regulatory capital requirement exceeds what the firm would voluntarily hold, the cost of its failure to equity holders and subordinated debt holders increases: the cost of failure is thus shifted towards the owners, and away from other firms and their customers. Although the probability of failure should fall because of the higher capital buffer, the net impact may nevertheless be stronger incentives on the capital holders to operate effective oversight over the firm's management. The firm is then less likely to be operated in a way that threatens its solvency, or infringes conduct of business or client money regulations.

Finally, higher capital levels also give a signal to the public. Markets and customers will see the benefits of higher capital levels and be more likely to trade with these highly capitalized firms. In aggregate this can increase market and public confidence, another of the objectives of regulation.

The regulation of capital adequacy has always been an important tool for supervisors to ensure the stability of each individual bank and the banking system as a whole. Nevertheless it needs to be said that capital requirements are only one of many tools available to supervisors. Indeed, capital should be regarded as only mitigating risk rather than preventing bank failure altogether. Prevention itself would be achieved through good risk management, which, as we have seen, implies effective systems and controls. At the very least, without some assurance that the firm's systems for monitoring and measuring risk are adequate, the regulator cannot even be sure that the notional reported capital strength reasonably reflects the true risk position of the firm.

Similarly capital levels, and capital ratios, are an important element in market discipline. Market discipline is the concept that market participants themselves will promote sensible risk management and capital levels. Market discipline requires that market participants be provided with information that will allow them to judge whether a firm is weakly capitalized or poorly run. The markets may then penalize the firm in various ways, such as charging a higher rate for borrowing, or discounting the firm's share price. Historically, market discipline has primarily worked through the information provided by capital ratios.

Regulators thus have a considerable interest in ensuring that banks have adequate capital levels. They have thus introduced capital requirements and these are generally known as capital adequacy rules. For banks, capital ratios are only meaningful in relation to the assets that they need to support. There is also a risk dimension: the higher the risk of the assets, the more capital is needed.

16.2 The Basel Capital Accord

Historically capital ratios have been falling more or less continuously ever since banks became important economic agents in the early 1800s. This fall is thought to have been driven by increased legislation, the more formal role of central banks as lenders of last resort and finally banking regulation. By the beginning of the 1980s capital ratios were thought to be so low as to require concerted action by the main national regulators. This was partly due to the third-world debt crisis that occurred at the time. At the time deposits, often coming from rich oil-producing countries, were channelled to developing countries. By the 1980s this lending became unsustainable, partly due to high interest rates and partly due to overborrowing. The high provisioning levels required led to capital ratios falling further. At the same time worldwide financial markets were becoming increasingly integrated. This created a volatile combination of low capital levels and increased vulnerability as financial instability in one country could easily have destabilizing effects in other countries. National supervisors, meeting under the aegis of the Basel Committee, agreed the so-called Basel Accord, with the aim of stabilizing capital ratios across the internationally active banks. Its other aim was to secure international convergence of supervisory regulations governing the capital adequacy of international banks in order to reduce regulatory arbitrage. Regulatory arbitrage is the notion that banks would move towards those jurisdictions with the weakest capital requirements. In time the Basel Accord became the internationally accepted norm for bank capital adequacy.

The Accord achieved this by setting up a framework which national supervisors and banks themselves can use to calculate capital ratios. In the first instance the Accord defines what constitutes capital. It acknowledges the differences between various types of capital and thus splits capital into core capital and supplementary capital. The Accord then goes on to specify the various risk weights that should be applied to assets for the calculation of capital ratios. It then sets a minimum ratio of capital to weighted risk assets of 8%, of which at least half needs to be core capital. These ratios are sometimes referred to as the Cooke ratios.

The formula for the capital calculation is:

$$\frac{\text{Capital}}{\text{Risk Weighted Assets}}$$

Because the calculation is based on assets, and because banking assets mainly contain credit risk, the initial Accord is entirely driven by credit risk. Finally the Accord provided for a transitional period to the end of 1992 to give banks time to adapt.

16.2.1 Definition of capital

The Accord begins with defining the numerator, ie what is to be counted as capital. Core capital is defined as basic equity: issued and fully paid ordinary shares/common stock and non-cumulative perpetual preferred stock. In contrast cumulative preferred stock are excluded on the basis that the cumulating of unpaid dividends goes against the notion of the buffer function that core capital needs to fulfil. As noted previously when looking at capital as part of funding, reserves from post-tax retained earnings should also be included as part of core capital. Another name for core capital is Tier 1 capital. Overall, Tier 1 capital has to represent 50% or more of total Tier 1 and Tier 2 capital.

Tier 2 capital, also known as supplementary or secondary capital, includes those items that have some but not all of the features of core capital. Undisclosed reserves, also referred to as unpublished or hidden reserves, are in many ways similar to retained earnings, as long as they have been passed through the profit and loss account and are accepted as core capital by the bank's supervisory authorities. At the same time many countries do not recognize hidden reserves at all. Indeed, over time, hidden reserves have become less common as accounting practice has moved towards ensuring that accounts represent a timely and accurate reflection of the financial position of a company. Instead current practice now favours putting such items in revaluation reserves, another type of secondary capital. Revaluation reserves arise where, under national regulatory or accounting arrangements, certain assets are revalued to reflect their current value, or at least to something closer to their current value than historic cost suggests. The resultant revaluation reserves can be included in the capital base under the condition that assets are prudently valued, fully reflecting the possibility of price fluctuations or forced sale.

General provisions or general loan-loss reserves are another type of capital recognized as Tier 2. They form a reserve held against future losses, currently unidentified, and are freely available to meet losses that subsequently materialize. Provisions relating to specific exposures, such as those created when a loan is in default or impaired should be excluded, as they are no longer deemed to be freely available. Nevertheless the Committee believed that double counting could occur and it has therefore limited the eligibility for inclusion in the capital calculations. They are thus limited to 1.25% of risk weighted assets.

Moving away from reserves there are certain hybrid debt capital instruments, which have characteristics close to equity. The Accord states that some of these may be treated as Tier 2, particularly when they are able to support losses on an ongoing basis without triggering liquidation. To be available for inclusion, the instruments need to meet following requirements:

- they are unsecured, subordinated and fully paid-up;
- they are not redeemable at the initiative of the holder or without the prior consent of the supervisory authority;
- they are available to participate in losses without the bank being obliged to cease trading (unlike conventional subordinated debt);
- although the capital instrument may carry an obligation to pay interest that cannot permanently be reduced or waived (unlike dividends on ordinary shareholders' equity), it should allow service obligations to be deferred (as with cumulative preference shares) where the profitability of the bank would not support payment.

This category includes a variety of instruments, such as perpetual preference shares, and a number of instruments that are country specific. Examples of these are perpetual debt instruments in the UK and mandatory convertible debt instruments in the USA.

Hybrid debt instruments, generally categorized as subordinated term debt, that do not meet the above criteria, may be counted as Tier 2 capital under the subordinated debt heading. Such debt, however, is least like equity, particularly given its fixed maturity and inability to absorb losses except in the case of liquidation. Therefore, in order to be counted as Tier 2 capital, these instruments need to have an original maturity exceeding five years. Furthermore it may not amount to more than 50% of the core capital element and must be subject to adequate amortization arrangements.

To ensure a prudent approach to what can count as capital, the 1988 Accord also requires some deductions from capital. Goodwill has to be deducted from Tier 1 capital. The rationale is that goodwill is unlikely to be available to support the bank's operation when it is most likely to be needed. In this the regulatory treatment of goodwill is very different from the accounting treatment. This difference is justifiable, as goodwill, like other intangible assets, is an important element of commercial strength and thus should be reflected in the accounts if these are to give a true and fair picture. In contrast capital adequacy deals with prudence rather than commercial opportunities.

Deduction from capital is also required for investments in subsidiaries engaged in banking and financial activities not consolidated in national systems. The normal practice will be to consolidate subsidiaries for the purpose of assessing the capital adequacy of banking groups. Where this is not done, deduction is essential to prevent the multiple use of the same capital resources in different parts of the group. The deduction for such investments will be made against the total capital base. The assets representing the investments in subsidiary companies whose capital had been deducted from that of the parent would not be included intotal assets for the purposes of computing the ratio.

At the discretion of national authorities the Accord also allows investments in the capital of other banks and financial institutions to be deducted. The rationale is that if these are not deducted there could be double counting across a banking system as capital in one bank could also be used to support capital in a second bank.

16.2.2 Risk weighting

Having defined the numerator of the capital adequacy calculations it is time to look at the denominator, ie the calculation of the risk-weighted assets. To undertake the calculations the Committee broke assets down into several risk categories. Table 16.1 shows the main weighting categories.

Table 16.1: Risk weightings for on-balance sheet assets

0%	20%	50%	100%
◆Cash ◆Claims on central governments and central banks denominated in national currency and funded in that currency ◆Other claims on OECD central governments and central banks	◆Claims on multilateral development banks ◆Claims on banks incorporated in the OECD ◆Claims on other banks with a residual maturity of up to one year ◆Claims on non-domestic OECD public-sector entities, excluding Central government ◆Cash items in process of collection	◆Loans fully secured by mortgage on residential property that is or will be occupied by the borrower or that is rented	All other assets

Where loans are guaranteed they attract the same risk weighting as if the exposure was directly with the guarantor. There are also some national discretions of how to treat claims on domestic public-sector entities, such as local authorities. Depending on the country where these are based they could face a risk weighting of either 0%, 10%, 20% or 50%. The table below shows how the capital calculation would be done in practice, based on three exposures.

Table 16.2 Examples of capital adequacy calculations

Exposure	8% charge	Risk weighting	Minimum Regulatory Capital needed to support exposure
1mn UK 10 year Treasury Bond	8%	0%	0
1mn overnight money	8%	20%	16,000
1mn corporate loan	8%	100%	80,000

Using the above methodology will ensure that a bank will meet the Basel requirement of 8% capital. As an additional safety measure, banks generally have a buffer of capital in addition to the regulatory requirements. Although there are several potential reasons why such a buffer is held, one of the key explanations is that regulatory interference is costly. It is thus cheaper to have additional capital to enable senior management to focus on business-related issues, rather than having to answer capital-related questions from the regulatory authorities.

16.2.3 Treatment of off-balance sheet items

To ensure it is comprehensive, the Accord provides details of how to take account of credit risk on off-balance sheet exposures. It does this by applying credit conversion factors to the different types of off-balance sheet instrument or transaction. The credit conversion factors are derived from the estimated size and likely occurrence of the credit exposure, as well as the relative degree of credit risk. The credit conversion factors would be used to determine the credit risk inherent in the instrument. The weights applicable to the category of the counterparty for an on-balance sheet transaction would then apply to that exposure.

Table 16.3: Credit conversion factors

Instruments	Credit conversion factors
Direct credit substitutes, eg general guarantees of indebtedness (including standby letters of credit serving as financial guarantees for loans and securities) and acceptances (including endorsements with the character of acceptances)	100%
Certain transaction-related contingent items (eg performance bonds, bid bonds, warranties and standby letters of credit related to particular transactions)	50%
Short-term self-liquidating trade-related contingencies (such as documentary credits collateralized by the underlying shipments)	20%
Sale and repurchase agreements and asset sales with recourse, where the credit risk remains with the bank	100%
Forward asset purchases, forward forward deposits and partly-paid shares and securities, which represent commitments with certain drawdown	100%
Note issuance facilities and revolving underwriting facilities	50%
Other commitments (eg formal standby facilities and credit lines) with an original 2 maturity of over one year	50%
Similar commitments with an original 2 maturity of up to one year, or which can be unconditionally cancelled at any time	0%

The above methodology does not, however, work for credit or counterparty risk on foreign exchange and interest related items. This is because banks are not exposed to credit risk for the full face value of their contracts, but only to the potential cost of replacing the cash flow (on contracts showing positive value) if the counterparty defaults. The credit equivalent amounts will thus depend, at least partially on the maturity of the contract and on the volatility of the rates underlying that type of instrument.

Instruments covered under this replacement cost method would be OTC items, such as interest-rate swaps and forward foreign exchange. The aim of the treatments is to calculate the approximate cost to banks of replacing cashflows if the counterparty defaults. The first step will be to convert the transaction to its credit risk equivalent amount (CEA) by multiplying the nominal principal amounts by a credit conversion factor, the resulting amounts then being weighted according to the nature of the counterparty. No CEA applies to contracts traded on exchange, as these are subject to margin requirements.

The Accord proposes two different methodologies. Under the current exposure method a bank calculates the current replacement cost by marketing contracts to market, thus capturing the current exposure without any need for estimation, and then adding a factor (the 'add-on') to reflect the potential future exposure over the remaining life of the contract. The add-ons applicable in the UK differ slightly from those provided in the 1988 Accord. The Accord also allows a more simplistic original exposure method, but this method has not been implemented in the UK.

Table 16.4: Potential future exposures additional risk factors

Residual maturity	Interest rate contracts	Exchange rate contracts
1 year or less	0.0%	1.0%
Over 1 year to 5 years	0.5%	5.0%
Over 5 years	1.5%	7.5%

Example using replacement cost method

Assume a swap granted for five years for USD 100,000,000 where the bank is due to receive annual fixed-rate payments of 5.5%. The corporate counterparty has failed at the end of the first year and four year fixed rates for swaps are quoted at 6.25 – 6.35. The income stream of 5.5% fixed can be replaced by one for 6.25%, so there is no capital charge for this element of the swap.

The potential future exposure, from the table of risk factors, is 0.5% of USD 100 million, ie USD 500,000. Assuming the counterparty weight is 20%, a minimum capital of USD 8,000 is required to support the swap (USD 500,000 x 20% x 8%). If the four-year fixed rates were below 5.5%, capital would have to be provided for the net present value of the future outflows of interest, which cannot be calculated easily without the help of computers.

16.2.4   1996 Market Risk Amendment to the Accord

Soon after 1988 it became evident that there was no effective way to allocate capital uniformly to activities that were driven by market risk rather than credit risk under the Accord. This was because it only dealt with credit risk. Thus, in 1993, the Basel Committee issued a proposal for a standardized measurement framework for market risk. Following the consultation the Market Risk Amendment was agreed in 1996. The risks covered by the framework were: (a) the risks in the trading book of debt and equity instruments and related off-balance sheet contracts, and (b) foreign exchange and commodities risk.

The amendment contains two elements, a standardized methodology and the ability for supervisors to allow banks to use their own internal models.

The standardized methodology is based on a building-block approach. It introduced specific capital charges to be applied:

- ◆ to the current market value of open positions (including derivative positions) in interest rate related instruments and equities in banks' trading books; and
- ◆ to banks' total currency and commodities positions in respect of foreign exchange and commodities risk.

This is done with a variety of multiplication factors, which were based on the riskiness of the underlying instruments.

The amendment differentiates between requirements for specific risk (ie, the risk of loss caused by an adverse price movement of a security due principally to factors related to the issuer of the security) and those for general market risk (ie, the risk of loss arising from adverse changes in market prices).

The alternative approach suggested by the Basel Committee was for supervisors to validate proprietary internal models of banks. In order to ensure a minimum degree of prudence, transparency and consistency of capital requirements across banks, the Committee proposed a number of quantitative and qualitative criteria for those banks which wish to use proprietary models. These require that value-at-risk be computed daily, using a 99th percentile, one-tailed confidence interval; that a minimum price shock equivalent to ten trading days (holding period) be used; and that the model incorporate a historical observation period of at least one year. The capital charge for a bank that uses a proprietary model will be the higher of:

- ◆ the previous day's value-at-risk;
- ◆ three times the average of the daily value-at-risk of the preceding 60 business days.

This 'higher-of' approach is designed to account for potential weaknesses in the modelling process. Such weaknesses exist because:

- ◆ market price movements often do not follow the normal distribution that many models assume and that was shown in Figure 5.1. Instead they tend to show other patterns, such as 'fat tails';
- ◆ the past is not always a good indicator of the future. In particular volatilities and correlations can change significantly;
- ◆ value-at-risk estimates are typically based on end-of-day positions and generally do not take account of intra-day trading risk;
- ◆ models cannot adequately capture exceptional market circumstances;
- ◆ many models rely on simplifying assumptions to value the positions in the portfolio, particularly in the case of complex instruments such as options.

The Committee also proposed to add to the minimum multiplication factor a so-called plus factor. This is based on the outcome of backtesting. We saw previously that backtesting is a comparison of the risk measure generated by the model against actual daily changes in portfolio value. This provides an incentive to construct models with good predictive quality.

Finally the market risk amendment introduced a so-called Tier 3 capital in addition to Tier 1 and Tier 2 capital. Tier 3 can only be used to meet market risk capital requirements. Of course Tier 1 and 2 capital continues to be able to cover for market risk capital requirements. Additional requirements of eligibility to be classed as Tier 3 capital are:

◆ it should have an original maturity of at least two years and will be limited to 250% of the bank's Tier 1 capital that is allocated to support market risk;
◆ it is only eligible to cover market risk, including foreign exchange risk and commodities risk;
◆ as long as the overall limits in the 1988 Accord are not breached, Tier 2 elements may be substituted for Tier 3 up to the same limit of 250%;
◆ it is subject to a lock-in provision, which stipulates that neither interest nor principal may be paid if such payment means that the bank's overall capital would then amount to less than its minimum capital requirement.

In calculating a bank's overall capital ratio, an explicit numerical link between credit and market risk was created by multiplying the measure of market risk by 12.5 (ie the reciprocal of the minimum capital ratio of 8%) and adding the resulting figure to the sum of risk-weighted assets compiled for credit risk purposes. The numerator of the calculation thus remains the whole of the banks' Tier 1 capital, its Tier 2 capital under the limits imposed in the 1988 Accord, plus (at national discretion) those Tier 3 capital elements which can be used to support market risks.

16.3   Basel II

Since 1998 the Basel Committee has been working on updating the Accord. The new proposals include:

◆ new rules on consolidation to capture the increasingly complex structures of financial groups;
◆ more risk sensitivity than the 1988 Accord allowed;
◆ the use of internal ratings for the calculation of capital weightings for credit and operational risk;
◆ more recognition of techniques used to reduce credit risk, such as collateral and credit derivatives;
◆ more discretion for supervisors to set stiffer capital ratios for institutions they see as riskier than the minimum capital requirements suggest.

16.3.1   Deficiencies of existing Accord

The 1988 Accord managed to secure international convergence of supervisory regulations governing the capital adequacy of international banks. This helped reduce the incentive for regulatory arbitrage that led to competitive inequalities between international banks. It also strengthened the soundness and stability of the international banking system.

Despite the achievements of the 1988 Accord it became evident over time that it was not foolproof, even taking into account the market risk amendment. A key criticism of the Accord is that it provides an incentive towards risk taking. This is because the 100% risk weight bucket includes anything from a AAA rated company to a below investment grade bond. Both exposures require the same underlying capital according to the Accord, even though from an economic point the highly rated exposure ought to require much less capital as it is less risky. As a result some banks took the view that, given they had to provide the capital one way or another, they might as well invest it in risky exposures to earn more profit from it.

Almost more worrying for the Basel Committee were the developments of securitizations and other credit risk mitigation techniques, such as credit derivatives. Although these are very useful instruments from a credit risk management point of view they can also be used to undermine the regulatory capital requirements determined by the Basel Accord. In particular securitizations can be used to remove from the balance sheet assets that require too much capital. This means that in effect they can be used to achieve almost any capital adequacy ratio, even if this means that the balance sheet is no longer an accurate reflection of the bank's exposure. This is the case with securitizations as, from a market perspective, only under very restricted circumstances, do they represent a full clean break from which a bank could walk away. This means that banks securitizing parts of their portfolio keep what is an implicit requirement to support their issues, even if legally they are no longer obliged to do so. Similar problems occur with credit derivatives. A different set of problems arose with the use of collateral, which was not addressed in the original accord.

A further consequence of the Accord was that it allowed some banks to focus almost exclusively on the capital adequacy calculations to the detriment of good risk management. This resulted in those banks focusing on the pure calculations to benefit from poorer risk management, in effect penalising those banks attempting to follow best practice. An example here is that over time the more sophisticated banks developed economic capital models that were increasingly at odds with the old Basel Capital Accord. This created additional costs for them as they had to maintain both systems, even if supervisors agreed that the economic capital allocation model was a better way of managing risks and capital.

It is these deficiencies which led the Basel Committee to propose a new capital accord. A first consultation paper was issued in 1999, soon followed by a second consultation paper in January 2001. A third consultation paper was issued in April 2003. The Committee believes the proposals contained therein will be close to the final version that the Committee hopes to agree by the end of 2003.

16.3.2   The Revised Basel Capital Accord

The new Accord, often referred to as Basel II, will be based on what the Basel Committee describes a three pillar approach. The first pillar will contain the minimum capital requirements. This will cover capital requirements for credit risk, operational risk and market risk. The second pillar involves supervisory review of capital adequacy, allowing supervisors to require additional capital when justified by circumstances. The third pillar is about public disclosure so as to help promote market discipline. It is a significantly more complex accord than the 1988 Accord and is likely to shape banking practices for many years to come. Indeed the Basel Committee has stated that the new Accord is to be seen as an evolutionary accord that will be amended as market practices evolve.

The Basel Committee envisages the new Accord being finalized by the end of 2003. Banks can then start data collection so that they can undertake parallel running during 2006, ready for final implementation by the end of 2006. Given such an implementation timetable, banks already have to take the new Accord into account for structuring and pricing products that have maturity later than 2006. Readers are therefore advised to keep abreast with the changes and implementation issues raised by the new Accord. This section is based on the assumption that the proposals contained in the third consultation paper of the Basel Committee, which was issued in April 2003, will be close to the final text.

While Basel II is very different from the 1988 Accord, the two also build on each other. The current Accord is based on the concept of a capital ratio where the numerator represents the amount of capital a bank has available and the denominator is a measure of the risks faced by a bank. Under the proposed Accord, the definition of what counts as capital remains unchanged. Similarly, the minimum required ratio of 8% is not changing. The major changes thus relate to the definition of risk-weighted assets. The aim of the changes is to improve the risk sensitivity of the capital requirements. The market risk charges, which are already risk sensitive and allow models, will remain unchanged.

The new Accord also introduces an explicit operational risk capital requirement. Under the old accord this was implicitly covered by the credit and market risk capital requirement. Now, in order to focus banks' minds on operational risk management the operational risk capital requirement will be added to the credit risk and the market risk capital requirement.

The Committee believes that it is not feasible, or desirable, to apply the same capital requirement for every institution. Instead banking supervision is likely to benefit from improved risk management. In order to provide incentives for banks to improve risk management, the new proposals include three approaches to each credit and operational risk capital requirement. The aim is that the approaches reflect different trade-offs between capital requirements and risk management. Thus as risk management improves there will be lower capital requirements. It will also allow banks and supervisors to select the approach or approaches that they believe are most appropriate to the stage of development of banks' operations and of the financial market infrastructure. The following table identifies the three primary approaches available by risk type.

Table 16.2: The three approaches to credit/operational risk

Credit Risk	Operational Risk
(1) Standardized Approach or Revised Standardized Approach	(1) Basic Indicator Approach
(2) Foundation Internal Ratings Based Approach	(2) Standardized Approach
(3) Advanced Internal Ratings Based Approach	(3) Advanced Measurement Approaches (AMA)

Standardized approach for credit risk

The standardized approach for credit risk has many similarities to the 1988 Accord. Every bank on this approach will be required to slot their credit exposures into risk buckets. However, there are more risk buckets in the new proposals. Indeed the various risk buckets will be directly correlated to external credit assessments by rating agencies or OECD export credit agencies. Strict eligibility criteria are planned for the rating agencies that are to be acceptable to regulators.

Risk weights will be different depending on whether the exposure is of a corporate, bank, sovereign or retail nature. An example of the proposed corporate risk weights is shown below. All of these exposures would have faced a 100% risk weighting under the existing Accord:

Table 16.3:

Credit Assessment	AAA to AA-	A+ to A-	BBB+ to BB-	Below BB-	Unrated
Risk weight	20%	50%	100%	150%	100%

The standardized approach retains the 8% limit of the existing Accord. All exposures that are in default, as defined by the Basel Committee, should face the 150% risk weighting even if the exposure is unrated. A further addition to the current Accord is the expanded range of collateral, guarantees, and credit derivatives that banks using the standardized approach may recognize. Almost all traded financial instruments will, for example, be eligible as collateral. The treatment of securitization is also covered.

Internal ratings-based (IRB) approaches

The New Accord proposes two variants of the IRB: a foundation version and an advanced version. Similar to the market risk amendment the IRB approaches are based on the bank's own internal credit ratings. Because the approaches are based on banks' internal assessments, the potential for more risk sensitive capital requirements is substantial. As a result there are numerous conditions that banks have to meet before they can rely on their own internal ratings. The difference between the foundation and the advanced approaches is that the former allows less flexibility than the latter.

Banks will have to split their exposures into various categories; the main categories being corporate, bank and sovereign exposures. For each of these portfolios banks will require four quantitative inputs, most of which we have already seen in the chapter on credit risk:

- ◆ probability of default (PD), which measures the likelihood that the borrower will default over a given time horizon;
- ◆ loss given default (LGD), which measures the proportion of the exposure that will be lost if a default occurs;
- ◆ exposure at default (EAD), which for loan commitments measures the amount of the facility that is likely to be drawn if a default occurs; and
- ◆ maturity (M), which measures the remaining economic maturity of the exposure.

Both IRB approaches require banks to determine the PD values based on their own internal models. For the foundation approach, supervisors will set LGD and EAD values; the assumptions on maturity will depend on regulatory preference. In the advanced IRB approach they will have to determine LGD, EAD and M based on internal models. Internal models will have to be validated by supervisors before banks can use them for capital requirement calculations.

For retail exposures there will only be an advanced IRB approach available. The biggest difference that retail exposures can be combined into pools of similar exposures, rather than having to be reviewed on an individual basis. The retail portfolio can be split into three different types, each of which has slightly different proposed treatments:

- ◆ exposures secured by residential mortgages;
- ◆ qualifying revolving retail exposures, such as overdrafts or credit cards; and
- ◆ other non-mortgage exposures, also known as 'other retail'.

The new Accord proposes additional portfolios such as specialized lending (eg project finance) and equity portfolio. These should, however, be less relevant to treasury functions. In addition the Basel Committee proposes a detailed capital requirement for securitization. The aim of the securitization proposals is to ensure that capital requirements are neutral and do not give artificial incentives in favour of securitization. This is done by looking at the economic substance of a securitization transaction when determining the appropriate capital requirement. The exception is that lower quality and unrated securitizations will have a worse treatment than comparable corporate exposures. In particular, for banks using the standardized approach, unrated securitization positions must be deducted from capital.

For IRB banks that originate securitizations the treatment will look at the bank's exposure as if they held the exposures directly, rather than via securitizations. This treatment has been introduced to provide an incentive for banks to sell off the whole of their risk, rather than retaining some of it on their books. Only that way can there be some degree of comfort that an originator will not be expected to support a securitization.

It should be noted that the US currently propose to remain on their existing well capitalized bank approach for the majority of their domestic banking system. In addition to those that will be told by their regulator to implement the advanced IRB approaches and the AMA, US banks may voluntarily move onto the Basel II proposals. This is on the basis that the current domestic requirements are harsher than the requirements of the 1988 Accord and potentially the revised Accord. Furthermore those banks that will be on the advanced approaches will have about 99% of the US foreign banking assets on their book.

Operational risk

The Committee defines operational risk as the risk of losses resulting from inadequate or failed internal processes, people and systems, or external events. Again its approaches are built on providing incentives to improve risk management by accepting internal models for the more advanced approaches. The basic approach provides a simple capital requirement of 15% of the annual gross income over the last three years. However, the definition proposed by the Basel Committee for gross income is in many ways more akin to net operating income, being based mainly on net interest income.

The standardized approach will require banks to split their business into eight categories for capital calculation purposes. Each of the eight categories will have a factor of either 12%, 15% or 18% applied to the gross income generated by the activities in the category. There are additional risk management criteria that banks need to meet before supervisors will allow a bank to move onto the standardized approach for operational risk.

Finally the AMA builds on banks' rapidly developing internal assessment techniques and seeks to provide incentives for banks to improve upon those techniques, and improve their management of operational risk more generally. The AMA will allow banks to demonstrate, on the basis of models validated by supervisors, what the appropriate operational capital requirement, is given the business of the institution in question.

Pillar 2: Supervisory review

The second pillar of the new Accord is based on a series of guiding principles, all of which point to the need for banks to assess their capital adequacy positions relative to their overall risks, and for supervisors to review and take appropriate actions in response to those assessments. This will allow supervisors to impose additional capital requirements if they believe that there are additional risks that banks have not taken into account in their existing capital. This, to some extent, has already been the approach of the FSA, which does set individual capital requirements for its banks. Specific areas mentioned under the supervisory review include interest rate risk, a need for banks to stress test their portfolio and to take account of concentration risk. There is an additional part on the treatment of residual risk that may arise from the use of collateral, guarantees and credit derivatives. Lastly the Committee has provided guidance on how to interpret the quantitative securitization proposals.

Pillar 3: Market discipline

The purpose of pillar three is to harness market discipline to help provide the incentives that it aims to set. The proposals are based on the notion that increased disclosure by banks can help market participants to assess key information about a bank's risk profile and level of capitalization. It should thus be seen as complementary to both pillar 1 and 2. The proposals for pillar 3 are still in flux. This is partly because they are closely related to the disclosure requirements that are being discussed as part of the move towards the International Accounting Standards (IAS) and the need to ensure that the two do not compete with each other. Another reason that the pillar 3 proposals remain contentious is that some banks are concerned about the level of detail that is due to be disclosed.

Relevant disclosures are likely to fall into the following categories:

- ◆ financial performance;
- ◆ financial position;
- ◆ risk management strategies and policies;
- ◆ risk exposures;
- ◆ accounting policies;
- ◆ management and corporate governance.

The Basel II proposals broadly suggest the following disclosures:

◆ Disclosures on the scope of application
  ● The name of the top corporate entity in the group to which the Capital Accord applies.
  ● An outline of differences in the basis of consolidation for accounting and regulatory purposes, with a brief description of the entities within the group and how they are consolidated.
  ● Any restrictions, or other major impediments, on transfer of funds or regulatory capital within the group.
  ● The aggregate amount of capital deficiencies in all subsidiaries not included in the consolidation.
  ● The treatment of insurance entities in the group.
◆ Disclosures on capital
  ● The main features of all capital instruments, especially in the case of innovative, complex or hybrid capital instruments.
  ● Breakdown of Tier 1 capital.
  ● Aggregate of Tier 2 and Tier 3 capital.
  ● Details of any deductions and total eligible capital.
◆ Disclosures on capital adequacy
  ● A summary discussion of the bank's approach to assessing the adequacy of its capital to support current and future activities.
  ● Capital requirements for credit risk by portfolio.
  ● Capital requirements for equity risk.
  ● Capital requirements for market risk.
  ● Capital requirements for operational risk.
  ● Total and Tier 1 capital ratios.

For each separate risk area (eg credit, market, operational, banking book interest rate risk, equity) banks would have to describe their risk management objectives and policies, including:

  ● strategies and processes;
  ● the structure and organization of the relevant risk management function;
  ● the scope and nature of risk reporting and/or measurement systems;
  ● policies for hedging and/or mitigating risk and strategies and processes for monitoring the continuing effectiveness of hedges/mitigants.

16.4 EU capital directives

As part of ensuring a single market for financial services, the EU has implemented the 1988 Accord and the market risk amendment via two separate directives. Capital requirements for the banking book are included in the Banking Consolidation Directive. This directive consolidates various other banking related directives into a single directive. From a capital adequacy point of view it includes the Own Funds Directive and the Solvency Ratio Directive, both of which were put on the statute books after the Basel 1988 Accord and therefore incorporate the provisions described earlier in this chapter.

The Market Risk Amendment to the Accord was incorporated into EU law via the Capital Adequacy Directive in 1993, as subsequently amended. However, the Capital Adequacy Directive has a much wider scope than the market risk amendment to the Basel Accord, mainly because it is also applicable to investment firms. As a result, it retains a number of clauses that are not relevant to banks, although they may be relevant to investment banks that are registered as investment firms.

Following the precedent set by the above mentioned directives the European Commission is proposing another directive to implement the new Basel Capital Accord. The working title of this directive is 'Risk Based Capital Directive'. However, another common name for the proposed directive is CAD3, as it can be seen as the third version of the Capital Adequacy Directive. Although this directive is likely to amend the Banking Consolidation Directive and the Capital Adequacy Directive, these two directives will remain in force in addition to the Risk Based Capital Directive.

In line with the Capital Adequacy Directive the Risk Based Capital Directive is likely to have a much wider scope than the new Basel Accord, as it will also be applicable to investment firms. As a result the directive is likely to take account of European specificities. However, given that the final version of the new Basel Capital Accord is not yet available, and that the European legal process for the new implementing directive is just beginning, the extent of any divergences between the Basel text and the European Directive is as yet unknown. Indeed the final European directive is not likely to be available before the end of 2004 at the earliest. Readers need to be aware of this, as EU countries will have to abide by the European Directive as opposed to the Basel text, which will not be legally binding. Nevertheless the Basel text will be a useful guide to the general direction of the EU directive. Such an awareness of general direction is very important for treasury functions, as systems and controls, pricing structures and deal structures are already beginning to be significantly influenced by these developments. It is therefore important to remain aware of developments in this area.

16.5   UK capital adequacy rules

The focus of this chapter has been primarily on the Basel Accord and its revisions. However, from a purely legal point of view, it is the UK implementation of the EU rules that is of importance. This is particularly important where EU law allows national discretion, which will only be reflected in the FSA Handbook. The FSA Handbook also describes the processes to which firms have to adhere in order to obtain recognition for their market risk models or the basis on which regulated firms have to provide regulatory returns to the FSA.

Just as the international and EU approach to capital adequacy is currently in flux, the UK implementation of these rules is changing to reflect other developments. The current FSA rules on capital adequacy are contained in the Prudential Sourcebooks, which still reflect the rules that were set by the Bank of England, as banking regulator prior to 1998, and the rules of the SROs which only ceased to apply in November 2001. Both the Prudential Sourcebook for Banks and the Prudential Sourcebook for Investment Firms directly implement the Banking Consolidation Directive (including its predecessor directives) and the Capital Adequacy Directive.

The UK rules thus indirectly implement the 1988 Basel Accord plus the market risk amendment. In addition, however, the Bank of England, and now the FSA, have a history of imposing capital adequacy requirement on a bank-by-bank basis in excess of the minimum requirements suggested by the Basel Accord and its EU implementation. One can thus say that the UK has already implemented a form of Pillar 2 of Basel II, as it considers that the 8% minimum requirement would only be sufficient for well diversified banks, which have strong management and systems and controls in place. The assessment of whether this is the case will be undertaken as part of the general supervisory approach of the FSA, and particularly its ARROW methodology. For banks this includes a review of the various risks reviewed in previous chapters, as well as the systems controls put in place to manage these risks. The FSA also looks at more qualitative factors such as strategy, business continuity (including access to capital) and environmental risks.

The FSA has already stated that it intends to issue a single Prudential Sourcebook for all the activities that it regulates. However, given that neither the Basel Capital Accord nor the Risk Based Capital Directive are as yet available, the FSA decided to issue its revised unified rules only after 2005 when both texts should be available. This decision was partly taken to avoid the need for companies to introduce changes in their processes at present when it was already public knowledge that the rules would have to be changed as a result of the EU legislative process. In the meantime the FSA has already issued several papers looking at implementation issues relating to the Risk Based Capital Directive.

Seventeen

The functions and structures of financial markets

Objectives

This chapter will cover the following topics:

- ◆ function of financial markets;
- ◆ participants in financial markets;
- ◆ processing of transactions in both front and back-offices;
- ◆ payments using real-time gross settlement (RTGS) systems;
- ◆ the role of clearing houses and stock lending.

17.1 Function of financial markets

It is hard to imagine how market economies could function effectively without financial markets. They are to some extent the lubricants that ensure market economies function. They do this by fulfilling several roles:

- ◆ transformation of risk;
- ◆ transformation of maturities and provision of liquidity;
- ◆ transformation of transaction costs.

Financial markets reduce risk through risk spreading or risk pooling. Risk pooling is undertaken by spreading any risky investment across a sufficiently large number of lenders. Although some of these will fail, the specific risk of each individual loan will be low compared to the aggregate portfolio. Risk spreading refers to the benefit achieved by constructing a portfolio so that various risks offset each other. This is also known as diversification. This role of risk transformation implies that financial intermediaries, such as banks, can benefit from their information advantage to assess investment opportunities and allocate resources according to their assessment.

The role of transformer of maturities is another key economic function of financial markets. Financial intermediaries have the ability to hold assets that are less liquid than their liabilities. In less economic language this means that banks transform short-term liabilities, such as deposits, into long-term assets such as loans. Long-term loans are an important source of finance for commercial business. They provide businesses with the ability to plan business activities and manage the business accordingly. This would not be possible using short term financing only. From the depositor's point of view the fact that financial intermediaries accept short-term deposits, which can be redeemed at short notice, while still obtaining a revenue from them, improves liquidity and thus economic performance of the economy. Clearly the larger a financial intermediary, the more it can take advantage of economies of scale.

Finally financial intermediaries can, by virtue of their size, reduce the cost of transactions to significantly below what an individual investor could achieve. They achieve this by providing convenient and safe locations for borrowers and lenders to transact, which reduces the resources needed to find counterparties. They thus provide a cheap and simple way of bringing borrowers and lenders together. Similarly the standardization of contracts and the advantage of expertise gained from transacting large volumes provides another opportunity to benefit from economies of scale.

Initially exchanges and banks undertook these roles. They developed procedures and regulation to ensure participants were certain of others' behaviour and thus could plan. With disintermediation the central role of banks has diminished and other participants increasingly participate in the financial markets, but banks continue to play a key role.

17.2   Participants in financial markets

17.2.1   Exchanges

Although exchanges are not really participants in the financial markets, they are key intermediaries allowing other market participants to deal with each other. Many financial exchanges began as exchanges where commodities were sold and bought in a single location. These days exchanges can be virtual without a single physical location. Trading can being undertaken via screens all over the world. In the UK the largest exchange is the London Stock Exchange, on which stocks and shares are traded. LIFFE, another large exchange, deals in futures and options on a variety of instruments. The competition between exchanges is international with competitive advantages being obtained from low costs per transaction and the depth and liquidity of the market. In addition they face the competition of over the counter (OTC) trades, which refers to all trades not undertaken on an exchange.

17.2.2   Credit institutions

The term credit institutions is used to include all commercial deposit-takers including banks, building societies and other savings institutions. Many of these only have retail customers, but they would interface with the financial markets for wholesale funding; the issuing of subordinated debt and other financial activities. On the other hand there are investment banks that almost exclusively deal with large corporates and other financial institutions. Some are large proprietary traders, while others only pass through customer orders. Banks also interface with the financial markets to hedge other positions or to invest as part of their liquidity management. A sector of the financial markets is the interbank market, where only banks trade with each other. Credit institutions often also perform the roles of other market participants. As proprietary traders they are investors into the markets, or they are active borrowers and lenders. Some banks run Alternative Trading Facilities, also known as multilateral trading facilities, which are similar to exchanges. Other banks also act as market makers.

17.2.3   Investment banks

Whether an investment bank is also a credit institution will depend on whether it accepts deposits or not. Those that do not accept deposits act in effect as agents for their customers. Customers tend to be large commercial corporations and institutional investors. Their activities include, among others, corporate finance, asset management, international investment advice, agency broking and market making. They often compete with banks in the areas of concern to treasury functions.

17.2.4   Brokers

Wholesale brokers facilitate trades between market participants by bringing buyers and sellers together. In some markets they act purely as intermediaries, while in others they act as principals. Market participants use them because brokers have specialized market knowledge and this benefits their customers. Another added value brokers can provide is anonymity. This is particularly useful when one bank does not want competitors to know about the transactions that it is undertaken. More generally the intermediary role of brokers makes markets more liquid and increases depth.

17.2.5   Market makers/dealers

In order to provide liquidity to a market it is important that prices are quoted on a continuous basis. This is the role of market makers who will always quote prices at which they will buy or sell relevant financial instruments. Prices are generally published on screens via information systems such as Bloomberg or Reuters. Their profits will arise from the spread between the bid and offer prices. In addition, many will also have profits from the profits they make on their own positions.

17.2.6   Investors and issuers

Market participants can also be split into investors and issuers. Both categories include large commercial companies and public sector bodies. Both of these tend to manage large cashflows, which their respective treasury functions will need to invest with other market participants to maximize their organizations' net worth. Similarly they will need to finance their working capital, again an area in which the financial markets can provide the necessary funding. A company could for example issue subordinated debt, which can also be useful to maintain contacts with the investors.

Other market participants are those that invest funds on behalf of others. This includes pension funds, collective investment schemes (such as unit trusts or investment trusts), asset management companies or hedge funds. Insurance companies also tend to have large sums to invest into the financial markets.

Market participants may also have different reasons for their participation. Life insurers for example will be investors with a long-term outlook. Commercial companies will also participate in the financial markets to hedge their exposures. Internationally active companies very often like to hedge their foreign exchange exposures to ensure they do not face volatile trading results. The market will thus take on the risks that the company itself wishes to avoid. Others will be involved for purely speculative reasons. They will take positions in anticipation of certain market movements. Arbitrage is a special type of speculation, which allows traders to benefit from price differences of certain financial instruments from one market to another. Prices are generally the result of supply and demand, which may be slightly different between markets. Thus the USD/EUR rate may be slightly different in Frankfurt and New York. A trader having access to both markets may use this to his advantage. Arbitrage opportunities also exist between financial instruments. Thus future prices should in theory always be calculated from the prices of the underlying instruments, in reality supply and demand may result in this relationship being altered. This would again enable traders to make a profit from arbitrage.

17.3 Processing of transactions in both front and back-offices

17.3.1 Front-office

The term front-office is used for dealing activities. In order to trade, dealers need access to telecommunication systems, be they telephone or computer based. This is not only required to pass and agree trades with counterparties, but also to monitor positions and to undertake research. Analysts and other research personnel that support the dealing activities may be part of the front-office, depending on each organization's structure.

Dealing activities are undertaken by both market makers and dealers. The difference is that market makers will quote prices on an almost continuous basis, while dealers will only be active in the market when it suits them. Thus the former are necessary to ensure a market exists in the first place, while dealers only add additional liquidity to a market. In practice, the term dealer will often cover both market makers and dealers. Both will need to remain aware of quotes in the market to decide whether to deal or not. Additionally market makers will need to keep their own quotes under constant review to ensure that they accurately reflect market conditions. If they did not, they would lay themselves open to losses, as other market participants would either not deal with them (if quotes are to expensive) or rush to deal with them to take advantage of the 'cheap' quotes.

When determining prices, dealers and market makers will take into account existing demand and supply and how these are likely to change. Developments in other markets may also affect prices and participants need to keep track of what market prices do to ensure that their own prices do not diverge without good reason from the market trend. The positions that the market maker has on its books may be a reason to diverge from the market price. Depending on the financial instrument that is being traded other factors may also be involved in price determination. Interest rates for example may be influenced by the creditworthiness of the counterparty or by economic factors, such as expected changes in the official interest rate. The volume of data that will be available to help pricing decisions will require front-office staff to be very good at assimilating new information as it is made available during a typical trading day. This is where a good team working together can make quite a difference in improving performance.

A dealer may either initiate a deal or, if the dealer quotes prices, may be contacted by other market participants. In some markets it is also common to use a salesperson to interact with customers and it will be the salesperson that will pass the trade to the dealer who will then execute it in the market. Dealers that do not quote prices themselves will need to contact other dealers or brokers to quote prices.

Prices will be either on a bid or offer basis. A bid price is the price at which dealers are prepared to borrow or purchase. The offer price is the price at which they are prepared to lend or sell. It is also important to check that any proposed value dates are business days in the relevant jurisdictions. If they are not, costly overdraft charges will be incurred. Foreign exchange transactions can only be executed when the countries of both currencies involved are open for delivery. Thus a USD/GBP trade will require both London and New York to be open for business.

Contact with dealers and market makers may be established via telephone or screen. The first thing that a dealer will then have to check is that the proposed deal does not breach the limits that have been set internally. It is then time to agree a deal. Depending on the financial instrument involved, details to be agreed include price, amounts, maturity and settlement details. Only once all the relevant details are agreed can it be said that a deal has been done. Clearly if the traders cannot agree on the details no deal will take place.

The next step is that the details of the deal will have to be input into the systems. Only then will it be possible to incorporate the deal into the risk management systems of the bank. It is at that point that a deal will be included into the bank's accounting records. Recording is also required to ensure that any payments that are due under the deal will be made in time. It is increasingly common for banks to use straight through processing (STP).

STP attempts to reduce manual keying in of information to a minimum. With STP, a trader will type deals directly into their computer, which will then be caught by the system. The computer system will then automatically verify the details of the deal to make sure no limits are breached. It will also produce the necessary accounting entries, send out a confirmation to the counterparty and if appropriate make the necessary payments, once confirmation has been matched with that from the other counterparty. Where manual intervention is still required this will be undertaken by the back-office, particularly for the authorization of payments and reconciliation.

17.3.2 Middle office

Middle offices arose from the need for improved risk management. Middle offices produce the risk management reports and check for compliance with internal limits. Another role of the middle office tends to be liaison with the back-office. Thus when manual dealing slips were still common they were collated by middle office staff for onward transmission to the back-office. It was also the middle office role to check that dealing slips were completed correctly and that settlement instructions made sense. Queries from the back-offices on deals would be filtered through the middle office.

Other roles of a middle office are to check valuations for inputting into integrated risk reporting. Valuation checks are particularly important for mark-to-market valuations. Staff would also verify adherence to VaR and other limits. This is best done on a real time basis. In practice, with STP becoming increasingly common, middle offices have tended to take on a much more direct risk management role. For example, they would be running VaR models, including stress testing and backtesting.

17.3.3   Back-office

Sometime the activities undertaken by back-offices are collectively known as settlement activities. These include making sure that accounting entries are correct, confirmation received, payments are authorized, and accounting records for funds or securities are reconciled with actual payments/deliveries. Nostro accounts may also have to be reconciled and margin payments may have to be made.

From an operational risk point of view it has always been important to split the role of arranging a deal and executing it. In line with this principle banks require dealers to pass any deal they have undertaken to the back-office for actioning. Even in an STP system it is still the back-office that reviews the deal and authorizes payment. In manual systems it is important that any re-keying undertaken in the back-office is counterchecked by another person.

After the back-office receives a deal it will need to be confirmed. Systems where confirmations are sent automatically after the dealer input have certainly reduced the need for manual input, but where they are not received, back-office staff will need to chase it. Where deals are due to be processed within a short time period, or on the same day, it may be necessary to undertake initial checks by telephone. Certainly all discrepancies between dealing slips and confirmations need to be followed up to ensure that the company can still deliver on its contract. This is important because legally it is the deal undertaken by the trader that is the contract. If there are differences this could give rise to additional costs as the terms of the contract may not have been met.

The work of back-offices has been significantly streamlined with software that enables automatic reconciliations between confirmations received and deals undertaken. Particularly when combined with STP does this reduce settlement disputes and thus costs. It also allows back-office staff to become risk focused and spend time on following up real discrepancies and settlement errors.

International transactions are most commonly confirmed using SWIFT, a communication system that has been set up specifically for banks. Another commonly used system is the Crossmar® Matching Service for money market and foreign exchange deals. For Eurobonds the TRAX system can be used to match transactions.

While confirmation checking is important it is only a means to avoid wrong payments. Ultimately it is at the payment point that money leaves the organization and risks are crystallized. We will look at the various clearing systems that can be used for domestic transactions later in this chapter. For foreign currency payments that cannot be passed through clearing systems, banks will have to rely on their correspondent banks or overseas bankers, if applicable. Again SWIFT is the main means of communicating such transactions. In the case of a currency payment the correspondent bank will be sent a SWIFT message telling it to debit the nostro account and send the funds through the domestic payment system to the ultimate beneficiary. It should also be noted that payments can only be made in the country that issues the currency. Thus a US dollar payment will always have to be made in the US, even for Eurodollar transactions.

In addition to ensuring payment instructions are correct and sent out on time, back-offices will also have to make sure that any netting arrangements are taken into account. For non-money market or foreign exchange transactions it is common to use clearing houses, particularly for international securities transactions.

Once payment has been made it is important to reconcile accounts to ensure that all due payments have been received and that the bank's funds can be invested, rather than being tied up while awaiting receipts for outstanding transactions. Again reconciliations are now commonly undertaken electronically, allowing back-office staff to look at those transactions that do not match.

Margin payments would also be made from the back office. Margin payments exist particularly with futures contracts where counterparties are required to provide collateral for contracts that have not yet matured.

Finally back-offices have to ensure that the bank's systems reflect the accurate position of the deals. Only once that is done can senior management rely on the information provided by its internal systems to take management decisions. It is also important to ensure that regulatory returns, such as capital adequacy returns, are accurate.

17.4   Payment systems

Ultimately deals will have to end in either delivery or in a cash transfer. Cash transfers will depend on the quality of the mode of transfer. Efficient and secure systems will improve financial stability. It is thus generally central banks, as the guardians of financial stability, that ensure payment systems meet the necessary standards.

Developments in clearing occurred to reduce settlement risk. The settlement risk is the risk that the funds which a bank has been expecting to receive, and on which it is relying to honour its own commitment to make payments or transfer assets, do not arrive. As the size of exposures within the financial system and the interdependence of financial intermediaries have increased, so has the risk that a payments or settlement failure by one institution could bring down another and ultimately disrupt the whole financial system. To avoid this it has increasingly been accepted that payment systems need to provide Real Time Gross Settlement (RTGS) in order to meet the needs of advanced economies.

17.4.1   United Kingdom

The main same day payment system in the UK is known as CHAPS Sterling. From 1854 to 1996 the clearing system in London involved an end-of-day net settlement of balances across accounts at the Bank of England. CHAPS, the electronic, same-day large-value credit transfer system was introduced in 1984 to complement the Town Clearing (last used 1996) for same-day large-value debit clearing. Average value of individual payments in CHAPS Sterling in 2000 was £2.3 million. The average daily volume of large-value payments passing through CHAPS Sterling was around £195 billion, with peaks up to £318 billion.

There are currently 13 direct participants in CHAPS Sterling. Operationally it is run by a company called CHAPS Clearing Company Ltd. The company is run by the Association for Payment Clearing Services (APACS) that also runs BACS and Cheque and Credit Clearing, the UK's retail clearing systems. The CHAPS system runs on a platform based on the SWIFT methodology, which enables easy integration into banks' wider systems.

Pre RTGS

While the receiving or collecting banker would typically make the relevant funds available to his customer when the CHAPS instruction was received, it did not receive value from the paying banker until the relevant settlement was completed at the end of the day. This exposed banks to unquantified risks vis-à-vis each other. In practice, if a bank found itself unexpectedly short of immediate liquidity at the end of the day, it was able to borrow from the other clearing banks or from the Bank of England at a penal rate.

An interim step to reduce settlement risk was to impose intra-day limits on the extent to which a CHAPS bank could build up a net sender position vis-à-vis another CHAPS member. This means that banks know the extent of their exposures within the system, can impose limits on them, and actively manage them to avoid payment delays.

RTGS

In April 1996, Real Time Gross Settlement was introduced. Individual large-value sterling payments are now paid gross across accounts at the Bank of England in real time during the course of the business day. This ensures finality and eliminates payment risks all along the line. Customers can ask a bank to debit their account, the bank will then instruct to debit its own account at the Bank of England, and credit the corresponding account of the receiving bank. This bank can then in turn confidently credit the payee's account in its books in instantly available cleared funds.

A bank must have cash in its account at the Bank of England before it can make a payment to another bank. This means that there has to be liquidity somewhere in the system or the whole system could become gridlocked as banks waited for incoming payments. If there are real liquidity blockages there is a facility to settle some transactions simultaneously, rather than sequentially, where collective settlement would overcome the blockage. This is, however, restricted to unusual market circumstances.

Normally liquidity is provided partly by the cash balances banks held with the Bank, but this is an expensive form of liquidity for the banks. The Bank of England stands ready to provide the settlement banks with intra-day cash advances, without limit and without charge, but always against first-class security. A list of assets that are eligible for the sale and repo transactions to provide liquidity is maintained by the Bank of England. It is important that all repos be reversed at the end of the same day. Penal rates of interest are applied to any inter-day advances, which become overnight credit. Liquidity is also made available by including the cash ratio deposits that each bank is obliged to hold with the Bank of England as being available for the clearing process.

Operationally CHAPS is controlled by the Bank of England and it is the Bank of England that provides back-up facilities. CHAPS retains the ability to return to net end-of-day systems as a final back-up process.

CHAPS Euro

In January 1999 CHAPS Euro was launched to cater for Euro-denominated payments. It is linked to the TARGET system, which we will review in the next section. CHAPS Euro has 20 member banks and uses the same underlying systems and processes as CHAPS Sterling.

However a difference from the CHAPS Sterling system is that the Bank of England is restricted by the European Central Bank (ECB) in the intraday liquidity that it can provide. This is presently EUR 3 billion credit in aggregate with a maximum for an individual participant of EUR 1 billion.

17.4.2   Euro area

The main interbank exchange and settlement system for Euros is TARGET, which stands for Trans-European Automated Real-time Gross settlement Express Transfer. It is a decentralized system based on the 15 national RTGS systems in the EU, including CHAPS Euro, as well as the ECB's payment mechanism. Thus the system allows transfer of central banks' money across borders. As participation of CHAPS Euro shows, the TARGET system is not restricted to countries that have adopted the Euro as their domestic currency.

TARGET was developed to meet three main objectives:

◆ facilitate integration of Euro money markets and thereby a single monetary policy;
◆ improve the soundness and efficiency of Euro payments;
◆ minimize risks of making payments.

This does not mean that all national RTGS systems need to use the same systems, but it does mean that there are certain rules and procedures and minimum requirements that each system must meet before it can be linked to TARGET. For instance access must be restricted to supervised credit institutions established in the European Economic Area. Exceptions are only allowed for other supervised clearing and settlement services, governmental treasury departments, certain investment firms and some public-sector bodies of member states authorized to hold accounts for customers.

The role of the ECB is to ensure correctness of processing within the system and the balance positions between the national central banks (NCBs) resulting from this. Operationally no NCB may close before it has finalized all of its positions with bilateral partners. To support the system each transaction carries a charge of between EUR 1.75 and 0.80 depending on the number of transactions undertaken per month. The fees are charged by NCBs/ECB on the sending participant.

TARGET is becoming an increasingly important settlement system. Daily average volumes for 2001 was EUR 1,299 billion. The average cross-border interbank payment was EUR 17.7 million.

The main commercial settlement system for Euros is the Euro 1 system of the Euro Banking Association. It is not a real time gross settlement system, but has the advantage of lower operating costs. Clearly banks can still use their correspondent banking network to transfer money, although this is becoming less common. In addition there are a number of retail credit transfer systems available, such as TIPANET and Eurogiro.

17.4.3   United States

The main large-value payment transfer systems in the United States are Fedwire and CHIPS. Fedwire is operated by the Federal Reserve, and CHIPS is operated by the Clearing House Interbank Payments Company L.L.C. (CHIPCo) in New York. Other settlement processes continue to be available, as they do in other jurisdictions.

Fedwire funds transfer system

The Fedwire funds transfer system is a real-time gross settlement system that is open to all institutions that maintain an account with a Federal Reserve Bank, subject to meeting additional participation criteria. These criteria may differ between Federal Reserve Banks, but include requirements to meet appropriate security procedures and have sufficient funds available. Payment to a receiving participant over Fedwire is final and irrevocable once the amount of the payment order is credited to the receiving participant's account or when notice is sent to the receiving participant, whichever is earlier. Transfers may be initiated either electronically or by telephone.

The BIS reported the following statistics in its Red Book on clearing and settlement:

> 'Fedwire processed an average of nearly 430,000 payments per day in 2000. The total value of transfers originated during 2000 was USD 380 trillion. The distribution of the value of these payments is not uniform. The median Fedwire payment during 2000 was approximately USD 25,000, and the average payment was approximately USD 3.5 million.'

Liquidity is provided by the Federal Reserve, which may make intra-day overdrafts available to holders of Federal Reserve accounts. To ensure that the Federal Reserve does not take undue credit risk on these overdrafts it undertakes risk assessments, provides limits and may require collateralization. Overdraft fees are also used to reduce exposure.

Charges for using the Fedwire system are introduced to cover the cost of running the system. Similar to TARGET, the Fedwire service is charged on a volume-based fee schedule. In 2003, the fees charged by Federal Reserve Banks for an online Fedwire transaction range from USD 0.10 to USD 0.30 per transfer, per institution. A surcharge of USD 15 is required to initiate or receive an offline transfer. Electronic access fees (connection and terminal charges) are assessed separately. Unlike TARGET, Fedwire's transaction fees are charged to both the sending institution and receiving institution.

Clearing House Interbank Payments System (CHIPS)

CHIPS became an electronic settlement system in 1970. It was previously paper based. It began as an end-of-day, multilateral net settlement system before converting in 2001 to a real time final settlement system that works through orders sequentially. Instructions that are unsettled at the end of the day are tallied and funded on a multilateral net basis prior to releasing the payments. The system continuously matches, nets and settles payment orders. On a daily basis, the new system provides real-time finality for all payment orders released by CHIPS from the CHIPS queue. To achieve real-time finality, payment orders are settled on the books of CHIPS against positive positions, simultaneously offset by incoming payment orders, or both.

As a commercial system CHIPS is supervised by state and federal banking authorities. It is open to commercial banking institutions, including non US-banks. By end-2000 CHIPS had 63 participants. Banks that are not participants need to use one of the participants as agents. During 2000 transfers worth USD 292 trillion were made via CHIPS, with an average of 263,000 payments per day. The system is mainly used for interbank transactions and, in particular, payments relating to foreign currency transactions. We have already mentioned that any USD transaction needs to be passed through the US and CHIPS is used for many of these. It is thus primarily to transfer value as part of spot and currency swap contracts and Eurodollar placements and returns. Payment orders are also sent via CHIPS for the purpose of adjusting correspondent balances and making payments associated with commercial transactions, bank loans and securities transactions.

To reduce settlement risk each CHIPS participant has a pre-established opening position requirement, which needs to be funded via a Fedwire funds transfer to the CHIPS account with the Federal Reserve Bank of New York. Only once funds have been received can participant send or receive CHIPS payments. Operationally CHIPS also differs from RTGS systems.

CHIPS maintains a centralized queue of submitted payment orders. This is searched continuously for payment orders to settle. When an opportunity for settlement involving one, two or more payment orders is found, the optimization algorithm releases the relevant payment order(s) from the central queue and simultaneously marks the CHIPS records to reflect the associated debits and credits to the relevant participants' positions. It is at that time that payment is final. There is a facility for participants to revoke unsettled transactions prior to the daily cut-off.

At the daily cut off, which is at 17.00hrs New York time, the system attempts to match, net, set off and release as many of the remaining payment orders as possible, without creating any overdrafts. Any remaining unreleased payment orders in the queue are tallied on a multilateral net basis. The resulting net position for each participant is provisionally combined with that participant's current position (which cannot be negative) to calculate the participant's final net position. Any negative final net positions must be covered via Fedwire to the CHIPS account. Only once this is received does CHIPS release and settle all remaining payment orders. Finally, at the end of the day, all remaining balances are transferred to the participants so that the CHIPS account will not have any balances at the end of day.

To further reduce credit risk and to increase liquidity, only those banks can participate in CHIPS that meet the specified credit criteria. Prospective participants must also be regulated by the New York State Banking Department or a federal bank regulatory authority. This will ensure that participants are examined on a regular basis and are operating in a sound manner.

Federal Reserve National Settlement Service

In addition to the normal correspondent banking settlement procedures, US institutions can use the Federal Reserve's National Settlement Service (NSS). It allows participants in private clearing arrangements to settle transactions on a net basis using account balances held at the Federal Reserve. Users include cheque clearing houses, ACH networks and some bank card processors. In 2002, more than 70 local and national private sector clearing and settlement arrangements used NSS to settle a netted value of about USD 15 billion daily.

17.4.4   International payment arrangements

The main international payment services are provided by SWIFT, as an infrastructure provider, and CLS Bank.

SWIFT

The best known international payment arrangement is SWIFT, the 'Society for Worldwide Interbank Financial Telecommunication'. It was founded in 1973 to provide payment and communication services across all financial markets through member banks. It has over 2,200 members and provides services to over 7,400 financial institutions in 198 countries. In 2002, over 1.8 billion messages were processed. Average daily traffic exceeds seven million messages. Up to 70% of these are payments messages. SWIFT provides or is involved with several national RTGS systems and netting systems. The average daily value of payment messages is estimated to total more than EUR 6 trillion.

SWIFT has its headquarters in Belgium, where it is also incorporated. Its role is to provide secure messaging services and interface software. The underlying aim is to contribute to greater automation of financial transaction processes. Messaging services are provided to banks, broker/dealers and investment managers, as well as to market infrastructures in payments, treasury, securities and trade.

There are three categories of SWIFT users: members (shareholders), sub-members (ie subsidiaries controlled by members) and participants. Participants will only have access to a restricted range of services. Securities brokers, dealers and investment management firms are mainly participants. In contrast members can benefit from all the services offered by SWIFT.

Although SWIFT is not a bank and is therefore not regulated or authorized, it has such a key role in international finance that oversight arrangements have been put in place by the central banks of the G10 countries. The National Bank of Belgium (NBB), the Belgian central bank, acts as lead overseer of SWIFT with a day-to-day oversight relationship. It is supported in this by the other G10 central banks. The primary focus of the oversight of SWIFT is on the security and operational reliability of the SWIFT infrastructure. Where appropriate, the central banks raise issues and make recommendations to SWIFT to which SWIFT will respond. But the central banks have no direct power of enforcement and it is SWIFT on its own which bears responsibility for the security and reliability of its systems, products and services.

SWIFT increasingly offers a market infrastructure service. It provides messaging and connectivity services to other market infrastructure providers, such as CLS Bank, The Euro 1 and Step 1 netting services and various national RTGS services, such as TARGET and CHAPS. It also provides the communication infrastructure to various stock exchanges and clearing houses.

CLS Bank

CLS Bank began operating from New York in 2002. It is run by CLS Services, which is incorporated in England. The group's holding company is based in Switzerland. The aim of CLS, standing for continuous linked settlement, is to reduce significantly foreign exchange settlement risk by providing multicurrency payment services. Unlike CHIPS or CHAPS it provides settlement for foreign exchange transactions involving the Australian dollar, the pound sterling, the Canadian dollar, the Euro, the Japanese yen, the Swiss franc and the US dollar, with other currencies due to be added.

CLS Bank reduces risk by eliminating Herstatt risk, ie the risk that one part of a foreign exchange transaction would be settled without the other leg being completed. It does this by simultaneously settling both legs in its books. In order to provide this service CLS Bank maintains an account at each of the central banks whose currencies it settles.

After validating and matching foreign exchange settlement and ensuring their eligibility CLS Services will pass these on to CLS Bank on the date prior to the settlement (value) date. To enable CLS Bank to undertake transactions, each CLS Bank settlement member is required to hold an account at CLS Bank that is divided into subaccounts for each currency that the settlement member settles. CLS Bank settles instructions individually on the members' accounts by simultaneously debiting the subaccount of the currency being sold and crediting the subaccount of the currency being bought. Finality of settlement is achieved upon transfer of funds in CLS Bank's books. This will create net debit and credit position in each currency and settlement members must provide funds in the correct currencies to cover projected net debit positions. Net credit balances are paid out during the settlement day, although the sum of all currency balances (positive and negative) in a member's account, converted into US dollars, must never be less than zero.

For execution of transfers with settlement members, CLS Bank relies on its central bank accounts and the respective RTGS systems associated with them. In normal circumstances, settlement members will have zero balances in their CLS Bank accounts at the end of each day, and CLS Bank will have zero balances in its central bank accounts at the end of each day. Unlike CHAPS, transactions that are not settled at the end of the day are returned to the sender.

CLS Bank significantly reduces settlement risk, but it does so by creating credit risk for the settlement members. To overcome this problem CLS Bank is supervised by the Federal Reserve Bank of New York as a fully-fledged bank. It also needs to meet the standards for payment systems and interbank netting schemes. Like other banks it will need to manage its outstanding credit, operational and liquidity risks. As part of this it will impose short position limits both on aggregate and currency specific. As backup it also has liquidity support from contracted liquidity providers. A final backstop would be its loss-sharing agreement with users.

17.5 Securities settlement

We noted earlier that exchanges are an integral part of financial markets. Because exchanges trade standardized products they can provide lower dealing costs than OTC markets can provide. They also offer better liquidity and market depth. Securities markets, in particular, face the high cost of delivery once a deal has been agreed, either on exchange or in the OTC market. Clearing houses and depositaries have developed to reduce the cost of delivery and take advantage of economies of scale.

17.5.1 Clearing houses

The nature of each clearing house will be slightly different and will depend on the type of financial instrument involved. Nevertheless there are certain overall characteristics. Clearing houses facilitate the settlement of securities by handling the transfer of ownership of securities. This can either be done by what is known as Delivery versus Payment (DvP) or Delivery by Value (DbV). The latter occurs when holdings of different securities are exchanged for each other rather than having a monetary cashflow as under DvP.

The trend has been for clearing houses to become Central Counter Parties (CCPs). If a clearing house is a CCP it will mean that every transaction will have the clearing house as the counterparty. This has significantly reduced counterparty risk and is an important element in risk management.

Some clearing houses also provide custody services. Many securities now exist in a dematerialized form, which avoids the need to deliver securities physically. Additional work undertaken involves the administration of interest and dividend payments.

Clearing houses can also allow the cheap lending and borrowing of securities. This increases liquidity in the markets. For some short-term instruments, such as CDs, clearing houses also undertake issuing and paying agent functions. We have already seen that repurchase transactions are often used in the payment systems to provide additional liquidity. The borrowing of securities may be undertaken to cover short positions in securities that need to be delivered.

17.5.2   UK clearing houses

In the UK those clearing houses that fall under the FSA's remit are known as Recognized Clearing Houses (RCHs). The main RCHs are Crest and the London Clearing House (LCH). The main international clearing houses are Euroclear and Clearstream.

Crest

CREST was inaugurated in 1996, and was originally owned and operated by CRESTCo. CRESTCo was itself owned by a range of CREST users. In September 2002 it merged with Euroclear and CRESTCo became a wholly owned subsidiary of Euroclear Bank.

Participation is open to bodies corporate and individuals regardless of domicile or location. Participants comprise most firms active in the UK and Irish equity markets and the gilt market (or their custodians), and a large number of individuals.

CREST's remit is very wide. It settles the purchase, sale, loan and repo of UK and Irish equities and UK government and corporate debt. As a result of links to other settlement systems it can also be used to hold foreign securities.

Since November 2001 CREST provides real-time DvP with settlement in central bank money and irrevocable electronic transfer of title for securities denominated in sterling and Euros. CREST records are the register for dematerialized UK securities. This means that at the point of settlement in CREST the transferee/buyer receives immediate and irrevocable direct legal title to the dematerialized securities. CREST is not responsible for other functions carried out by securities registrars, such as dividend payments and other corporate events. The CREST payment also discharges the buyer's obligation to the seller, as it is accompanied by a simultaneous real-time payment from the buyer's settlement bank to the seller's across settlement accounts at the Bank of England.

Central Moneymarkets Office (CMO)

The CMO system was initially operated and owned by the Bank of England. It was sold to CRESTCo in September 1999. Once legislation for the dematerialization of Treasury bills and other money market instruments was passed it is the intention to close the CMO and incorporate settlement into the CREST DvP arrangements. The aim is to close the CMO at the end of 2003.

Membership was open to all London money market participants subject to arrangements being made with a settlement bank to make payments on their behalf. There are currently 31 members of the CMO, which are drawn from a wide range of UK and overseas institutions. Over 200 firms also participate indirectly in the CMO through agency arrangements with CMO members.

The CMO provides safekeeping and settlement facilities for sterling- and Euro-denominated Treasury bills, local authority bills, bank bills, trade bills, bank and building society CDs and commercial paper. All of these instruments are immobilized in the CMO depository (which is operated on CRESTCo's behalf by the Bank of England), except for CDs, which are dematerialized using a contractual structure. Settlement occurs in real time by means of book-entry transfer between accounts in the CMO system.

London Clearing House (LCH)

LCH acts as CCP to trades executed on LIFFE, the LME, the IPE and the London Stock Exchange (trades on the SETS electronic trading platform) and a limited number of contracts on the US-based Intercontinental Exchange. Since 1999, LCH has acted as CCP for cash and repo trades in European (Austrian, Belgian, Dutch, German and UK currently, with more planned) government bonds, supranational and agency bonds and Jumbo Pfandbriefe ('Repoclear') and plain vanilla interest-rate swaps ('Swapclear').

From an ownership and governance point of view LCH is a public limited company. It is owned by its members (75% of the share capital) and LIFFE, the LME and the IPE (25% of the share capital intotal).

Because the LCH assumes counterparty default risk when it accepts trades into clearing it will cover its risk by requiring payment of margin. Initial margin (collateral), which is collected on all trades, is intended to protect LCH against the potential loss of a defaulter's positions before closeout. LCH also collects variation margin to re-establish this protection at close of business and, if necessary in fast-moving markets, makes intraday calls for more margin. LCH restricts, mainly to cash, government bonds and bank guarantees, the types of collateral that it will accept as initial margin.

17.5.3 International clearing and settlement

The Euroclear System

The Euroclear System used to be operated by Morgan Guaranty Trust Company of New York (MGT), via its Belgian branch. In 2000 MGT transferred these activities to Euroclear Bank, a new Belgian credit institution that was set up for the specific purpose of operating the Euroclear System.

Euroclear Bank also owns various other clearing systems, such as a 20% stake in the capital of Clearnet, the French credit institution responsible for the clearing of

Euronext transactions. Euroclear is also responsible for the settlement of Irish government bonds (Gilts) following the decision of the Irish government and the Central Bank of Ireland to delegate this activity to Euroclear. In September 2002, Euroclear Bank acquired 100% of the capital of CRESTCo, which, as we have seen, operates the real-time settlement systems settling UK, Irish and international securities through the CREST system, and money market instruments through the Central Money markets Office (CMO).

Euroclear Bank provides both international and domestic securities settlement services, including new issues distribution. In addition, it provides other services such as custody, securities lending and money transfer. Acting as a limited purpose bank, it also provides the system participants with the banking services directly bound to the settlement activity, including credit, securities lending and borrowing and collateral management services. In 2001, the Euroclear Group had a turnover exceeding EUR 130 trillion and settled more than 161 million transactions (pre-netted). The total value of securities held in custody was almost EUR 8 trillion. There are over 208,000 different issues of securities accepted in the Euroclear System issued by entities from over 110 different countries. The Euroclear System currently has about 2,000 participants from more than 80 different countries, the vast majority of which are banks, broker-dealers and other institutions professionally engaged in managing new issues of securities, market-making, trading or holding the wide variety of securities accepted by the system. Applicants must meet four criteria to be admitted:

- ◆ adequate financial resources;
- ◆ technological ability to use the Euroclear System;
- ◆ need to use the Euroclear System;
- ◆ sound reputation in the market.

In addition, the internal anti-money laundering measures of the applicant institution are considered prior to admission.

Over 190,000 national and international securities issues are accepted in the system, covering a broad range of internationally traded fixed and floating rate debt instruments, convertibles, warrants and equities. This includes domestic debt instruments, short- and medium-term instruments, equities and equity-linked instruments as well as international bonds from the major markets of Europe, Asia-Pacific, Africa and the Americas. Euroclear participants can confirm, clear and settle trades by book-entry in more than 40 settlement currencies on a simultaneous DvP basis.

Real-time settlement is possible for internal settlement and most cross-border trades. Upon receipt of the instruction from the participant, it allows for both the recycling of previously unmatched or unsettled transactions and the processing of new instructions for same day settlement. 75% of the Euroclear turnover settles within its own books, 12.5% on the 'Bridge' with Clearstream Banking Luxembourg (CBL), and 12.5% externally.

Euroclear also offers a custody function and subdeposited securities with a network of more than 70 custodians (called depositories) covering 32 markets. Some of these custodians in turn may subdeposit the securities with their own subcustodians. Euroclear Bank offers a large number of custody services facilitating the exercise of securities holders' rights and corporate actions, including tax services, proxy voting, information on corporate events and processing for collection of income and redemption proceeds, market claims, and exercise of subscription rights.

Furthermore, Euroclear Bank offers a securities lending and borrowing programme fully integrated into its overnight settlement process. As a general rule, all securities accepted by the Euroclear System are eligible for securities lending and borrowing except those bound by liquidity, fiscal or legal restrictions. Euroclear Bank also guarantees income and redemption proceeds and other entitlements on lent securities.

Euroclear provides its participants with integrated collateral management services facilitating collateralization of all types of exposures from a single pool of collateral. Collateral services offered in the Euroclear System include marking to market, substitutions, margin calls and other monitoring associated with collateralized securities. Integrated collateral management supports standard market agreements for repos, securities lending, derivatives support and secured loans.

Clearstream

Clearstream was set up in 1970 under the name of Cedel to provide for the clearing, settlement, custody and management of securities and precious metals. In 1999 Cedel merged with Deutsche Börse Clearing AG. The joint venture was renamed Clearstream International, of which 50% was owned by Cedel International Holding (itself held by international financial institutions), the other 50% being held by the Deutsche Börse AG. Deutsche Börse is the company managing the Frankfurt stock exchange. In 2002 Deutsche Börse took full control of Clearstream.

Participation in the system is essentially open to banks, broker-dealers, investment banks, central banks and other clearing houses. New members have to meet certain criteria when applying for membership and their credit standings are assessed on an ongoing basis. Criteria against which membership is assessed include the institution's net worth, its legal structure, its management reputation and the underlying country risk. Today, Clearstream maintains customer relationships with all major financial institutions from over 100 countries.

Clearstream currently accepts over 230,000 securities issues for clearance and settlement. They include fixed income bonds such as eurobonds, foreign bonds, domestic bonds and convertibles, money market instruments (including short- and medium-term notes, commercial paper and certificates of deposit), as well as equities, depository receipts, units in investment funds, warrants and precious metals. It also offers securities and cash lending facilities. It does so by acting as intermediary between the lenders and the borrowers, rather than as principal. In addition, Clearstream offers two types of credit facilities against collateral. Unsecured credit lines are only granted to top names in the financial sector after a rigorous credit assessment.

Eighteen

Offshore financial centres (OFCs)

Objectives

This chapter will cover the following topics:

- ◆ offshore banking centres;
- ◆ functions of offshore currency markets;
- ◆ selection of offshore centres;
- ◆ control of money laundering.

18.1 Introduction

The common characteristic of offshore financial centres (OFCs) is that they cater for clients based in other jurisdictions, rather than domestic clients. Thus places like London and New York are often considered offshore centres, as many of the banks located in these cities are only there to provide services into other countries rather than into the UK or US. Nevertheless they have sizeable domestic operations and therefore other definitions would not include London and New York.

The Financial Stability Forum, in its report on OFCs, defines them as jurisdictions with at least some of the following characteristics:

- ◆ low or no taxes on business or investment income;
- ◆ no withholding taxes;
- ◆ light and flexible incorporation and licensing regimes;
- ◆ light and flexible supervisory regimes;
- ◆ flexible use of trusts and other special corporate vehicles;

♦ no need for financial institutions and/or corporate structure to have a physical presence; and
♦ unavailability of similar incentives to residents.

OFCs have recently come into difficulties with onshore bodies as a result of increased international cooperation against money laundering and the financing of terrorism. Many OFCs have strict banking secrecy laws that are thought to facilitate both money laundering and the financing of terrorism. Other critics, such as the OECD, dwell on the harmful tax competition that they think OFCs create. Banking supervisors are concerned about possible lax regulation, which may affect financial stability and cause contagion to the wider financial markets. Lack of consolidation by many of the offshore supervisors and insufficient co-operation between offshore supervisors and mainstream regulators is also thought by some observers to be an issue. As a result of these concerns, the activities of OFCs have come under increasing scrutiny in recent years.

At the same time OFCs offer many benefits to legitimate banking activities. Maximizing profits by reducing the cost of running the business has always been a prime objective of commercial companies and OFC offer the facilities to do just that. Low taxation has attracted numerous businesses to offshore centres. Particularly the absence of withholding tax has been an attraction. Profits booked in offshore centres may also face low or nil tax rates. A further cost saving may come from reduced compliance costs. Regulation may not be quite as onerous and this may enable banks with presences in OFCs to offer better terms than competitors can.

It is not thought that treasury functions would be attracted to OFCs solely because they offer improved banking secrecy and reduced international co-operation. Nevertheless some customers may value this for legitimate reasons and in that case it can be beneficial to offer services from those offshore locations. Instead the ease of setting up special purpose vehicles for risk management purposes and tax reasons is a consideration that treasury functions need to take into account.

A decision to operate from an OFC is not a simple one, particularly since each OFC has specific advantages over others. Indeed not all financial centres cater for banking activities. Some, like Bermuda, are OFCs that are particularly known for the insurance and re-insurance sectors. Other centres, like the Cayman Island, have a track record in collective investment schemes. What is clear from this is that utilising offshore centres is a complicated business and in-depth research is required before beginning operating from them.

18.2 Historic developments

The offshore banking market has arisen from the anomalies that exist from the regulation of domestic markets, and the attempts to regulate on both a European and international basis. A less strict regulatory framework combined with favourable fiscal and monetary policy in relation to the home market can make offshore banking very attractive. For example, Euromarkets are where deposits are made outside the regulations and constraints that might apply in the local economy. Despite its geographical connotation, 'Euromarket' has become the term used to describe the collective international offshore banking market.

The markets became significantly active in the 1950s. Many Eastern European countries utilized offshore facilities in order to avoid, on the one hand, the political embarrassment of lodging US dollar deposits in the US, and on the other, the expensive regulation under the US Banking Act of 1933. By not having to follow regulatory conditions, banks can find themselves very competitive in the lending markets and in the interest bearing deposit markets. Various regulatory restrictions on the ability of American banks to pay interest on deposits paved the way for the Euromarkets to plug the gap without the shackles of restrictive supervision and control. While these markets involve more risk by definition, the risks are known and limited as the banks operating in these markets tend to be well known and generally reputable. It has become so lucrative and competitive that reputations have become as important as those in regulated markets. Many banks in this sector take great pride in their prudential control based on their own set of internal standards.

In the 1970s the massive dollar earnings of the oil rich Middle Eastern countries were diverted from regulated US markets and towards the less regulated Euromarkets. Even though the restrictions of 'Regulation Q' of the US Banking Act 1933 have since become insignificant, the Euromarkets had been born and have now gone on to become the largest deposit and funding market in the world, dealing in dollars (dollar markets form half the total), Euros, Swiss francs, yen and sterling. In all the countries issuing these currencies regulations exist that restrict nationally based banking operations, including the requirement to deposit non-interest bearing moneys with the central bank.

Traditional banks have now joined the more specialized banks in setting up offshore branches, subsidiaries or affiliates to take advantage of the demand for tax havens and the ease, through electronic transmission, with which these activities can take place. There has also been a growth in consortium and syndicated operations in these markets ensuring a presence in the market while sharing the risks involved.

More recently the activities of OFCs have come under close scrutiny. The Financial Stability Forum issued a report on Offshore Centres in 2000. It found that 'inadequate supervision in OFCs can hinder supervision in "onshore" centres, posing a potential threat to the global financial system'. It also noted that implementation of international standards was markedly different between centres and that one therefore needed to differentiate between them.

Similarly the Financial Action Task Force (FATF) on Money Laundering has reviewed OFCs from an anti-money laundering point of view. The FATF has established international standards for effective anti-money laundering measures. Its 2000 review identified numerous OFCs that were deemed uncooperative and international pressure is now being exerted bon those countries or territories.

Despite the FATF's work most observers believe that a majority of money-laundering activity occurs onshore, and particularly in onshore major financial centres.

Another report issued by the OECD, also issued in 2000, identified 35 jurisdictions meeting its criteria for being tax havens. Such work is ongoing, particularly since many of the OFCs fundamentally disagree with the assumptions underlying these reports. Others disagree with the findings from these reports on the basis that they have not been consulted or are in the process of changing legislation to address concerns.

Table 18.1: International ratings of offshore centres (2000)

OFC	FATF rating	FSF rating	OECD rating
Andorra		II	Uncooperative
Anguilla		III	Uncooperative
Antigua & Barbuda	Cooperative	III	
Aruba		III	Uncooperative
Bahamas	Non-cooperative	III	Uncooperative
Bahrain		II	Uncooperative
Barbados		II	Uncooperative
Belize	Cooperative	III	Uncooperative
Bermuda	Cooperative	II	
British Virgin Islands	Cooperative	III	Uncooperative
Cayman Islands	Non-cooperative	III	
Cook Islands	Non-cooperative	III	Uncooperative
Costa Rica		III	
Cyprus	Cooperative	III	
Dublin (Ireland)		I	
Dominica	Non-cooperative		Uncooperative
Gibraltar	Cooperative	II	Uncooperative
Grenada			Uncooperative
Guernsey	Cooperative	I	Uncooperative
Hong Kong, SAR		I	
Isle of Man	Cooperative	I	Uncooperative
Israel	Non-cooperative		
Jersey	Cooperative	I	Uncooperative

Offshore financial centres (OFCs)

OFC	FATF rating	FSF rating	OECD rating
Labuan (Malaysia)		II	
Lebanon	Non-cooperative	III	
Liberia			Uncooperative
Liechtenstein	Non-cooperative	III	Uncooperative
Luxembourg		I	
Macao		II	
Maldives			Uncooperative
Malta	Cooperative	II	
Marshall Islands	Non-cooperative	III	Uncooperative
Mauritius	Cooperative	III	
Monaco	Cooperative	II	Uncooperative
Monserrat			Uncooperative
Nauru	Non-cooperative	III	Uncooperative
Netherlands Antilles		III	Uncooperative
Niue	Non-cooperative	III	Uncooperative
Panama	Non-cooperative	III	Uncooperative
Philippines	Non-cooperative		
Russia	Non-cooperative		
Samoa	Cooperative	III	Uncooperative
Seychelles		III	Uncooperative
Singapore		I	
St. Kitts and Nevis	Non-cooperative	III	Uncooperative
St. Lucia	Cooperative	III	Uncooperative
St. Vincent and the Grenadines	Non-cooperative	III	Uncooperative
Switzerland		I	
Tonga			Uncooperative
Turks and Caicos		III	Uncooperative
US Virgin Islands			Uncooperative
Vanuatu		III	Uncooperative

The above table is interesting in that it shows the large number of OFCs that exist around the globe. The FATFs ratings are purely based on anti-money laundering and identify those countries deemed to have serious systemic problems with their legislation. It should be noted that the standard of anti-money-laundering regulation is in some cases higher in OFCs than in a number of onshore jurisdictions.

The FSF classification is based on supervisory issues. A Group I rating applies to those jurisdictions that are 'generally perceived as … largely of good quality and better than in other OFCs'. Group II are 'lower' quality, and Group III 'lower' still. For an OFC to be deemed adequately supervised, its banking regulations need to conform to the Basel Core Principles for Effective Banking Supervision. As described in Chapter 15 the core principles set minimum standards which apply both to banks and their supervisors. Indeed there is a considerable degree of regulation in various OFCs and arguably, some OFCs have a greater degree of regulation and supervision than various onshore jurisdictions.

The OECD study shows those tax havens that it deems to have harmful tax practices. Its criteria are based on the lack of effective exchange of information, lack of transparency and the existence of ring fencing in combination with low rates of taxation.

18.3   Functions of OFCs

There are a variety of functions that OFCs perform. Benefits include the ability to:

- overcome regulatory constraints;
- provide trade finance and finance for overseas investment;
- take account of structural considerations;
- provide expatriate services;
- benefit from confidentiality;
- benefit from low taxes;
- ease of company incorporation and the setting up of trusts.

18.3.1   Overcoming regulatory constraints

Some countries place lending or gearing constraints on banks whereas OFCs may provide the means to operate outside such tight guidelines. The effect from the bank's point of view is that it can reduce its costs and provide lower-cost funding and higher returns on deposits. There is normally no requirement to deposit non-profit earning deposits with a central bank, which again helps to maximize profits.

As is usually the case with returns on investments, there is a trade-off between security and yield. Some offshore banks are potentially less secure than a domestic bank given the unpredictability of political events that might unfold. Many of the offshore centres, such as Bahrain, have been at pains to demonstrate their ability to maintain a liberal, yet secure, financial environment.

18.3.2 Provide trade finance and finance for overseas investment

The Euromarkets are a useful source of funding, particularly where large amounts are required, and may need to come from diverse sources. The Japanese have found offshore financing a very useful source of funds in their overseas trade and investment expansion, particularly as a large proportion of their transactions are in US dollars.

18.3.3 To take structural considerations into account

With banks maintaining portfolios across many locations, including offshore centres, they are able to influence certain transactions and the structure of the banks' portfolios. This often focuses on a bank's taxation position.

18.3.4 To provide expatriate services

The largest users of some offshore facilities are British expatriates. With limited allegiance to the British banking system, the expatriates can choose the ideal location for their money. This has led many banks to set up branches or subsidiaries offshore. These need to be integrated into the overall business strategy of the bank and that in itself will create additional requirements on treasury functions.

18.3.5 Benefiting from confidentiality

The lure of offshore banks as tax havens provides one of the strongest attractions to depositors. Those using the services of these financial centres will value the confidential framework within which they operate. This can be for legitimate reasons, such as tax planning, keeping transactions hidden from competitors or hiding money from corrupt regimes. However, confidentiality is also sought by those benefiting from criminal activities, wanting to launder money or finance terrorism. The balancing act between taking account of legitimate reasons for seeking confidentiality and stopping criminal activities is one that many OFCs have to deal with.

18.3.6 Tax planning

Because of low or nil taxation regimes implemented in many OFCs, judicious tax planning can considerably improve organizations' cashflows. This can be achieved via transfer pricing for example. Profits are booked in the low taxation area, while costs are booked onshore to minimize tax liabilities. Many countries, such as the

UK, have introduced tax laws to minimize the use of such tax planning. Again the border between tax planning, which is legal, and tax evasion, which is not, is a grey one that OFCs will have to evaluate accordingly.

18.3.7 Ease of company incorporation and the setting up of trusts

In many onshore jurisdictions it can be relatively expensive to set up corporate vehicles or trusts. Some offshore jurisdiction specialize in these by offering low registration fees and few on-going costs in terms of reporting and public disclosures. Some jurisdictions even dispense with the need for audited accounts.

18.4   Characteristics of OFCs and selection of OFCs

An OFC may demonstrate one or more of the characteristics described earlier. It might be a major centre already for deposits or loans, such as London, or it might be a large net supplier of funds to the world financial markets such as Switzerland. Markets might offer stability in political and economic terms as well as being a sound, efficient and experienced financial community. Some markets such as the Bahamas and the Cayman Islands are an intermediary or pass-through for international loan funds. Some regimes foster a favourable regulatory climate according to the prevailing needs.

OFCs can be considered either as operational centres or booking centres. London is an active operational centre with a well-developed and experienced financial centre, whereas the Cayman Islands to a considerable degree is a booking centre. A booking centre is where there are few actual banking activities, but where transactions are recorded to take advantage of secrecy and low tax rates.

18.4.1   Criteria for selecting an offshore bank

Given that OFCs have recognizable advantages and functions, it is appropriate to focus on the sorts of considerations that should be taken into account when selecting an OFC. Below are a number of factors that should be considered.

- ◆ Accessibility – The availability of day-to-day communications, for example by fax, telephone, post, courier, and so on. This includes the time zone in which a centre is located.
- ◆ Availability of personnel – There should be an established choice of qualified personnel, such as lawyers, tax consultants, finance experts and administrative skills. Potential language barriers should also be taken into account.

◆ Confidentiality – Where confidentiality is needed the level of banking secrecy law will have to be ascertained. Level of reporting is also important. Some jurisdictions do not disclose beneficial ownership and do not require registration of trusts.

◆ Cost – Not only will the cost of personnel be relevant, other cost considerations will include the fees for incorporation and other annual fees that need to be paid as part of doing business in the relevant centre.

◆ Financial development – An established financial centre breeds confidence and therefore attracts certain types of investor, particularly those more averse to risk.

◆ Foreign exchange controls – The free movement of funds from offshore will be a prerequisite. It is now common to allow this for non-residents in most OFCs.

◆ Legal system – The legal system in existence will be of major importance. Preferred systems are likely to have a strong background in commercial law. A history of common law as in Britain is likely to be favoured. Independence of the judiciary and acceptance of the rule of law are also likely to be very important to provide stable business conditions.

◆ Reputation – The reputation of each OFC should be considered to ensure that it is compatible with the image that the bank wishes to portray of itself.

◆ Stability – The level of political and economic stability in the host country is significant. Absence of corruption should be considered as an important condition.

◆ Taxation – If the use of tax planning is envisaged detailed research is needed on the level of income or withholding taxes. Other taxes that may be relevant are inheritance taxes or VAT equivalent taxes. Double taxation agreements will be of major benefit.

18.5 Description of selected OFCs

The largest offshore centres are London and New York. Ireland, Hong Kong and Switzerland also have a sizeable amount of offshore activities. Many would not, however, include these as offshore centres as they do not provide special legislation for offshore activities, although Ireland did provide tax incentives. Also these centres do not tend to provide as flexible supervisory regimes, light incorporation and licensing regimes, while at the same time requiring a physical presence.

Singapore also has specific legislation for offshore activities, in addition to being domestic banking centres. Significant other OFCs include Bermuda, the Channel Islands and the Isle of Man. Bermuda is particularly known for its insurance related offshore activities. The Bahamas, the British Virgin Islands, Cayman Islands and Panama are known for their ability to provide international corporate domiciles with strict confidentiality. A more comprehensive list of OFCs was shown in Table 18.1.

18.5.1   London

London has become an offshore centre because of its expertise and maturity as an operational financial centre. It also offers favourable treatment of foreign currency in terms of taxation, absence of mandatory reserve requirements, and convertibility. These three factors are important in determining the suitability of a country for Eurocurrency business. Unlike many other offshore centres, London does not have specific legislation relating to offshore activities.

18.5.2   Hong Kong

Hong Kong has proven to be a key offshore banking centre because of its position in relation to Britain and China, its wealth-creating culture and its geographical position on the Pacific Rim. Hong Kong has, however, faced significant competition since it became a Special Administrative Region of China. The Hong Kong Monetary Authority (HKMA) is seen as a strong regulator, which closely follows international standards. It has an approach of 'continuous supervision', which includes on-site inspections, prudential reviews and meetings. It also works together with external auditors and other supervisory agencies.

18.5.3   Singapore

The Monetary Authority of Singapore (MAS) can issue full banking licences, restricted licences and offshore licences, all of which enable banks to operate in the offshore markets. Banks have ACUs or Asian Currency Units within their banks, which are integral parts of the bank, but with separate offshore accounting and regulatory procedures.

Banks must be adequately capitalized, and are limited in the extent to which they can deal in Singapore dollars, because the government wishes to control the growth of its currency as a major international denomination. The MAS applies strict regulation, and operates through a licensing system, which involves three types: full, restricted and offshore. Unlike some centres, the licences require a physical banking presence in Singapore. The MAS scrutinizes applications for licences very carefully, reflecting the local culture of rigid enforcement of codes of behaviour.

18.5.4   Ireland

In 1987 the Irish Government established the IFSC (International Financial Services Centre) in Dublin to attract financial services industry to the island. Those IFSC entities that do not provide services to residents enjoyed a low corporate tax rate of 10%, although this will be phased out by 2005. IFSC entities are fully incorporated in the general supervision undertaken by the Central Bank of Ireland. However, reduced cost, the availability of a skilled workforce and good infrastructure, combined with the tax benefits, have made Dublin a large financial centre. Funds under management for example stand at over Euro 180 billion, partly as a result of the establishment of many collective investment schemes.

18.5.5   Jersey, Guernsey and Isle of Man

These centres have benefited from close proximity to the UK mainland, combined with their separate legislative regimes. The authorities in these centres have also been keen on ensuring that regulations are strict enough to avoid reputational problems, while still allowing considerable tax benefits. They are often used for the incorporation of investment vehicles, be they investment trusts or other collective investment schemes.

18.5.6   New York

New York is mainly built on being the financial centre for the US domestic financial markets. In addition the fact that all US dollar transactions need to be booked in the US has lead to many foreign banks opening branches or subsidiaries in New York. This was made even easier in 1981 when international banking facilities (IBFs) were exempted from some restrictive US regulations. Additionally the Edge Act permits US banks to conduct international banking business from offices in financial centres outside of their home state.

18.6   International Banking Facilities (IBFs) and managed banks

Many offshore centres were the result of restrictive regulations in the US (Regulations D and Q). In 1981 IBFs, or international banking facilities, were made exempt by the Federal Reserve from these regulations. This enabled banks operating in the state of New York to introduce offshore units. This facilitated growth of New York as an operational banking centre. In 1986 Japan began to offer similar services. In both centres it reduced the incentives for banks to move some of their business into offshore jurisdictions.

In the US IBFs are authorized to transact business in US dollars and in other currencies, with non-residents and with other IBFs. Individual deposits cannot be accepted if they are below $100,000. IBFs can operate in certain secondary transactions. IBFs are an integral part of a banking operation, and as such are subject to regulatory control applied as part of normal review processes.

In practice IBFs are often part of existing branches, but they need to maintain separate books/records to be able to demonstrate that they abide by the restrictions imposed on them. This includes the restriction of not dealing with residents and not issuing negotiable instruments that may end up with residents. In return they can undertake business without being subject to all of the country's taxes and regulations. IBFs are exempt from deposit insurance coverage, foreign deposits do not face reserve requirements and there are no interest rate limitations. At the same time such IBFs do not have all the advantages of full OFCs. Thus the growth of the offshore market has continued despite the availability of IBFs.

18.6.1   Managed banks

An important advantage of OFCs has been the ability to open managed banks. These are also known as administered banks. The name comes from the requirements that all of the books and records be managed by an administering bank. In some jurisdictions administering banks require a special license to provide that service.

The outsourcing arrangements will need to address confidentiality issues, service level agreements, conflicts of interest, termination clauses, etc. At the simplest level all services can be outsourced. This enables institutions that want a simple entry into the offshore market to buy in expertise, without having to go into the administrative complications of establishing a full presence. On the other hand there are arrangements that fall just short of establishing a full stand-alone bank. For example, a bank could operate its own front-office, with the back-office functions being outsourced to an administering bank. However, not all OFCs allow the establishment of managed banks.

18.7   UK regulation of offshore activities

The main aim of FSMA is to regulate the provision of financial services in the UK. Thus FSMA prohibits the carrying on of regulated activities in the UK without authorization or exemption. There are two main tests for establishing whether the regulated activity is being carried on in the UK. In the first test, an authorised person is classed as carrying on regulated activities in the UK if it is conducted from a permanent place of business maintained in the UK. This applies even if all customers are located overseas. Furthermore, the place of business does not have to be the person's main place of business, eg a bank could conduct its investment business with customers based solely in the bank's home country but it could also have a London office. In the second test, an authorised person is classed as carrying on regulated activities in the UK if he engages in certain activities which the FSA lists.

This applies even if it does not have a place of business in the UK. It covers investment business, which is carried on in the UK from a location overseas on a recurring basis. Advising or selling investment products by telephone or in writing to UK-based customers is thus also covered by FSMA.

Unsolicited or legitimately solicited transactions with unauthorized and non-exempt persons are exempt from the need for authorization. This covers transactions which arise from a UK customer approaching an overseas company, ie unsolicited transactions, and transactions which arise from advertising and cold calling by the overseas company which complies with the Act.

If the overseas company wants to advertise its products in the UK, the financial promotion must be approved by an authorised person in accordance with the financial promotion rules. This imposes a duty on the firm that approves the advertisement. Communicating financial promotions without approval is classed as a criminal offence and the transaction may become invalid. Furthermore, breach of the rules relating to unsolicited real-time communication can also be treated as a criminal offence. This is, however, mainly a protection for retail customers and is therefore less relevant to Treasury activities.

A person in the UK may promote the products and services of an overseas company in the UK providing the products are not unauthorized unit trusts or unregulated collective investment schemes. Again, the financial promotion requirements issued under FSMA must be adhered to. This person would not be classed as carrying out investment business if the customer subsequently instructed the overseas company directly. Again, the authorized firm must be satisfied that the overseas firm will act with customers in a reliable and honest way. The financial promotion must include all the prescribed information that a UK financial promotion has to contain.

18.7.1 Impact of FSMA on UK firms overseas

An overseas branch of a UK firm is treated as having a separate legal personality, ie as if it were an overseas company. This exemption from FSMA, which applies to an overseas person when transacting with or through an authorized or exempt person or when undertaking unsolicited or legitimately solicited transactions, also applies to overseas branches of UK firms. This means that if an employee or representative of a UK firm conducts investment business when travelling overseas, the transactions will continue to be subject to the FSA rules. However, if the person operates from an overseas branch, he could take advantage of the exemptions from FSMA for an overseas company.

The FSA will nevertheless want to make sure that firms act in a fit and proper way both in the UK and overseas. The FSA also requires notification of events, which happen overseas, which have a regulatory implication. This includes disciplinary actions taken against the firm by an overseas authority or convictions for fraud or dishonesty. Due to increased international co-operation, the regulators in the UK are able to obtain information from most overseas regulators and the increased pressure on OFCs to become more cooperative is likely to close many existing loopholes.

18.8 Taxation

Governments find themselves in a difficult situation when it comes to the issue of taxation in the offshore context. On the one hand they actively seek an active banking sector, which might well include the increasingly important offshore sector, yet they realize that they stand to lose a lot of revenue when citizenship is renounced and capital moved offshore, out of the reach of the treasury. The US is currently looking at introducing legislation to limit the ability of people to find a way of not paying domestic taxes.

As far as companies are concerned, the UK legislation in 1984 limited the use of foreign companies to real value-added activities, rather than as a tax shelter alone. Tax breaks can no longer be the sole reason for using offshore centres in business. Companies must meet certain criteria before they can go ahead and use an offshore bank to reduce domestic taxation:

- ◆ a proportion of profits must be distributed back to the UK;
- ◆ based on premises, numbers of local staff employed etc. The company has to demonstrate that it has genuine business interests in any given country;
- ◆ the main motive must be to do business, not avoid tax.

18.9 Money laundering

Most offshore centres have been observing the trend by major onshore countries towards strict measures aimed at eliminating the threat of money laundering. With the risk of being branded soft on criminal activity, thus threatening their own reputation for security, most offshore centres are now looking at implementing their own measures. It is also important that all parts of banking operations are trained up on money-laundering issues, particularly those dealing with customers or with offshore centres.

Money laundering is the process by which money, which is illegally obtained, is made to appear to have been legally gained. The nature, source and ownership of those criminal proceeds are concealed by a large variety of methods. The consequence is that the origins of entitlement to the money are disguised and the money can again be used to benefit the criminal and/or his associates.

The criminal activity from which the proceeds are derived can be of any kind, ranging from tax evasion (though current guidance is that in the UK it is only the actual evasion of UK taxes that would constitute an offence) to drug trafficking. The methods used to disguise the origin and/or ownership of these proceeds are infinite and varied. Essentially however, the money launderer has two weapons – secrecy and the ease with which property can be transferred within the international financial markets.

The reason for anti-money laundering legislation is that it has increasingly been recognized that the ease with which money can be laundered has in itself facilitated and encouraged criminal activity. Unless a criminal is able to exploit the financial gains accruing from his criminal activity, there is little point in his embarking upon such a course of action. In addition, the integration of the international financial markets has made it easier for 'dirty' or 'hot' money to be transferred across national boundaries.

Once cross-border transfers of property have taken place, it becomes more difficult for law enforcement agencies to trace the source of that property. Accordingly, the globalization of financial markets has in itself assisted the money launderers in their aim of disguising the origin of criminal proceeds so that those proceeds can again be used, often for a criminal purpose.

In recognition of these factors, various national governments have in recent years collaborated on a international scale to combat money laundering. Action taken has concentrated not only on the law enforcement process but also on recommendations to banks and financial institutions to put in place procedures which will assist in the detection of money laundering.

In 1991, the European Community adopted Council Directive 91/308 on prevention of the use of the financial system for the purposes of money laundering. This Directive must be implemented by all member states. In part, the impetus for the Directive was the removal of obstacles to free movement of capital and freedom to supply financial services, which was to come about upon completion of the Single European market. The Directive provides that all European Union member states should ensure that all financial and credit institutions located within the national member states should implement certain internal procedures and controls.

Let us first look at how the money laundering process works. In the first instance, if the money launderer is able to deposit illicit proceeds within an institution or a state (this is known as **placement**) which requires little or no disclosure concerning the ownership of those funds, it may be difficult, if not impossible, to trace the property back to its criminal source.

In the second instance, if property is passed through a complicated series of transactions (this is known as **layering**), involving legitimate as well as illegitimate enterprises, it may again be impossible to identify the true ownership of that property.

If the ownership of the funds cannot be ascertained, it is virtually impossible to establish that they are the product of criminal activity. The funds can then be reused in legitimate activity (this is known as **integration**).

In the UK the Criminal Justice Act 1993 and the Money Laundering Regulations 1993 were enacted in order to implement the European directive on money laundering. The focus of these was on the financial sector, while other laws relating to anti-money laundering applied to all individuals independent of their employment, but these go beyond the scope of this syllabus. For financial services companies and their employees the FSA Handbook includes further requirements that they need to comply with. The aim of these laws and rules is threefold:

◆ Deterrence: to prevent credit and financial institutions being used for money laundering purposes.
◆ Co-operation: to ensure that there is co-operation between credit and financial institutions and law enforcement agencies.
◆ Detection: to establish customer identification and record-keeping procedures within all financial and credit institutions which will assist the law enforcement agencies in detecting, tracing and prosecuting money launderers.

The anti-money laundering framework now provides that failure by a financial institution to implement and maintain the internal systems and training required by the regulations will result in criminal liability on the part of the financial institution's directors, managers, partners or officers. This is a radical departure from the previous position and reflects the seriousness with which the authorities intend to tackle the problem of money laundering.

The UK's Proceeds of Crime Act 2002 replaces the money laundering provisions of the Criminal Justice Act 1988, and the Drug Trafficking Act 1994. The major change is that money-laundering offices are applicable throughout the UK to the proceeds of all crimes, including tax evasion. There is an obligation to report a suspicious transaction no matter what the sum involved is, and it is immaterial who carried out the criminal conduct or who benefited from it. It is now a criminal offence to fail to report when there is knowledge, suspicion or reasonable grounds to know or suspect that another person is laundering the proceeds of criminal conduct, or is engaged in terrorist financing.

18.9.1   Individual liability

The legislation in relation to individual liability is contained in different statutes depending on the source of the criminal proceeds, that is, whether the money to be laundered results from terrorist activity, drug trafficking or other criminal conduct. In essence, however, it is an offence for an individual to commit any of the following types of actions:

◆ to assist another person to launder proceeds obtained from drug trafficking or other criminal conduct, or terrorist funds;
◆ to fail to report knowledge or suspicions of the laundering of drug trafficking proceeds or terrorist funds;

♦ to provide information to another person which is likely to prejudice an investigation into drug trafficking, criminal conduct or terrorist activity. This is known as tipping off.

Assistance

If any person helps another person to launder the proceeds of drug trafficking or criminal conduct, or to launder terrorist funds, he will be committing an offence. Assisting a money launderer, as defined by UK legislation can take many forms. Any of the following actions will constitute such an offence:

♦ to obtain, use or do any act in relation to property which represents the proceeds of drug trafficking, criminal conduct or which are terrorist funds;

♦ to assist a person to retain control over, ownership of or the benefits from the proceeds of drug trafficking, criminal conduct or terrorist funds;

♦ to hide property or transfer property out of the UK or to assist a person to hide property or transfer property out of the UK for the purpose of avoiding prosecution and/or the making of a confiscation order in relation to that property.

The person who provides the assistance to a criminal must, in order to be guilty of an offence of this type, do more than simply commit the act of assistance. He must do so with the requisite knowledge. That is to say:

♦ in the case of the laundering of the proceeds of drug trafficking or criminal conduct, a person must either know or suspect that the property represents the proceeds of drug trafficking or criminal conduct, or that a person is helping someone who is or has been engaged in drug trafficking or criminal conduct;

♦ in the case of terrorism, a person must either have known or have had reasonable cause to suspect that the funds were derived from terrorist funds or that the person being assisted is or has been engaged in terrorist activities.

It is important to note that in the case of the money laundering offences relating to drug trafficking and criminal conduct, a person can only be found guilty of assistance if the prosecution is able to prove that that person did actually know or have suspicions concerning the origin of the property. However, in the case of terrorist funds, a person can be found guilty of the offence of assisting if the prosecution is able to prove that that person either knew or ought reasonably to have known about the origins of those terrorist funds.

It is a defence to the above offences that a person disclosed his knowledge or belief concerning the origins of the property either to the police or to the appropriate officer in his employment.

The maximum penalties for any offence of assisting a money launderer are 14 years imprisonment and/or an unlimited fine.

Failure to report

If a person discovers information during the course of his employment which makes him believe or suspect that drug trafficking proceeds or terrorist funds are being laundered, a person must inform the police or the appropriate officer designated as such by his employers as soon as possible. Such officer tends to be called the Money Laundering Reporting Officer (MLRO). If an employee fails to make the report as soon as is reasonably practicable, the employee commits a criminal offence. The role of the MLRO is to assess reports made and where deemed relevant pass any such reports on to NCIS, the National Criminal Intelligence Service.

The only defence to this charge is if a person charged can prove that he had a reasonable excuse for failing to disclose this information. Whether an excuse is reasonable will depend on the circumstances of the case, but it is noteworthy that the person charged has the burden of proving that he had a reasonable excuse for his failure to disclose.

The relevant legislation specifically provides that any person making a disclosure of this kind will not be in breach of any duty of confidentiality owed to a customer. This offence of failing to report is punishable with a maximum of five years' imprisonment and/or an unlimited fine. Even where a firm or individual does report they must be careful not to alert the suspicions of the alleged launderer since this is itself an offence.

Tipping off

If a person either knows or believes that the police are or will be investigating the laundering of the proceeds of drug trafficking, criminal conduct or terrorist funds, that person must not disclose to any third party any information which might prejudice such an investigation. If he does so, he will commit the offence of tipping off.

This offence is committed if:

- ◆ prejudicial information is disclosed to any third party, not just the person suspected of money laundering;
- ◆ if prejudicial information is disclosed to a third party who is aware that a report of a suspicious transaction has been made either to the police or to the appropriate officer in a place of employment.

It is a defence to this offence if the person charged can prove that he neither knew nor suspected that the disclosure would prejudice an investigation.

There is an additional defence in relation to a charge of tipping off in respect of an investigation of the laundering of terrorist funds. In that case, it is a defence if a person charged can prove that he had either lawful authority or reasonable excuse to make the disclosure. Once again, the burden of proving the defence rests upon the person who has been charged with an offence.

In relation to terrorist funds only, it is also an offence to hide, destroy or tamper with material which may be relevant to any police investigation, if the person who does so knows or believes that the police either are or will be conducting an investigation, or knows or believes that a report concerning terrorist funds has been made to the police or to an appropriate officer.

It is a defence to this charge to prove that there was no intention to conceal material from anyone carrying out an investigation.

All these offences are punishable with a maximum of five years' imprisonment and/ or an unlimited fine.

18.9.2   Record-keeping procedures

Records of certain matters must be maintained by institutions; those records must be kept for a least five years after the relevant business has been completed.

Those records must contain:

- ◆ details of the evidence obtained to verify the identity of an applicant for business;
- ◆ a copy of that evidence, or details of how such a copy could be obtained, or if it is not reasonably practicable to keep a copy of that evidence, enough information to enable the evidence to be obtained again.

These records must be retained for five years after:

- ◆ the business relationship has been ended. (If the business relationship has not been formally ended, the five-year period commences on the date of the completion of the last activity in that business relationship);
- ◆ the date on which all activities taking place in the course of a one-off transaction or series of transactions have been completed;
- ◆ proceedings to recover any debt payable by an applicant for business, who is reasonably believed to have become insolvent, have been commenced.

The records must also contain information concerning individual transactions. This should provide information on all transactions undertaken by the institution. These records must be retained for five years after the date on which a transaction has come to an end and must be maintained in an easily retrievable form for the benefit of law enforcement agencies.

Those records which related either to a suspected money laundering transaction, or to a customer suspected of involvement in money laundering activities must only be destroyed at the expiry of the five year period if the consent of the appropriate law enforcement agency has been given.

Where the firm is aware of any investigation or has itself submitted a report to the authorities, they must not destroy any records regardless of the five-year limit without the express permission of the authorities.

18.9.3   Financial Services and Markets Act 2000

The FSA has translated the requirements imposed by the European Directive into rules applicable to authorised persons. Breach of the provisions thus means that the FSA can also take disciplinary action against authorised persons and approved persons. Section 402 of FSMA also allows the FSA to institute proceedings relating to money laundering under criminal law.

The FSA handbook requires firms to ensure that staff are adequately trained in the prevention of money laundering, and have appropriate processes in place. In addition, firms will need to maintain records to show that they have complied with the rules.

Nineteen

The foreign exchange market

Objectives

This chapter will cover the following topics:

- ◆ the market in foreign exchange, its history, definitions, size and participants;
- ◆ the methods of trading including electronic broking;
- ◆ spot and forward foreign exchange calculations;
- ◆ swap and interest arbitrage calculations;
- ◆ the Bank of England's role in the money markets in the UK, including the repo market.

19.1 Introduction

The foreign exchange (FX or forex) market enables companies, fund managers, banks and others to buy and sell foreign currencies, if necessary in large amounts. Capital flows arising from trade in goods and services, international investment and loans together create this demand for foreign currency. The sums involved are very large, with global turnover in April 2001 in all currencies estimated at USD1.2 trillion daily, according to the Bank for International Settlements. These represents a fall compared to previous surveys that were undertaken prior to the arrival of the Euro. Typical wholesale deals are for amounts of USD 1 million to USD 5 million, although much larger transactions are often done. The foreign exchange markets are much more volatile than the money markets, where rates may not change during the day.

The foreign exchange market has no single location. Trading is via telephone, conversational screen systems and electronic broking systems, which link financial centres. There is 24-hour trading in the foreign exchange markets. When banks in London open for trading at around 7.00 am, they can deal with banks in Tokyo, Hong Kong and Singapore. From 1.00 pm onwards, London can trade with banks in New York. Trading by US banks will overlap with the Far East at their closing time. Liquidity for trading is affected by these time overlaps.

The foreign exchange market is now a mature market and is subject to rationalization in terms of numbers of dealing rooms, currencies traded (following the introduction of the Euro), methods of trading (the introduction of screen-based trading systems) and settlement efficiencies. With modern communications, a single settlements service can process the work of a number of dealing rooms, for example covering a bank's foreign exchange trading in other European countries.

19.2 History

The Bretton Woods Agreement of 1944 established a fixed exchange rate system, subject to occasional realignment. In the 1950s and 1960s, substantial international payment imbalances developed, with the two major reserve currencies, the US dollar and pound sterling, being overvalued and both countries running large balance of payments deficits. It was modified by the Smithsonian Agreement in 1971, after a devaluation of the US dollar.

On 23 June 1972, the British government floated the pound sterling and effectively disbanded the sterling area in its broader context. On 13 February 1973, the US government devalued the dollar by a further 10% and the foreign exchange market closed. When it reopened, all major currencies were floating against each other and the Bretton Woods and Smithsonian Agreement had become virtually irrelevant. Since then, a number of formal and informal agreements have linked various currencies to each other, the European Exchange Rate Mechanism (ERM) being the most significant. It ultimately evolved into the Euro. It should be noted that the Euro is not a fixed exchange rate system. Instead it has completely replaced the previous legacy currencies.

Within a floating exchange rate structure, the rate of exchange of one currency in terms of another should be determined entirely by market forces. Governments, both collectively following G7 agreements and using individual initiatives, occasionally seek to influence the level of exchange rates through open market intervention or the setting of exchange rates.

Although foreign exchange trading in London is free from restrictions, regulations in other countries may affect exchange rates of those currencies and also affect individuals' freedom to access international currencies on a competitive basis. Regulations can include exchange controls and other monetary directives, constraints on capital flows reserve requirements, official exchange rate policy and similar constraints.

19.3   Definitions and description

Foreign exchange trading may be for spot or forward delivery:

◆ Spot transactions are undertaken for an exchange of currencies (delivery and settlement) on the value date, which is two business days after the trade date.
◆ Forward transactions (outright forwards) involve a delivery date further into the future, normally for periods up to one year and in some cases longer. By buying or selling in the forward market a bank can, on its own behalf or that of a customer, protect the value of anticipated flows of income from exchange rate volatility.
◆ Swaps are the simultaneous spot sale and forward purchase (or spot purchase and forward sale) of currencies and are extensively used for trading, matching and arbitrage purposes.

19.3.1   Size of the market

A three-yearly survey is conducted by the Bank of International Settlements (BIS)/ central banks on the foreign exchange markets. The results of the 2001 survey showed the following daily turnover:

Centres:	United Kingdom USD 504bn, United States USD 253bn, Japan USD 147bn
	The estimated global daily turnover is USD 1.2 trillion after adjustments for double counting.

London

Turnover	Spot USD 151bn, outright forward USD 53 bn, Swaps 300 bn.
Currencies	USD 92%, Euro 41%, Yen 17%, Sterling 24%, Swiss franc 6%
	Total of all currencies amount to 200%.
Counterparties	95% of business was between financial institutions, 5% was with non-financial institutions.
Brokers	67% of business was conducted through brokers

The top 17 firms accounted for 75% of the market.

19.3.2   Participants

Broadly speaking, there are three types of participant in the market: banks, brokers and customers.

♦ *Banks* participate as market-makers. That is, their dealers will at all times quote buying and selling prices for currencies. Other banks or corporations seek rates from the market-makers and may then buy or sell, giving the market-maker the opportunity to make a profit from the difference between the buying and selling rate, ie the spread. Dealers have to be ready to change their prices very quickly to avoid holding onto a depreciating currency or being short of rising currency, because exchange rates are constantly moving, particularly in volatile market conditions.

♦ *Voice brokers* act as intermediaries with telephone lines to banks throughout the world so that at any time they know which banks have the highest bid and offered rates. By telephoning a broker or listening to voice boxes it should be possible for banks to find the best dealing rate currently available. The broker does not deal on its own account but charges a commission for its services. Commission rates are not set, they are negotiable. Voice brokers have become less prevalent with the arrival of *electronic broking*.

♦ *Customers*, such as multinational corporations, are in the market because they require foreign currency in the course of their cross-border trade or investment activities.

19.4   Trading practice and procedures

19.4.1   Traditional dealing in the spot markets

To execute a spot deal in the market a dealer may telephone his counterpart at the market-making bank and ask him for his price, for example 'dollar-Swiss franc' (ie how may Swiss francs to the base currency, one US dollar). The market-maker normally quotes a two-way price. He stands ready to bid for or offer (up to some standard amount). The spread is the difference between these two prices and favours the market-maker. The spread of 10 'pips' or 'points' is the difference between the two prices. Each 'pip' is one hundredth of one cent. The sterling/dollar quotation is known as 'cable', which is a reference to the time when communications between London and New York was by undersea cables.

During interbank trading where participants know the 'big figure' (ie dollars and cents, Euro and cents), the dealer might quote only the points (the last two figures of the price). For example, if the rate for Euro against the dollar is 1.050-1.060, then the market maker will quote 'fifty-sixty'. He bids to buy Euro (the *base* currency in the case of the Euro) at Euro 1.050, selling dollars which is the currency or the *quoted* currency, and offers to buy dollars (sell Euro) at Euro 1.060.

If the caller wishes to deal he will hit, that is accept, one side of the price. The dealer will note the deal in his position records and pass the details of the trade to the back-office. Utilization against credit limits will be updated. Settlements staff will exchange confirmations and confirm instructions for payments. Nostro reconciliations staff will subsequently ensure that the respective currency amounts have been transferred into the designated accounts on the value date. If straight through processing is used these will be undertaken automatically.

19.4.2 Electronic trading and electronic broking

Dealing is conducted electronically either using *conversational trading systems* or using *automated-matching systems*. There are now several conversational trading systems available from a variety of providers. These follow the success of Reuters Monitor Dealing System, which was first used in 1981. The most up-to-date version from Reuters is Reuters Dealing 3000 Direct.

Anonymous electronic matching, or automated matching systems, of spot foreign exchange orders have became increasingly prevalent. Subscribers enter their bid or offer and the size of deal they will do at this rate into the system. The system automatically matches counterparties if there is mutual credit. Credit limits would have to be maintained on the system separately. Common platforms are the Reuters Dealing 3000 – Spot Matching and the solutions provided EBS (Electronic Broking Service). EBS is owned by 13 banks that are major participants in the foreign exchange market.

Deal sizes transacted tend to be in the USD 1m–5m range, which makes it an ideal way for smaller banks to execute trades. Previously small banks wishing to buy or sell would approach the large banks that would provide liquidity while taking a profit. Because of the transparency of the system – the amount, size and rate of the latest deals are posted on screens throughout the system – the spreads on trading have reduced significantly.

These systems cannot cover the whole of the market but only certain currency pairs. All the settlement details are pre-advised between the participants for each currency paid. More than half of spot trading in London is now done using electronic broking. Reuters states that its Reuters 3000 system has more than 19,000 users from over 6,000 organizations, providing considerable liquidity to the market. It allows straight-through processing and reduces back-office work.

Internet trading

E-commerce forex trading is developing as an additional distribution channel. Several new systems have been introduced – FXAll and Currenex being the most prominent at the time of writing. Some have already failed. EBS introduced an internet direct dealing facility in 2002 and Reuters has a competing product. Different groups of banks are involved in the different systems. Some banks may join several systems and some may be waiting to see which system will predominate before joining. The benefits are:

- ◆ simultaneous pricing – a search engine is the best way to get quotes from many sources;
- ◆ finer pricing, because pricing is more transparent. However, liquidity may be diluted and personal contact is lost. Will the lack of margins and profit reduce the number of banks who are market-makers?
- ◆ straight through processing – automation can be extended to front- and back-office systems, resulting in lower costs and better audit trails;
- ◆ free research and information is usually available on the sites.

Electronic broking, as opposed to voice broking, has now become the more prevalent way doing business. Its advantages are:

- ◆ transparent pricing;
- ◆ system checks credit availability;
- ◆ can support 24-hour trading;
- ◆ once the technology is set up, transaction costs are low;
- ◆ there is automatic position keeping and exchange of confirmations, enhancing risk monitoring and audit trails;
- ◆ reduced risk of error;
- ◆ there is no obligation to reciprocate quotes.

There are, however, some disadvantages, keeping some transactions away from electronic broking. The disadvantages are:

- ◆ the number of currency pairs traded is limited;
- ◆ deal sizes tend to be small (USD 1–USD 5m);
- ◆ deals are transacted only in round amounts;
- ◆ electronic broking fragments the spot market, which reduces overall liquidity;
- ◆ there is no exchange of information as with brokers which helps dealers to build up a picture of market sentiment.

19.4.3   Dealing in the forward markets

Forward exchange rates are derived from current spot rates, adjusted to take account of the interest rates for the respective currencies up to the forward value date. Trading and settlement is similar to spot trading, but systems must be in place to ensure payments with future value dates are not forgotten.

Reuters Dealing 3000 – Forward Matching includes automated forward foreign exchange dealing for a number of currency pairs and periods. A problem that this raises is limit setting. In spot dealing, it is relatively easy to agree a system for setting limits. Banks can apply straightforward dollar values to define the amount they are willing to trade with a particular counterparty. However, no two banks are likely to handle the allocation of forward credit limits in the same way. Reuters has a system of soft matching, which allows banks to give a simple yes or no credit indication for each participating bank.

Non-deliverable forwards (NDFs)

There is a forward market for non-convertible currencies, but delivery is by way of net payments in US dollars. Official 'spot' exchange rate fixings in the currency determine the amount payable.

SAFEs

There is a small market in synthetic agreements for forward exchange (SAFEs). This is a method of trading forward-forward positions (eg a three-six month SAFE transaction) without having to exchange principal amounts. This is a similar to using FRAs in the money markets. The SAFE market has not developed significantly and you do not need to know calculations relating to them for the examination.

19.5   Risks in foreign exchange dealing

The risks in foreign exchange dealing include trading and settlement risk.

19.5.1   Trading risks

Trading risks are operational risks, counterparty risk, open position risk and mismatch risk. Limits are applied and monitored to minimize these risks.

Operational risks includes accidental errors and deliberate concealment of errors. These can be avoided by training and experience, and by adequate control and audit procedures, the most important being the division between trading and settlements.

Counterparty risk for *spot* dealing covers the settlement risk. The risk of *forward* deals is that, if the counterparty is liquidated, the deal will have to be replaced at current market rates. A percentage, say 10 or 20% of the principal amount is taken as the amount at risk. Limits will take into account credit ratings, the period remaining on current deals and the volatility of the currencies traded.

Open positions are the extent to which a dealer is long on or short of, on its own account, for particular currencies and on which an exchange risk is run. Spot dealers need to adhere to their end-of-day and any intra-day open position limits.

Mismatch limits relate to forward positions. One way to unwind forward deals is to borrow or lend the respective currencies up to the value dates of the forward maturities. Potential losses or profits can then be calculated using current interest rates.

Stop-loss limits or the necessity to report adverse dealing positions at particular levels of loss must be clearly defined. Decisions can then be taken as to whether to close out the positions and crystallize losses.

19.5.2   Settlement risk

Traditionally, settlement risk had been considered a *daylight* exposure of a bank to the risk that the counterparty fails to deliver the bought currency when the sold currency had been paid away. The collapse of Bankhaus Herstatt in 1974 first highlighted these risks. The banking licence for this bank was withdrawn after it had received payment in D-Marks, but *before* its dollar payments had been processed in New York. We have already looked at settlement risk in previous chapters.

19.6   Spot and forward foreign exchange conventions and calculations

19.6.1   Spot foreign exchange

The following is an exchange rate of sterling and the US dollar, also called 'cable':

GBP 1 = 1.6110 – 1.6120

In this case the sterling is the **base currency**. Dollars are the **quoted currency** or the variable in the exchange rate quotation. The market practice as to what is the base currency is as follows:

- ◆ The Euro is the base currency in any exchange rate.
- ◆ Sterling is the base currency if it is one of the currencies, exempt when traded against the Euro. This practice still dates back from before the time of decimalization of sterling, where it would have been very complicated to use other currencies as base currencies.
- ◆ Australian and New Zealand dollars are the base currency, except against sterling and Euro.
- ◆ The US dollar is the base currency except against any of the above.

The rate quoted indicates that the market-maker is willing to buy sterling (sell dollars) at the bid price of 1.6010. The market-maker is willing to sell sterling (buy dollars) at the offered rate 1.6120. When market-makers are quoting prices, they quote only '10-20' (using the rates 1.6110–1.6120), because they assume that the counterparty knows that the 'big figure' is one sixty one.

Quoting a variable amount of dollars (the foreign currency) to one pound of sterling (the domestic currency) is called an indirect or reciprocal quotation. International practice is generally to use indirect quotations. If we said that we can sell one dollar for GBP 0.6242 and buy one dollar for GBP 0.6246 (USD 1 = GBP 0.6242 – 0.6246), this would be a direct quotation.

Where the quoted currency has less than 20 units per unit of base currency, rates are quoted for four decimal places. Japanese yen are quoted to two decimal places. The last decimal place is known as a 'pip' or 'point'.

19.6.2 Cross rates

A cross rate is an exchange rate that is calculated from two other rates. A NOK/ CHF rate (Norwegian krone to Swiss franc) can be calculated from a USD/NOK and a USD/CHF rate. Most trading is against the US dollar and exchange rates involving two currencies, neither of which is the US dollar, are referred to as cross rates.

The method of calculation depends on whether the currency rates in the calculation are both indirect (or both direct) *or* one rate is direct and one indirect.

(i)   Both indirect and reciprocal. You are given two rates against the USD, eg,

$$USD\ 1 = NOK\ 7.6484 - 7.6548$$
$$X$$
$$USD\ 1 = CHF\ 1.2965 - 1.2982$$

You, as a trader, want a NOK/CHF exchange rate. CHF will be the base currency. To calculate the rate at which *you* buy CHF/sell NOK, select the rates quoted by other banks at which you are able to:

- ◆ Buy the CHF in the market versus USD – use other bank's bid rate of 1.2965.
- ◆ Sell the NOK in the market versus USD – other bank's offered rate of 7.6548

The rule is to *divide* by the new base currency, ie,

$$NOK\ 1 = \frac{CHF\ 1.2965}{NOK\ 7.6548} = 0.1694$$

To calculate the rate at which you (as dealer) will sell CHF/buy NOK, select the rates at which you sell CHF v USD and buy NOK v USD, and *divide* by the new base currency.

$$NOK\ 1 = \frac{CHF\ 1.2982}{NOK\ 7.6484} = 0.1697$$

The cross rate is: NOK 1 = 0.1694 – 0.1697

The CHF/NOK is calculated as follows:

$$\text{CHF 1} = \frac{7.6484}{1.2982} = \text{NOK 5.8915} \qquad \text{CHF 1} = \frac{7.6548}{1.2965} = \text{NOK 5.9042}$$

(ii)   Where one currency is quoted directly and the other indirectly, the rule is to multiply the two bid and the two offered rates as in the following example using sterling and the South African rand:

$$\text{GBP 1} = \text{USD 1.6000} - 1.6010$$
$$\text{x} \qquad\qquad \text{x}$$
$$\text{USD 1} = \text{ZAR 7.8300} - 7.8400$$

Cross rate GBP/ZAR: 12.5280 – 12.5518

19.6.3   Outright forward foreign exchange calculation

A forward exchange rate is equivalent to the spot rate *minus* a premium or *plus* a discount. The forward premiums are determined according to the interest rates for the respective currencies and period.

Say a forward rate is sought by a client who wishes to buy dollars (sell sterling) in one month's time. The dealer will (in theory) buy the dollars now and invest them for one month and borrow sterling, to be repaid from the sterling he is due to receive.

In one month's time he will give the dollars to the client and use the client's sterling to repay his sterling loan. If dollar interest rates are lower than sterling rates, the dealer will earn less interest and will charge the 'loss' to the client by giving fewer dollars. Because he receives fewer dollars, dollars are said to be at a premium. The dealers calculate the forward rate using the spot rate *minus* the premium.

If dollar interest had been higher than sterling, the dealer would have earned more interest and would have given more dollars to the client. The dollars would be at a discount. The forward rate is the spot rate *plus* the discount.

Calculation of premium and discounts can be made in more than one way. Let us assume USD 1,000,000 is being sold by the dealer value in 30 day's time. Spot is GBP 1 = USD 1.6000 – 1.6010. The USD one-month rate is 2% (bid) and sterling 5% (offer).

(i)   Steps:

      Spot   Buy USD 1,000,000 now at GBP 1 = USD 1.6000

           Sell   GBP 625,000

Spot Invest USD 1,000,000 now at 3%, interest USD 2500.00, total USD 1,002,500.00

borrow GBP 625,000 at 5%, interest GBP 2,568.49, total GBP 627,568.49

Forward rate $= \dfrac{1,002,500.00}{627,568.49} = 1.5974$

Forward points $=$ 1.6000 less 1.5974 = 0.0026 (26 points) premium.

The quoted currency (USD) rate is at a premium because interest rates of the base currency (GBP) are higher than those of the quoted currency.

(ii)   The figures can be expressed in tabular form:

Interest calculation	USD amount	FX rate	GBP amount	Interest calculation
	1,000,000.00	1.6000	625,000.00	
3% x 30/360	2,500.00	0.0026	2,568.49	5% x 30/365
	1,002,500.00	1.5974	627,568.49	

Assuming the offered side of the forward quote is 0.0022, the two-way outright rate is:

$$1.6000 - 1.6010$$
deduct premium $$0.0026 - 0.0022$$
$$1.5974 - 1.5988$$

(iii)   The following formula gives an *approximate* figure for the premium or discount. The calculation uses the figures from the above example.

$$\frac{\text{Spot rate x interest rate differential x term}}{360 \times 100}$$

$$\frac{1.6000 \times 2.0 \times 30}{360 \times 100} = 0.0026$$

Where the forward rates are at a discount (interest rates for the quoted currency rate higher than those for the base currency), the discount is added to the spot rates. When calculating cross and forward rates, the spread will be wider than for the rates used in the calculation. If the spread has narrowed, then the calculation is incorrect.

19.6.4   Swaps and interest rate arbitrage

Swaps are a more common instrument than forwards. For swap calculations, if we know the interest rate for one of the currencies, the forward point and the spot rate, we can calculate the interest rate for the other currency when an FX swap is done.

There are three points to note:

♦ Where the spot rate is set it does not have a material effect on the calculation, it needs to be a market rate. Frequently the mid rate is used.
♦ When forward dealers agree a swap, it is normal practice in the interbank markets for the amount of the base currency to remain constant. A USD/EUR swap for USD 10m implies that the spot and forward dollar amounts are the same and that the currency amounts are different. If this is not the case, there is mismatch, which is taken account of in the trader's spot position.
♦ Dealers trade the forward points in the market.

Example: The forward dealer sells and buys USD 10,000,000 against CHF when the market is quoting 110 – 100 points. (Higher points on the left hand side indicate a premium.) Spot is set at USD = CHF 1.2965. The dealer is (buying dollars and) selling the Euro forward at 110 points premium (left hand side of the forward points). The payment flows for the dealer to record are:

Value			FX		
Spot	Pay	USD 10,000,000	1.2965	Receive	CHF 12,965,000
Forward	Receive	USD 10,000,000	1.2855	Pay	CHF 12,855,000

Two uses of swaps for trading purposes are:

♦ Interest arbitrage swaps to enable money market dealers to access a currency where the deposit market is not liquid, or swap surpluses into another currency to obtain a better return.
♦ Commercial paper arbitrage. For example, a Euro investor could enhance his return in Euro by investing in higher-yielding US commercial paper with a related forward exchange swap. This will not be tested for.

Interest arbitrage

A money market dealer has received a request for a loan of Swiss Francs 10,000,000 for 122 days. The Swiss Franc deposit market is thin, so he checks the USD = CHF 1.2965 and the forward points are 35-25. The money market dealer will 'buy and sell' CHF (right-hand side of the forward rate). The forward points tell you that CHF are at premium, ie, CHF interest rates are lower than USD rates. What is the cost of funding CHF?

Calculate: Amount of USD to be borrowed using spot FX rate

USD repayable at maturity

The CHF forward rate

The forward amount

The Swiss interest rate

In tabular form, the calculations are:

Interest	CHF amount	FX rate	USD amount	Interest
	10,000,000.00	1.2965	7,713,073.66	
? x 122/36,000	48,364.40	0.0025	52,277.50	2% x 122/360
	10,048,364.40	1.2940	7,765,351.16	

$$?CHF \text{ rate} = \frac{48,364.40 \times 36,000}{10,000,000.00 \times 122} = 1.42715\%$$

Note the following points:

◆ The forward dealer deals in constant amounts for one currency of the swap. However, there is a mismatch in the CHF spot and forward amounts. If the money market dealer is dealing with the forward dealer in his own bank, the forward dealer may take the mismatch into his position. If dealing with another bank, the money market dealer will have to cover the mismatch separately. The CHF interest would be sold forward for USD so that the profit on the deal is the USD.

◆ The money market dealer would round the CHF rate upwards to allow for costs and a profit margin.

Twenty

The London money markets

20.1 Trading practices and procedures

This chapter describes the characteristics of trading in the London money markets.

Currencies

Some 40 currencies are traded in London although most activity is in pound sterling, then US dollars and Euros. Liquidity in many of these less actively traded currencies will be thin.

Amounts

The rates quoted on screens are for market amounts. What constitutes a market amount is determined by market practice. In domestic sterling, this may be between GBP 5 to 10m. Below GBP 5m may be considered 'small', above GBP 50m may be considered 'large', and rates may be shaded (the spread widened) for such amounts. For US dollars, market amounts are, say, USD10m – USD 50m. The rates quoted may also differentiate the counterparty to the deal.

Periods

Most dealing is in overnight trading as banks and companies seek to balance their books. Money market trading is essentially short-term in nature and does not extend beyond 12 months. Although rates on screens are displayed for standard periods, eg, one, two and three months, most currencies are traded by dealers on a portfolio basis and it is possible for counterparties to deal for any period or 'odd date'.

Rates

Rates are quoted on an offer and bid basis, eg 7.125% – 7.000%. The offer rate is the rate at which the trader is prepared to lend money. The bid rate is the rate at which he is prepared to take deposits. In the London market the offered price is quoted first. The difference is the 'spread' but this is not an in-built profit for the dealer. It is only profit if other banks come to him and deal on his rates in matching amounts and periods. A single deal merely gives him the opportunity to make a profit.

Rates are usually quoted in basis points but may still be quoted in fractions for sterling. One basis point (bp) is $1/100$ of 1% or 0.01%. One quarter of 1% is 25bps.

Trading and settlement dates and times

Sterling is normally traded for same-day value. The cut-off time for trading is 16.20hrs when the CHAPS (Clearing House Automated Payment System) closes. Movements on call and notice accounts should be given by 12.00hrs. There is no minimum amount that can be transferred via CHAPS.

Eurocurrencies are traded for 'spot' value with settlement two business days after the trade date. These business days take account of holidays in London, or the country of the currency in question and, for most currencies, New York. Currency dealers generally balance their books at the beginning of the day after spot, which is known as 'tom' (for value tomorrow). For some currencies, eg Euros, dealers may trade until late morning on the 'tom' date.

The exceptions are US dollars and Canadian dollars where most dealing is for same-day value because the trades can be settled in New York or Toronto which are still open to settle the deals. Sterling deals can be concluded for value tom or spot.

Trades for standard periods, eg, one month, mature on the corresponding date in the month of maturity or on the next business day if that day is a weekend or a holiday. There is an exception to this: the 'end-end' rule. When a trade is completed on the last business day of a month for, say, a one-month period, it will mature on the last business day of the next month. For example, a deal for one month value 31 January will mature on 28 February (or earlier if the 28 February is a holiday).

LIBOR

The London interbank offered rate is the lending rate. The LIBOR for a given currency and period may change during the day. Banks 'fix' their LIBORs at 11.00 am each day and these rates are displayed on the screens. 11.00 am LIBORs are used where there is a contractual agreement to lend or fix rates in this way, as in syndicated loan or interest-rate swap agreements. All other rates quoted on brokers' screens are indicative rates only.

Both Reuters and Telerate display 11.00 am fixings as calculated by the British Bankers' Association (BBA) for seven currencies: US dollar, pound sterling, Euro, Swiss franc, Japanese yen, Australian dollar, and Canadian dollar. The following is the definition of the BBA Interest Settlement Rates (BBAISRs):

◆ USD, GBP, EUR, JPY, CHF: The rates from 16 banks are taken. The four highest and four lowest are disregarded. AUD, CAD: The rates from eight banks are taken. The two highest and two lowest are disregarded. The remaining rates in each case are averaged to five decimal places. The value date for sterling is same day, for other currencies the value date is spot, taking into account TARGET business days for the euro.

◆ The periods are overnight (spot-next for AUD, CHF and JPY), one and two weeks, one month through to twelve months.

◆ The panel of banks for each currency will be broadly representative on the market's liquidity in the currency.

Other centres have similar offered rates and fixings eg:

◆ Euribor: is the rate calculated for the Euro (fixed in Brussels).
◆ Sibor: Singapore interbank offered rate.

Day-count conventions

Interest in sterling is calculated on the basis of the number of days elapsed and a 365-day year (365/365), as is interest in South African rand, and Singapore and Hong Kong dollars. Interest on all other eurocurrencies is calculated on the basis of the actual number of days elapsed and a 360-day year (365/360). In the interbank market, interest is payable at the end of the fixture and annually if deposits are traded over 12 months. It is market custom for corporates to pay interest semi-annually on loans.

20.1.1 Trading practice and procedures

Trading between bank counterparties may be conducted with voice brokers, via Reuters dealing screens or telephone. Loudspeakers are also used in dealing rooms and brokers offices for brokers to convey current prices to the market. Deals with brokers are completed on the telephone.

Reuters dealing screens are the modern version of telexes. A dealer can call up another bank on his screen using that bank's code and request a price. A trade can be confirmed if the price is acceptable. Cryptic messages are the norm, eg this is a Norwegian krone trade:

- HIHI WHERE IS YOUR NOK ONE MONTH IN ABOUT 50 MIO

- 5.25 – 5

- MINE 50 MIO AT 5.25 WE TAKE AT DEN NORSKE OSLO

- OK DONE USUAL INSTCTIONS FOR US BIBIFN

The calling bank has borrowed NOK (Norwegian krone) 50 million for one month at 5.25%.

Credit limits must be in place and checked for all counterparties with which the bank is prepared to deal, that is, when funds are placed with the counterparty. When dealing through a broker, the name of the lender will be disclosed only when the borrower's name has been accepted by the lender.

The process without straight through processing is complex. As each trade is completed, a dealing ticket is prepared or the deal is keyed onto the screen. Keying allows the deal to be recorded directly in the dealer's position. The positions clerk records all money coming in and all payments out on the current value date(s). The dealer notes the deal in his maturity ladder and profit records. His aim is, first, to match all inflows and outflows during the day and then to ensure that the interest rate mismatch or gap position is within the pre-defined limits where individual deals are not matched.

Deposits received tend to be for shorter periods than placings (loans) and these mismatches may be maintained deliberately to take advantage of the yield curve (longer-term rates normally being higher than short-term rates). Where action has to be taken to reduce the interest rate gap, other markets or instruments may be used to achieve this, eg financial futures, repos, the issue of certificates of deposit or interest-rate swaps.

In less liquid currencies, it is quite usual to match deposits and loans through deposit arbitrage deals. For example, a deposit is taken in Norwegian krone where the dealer does not run a book and there are no other banks with which to place the funds profitably. The kroner are sold for dollars which are invested for the period in question. A forward swap is done to sell the dollars received at maturity in return for the kroner, which are returned to the original depositor. The calculations for this type of transaction are given in the previous chapter.

20.1.2 Settlement

The back-office receives details of the deal either from the dealing slip or the electronic entry. The back-office is responsible for making payments and monitoring receipt of funds, confirmations and recording the deal in the books of the bank.

Payments of currencies are made using the services of the bank's correspondent bank abroad, most likely using the SWIFT system (Society for Worldwide Interbank Financial Telecommunication). Banks use Standard Settlement Instructions. Risks are reduced by using CLS Bank for currency transactions.

Smaller corporate customers who maintain currency accounts at a local branch are sometimes unaware of the full instructions that must be given for payments. 'Pay USD to Barclays London' is insufficient. The full instruction might be 'Pay USD to Barclays New York, for account Barclays London, account XYZ'. As well as requesting its correspondent bank to transfer funds to Barclays Bank New York, the settlements area will send a SWIFT advice to Barclays, London, to advise the transfer of funds in New York.

A confirmation should be sent for each deal. This will identify the parties to the deal including brokers if used, the currency and amount, the trade, value and maturity dates, the interest rate and amount and payment instructions. Confirmations should be sent electronically and on the trade date where possible. An essential task is to monitor receipt and check the details of the counterparty's confirmation. Where confirmation is not received, systems should be in place to chase receipt after a short period.

It is an essential task of the nostro reconciliations section to check statements received from banks abroad, usually daily via the SWIFT system, in order to reconcile payments, monitor receipts and investigate any discrepancy in the bank's own records.

Recording the deals in the main books of the banks ensure that reports are generated for gap positions and profit records are checked against dealers' own records and by senior dealing management. Treasury, Financial Control, Risk Management and Audit units also have an interest in the trading exposures, balance-sheet assets and liabilities and profits.

20.2 Calculations

Examples of the following calculations are given:
- simple interest;
- given an interest amount, a period and a principal amount, calculate the rate of interest;
- annualized cost;
- the cost of breaking a fixture.

Simple interest

The formula is: $\dfrac{\text{Principal} \times \text{Rate} \times \text{Term}}{100 \times 365 \text{ or } 360}$

Example: A bank places USD 10,000,000 from 15 January to 15 February at 5.50%.

$$\dfrac{\text{USD } 10,000,000 \times 5.50 \times 31}{100 \times 360} = \text{USD } 47,361.11$$

You could say that USD 47,361.11 is the future value of USD 10,000,000. The calculation to give you the future value directly is:

$$\text{USD } 10,000,000 \times \left(1 + \dfrac{(5.50 \times 31)}{36,000}\right) = \text{USD } 10,047,361.11$$

If you are given an interest amount, a period and a principal amount, calculate the rate of interest.

Formula: $\dfrac{\text{Interest} \times 36,000 \text{ (or } 36,500)}{\text{Principal} \times \text{Term}}$

Using the interest amount above:

Calculation: $\dfrac{\text{USD } 47,361.11 \times 36,000}{\text{USD } 10,000,000 \times 31} = 5.50\%$

Annualized yield

Interest paid on a 360-day basis is more expensive that interest payable on a 365-day basis. But by how much? Simply multiply the rate of interest (eg 5.50%) by 365/360:

Calculation: $5.50 \times \dfrac{365}{360} = 5.5764\%$

Breaking a fixture

Money market deposits are non-negotiable and interbank deposits always go to maturity. However, banks may receive requests from commercial customers to repay deposits or loans early.

In the case of a loan fixture, the bank will seek to be compensated for any lower return on reinvesting the funds paid back early for the remaining term of the fixture. For example, a borrower asks to repay a 183-day loan of £ 5,000,000 at 10% pa after 140 days. The bank can only reinvest the funds at the current 43 day 'bid' rate of 9.5% pa. The cost of 0.5% pa of £ 2,945.21 (as calculated below) is added to the interest payable to the customer.

$$£5,000,000 \times \frac{0.5 \times 43}{36,500} = £2,945.21$$

The compensation is usually paid when the fixture is broken rather than at the maturity of the original loan. Where the compensation is significant, it may be discounted to present day value as follows:

$$£2,945.21 \times \frac{1}{1 + \frac{(9.5 \times 43)}{36,500}} = £ 2,912.61$$

Twenty one

Money market instruments

Objectives

This chapter will cover the following money market instruments:

♦ eligible bills;
♦ certificates of deposit;
♦ commercial paper;
♦ UK Treasury bills.

21.1   Introduction

Money Market Instruments (MMIs) in the London market are sterling eligible bills (also known as bankers acceptances), certificates of deposit (CDs), commercial paper (CP) and UK Treasury bills. MMIs are widely used for liquidity and collateral purposes by banks and the Bank of England (the Bank). Trading in MMIs is mainly a telephone market. However, there are two separate and distinct settlement processes. Either:

♦ MMIs in sterling are settled mainly as Eligible Debt Securities (EDSs) in CREST. The Bank conducts its daily Open Market Operations (OMOs) through the repo and outright purchase of a variety of instruments, of which sterling EDSs are a significant part;

or:

♦ MMIs in any of the currencies traded can be settled through the international clearing houses, Euroclear, Clearstream and BankOne.

21.1.1 Eligible Debt Securities (EDSs) in Sterling and Euro

CREST has been the clearing house for custody and settlement of sterling and euro EDSs in London since September 2003, when it took over the role of the Central Moneymarket Office (CMO). EDSs lodged and transferred within CREST have the following common features:

- ◆ They are fully dematerialized. There are no separate definitive certificates.
- ◆ They are distributed as 'issues' rather than separate physical instruments. An issue represents all instruments with the same features.
- ◆ Trading is possible in denominations of one penny. The minimum issue is usually £100,000 and higher trading amounts may be specified.
- ◆ Issues are fungible. Any part of an issue has exactly the same characteristics as another part (so further tranches of an existing issue can be made).
- ◆ Issues of MMIs are identified by an International Securities Identification Number (ISIN), which is allocated by CREST, bringing them into line with other internationally traded instruments.
- ◆ CREST records will serve as the definitive record of ownership of dematerialized MMIs.

In the CREST settlement system, title and transfers of title are evidenced by entries on an electronic register. This is different from physical or paper MMIs, which are negotiable instruments, where full rights are transferred to new holders on delivery on the instrument.

Issuers of EDSs sign 'Deeds' which ensure that holders of securities issued under it acquire directly enforceable rights against the issuer. There are two versions of the Deed, one for CDs and CPs, and the other for sterling eligible bills. This is because sterling eligible bills are 'two name' paper. The accepting bank signs the Deed and the 'drawers' of bills sign a Deed of Adherence and Issuer Application Form.

Settlement procedures follow CREST practices and daily timetable. Participation in CREST will be either direct or through a direct member. Accounts are held in CREST for cash and instruments. There is an assured payment system on a Delivery versus Payment basis.

21.1.2 MMIs settled through clearing houses

The clearing houses, Euroclear, Clearstream and BankOne, act as Issuing and Paying Agents (IPAs) for issues of CDs and CP in physical format (definitive certificates or global notes) in the currencies in which these instruments can be issued. These need to conform to the British Bankers' Association requirements for physical instruments, which are set out at the end of this chapter.

21.2 Eligible bank bills

The definition of a bill of exchange is contained in the Bills of Exchange Act 1882:

> 'A bill of exchange is an unconditional order in writing, addressed by one person to another, signed by the person giving it, requiring the person to whom it is addressed to pay on demand or at a fixed or determinable future time a sum certain in money to or to the order of a specified person or to bearer.'

An eligible bank bill is a bill that is accepted by a bank listed by the Bank of England for eligibility. It must meet the strict criteria of the Bank for bill eligibility. Treasury bills and local authority bills are also eligible for rediscount at the Bank. The former are issued by the Debt Management Office and the latter by local authorities. Although such authorities do not have a lender of last resort, they are funded by government as well as locally and there is a general expectation that they would not be allowed to fail. More recently there have also been issues of Bank of England Bills.

Eligibility criteria for a bill to be eligible to be bought in the Bank's open market operations are:

- be in sterling for a tenor of no more than 187 days;
- not be payable outside the UK;
- not be drawn on a bank;
- no shareholding link or management control between the drawer of the bill and the acceptor;
- be accepted by one of the eligible banks.

All sterling eligible bills are settled as EDSs in CREST. The purpose of drawing sterling bills on banks and having them discounted is for banks and companies to obtain short-term finance. The holder obtains funding by selling the bills on a discounted basis. The terms 'acceptances', 'bills' and 'eligible bills' tend to be used interchangeably when bills are drawn. The volume of eligible bills outstanding at December 2001 was £11 billion.

21.2.1 Eligible banks

Most of the Bank's money market operations involve eligible bills. The Bank maintains a published list of institutions whose acceptances are eligible for discount at the Bank. Eligibility is based on the Bank's judgement about whether a bank has a substantial and broad-based existing sterling acceptance business in the UK and where they can command the finest rates in the market for ineligible bills. Foreign or foreign-owned institutions can be eligible if there are reciprocal arrangements for British banks in their domestic market. There is no official Bank limit on the volume of acceptance business written by eligible institutions, but the Bank does set its own internal limits on the proportion of its own portfolio that a particular acceptor's paper may represent.

21.2.2   Liquidity dealing and processing

The main advantage of bills to a corporate treasurer is that they may be cheaper than short-term borrowings or overdrafts. This is partly the case because of the liquidity in the market, which in turn is driven by the Bank of England's eligibility criteria. Furthermore, once accepted, they become the liability of the bank in the secondary market (as well as of the corporate) on the redemption date.

21.2.3   The primary market – acceptance and discounting

Dealing will take place before 12.00 noon for same day value but can be done for value 'tom' or 'spot'. Subject to the notice of drawdown being given, drawings by a company under a syndicated loan will usually have the discount rate set at 10.30 am Trades should be for a minimum of £250,000.

The bill dealer will agree the amount, period, discount rate and net proceeds with the counterparty. Discount rates are quoted in decimals in the market. Details of the trade are passed to the back office. The bill dealer has the options either of holding the bills or of rediscounting them in the market.

The Settlements office will arrange for the discounted proceeds to be paid to the counterparty's account with the bank or via the CHAPS system, for a confirmation of the deal to be sent and for details of the bill to be 'lodged' electronically at CREST.

At maturity, the face value of bills is settled through the CREST payment system. Companies may arrange new bills, the discounted proceeds of which will cover most of the amount due on maturing bills. They need then only pay the discount, plus acceptance commission to the accepting bank.

21.2.4   The secondary market

Banks hold bills as part of their liquidity portfolios, but those the bank has accepted itself will not qualify for liquidity purposes. This is because, if a bank has liquidity difficulties, it is unlikely it will be able to sell its own paper. This is why banks sell bills they have accepted and purchase bills accepted by other banks. Banks can 'swap' bills with each other in order to obtain instruments which qualify as liquid assets.

21.2.5   Other types of bills

There are no liquid markets in bills which are not eligible bills. The rates charged by banks when discounting ineligible or trade bills will be the same as 'cash' rates. Trade bills are drawn by one company on another company. They may be sight or term bills. They may be accompanied by trade documents, as with documentary credits and cannot be settled in CREST.

21.2.6   Calculations

The calculations relating to a bill are deceptively simple compared to some instruments, but the discount rate belies the true financial cost to the drawer, which is always higher. This is because, while it is a discounted rate on a nominal amount, it is actually a proportional cost on the slightly smaller discounted amount (ie the amount actually received, after discount and commission). For the purposes of the following calculations, we shall assume no commissions or fees.

The basic calculations are those of the discount the grossed-up yield, the net proceeds and the discount-to-yield differential. The basic formula is as follows:

$D = P \times R/100 \times T/365$

> Where D is the cost of the discount,
> P is the principal amount,
> R is the discount rate,
> T is the original tenor.

For example, a 60-day bill discounted at 6% for a principal amount of £1 million produces the following:

Discount cost = £1000000 x 0.06 x 60/365 = £9863.01p

The net proceeds for the drawer would be £1000000 – 9863.01 = 990136.99p

The yield rate is $\dfrac{D \times 365 \times 100}{Proceeds \times T}$ $\dfrac{£9863.01 \times 365 \times 100}{£990136.99 \times 60}$ = 6.06%

The discount-to-yield differential is 6.06 – 6.00 = 6 basis points

In order to 'gross up' a bill to a round amount, the formula is changed slightly, as follows:

Where A is the 'round' discounted amount to be received:

Amount (A) is $P - \dfrac{P \times R \times T}{365 \times 100}$

$= P - P \times 6 \times 60/36500$
$= P - P \times 0.009863013$

$$= P (1 - 0.009863013)$$
$$= 0.990136987 P$$

Therefore the principal for repayment, P, is A/0.990136987

So, if the required proceeds are £1,000,000 the principal is 1,000,000/0.990136987 = £1,009,961.26p

21.3 Certificates of deposit

Certificates of deposit (or CDs) are negotiable certificates, in bearer form, which in effect are evidence of an underlying deposit with a bank or building society. They were invented in the US and have become widely used throughout the world. The time or term bank deposit market has been in existence for centuries and particularly for short periods did not present liquidity difficulties until recent times. The volatility which has become characteristic of the last 35 years or so, has led to a need for a variety of short-term instruments which could be held to maturity, but have become negotiable in order to enhance the liquidity of funds. A bank deposit evidenced by a piece of paper was always in theory been negotiable, provided the necessary terms and protections were present. Indeed, non-negotiable CDs were in circulation but they did not become negotiable until 1961 in the US. Since then CDs have developed into a huge global feature of money markets.

21.3.1 Development history

Five years after the issue of CDs in New York, they were issued in London. Since then, they have developed in many different markets in a number of different forms, leading to a complex array of possible terms and equally complex calculations. London dollar CDs were first issued in May 1966 and represented the first new money market instrument since the previous century. Eurodollar CDs were issued in 1966 also, before sterling CDs started life in London in October 1968 as a result of provisions in the Finance Act of that year. This allowed for the payment of interest without deduction of tax. The Banking Act of 1987 took matters further.

The maximum term of dollar CDs had been extended to five years in 1967 and when sterling CDs were first authorized their term ranged from three months to five years. The shorter term has since been reduced to seven days and the London market has become highly liquid except in brief times of banking or monetary crisis.

Further developments included: the floating rate CD (FRCD) in April 1977 (there are now also renegotiable CDs), discounted Eurodollars in May 1981, the Special Drawing Rights-based CD (SDRCD) in June 1980 (London January 1981), the European Currency Unit (ECU) CDs in 1983, Euroyen in 1984, and other currencies (mainly limited to their own domestic markets) since. A UK-based buyer or trader (let alone an international fund) would need to take care and be clear about what was being bought and the specific terms accounting, dealing and settlement and tax consequences of each. FRCDs are now relatively rare.

The 1983 Finance Act permitted building societies to issue CDs of up to one year term and pay interest gross. From January 1987, following the Building Societies Act 1986, societies were permitted to issue CDs in any currency and from June 1987, the tax provisions were relaxed to allow payment of interest gross for maturities up to five years, thereby harmonizing the treatment with banks. Only societies with assets up to GBP 1 billion are able to issue CDs, but the market has developed well, based on the inherent security of these institutions. A credit rating is not needed for CDs, but a rating for a building society undoubtedly enhances the ability to issue in other currencies and markets.

21.3.2 Types of CDs

There is as wide a range of different types of CD as there is of any instrument dealt in the London money markets. CDs can be issued for terms from seven days to five years, in fixed- or variable-rate form, discounted or at par. Issues can be by tap, in a tranche or in a renewable, rolling programme. Issuers would be banks or building societies, in a range of currencies and composite currencies, such as the SDR, in London or overseas (mainly the US). In addition, they are issued in many other currencies in the financial centres relevant to the country of origin. Some markets are less well regulated or protected than others. By far the most important market is the US, where CDs and many of these associated practices in fact originated. There are certain differences however.

Gross interest is normally paid at maturity, but for tenures over one year and up to five years, interest is paid annually. If that is not enough, however, one-, two-, three- four- and five-year CDs may be issued for up to a few days beyond the anniversary because of the business day falling on a weekend or public holiday and dollar CDs are issued on the basis of a 360-day year.

21.3.3 Discount CDs

Discount CDs resemble ordinary CDs in every respect except that they carry no rate of interest. Instead they are issued at a discount which equates to a rate of interest when the CDs are repaid at par at maturity. They can be dealt with on a yield-to-maturity or a discounted basis in the market. The method of calculation of the interest rate purchase at issue or the interim proceeds if sold at maturity is a further feature of CDs, but is similar in principle to a Treasury or eligible bill. These are also known as zero-coupon CDs or 'zeros'.

21.3.4 The London Market for CDs

BBA guidelines

In March 1984, the British Bankers' Association (BBA) issued a book of guidelines on the sterling CD market. This incorporated for the first time the concept of London Good Delivery Standards. These standards were to become the basis of a common set of standards throughout the London market. In November 1990, the BBA booklet was updated by another BBA publication *Certificates of Deposit on the London Market: Market Guidelines*. Its latest version is the *London Market Guidelines for Certificates of Deposit* from October 1996. They are approved by the London Discount Market Association, the International Money Market Trading Association and the Building Societies Association. They incorporate the London Good Delivery Standards. The above are standard reference texts and should be read in conjunction with the present chapter, especially to obtain a wider understanding of the calculations and more detail on terms, conditions, etc.

Financial Services Authority and the London Code

The issue and trading of CDs in London are subject to the Financial Services and Markets Act 2000 (FSMA) and regulation by the Financial Services Authority. In addition the Bank of England (the Bank), in its role as guardian of financial stability, retains an important role for the market. The notice issued by the Bank of England in 1996, entitled 'Issues of Certificates of Deposit in London' remains as relevant as ever.

The primary market

The London market is effectively divided into two parts: the primary and secondary markets. Banks and building societies participate actively in both.

The primary market in London involves the process of a bank or building society issuing CDs to depositors. In other words, the depositor (or investor) is effectively placing funds with the institution, in return for which he gets a certificate acknowledging their deposit in negotiable bearer form. For a lower interest rate, the investor is making a deposit, which is repayable at the end of the term of deposit. In the event that he needs the cash sooner, he may negotiate the certificate in the secondary market. He will obtain most, if not all, of its principal value, depending on whether interest rates have risen or fallen in the intervening period. The CDs are issued 'prime' to the first investor and if the same investor holds them to maturity, he will be repaid at face value, together with the agreed rate of interest, never having entered the secondary market.

Banks wishing to issue CDs will approach counterparties direct or through brokers (without their name being divulged at this stage) with details of the period and amount they wish to issue. Investors wishing to purchase CDs will ask potential issuers directly or through brokers, indicating the period and amount they wish to invest. If the terms and issue size are acceptable to both counterparties, a trade will be agreed.

Sterling CDs are dealt before 12.00 noon for same day value. Currency CDs are normally dealt for spot value but US and Canadian dollar CDs can be dealt for 'tom' or same day value. Sterling CDs are lodged and settled either in CREST in dematerialized form or, for currency CDs, through one of the clearing houses, using definitive or global CDs.

The secondary market

The 'secondary market' refers to transactions in CDs that take place between issue and redemption. There are three main reasons for such transactions: first, a principal holder who originally intended to hold to maturity may find that he has need of liquidity before that date. If that likelihood is never going to arise, he would do better simply to make a time deposit for the same period and obtain a slightly better rate. Then there are two speculative reasons: some investors 'play the yield curve'. In normal circumstances, the rate of interest for longer-term deposits will be higher than that for short-term money. An investor in prime three-month CDs, for example, may intend to invest at the three-month rate and sell after two months, when the interest rate for one-month CDs would be expected to be lower. The speculation would then be that the effective return for the two-month period of investment would be better than simply having bought two-month CDs in the first place. Of course, interest rates in general and the shape of the yield curve may change during the investment period, which adds to the speculative nature of the investment. Finally, some investors may feel they have a better view of the future trend of interest rates than others. If they feel rates will fall over the next month, they might buy three- or six- month CDs, knowing that their value will rise with interest rates, enabling an 'extraordinary' short-term gain. Investors, who have to maintain short-term, liquid portfolios of money market investments are always looking for sensible ways to improve what might otherwise be a disappointing return on funds.

A secondary market is implicit in the concept of CDs, because if investors never intended to realize their 'certified' deposits, they could simply make an ordinary bank deposit, hold to maturity and collect a higher return. Buying CDs will therefore almost certainly mean that they will be traded before maturity. It is not unusual for a particular CD to be traded more than once in a day, in an active market. If an investor buys and sells the same CD in one business day, making a gain from the beneficial move in interest rates for that particular maturity, the return is effectively infinite because the sale and purchase transactions produce a profit for a net nil movement of principal.

The secondary market consists of a number of market makers (banks and investment houses who regularly quote buying and selling rates for various maturity dates), together with active investors such as the major building societies, which regularly trade in and out. It is augmented by the intervention of brokers who bring potential buyers and sellers together. Any principal investor would prefer to deal direct, if possible, because the brokerage can represent a major slice of the possible gain. The secondary market is important for four reasons:

- ◆ it provides liquidity for holders of CDs;
- ◆ it enables the widest possible choice of 'names' and maturities;
- ◆ it helps to avoid overissue of CDs by any one name (where this occasionally happens, the rate for that CD moves adversely or the paper 'sticks' until the issuer's supply is judged to have moderated);
- ◆ it provides one of the markets for trading and speculation in short-term liquid instruments.

London CDs

It is important to distinguish between 'London CDs', 'non-London CDs' and foreign currency 'London CDs'.

A London CD is a negotiable instrument in bearer form certifying that a stated principal sum has been deposited for a specified period with the issuing institution, at a specified rate of interest or discount, or at a floating rate set from time to time by a predetermined mechanism. Such CDs may be issued only by institutions authorized to accept deposits under FSMA. The Bank of England also requires standard terms and conditions in order to ensure homogeneity and minimize investor confusion. All CDs must show: the currency denomination, maturity, minimum denomination of certificate, and the bases and calculation process for interest. For good delivery in the secondary market, they must also meet the 'London Good Delivery' standards.

Non-London CDs are CDs issued by institutions that are not authorized as above, but which are nevertheless intended to be issued and traded in London. The Bank will allow these, provided they are clearly marked 'non-London' on their face, they meet the standards of London Good Delivery, they do not infringe FSMA, and purchasers are informed clearly where a UK issuing or paying agent is being used.

Foreign currency London CDs are London CDs issued in a Bank approved currency (eg USD, Yen, Canadian dollar, Australian Dollar, SDRs or Euros) or in another currency where the Bank is satisfied by written evidence that the relevant banking authorities in the parent country approve. Accordingly, foreign currency London CDs are either issued by UK-based institutions or the London branches of overseas-based banks (but governed by English law). Interest is paid free of all UK taxes, but the settlement arrangements are different (usually being made in the financial centre for the relevant currency on a two business-day money market basis). All the elements of interest, settlement and maturity can be handled by dealers in London. Holding and delivery should also be in London in order to minimize the possible consequences of mistakes.

Issue term

CDs can be issued for a term of seven days to five years. (Occasionally this may extend up to a few days over, due to the fifth anniversary date not being a business day. In this case, settlement would ordinarily be for the earliest business day thereafter and would be fixed at the time of issue. Where a maturity date later becomes a non-business day, settlement should be on the earliest business day following, unless this is in a new month, in which case the latest business day preceding would be used.)

CDs are issued by 'tap', by 'tranche' or under a medium-term re-issuable CD facility (known as a rollover facility or 'roly-poly'). Most issues are by tap, where the issuing institution wishes to issue direct to the market, without using a securities house as a medium. This allows the investor to meet the wishes of the buyer direct, without his having to resort to the secondary market at possible disadvantageous terms (eg where the original buyer has already taken a 'turn' or commission to a broker may be involved, thereby reducing the effective return to maturity). CDs are often issued for straight monthly maturities, such as one, two, three, six months, etc. Where the investor needs to match the maturity to a dated cash requirement, they may have to resort to the secondary market to buy secondary CDs to match. Alternatively, they could buy 'prime' CDs for a longer date, with the intention of selling secondary on the desired date. This does leave the investor hostage to fortune for the market conditions prevailing on the date of sale.

Tranche CDs are blocks of fixed or floating rate CDs which are placed privately with investors by securities houses, normally within an agreed programme. The securities house will balance investor interest, market conditions and interest rates for CDs, which may well be for names that might not normally be readily issuable, especially in such size. Many CDs may not see the light of day, or, if traded, the secondary market may be thin, requiring careful judgement by the investor or support by the securities house(s). An overseas bank with an authorized London branch might use this route. As with all issues, the volume must be carefully judged in order to avoid overissue because this will damage the secondary market for such paper and prejudice the possibility of future issues until the market position eases. A further consequence would be that the interest rate required to issue would be higher and although this increases the cost to the issuer, it also increases the possibility that an investor could achieve a better return from an acceptable name CD than a time deposit with a clearing bank.

21.3.5 Dealing and risks

Dealing

Clarity, flexibility, responsibility and adherence to the London Code are fundamental to efficient and secure dealing in the secondary market for CDs. Some of the characteristics have been discussed earlier. Fixed-rate CDs are dealt on a yield-to-maturity basis and FRCDs on price plus accrued interest. Being bearer instruments, passing without endorsement, there is no contingent liability after sale. Dealing for same-day value is up to 12.00 noon. Starting in the late 1980s this has led to very early dealing hours in London for eager traders. Foreign currency CDs are for two-day settlement. The normal practice on delivery is for the issuer to deliver prime CDs and the seller (or his holding agent) to deliver secondary paper. Initially this was done by messenger in bundles of physical paper, but this practice has reduced greatly since CDs were dematerialized.

Banks' use of CDs

Virtually all London banks play two or more roles in the CD market. Many issue CDs. Most will buy or trade secondary CDs, which have grown in volume to become a major component of short-term liquidity in the London markets. Some may act in the role of a securities house for the issue and support of tranches of CDs or roly-polys.

As traders of secondary CDs, they face the same risks as others, although some may have greater familiarity with the CD market by virtue of their long-term presence or their position as regular issuers of paper. Nevertheless, as for all highly tradeable negotiable bearer instruments, there are potential security and liquidity risks. CDs can have a material bearing on a bank's liquidity, both as issuer and trader and investor.

Banks as issuers

As issuer, a bank may well build up substantial amounts of issued CDs as part of its funding position. CDs should ideally be used for short-term liquidity purposes (except for the less liquid medium-term CDs, roly-polys and FRCDs). However, especially for the better quality names, a large total issuance can become a fairly stable sizeable liability. An interesting comparison would be commercial paper because in the US especially, what is essentially a very short-term instrument can be built up into a huge medium-term funding mechanism though a programme of issues. For as long as the market is stable and investors remain confident (reassured by the short-term ratings of the paper), the position can be sustained.

Markets are built on confidence and when that confidence is undermined only the very best names may trade at the keenest prices, or even at all in the same cases.

The problem becomes more acute as maturities come up for an issuer. If paper issues cannot be replaced, the only resorts are to borrow on short-term deposit or run down one's own holdings of short-term instruments. The latter can exacerbate the problem.

Even in a stable market, an issuer must guard against overissuing paper – not only intotal, but also in clusters around particular dates. Once an institution's paper starts to 'stick' for a particular maturity, it can affect the marketability of all but the shortest maturities and therefore also impact both the price and issuability of fresh supplies. The whole process is one requiring care, diligence and professionalism. Buying in and redeeming paper would not normally be allowed, except in extreme circumstances. Although CDs are not rated like other instruments, the rating accorded to instruments of a similar maturity is bound to impact on at least the price of CDs. Furthermore, while it is an instrument itself which bears the rating, the latter is a very public appraisal of the credit standing of the whole institution itself. High rating (the best) is an assurance that the issuer will have the stability and solvency to be able to repay principal and interest at maturity. If that rating slipped for, say commercial paper, it would clearly cast doubts on the similar viability of CDs of the same issuer. Relationship management is a highly desirable aptitude for any banker, but especially so with regard to the rating agencies. Banks may not wish to pay for a rating, but the need is determined by investor demand and therefore it will probably find that each institution carries a rating anyhow. This must be nurtured. Even where CDs are underwritten as part of a facility, the support of the underwriter could not be guaranteed if a rating was in doubt in the markets.

Banks as investors

As an investment, good-quality CDs are highly liquid. However, there is a massive cross-dependency between each other's deposits and short-term instruments. For a long time, cross-holdings of building society paper were tightly controlled by HM Treasury because of the concern that liquidity would become illusory. It would not take a doomsday scenario to make CDs unissuable in the short term for a large number of banks and building societies. In such circumstances, there is always a flight to quality and if the extreme did arise, it is doubtful whether even the very best names could be sustained as an alternative to government securities in times of uncertainty. The same could arise when, for example, interest rates change or are expected to rise. There is an inverse link between market expectations of rates and the capital value of CDs. As one or two worked examples will quickly demonstrate, the shorter the term to maturity, the smaller the capital deterioration in adverse circumstances. Of course, it may always be possible to hold the instruments to maturity, thereby suffering only the opportunity cost, while still accruing the investment return originally expected at the time of purchase. Where the investor is running a matched book, the loss on holdings will be offset by the savings on cost of funds as rates rise. In any case it would be a wise precaution to have limits for each institution whose paper a bank might hold. These might well be set in relation to the size of that institution's published capital resources.

21.3.6 Calculations

In the primary market, interest-bearing CDs have interest calculated on the same basis as money market deposits. Discount CDs are quoted on a discount to yield basis.

The proceeds formula for sterling CDs with a maturity of less than one year is:

$$A \times \frac{(365 \times 100) + (R \times T)}{(365 \times 100) + (Y \times D)} = P$$

Where   A =   Principal

R =   Interest rate on CD

T =   Tenor of CD in days

Y =   Yield purchased

D =   Days remaining at purchase

P =   Proceeds by seller

The yield earned by the original depositor during the period he held the CD is calculated by:

$$Y = \frac{I}{A \times D/365}$$

Where: Y =   Yield earned
I =   Income earned
A =   Face value of CD
D =   Number of days CD was held

Sale of a CD with an original maturity of up to one year: A £1,000,000 CD, issued with an original maturity of 91 days at 5.25%, is sold after 30 days (61 days remaining) when the secondary market dealer was quoting 5.00% – 5.125%.

The right hand side of the quotation, 5.125%, is used because that is the rate the seller has to pay or 'borrow' for the funds for the remaining period. This is the rate quoted in the Financial Times, ie the rate at which banks are prepared to buy other prime bank's CDs. There are two ways of calculating the sale proceeds.

The seller receives the amount payable at maturity, discounted to present day value:

$$\text{Maturity amount} = £1,000,000 + £1,000,000 \times \frac{5.25 \times 91}{100 \times 365} = £1,013,089.04$$

Discounted to NPV: $\dfrac{£1,013,089.04}{1 + (5.125 \times 61/36500)} = \dfrac{£1,013,089.04}{1.008565068} = £1,004,485.55$

Using the above example:

Proceeds $= £1,000,000 \times \dfrac{(5.25 \times 91) + 36500}{(5.125 \times 61) + 36500} = \dfrac{36,977.75}{36,812.63} = £1,004,485.55$

Yield: The seller received £4,485.56 for holding the CD for 40 days. In yield terms, this is:

$\text{Yield} = \dfrac{£4,485.55 \times 36500}{£1,000,000 \times 30} = 5.4574\,\%$

Expressed another way:

$\text{Yield} = \dfrac{\text{Income received}}{\text{Face amount} \times \dfrac{\text{days held}}{365}} \times 100 = \dfrac{4,485.55}{£1,000,000} \dfrac{\times\,100}{\times\,\dfrac{30}{365}} = 5.4574\%$

21.4   Commercial paper

Commercial paper (CP) is short-term promissory notes issued in programmes, mainly by corporates, but also by financial services organizations, banks, utilities, public authorities and sovereign borrowers, in a range of currencies, in the US, Europe, the UK and other markets such as Japan.

Promissory notes are in effect a written promise to pay an amount by an agreed future date. Thus a promissory note differs from a mere acknowledgment of debt, without any promise to pay. In its form a promissory note usually contains a promise to pay, at a time therein expressed, a sum of money to a certain person therein named, or to his order, for value received. It is dated and signed by the maker. A promissory note bears little resemblance to a bill of exchange; yet, when endorsed, it is exactly like one; for then it is an order by the endorser of the note upon the maker to pay to the endorsee. The endorser is as it were the drawer; the maker, the acceptor; and the endorsee, the payee. Most of the rules applicable to bills of exchange equally affect promissory notes.

Commercial paper originated in the US, in the early 20th century. To give some idea of scale, at the beginning of 2003 the Fed reported that there was about USD 1.3 trillion of outstanding commercial paper with thousands of diverse issuers. Financial companies and large companies undertake most of issuance. Nowadays, many British organizations tap the US markets, with issuance programmes up to USD 1 billion or more. Although commercial paper is short-term by nature and the average maturity varies up to 40 days or more, it has nevertheless provided what are effectively stable medium-term funds for issuers, because maturities are rolled over repeatedly. It has also helped to spawn a medium-term note (MTN) market. Both types of investment are now issued throughout the world and in many currencies.

The success of the US market not surprisingly encouraged the establishment of a sterling commercial paper (SCP) market, which came into existence in 1987. The BBA and the Association of Corporate Treasures jointly published 'interim guidelines' in December 1986, drawn from the experience in the USA and wide consultation. This has been replaced by the *Commercial Paper: The London Market Guidelines*, jointly published by the same organizations in November 1996 and now available from the BBA. Many of the detailed aspects of the issue, dealing and management of SCP programmes are covered in this document. Its latest update was issued in 2000: *London Market Guidelines: Commercial Paper 2000*.

It covers issues such as how to establish and operate a CP programme, the documentation involved, issuing and clearing procedures, legal and regulatory aspects and calculations. The appendices include information on exempt transactions and specimen examples.

The SCP market pales in size compared to the US CP market. The Bank of England reported that outstanding issues at the end of 2002 amounted to no more than sterling £20 billion. Reported issues during 2002 totalled £126 billions.

Much of this chapter will deal with sterling commercial paper (SCP) which takes the form of negotiable short-term bearer debt securities with maturities from seven to 364 days, denominated in sterling, issued and payable in the UK. It is similar in kind to US dollar commercial paper (USCP). Now mature in many markets around the world, CP has become a highly flexible and useful addition to the choice of short-term instruments available to borrowers and investors in the UK. CP is also issued in other currencies in London and Europe, including Eurocommercial paper (ECP). ECP paper can be issued into the Eurocurrency markets in a variety of currencies.

Euronotes are short-term, fully negotiable promissory notes, usually denominated in US Dollars, Euros or Sterling. As such they are a sub-sector of the eurocommercial paper markets. They are issued at a discount and are typically of 1, 3 or 6 months maturity. They are issued under facilities offered by banks to corporates. Some facilities include an arrangement to place the notes among potential investors. Other facilities are based on underwriting agreements. Under them the borrower will receive the funds from the underwriters, who then either take on the credit risk themselves or sell it on. Euronotes are no longer common.

21.4.1 Legal, regulatory and documentation

Legislation and regulation

The FSA regulates the banks and dealers involved in the CP process, based on FSMA. Proceeds received under a CP issue in the UK fall under the definition of deposit taking. However, these provisions do not apply for proceeds accepted outside the UK. This has helped the development of the ECP market, where proceeds are received in New York for US dollars, Tokyo for yen, etc.

FSMA is also relevant to SCP in relation to: authorization or exemption of dealers, regulation of investment business and advertisements, and its general provisions on misleading statements and practices relating to false markets and misleading investors. It is not practicable for each issue of SCP to be accompanied by a prospectus and therefore great care must be taken with the preparation of a document, which may come to be regarded as a prospectus for the purposes of the Companies Act. In general, issuers should take care before distributing any material relating to an issue, because it could fall foul of these statutes. A private limited company must also take very great care before it issues, if at all, because normally only public limited companies (plc's) are allowed to do so.

Documentation

The documentation of CP is in theory for agreement between the issuer and any other parties to the agreements. It is not necessary to 'reinvent the wheel' however. With the volume of issues that has taken place standard forms are readily available. The usual documents would be a dealership agreement, an issuing and paying agency agreement and an information memorandum for circulation to potential investors. SCP issues would normally be governed by English law.

The price of SCP is primarily a function of market rates and the credit standing of the issuer. Rating agencies play a role here. Some issues are guaranteed; this would ordinarily be to enhance the credit and therefore the price of the paper. In this case, the guarantee would be included in the issue documentation. Typically, the guarantee would be provided by the parent of an issuer, or a bank or sovereign guarantor.

The CP notes (or certificates) themselves may be in definitive or global form. In definitive form, they look like a sophisticated (and often ornate) share or bond certificate, but must conform to the London Good Delivery standards and be printed on security printed paper, unless they are held in a dematerialized form. In global form, they are merely evidence of a tranche of paper and therefore do not need to be security printed. Again the note will conform to London Good Delivery because it will be deposited with and settled through a recognized clearing system. It must be exchangeable at any time for definitive notes, conforming as above.

Dealer agreement

This is an agreement between the issuer (the guarantor, if relevant) and the dealers on the programme. Typically it would cover:
- ◆ issue and purchase duties, obligations and other arrangements;
- ◆ issuer's representatives and warranties, covenants and indemnities;

- securities laws and other relevant restrictions on the offer of paper;
- commission, fees and expenses;
- information provision arrangement for the Bank of England;
- conditions precedent to be provided by the issuer or guarantor.

Issuing and paying agency agreement

While the bank that acts as issuing and paying agent may also deal in the paper, this is not always so. Some banks specialize in this field. The agreement would cover, inter alia:

- the appointment of issuing and paying agents;
- arrangements for the authentication, issue and delivery of paper;
- the procedures for payment of proceeds on issue repayment by the issuer at maturity to the surrendering holders;
- arrangement for records of CP issues;
- fees and expenses payable by the issuer.

Issuing and clearing

A dealer may also be an issuing and paying agent. The issuing agent holds a stock of blank notes. SCP programmes will usually vary in size between £50 and £500 million. The size of the programme limits the maximum amount of paper that can be issued in total. Such a programme would be in place in addition to a number of other borrowing and funding mediums, affording the borrower the optimum choice in order to balance spreads of maturities and overall average cost of funds. It is advisable for the issuer to be prepared to issue every day if necessary, although this would not normally be the case. Not only does this increase the chances of funding at attractive rates, but it affords a degree of comfort to the markets. However, the issuer should never be seen to be in need of funds, because they could then become a 'hostage to fortune' to the market.

The issuer may invite bids from dealers, or dealers may make bids. They are under no obligation to bid. During the morning of the dealing day, the issuer and dealer may discuss possible needs, opportunities and terms. In the US, the networks of dealers and potential investors are vast. It is recommended that at maturity, CP should be presented for payment through an authorized institution known to the paying agent.

While there may be more than one dealer, especially in USCP, one dealer will often play a leading role. Dealers play a number of roles, including acting both as agents, to fill orders from investors, and as principals, taking paper onto their own books, with the intention of selling on at a profit. The secondary market is illiquid as most investors will hold the paper to maturity. Nevertheless a dealer will undertake to buy paper back to provide a measure of liquidity.

CP is usually issued, transferred and settled for same-day payment within Crest. However, where notes are cleared through Euroclear or Clearstream, settlement is the next day.

The relative attraction of CP over other short-term instruments has to be based on safety and a measure of liquidity. The investor will accept a lower return if he is certain of the return of the principal. Thus ratings will be the most important factor in investors' credit decisions.

21.4.2   Calculations for SCP issues

The purchase price for prime paper issued at a discount, or secondary paper bought at a discount or a stated interest rate, can be calculated from this formula. (Note that unlike some CDs, for example, interest is paid at maturity and therefore this complication is avoided):

$$\text{Purchase price} = \frac{F}{1 + \frac{(M \times Y)}{365 \times 200}}$$

where

   F is the face value
   I is the stated interest rate
   T is the original tenor in days
   Y is the purchased yield to maturity
   M is the number of days to maturity from the purchase date.

If SCP with a face value of £10,000,000 and 30 days to run is sold to yield 5.23%, the purchase consideration is:

$$\frac{£10,000,000}{1 + \frac{(30 \times 5.23)}{36500}} = \frac{£10,000,000}{1.00429863} = £9,957,197.69$$

Proof:

£10,000,000 less £9,957,197.69	=	£42,802.31 (interest)
£9,957,197.69 for 30days at 5.23% yield	=	£42,802.31

21.5   UK Treasury instruments

21.5.1   UK Government Sterling Treasury Bills

The most frequent, but not the most by volume, of types of government funding in the markets are issues of Treasury bills. For much of the post-war period, Treasury bills have been used as a means of implementing interest rate policy in the UK. First as bank rate and then as minimum lending rate, the Bank of England used Treasury bill issues and the secondary market as a means to control the amount of money in circulation in the money markets, thereby having an immediate effect on short-term interest rates.

If the Bank wanted to inject liquidity into the system, it could rediscount bill or redeem Treasury bills. By the same token, the weekly Treasury bill tender could be varied in size or rate to encourage take up of issues, at an attractive rate. This had the effect of taking liquidity out of the system and moving short-term rates higher. This did not, however, survive the monetary policy of the 1980s which created an unmanageable 'Bill mountain'. These days there are weekly tenders on a yield basis and no longer on tap. The yield is calculated in the same way as for commercial paper. They are redeemed at face value at maturity.

Since April 1998 Treasury bills are issued by the UK Debt Management Office (DMO), which assumed responsibility for the whole of the UK Government's debt programme. The DMO took over full responsibility for Exchequer cash management from the Bank of England on the 3 April 2000. Its main objective in carrying out its cash management operations is to offset, through its market operations, the expected cashflow into or out of the government accounts on every business day. The DMO also has to take account of the operational requirements of the Bank of England for implementing its monetary policy objectives.

The minimum denomination is £25,000 and bills are dematerialized in CREST. The volume of issue is announced a week in advance on a Friday. On the Friday allocation day, bids are phoned to the DMO before 11.00hrs. Bids must be for a minimum of £500,000 and in multiples of £50,000. Successful bids are issued on the following Monday on a Delivery versus Payment (DvP) basis.

Bills are allocated in full to bidders at the lowest yields until the tender is sold. Successful bidders pay the price they bid, so bills are sold at different prices. There is a market in 'hots', that is bills not yet issued but which will be available the following week.

There is also a secondary market. Trading is for same day value (T + 0). Rates in the secondary market are quoted on a discount basis, the same way as eligible bills. This shows the historic close association between the two instruments.

Twenty two

Eurobonds

Objectives

This chapter will cover the following topics:

- ◆ primary markets;
- ◆ secondary markets;
- ◆ types of issues;
- ◆ documentation;
- ◆ calculations.

22.1   Introduction

A bond is a negotiable debt instrument issued in bearer or registered form. It constitutes a commitment by the issuer:

- ◆ to pay a specified sum or sums of money to the holder at a predetermined rate or dates;
- ◆ to pay interest to the holder at stated intervals either at a fixed rate agreed at the outset or on floating-rate basis, often at a margin over a given benchmark, such as LIBOR.

The international debt markets are often thought of in terms of eurobonds only. Although the eurobond sector is the most visible, it is but one method of capital finance and but one option for investors, and there are many active domestic markets.

A domestic debt issue is one that an issuer raises within his own country and is denominated in its own country's currency. Such issues are more likely to appeal to investors resident in the country of issue because of withholding tax. They are generally in registered form and are generally quoted on official exchanges, although not always traded.

A foreign bond is one issued by a foreign borrower on a foreign capital market with the securities denominated in the currency of that market. The best known are Yankee bonds. A UK company raising US dollar debt in the US is a foreign debt and is known as a Yankee bond. They are particularly attractive due to the deep and liquid market that the US provides.

A Eurobond in contrast is a bond issued in one country and denominated in a currency other than that of the country of issue. Often they may not be sold into the domestic market of the currency they are issued in order to avoid local regulations. This is particularly the case in the US, which has a strict prohibition on the sale of eurobonds in the primary market to US citizens. Similarly the sale of eurobonds to UK investors is restricted. Eurobonds were first issued in 1963 and have since become the mainstay of capital market debt issues. Overall they have been issued in over 35 currencies. Because Eurobonds tap an international investor base, larger and more frequent issues are possible than in domestic markets.

The size of the bond market in 2001 was estimated at USD 33 trillion. Approximately 14.5% of this was issued in Eurobonds. 62% of these are issued by US entities, with bonds from the Euro area amounting to 14%.

Eurobonds generally have the following characteristics:

- ◆ They are unsecured securities. The only security they convey is the unpledged assets and creditworthiness of the issues.
- ◆ They are underwritten or bought by an international syndicate of investment houses and banks.
- ◆ They have interest paid without deduction of tax. If withholding tax were applied to payment in a particular currency, it would effectively terminate any meaningful activity in bonds in that currency. Issuers usually agree to gross up payment of interest in the event of withholding tax being imposed.
- ◆ They are listed on one or more exchanges. However, very few eurobonds are ever traded on them.
- ◆ They normally raise a single amount of funds on issue for the issuer.
- ◆ They may be issued at a discount or at a premium to the par value.
- ◆ They can be issued in the most favourable market at the time of issue. The proceeds of the issue are usually swapped to provide the issuer with his desired currency and interest basis.
- ◆ They are placed with investors internationally and this may exclude nationals of the country of the currency of issue.
- ◆ Originally the bonds were issued in bearer form with no register of holders and with ownership passing on delivery to the purchase. They are now mainly dematerialized and held in, for example, Euroclear or Clearstream.

Other features include:

◆ Size of issue: The usual range of issue size is USD 50m to USD 500m although larger issues are frequently made by governments and supranational issuers. The lower limit is dictated by the costs of issue. Floating rate notes (FRNs) can be much larger and longer term because the interest rate risks for investors is much lower. Some FRNs have been issued for much larger sums, for example USD 5 billion for sovereign issuers.

◆ Term: The usual term of eurobonds is five to seven or ten years, although longer terms are seen if market conditions are favourable. Issues for shorter periods are not unusual. Perpetual floating rate notes were popular but have now almost completely disappeared.

◆ Currencies: Eurobonds have been issued in about 35 currencies although the market in some currencies is very limited and issues infrequent. The main currencies of issue are US dollars, Euros, Yen and Sterling.

◆ Interest: Fixed rate eurobonds pay interest annually on the basis of a 360-day year. The interest is called the coupon because historically the printed bonds had coupons attached. The coupons, where still used, have the details of paying agents on the reverse and are clipped to claim the interest payments. Interest on floating rate issues is paid according to the terms of each issue, with the basis of the rate fixings needing to be defined.

◆ Denominations: The denominations of individual bonds within an issue may range from USD 1,000, for retail investors, to USD 100,000 to meet the needs of institutional investors.

22.2   Primary markets

Issuance of eurobonds can be divided into four phases: origination, syndication, placement and closing.

22.2.1   Origination

The primary market is overseen by the International Primary Market Association (IPMA), which issues recommendations on the methods and manner of issues. The IPMA makes recommendations on the methods and manner of issues and documentation. It has no formal powers. Its recommendations have included the need for lead managers to provide documentation at least one day before signing, limits on the deduction of fees for stabilization, minimum information in new issue invitations, minimum allotment amounts, penalties for late payment of fees and arrangements for custody of global notes.

Capital debt raising is an expensive exercise and it is important for potential fund-raisers to have an ongoing policy of examining their future debt requirements. Banks need to consider how a eurobond issue will meet their requirement for capital raising. The issuer will consult its advisers on its needs in terms of amount, currency, maturity and interest rate structure of the potential borrowing. It will consult potential lead managers about market conditions and the structure they can offer. It will have preliminary conversations with the rating agencies, who will make an assessment of the rating for the issue.

Lead Manager

The lead manager's role is to advise on:

- ◆ interest rate trends which might affect the cost of funding;
- ◆ the timing of the issue;
- ◆ the performance of recent bond issues;
- ◆ investor appetite and the demand for particular types of bonds;
- ◆ the possibilities for using swaps to reduce issue costs;
- ◆ the probable cost of funds, bearing in mind the rating the issue will be given;
- ◆ documentation of the issue.

Once the issuer is content with the outline terms offered, he will appoint a lead manager for the issue. The lead manager will, together with the issuer, select the other parties involved and will take responsibility for production of the documentation. It will also be responsible for ensuring that due diligence has been observed in the details of the issue. Other key parties to be appointed at this stage are:

- ◆ paying agents. One or more paying agents will be nominated to provide representation in the key financial centres. A principal paying agent will be nominated. These agents are responsible for payments made to investors in respect of principal and interest;
- ◆ trustee of fiscal agent to represent the interests of bondholders in monitoring administrative and substantive aspect of the issue;
- ◆ the issuer's accountants and auditors to advise on tax and accounting aspects and to certify the financial data as revealed in the issue prospectus;
- ◆ legal advisers to advise on all legal aspects;
- ◆ printers to prepare agreements, and where required a security printer if they are needed in definitive form;
- ◆ the listing agent to arrange for the issue to be listed on the desired exchanges.

The time it takes to complete origination of the issue will depend on whether the issuer is a new or regular issuer. If an issuer has a draft offering circular and documentation in place, perhaps under a medium-term note programme, the issue can be made very quickly.

22.2.1 Syndication and distribution

Once he has secured a mandate a lead manager will recruit other investment houses to assist in the underwriting of the issue, usually with the agreement of the issuer. The purpose of syndication is to spread the underwriting risk that the bonds will not be sold.

If the issuer is a new borrower, or is relatively unknown in the euromarkets, or is proposing an unusual structure for the bond, it may be necessary to undertake a programme of investor education by circulating information to or visiting potential investors. A series of presentations in various locations is known as a roadshow.

Under the process of syndication, the lead manager or bookrunner arranges for the launch of the issue on screen-based information services to alert potential syndicate members and investors. Informal invitations will usually be accepted by telephone. The lead manager will await returns of indications of interest from the syndicate member before allocating issues. If the price of the issue has been pre-set, which is usual, the lead manager will announce allotment within one working day of the launch.

The formal invitation will include:

◆ a list of managers and their underwriting commitments;
◆ details of commissions;
◆ the timetable for the issue;
◆ a summary of the terms and conditions of the bond;
◆ details of the managers' allotment and payment instructions;
◆ the deadline and wording for acceptance;
◆ the wording for the power of attorney to enable the lead manager to sign the subscription agreement. Signing will be within one or two week, with closing and payment usually within one month of the formal invitation being made.

Participating houses may be termed co-lead managers or co-managers depending on the extent of their agreement to underwrite the deal, their ability to add features to its structure (eg swaps) and their contribution to its distribution. The management group will maintain contact with potential investors so that they can assess likely future demand. As soon as an issue is launched, a grey market, effectively secondary market trading, is likely to develop. This is trading in bonds that have not yet been issued.

The lead manager should try to ensure an orderly market in the new issues he has arranged in the grey market. This is known as stabilization. This process of stabilization is undertaken under IPMA rules by the bookrunner. The managers in the issue must agree to stabilization and the bookrunner must maintain a separate account of stabilization transactions. The costs, within limits, can be passed on to the managers, although they are usually assumed by the stabilising manager itself.

22.2.3   Closing

Issuance is complete on the closing date. On this date, the syndicate pays the issuer and interest starts to accrue on the bond. The issuer delivers a global note into the custody of a clearing house with the ownership being assigned to individual investors by book entry transfer. Each issue will have an International Securities Identification Number (ISIN) assigned to it by the clearing house. On rare occasions the bookrunner will make physical delivery of definitive certificates.

22.3   Secondary markets

All trading after the closing of a eurobond issue takes place in the secondary market. This is an over-the-counter market, with bid and offer quotes, in which transactions are negotiated by telephone with market-makers who use the services of inter-dealer brokers. Brokers act as principals but do not take positions of their own. Trading between professional counterparties is either conducted by telephone or by screen trading using ISMA's COREDEAL, which was introduced in 2000. The Bloomberg system also provides securities information and has an electronic bond trading service, Bloomberg E-Trade, which enables participants to trade over the system with market makers throughout the world.

The International Securities Market Association (ISMA) has established rules for trading as well as setting out trading practice and providing conciliation and arbitration services. An important rule concerns deliverability of stock. If a seller cannot deliver a security within 21 days of the value date of the transaction, the buyer gives the seller 14 days' notice in which to complete the transaction. Failing that ISMA nominates a firm to buy the securities at the best rate available in the open market.

Some of the essential features of secondary market trading for cross border transactions, under ISMA rules, are:

◆ Settlement takes place on the third business day after the dealing day (T + 3), or as agreed by both parties.
◆ Prices are quoted in decimals as a percentage of par of 100.
◆ Accrued interest is added to the purchase price quoted for the period from the last interest payment date to the value date. For fixed rate bonds, this is calculated assuming a year of 12 months of 30 days (30/360 bond basis). This means that January and February both have 30 days in eurobond calculations.

22.3.1   Liquidity in the secondary market

Liquidity is a measure of the ease with which purchases and sales can be transacted. This depends on market conditions, which may be influenced by external events.

Large issues of USD 1 billion or more and issued by supranationals or the government of an OECD country are highly liquid and are regularly traded throughout their life on very tight bid/offer margins. They provide benchmarks along the yield curve for the market, which serve as measures of relative value for less liquid transactions. They are known as benchmark issues.

Liquidity in other issues is variable and is affected by the following factors:

◆ continued creditworthiness (and rating) of the issuer;
◆ size and currency of the original issue;
◆ availability of market makers;
◆ complexity of structure;
◆ time till maturity (most trading is done early in a bond's life);
◆ changes in interest rates.

22.4   Types of issues

22.4.1   Fixed-rate issues

These are the most common types of issue. The advantage of fixed-rate bonds to the issuer is that its financing costs are certain for the life of the bond. The disadvantages are that issue costs are heavy and the time of issue may depend on market conditions, not the issuer's preference. The advantages of fixed-rate bonds to the investor are that he obtains a certain rate of return and normally has the ability to sell his holding in the secondary market before maturity of the bond.

Step-up and step-down bonds allow for increases or decreases in coupon rates during the life of the bond. Deep discount bonds, convertibles and warrants are types of fixed-rate issues.

22.4.2   Floating rate notes (FRNs)

Borrowers who seek a long-term commitment of funds yet feel that interest rates are too high for a fixed-interest coupon may consider a floating rate note issue. FRNs are suitable for banks to raise capital because the issues can broadly match the assets of a bank. If needed they can be structured so as to count as Tier 2 or Tier 3 capital for regulatory purposes.

The interest rate payable on the borrowing will be brought into line with current market rates applicable usually to the three- or six-month LIBOR rates for the currency concerned. FRNs provide investors with a higher rate of return than they could expect to receive from a bank over the same interest period.

FRNs can be issued incorporating caps and/or floors (maximum and minimum rates payable). Reverse FRNs are issues where the interest rate is set at a fixed rate less the applicable LIBOR for the current interest period. They are thus notes whose rate fixes in inverse proportion to the level of interest rates.

22.4.3 Repayment types

The majority of bonds are issued with repayment in one sum at maturity. Staggered redemption could be in the form of a sinking fund or a note purchase programme. Redemption is by purchases in the open market or by repayment of bonds whose numbers have been drawn by lot. Others have call option integrated into the documentation. They give the issuer the right to redeem a bond early at or within set times. Repayments or call options are a useful tool for both corporate and bank treasurers. They can be used to take advantage of lower interest rates in the market or of lower interest rates as a result of improved creditworthiness on the part of the issuer. Other bonds include put options that give the investor the right to early repayment of the bond at or within set times.

22.5 Documentation

The following documents are prepared for a Eurobond issue:

◆ The *Offering Circular*, which provides detailed information on the issue and the issuer. It is a standard requirement for obtaining a listing on a stock exchange. It is used by the managers to promote the issue.
◆ The *Subscription Agreement*, between the issuer and the management group. This covers the managers' commitment to subscribe for bonds at the issue price, the issuer's obligations, commissions and fees, the terms of the issue and representations and warranties by the issuer as to the accuracy of the information provided.
◆ The *Agreement among Managers* sets out the responsibilities of the lead manager and managers between themselves for the underwriting, allotment of bonds and fees. This agreement is rarely produced as a separate document but is deemed to have been entered into at the same time as the subscription agreement.
◆ The *Trust Deed*, which constitutes the bonds and establishes the terms under which the trustee will act on behalf of the bondholders.
◆ The *Paying Agency Agreement* between the issuer and the nominated paying agents, outlining their responsibilities for timely payments.
◆ *Global Note* or bonds representing evidence of the debt owed by the issuer to the investor and including the terms of issue.
◆ *Legal Opinions* on various legal aspects of the deal will also be produced.

The terms of a public Eurobond issue will be set out in the trust deed and will also be printed on the bond and will cover:

- *Status of the bonds*: The bonds usually rank *pari passu* or equal, in terms of legal protection for the investor, with previous indebtedness of the issuer of similar type.
- A *statement* of the form and denomination of the bond.

Other terms and conditions will include:

- *Changes to terms and conditions*: What is allowable and for what changes bondholder approval is needed.
- *Conditions precedent:*, Which must be satisfied before any issuance takes place.
- *Events of default/enforcement of rights*: Non-payment of interest or principal and appointment of a receiver are the key events of default. If they occur, the trustees have the right to take proceedings against the issuer on behalf of the bondholders. It is also common to include breach of covenants (such as negative pledge) and conditions precedent.
- *Further issues*: Normally allowed without consent of the bondholders for this issue.
- *Governing law:* Usually English or New York.
- *Interest*: Floating rate notes will include definitions of interest periods, interest determination dates and how rates are determined.
- *Legal opinion(s):* That the documentation is valid and binding.
- *Meetings of Bondholders*: How they will be convened.
- *Negative pledge*: A negative pledge is an undertaking by the borrower that he will not offer security to investors in further bond issues. Bank issues ranking as capital must not contain a negative pledge or cross default clause which could accelerate payment.
- *Notices*: Where notices relating to interest rate fixings for FRNs and redemption will be published.
- *Payments*: How investors can obtain payment of interest and redemption proceeds.
- *Prescription*: The coupons and bonds normally become void unless presented for payment within respectively six and 12 years from the due dates.
- *Redemption*: For bullet repayment issues, the notes will be redeemed at a specific date in the future. If there is a sinking fund or a note purchase agreement, the redemption clause will include the details.
- *Representations, warranties and undertakings* given by the issuer, any guarantor and dealers.
- *Subordination*: Bank issues must be subordinated to count as regulatory capital. In the event of the winding up of the issuer, the holders of subordinated paper should not expect to receive payment from the liquidator until all senior claims and ordinary creditors have been satisfied in full. There may be several tiers of subordination.
- *Taxation*: Payments will be paid without deduction of withholding tax.

22.5.1   Listing

Eurobonds are listed on stock exchanges, usually in London and/or Luxembourg for three reasons:

♦ To qualify for the 'quoted Eurobond exemption', allowing payments to be made without deduction of tax.
♦ Some investors are only permitted to invest in listed securities.
♦ To generate greater confidence in the paper.

22.6   Calculations

The following calculations are explained.

♦ Current yield.
♦ Price of a Eurobond with annual coupon.
♦ Proceeds of a sale of bonds in the secondary market.

22.6.1   Current yield

The bond price is expressed in relation to a nominal value of 100. Increases in interest rates mean that anyone buying a fixed-rate bond in the secondary market will pay less than 100 so that he obtains current yields on his investment, but will pay more than 100 if interest rates have fallen. A bond purchased at 97.5, having a coupon of 12%, will give a current yield of 12.3%, calculated as follows:

$$\frac{\text{Coupon}}{\text{Net Price}} \times 100 = \text{Current yield} \quad \frac{12}{97.5} \times 100 = 12.3\%$$

22.6.2   Price of a Eurobond with annual coupon

What is the price of a Eurobond with a remaining life of two years, a coupon of 9% and a current yield of 8%? First, you must determine the cashflows, which are normally depicted as follows:

282

Then, discount each cashflow by the appropriate discount factor, ie, the yield of maturity, 8%.

$$\frac{Coupon}{\frac{(1 + yield)}{100}} + \frac{Coupon}{\frac{(1 + yield)^2}{100}} + \frac{coupon + face\ value}{\frac{(1 + yield)^3}{100}} = price$$

$$\frac{9}{\frac{(1 + 8)}{100}} + \frac{9}{\frac{(1 + 8)^2}{100}} + \frac{109}{\frac{(1 + 8)^3}{100}} = 1$$

$$8.333 + 7.716 + 86.527 = 102.58$$

This calculation shows the principle involved. The calculations become more complex as one takes into account more years, semi-annual interest payments and the fact that most trades do not conveniently have a value date on the anniversary of a bond issue. Most calculations require discounting for part of a year to the next coupon date, then for one year and part of a year, etc.

22.6.3 Proceeds of sale of eurobonds in the secondary market

Example: *Twenty bonds each with a nominal value of $100,000 are sold at 98.28, trade date 20 October, value date 23 October. The last coupon of 7.5% was paid on 23 January. The proceeds are the price plus accrued interest:*

Principal $2,000,000 x 98.28/100   = $ 1,965,600.00

Accrued interest for 9 months of 30 days (ISMA rules)

$$2,000,000 \times \frac{270 \times 7.5}{36000} \qquad\qquad = \$\ 112,500.00$$

Total proceeds   = $ 2,078,100.00

Twenty three

Medium term notes (MTNs)

Objectives

This chapter will cover the following topics:

- ◆ arrangers, dealers and paying agents;
- ◆ documentation;
- ◆ issuance procedure;
- ◆ secondary market.

23.1 Introduction

Whereas Eurobond issues normally raise a single large amount, MTNs are sold in smaller tranches either on a continuous basis or in response to investor demand. The financing resembles small Eurobond issues (which they sometimes are) but the method of distribution resembles that of commercial paper.

The Euro MTN market originated in London in 1986 when the US dollar was the dominant currency and issuers were encouraged to offer paper on a continuous basis. There is now a mature market in London in a variety of currencies. Notes are usually issued for periods between 18 months and five or ten years but exceptionally maturities can range up to 30 years. Individual notes are usually between $1 million and $20 million or the equivalent in other currencies.

23.1.1   Programmes

Prospective issuers are canvassed by investment houses to arrange programmes. These can take up to three months to set up. The matters that need to be considered by potential issuers are as follows.

Size and currency of programme

EMTN programmes are usually for USD one or two billion (or the equivalent in another currency). Smaller programmes being USD 500m, with some larger programmes being up to USD 5 billion. Recommendations to potential issuers on the appropriate size of the programme might be:

- ◆ setting a programme larger than necessary may give the impression of over-extending borrowing and send the wrong signals to potential investors;
- ◆ setting too low a programme size may require the administrative burden of updates;
- ◆ the level should be set to cover at least two years of the issuer's requirements.

Multi-currency programmes give issuers flexibility. Issuers should specify the currencies in which they expect to make issues in the Offering Circular.

Note Structure

To give the greatest flexibility, as many types of structures for individual note issues are set out in the Offering Circular. The following types of issue are usually included:

- ◆ fixed and floating rate notes, reverse floating rate notes;
- ◆ capped and collared notes, discount and zero coupon notes;
- ◆ dual currency notes, optional dual currency notes;
- ◆ index linked notes, commodity and equity linked notes.

Issuing patterns

The issuing pattern of EMTNs differs widely. Alternatives open to issuers are:

- ◆ to post aggressive rates continuously from one to five years and be willing to issue in any size up to USD 20m on request;
- ◆ not to post rates, but give dealers advance notice of funding requirements and be receptive to aggressively priced offers of funding. This issuer reacts opportunistically;
- ◆ to respond to 'reverse enquiry' where the investors specify the terms and timing of a transaction. The dealer's role is to match the requirements of investors and issuers by suggesting swap opportunities to the issuer;

- to circulate periodically to its dealers a list of forthcoming issuing requirements, accepting the lowest bid on each issuing date;
- to use its EMTN programme as a vehicle for public bond issues.

The majority of EMTN issues are swapped in order to meet each party's objectives.

A secondary market exists in EMTNs. However, the market relies mainly on the commitment of dealers to make a market in notes where they act as dealers, to back-up their continuing involvement in the programme. Market practice is similar to that for conventional eurobonds. Dealing houses need the ability to unwind swaps and to repackage structured notes.

23.2   Arrangers, dealers and paying agents

23.2.1   The arranger

The arranger's role is to deal with the administration when a programme is set up. The arranger also needs to ensure appropriate and timely liaison between the parties involved in the programme. The arranger's role will include:

- agreeing and monitoring a timetable for the documentation;
- negotiating and circulating draft documentation between the parties and arranging the signing of documentation;
- advising on the selection of dealers;
- providing advice on regulatory matters;
- acting as listing agent for the listing of the programme;
- liaising with legal advisers, stock exchange(s) and printers;
- ensuring the programme is presented to the market in a professional manner;
- assuring satisfactory answers to due diligence questions relating to the issuer's financial and business status.

The issuer will need to update the programme annually, renewing listings and updating the Offering Circular. New dealers may be added or existing ones deleted and the size of the programme may be increased or decreased. An issuer should consider annually:

- dealer performance;
- pricing objectives and results;
- operational procedures;
- relevant regulatory changes; and
- funding requirements for the year ahead.

23.2.2   Dealer group

A dealer's role is to approach the issuer with various funding opportunities that will satisfy the issuer's borrowing targets. Choosing an appropriate dealer group, in terms of size, expertise and geographic spread, is important to the success of the programme. For most issues, a group of four or six houses is normal. When assessing potential dealers, an issuer should consider:

- ◆ credit rating, since the dealer's firm will be a swap counterparty for at least some issues;
- ◆ market position of the bank: The firm must have appropriate technical expertise and distribution capabilities;
- ◆ currency and geographic diversity: A dealer may be chosen for his strengths in certain currencies or geographic areas;
- ◆ relationship banks and banks that have performed well in earlier programmes are likely to be on the proposed dealer list.

23.2.3   Paying agents

In a multi-currency programme, one or more paying agents will be appointed. The principal paying agent's responsibilities are to ensure that:

- ◆ the Pricing Supplement prepared for each trade is properly drawn up;
- ◆ the note is issued into the appropriate clearing systems and the issuer is paid;
- ◆ subsequent coupon payments and principal repayments are carried out in a timely fashion;
- ◆ all necessary reporting requirements are carried out for each particular currency regime.

23.3   Documentation

The principal documents for a programme are:

- ◆ *The Offering Circular*: This sets out the terms and conditions of the notes which will be issued under the programme, the financial information and business description of the issuer.
- ◆ *Dealers' agreement*: This sets out the mechanics of issuance and will contain:
  - ● The conditions precedent which must be satisfied before any issuance takes place.
  - ● Representations, warranties and undertakings given by the issuer, any guarantor and dealers.
  - ● A pro-forma example of the Pricing Supplement for trades.
  It may also include:
  - ● A syndication agreement that may be used for public syndicated issues.
  - ● A pro-forma Dealer Accession Letter for use when employing dealers not named on the programme when the 'reverse enquiry' facility is operated.
- ◆ The *Trust Deed,* as for Eurobond issues.

◆ *Settlement Procedures Memorandum*, which sets out the operational procedures of all parties who are involved in completing trades from initiation to settlement.
◆ *Listing Documents*, as for Eurobond issues.
◆ *Notifications* to the central banks of currencies in which issues are to be made.
◆ *Legal opinion(s)* that the documentation is valid and binding.
◆ *Auditor's comfort letter* covering the period since the last audited accounts
◆ *Issuer's board resolution* authorizing the establishment of the programme and the signing of the documentation.

23.4   Issuance procedure

Once the programme is in place, dealers who have identified an issuing opportunity will contact the potential issuer. After an initial telephone conversation, the process is generally that:

◆ the dealer faxes an indicative terms sheet to the issuer with all the details of the proposed trade, including how the funding level will be achieved if swaps are used;
◆ if the terms are satisfactory, telephone consent is given to the dealer to execute the trade. This 'working mandate' is given to the dealer for a specific period in order that the dealer can close a deal with an investor on a timely basis;
◆ once the trade is completed, a final terms sheet confirming the details of the trade is faxed to the issuer;
◆ a Pricing Supplement setting out the terms of the trade will be sent, together with any related swap confirmation;
◆ both parties will confirm the trade with the Principal Paying Agent who arranges for issuance of the notes. A global note will normally be issued for each tranche and is delivered into one of the clearing systems;
◆ the Paying Agent submits the pricing supplement to the respective stock exchange if that tranche is to be listed.

The benefit of issuing eurobonds under EMTN programmes is that much of the preparation (appointment of trustees, etc) has already been done. An offering circular, produced from the one on file, underwriting and placement of the notes are then the main tasks.

Twenty four

Gilt and repo markets

Objectives

This chapter will cover the following topics:

◆ gilt markets;
◆ repo markets;
◆ gilt repo markets.

24.1 Gilts

Gilts is the common term used to describe medium- to long-term debt securities issued and guaranteed by the British government. They are registered securities issued with fixed redemption dates for various periods up to 30 years. Gilts have now largely been immobilized and the transfer of ownership is carried out by computer 'book entry' in CREST. Since 1966, it has been possible to hold gilts in Euroclear or Clearstream (or its predecessor). Gilts coupons can be paid free of withholding tax on request. Gilts are listed on the London Stock Exchange. Each gilt stock has an ISIN, which incorporates the SEDOL (Stock Exchange Daily Official List) number for UK securities.

The Debt Management Office (DMO) began to assume responsibility for the British Government's debt programme in April 1998. It is responsible for issuing fixed rate and index-linked gilts and for monitoring secondary market trading in gilts.

Gilts are classified as: Short-dated (with remaining lives of up to seven years); medium-dated (remaining maturities between seven and 15 years) and long-dated, (maturities over 15 years). Fixed rate issues account for most of those outstanding, index-linked for about 15%. The largest benchmark issues are now over £15 billion. In June 2003, there were approximately £291 billion gilts outstanding.

Interest on gilts accrues and is payable on an 'actual/actual' or the actual number of days elapsed over 365 or 366 days. Gilts can be traded in units of one penny, which means that they can easily be traded on a delivery by value (DbV) basis. DbV is a mechanism in some settlement systems (including CREST) whereby a member may borrow or lend cash versus overnight collateral. The system automatically selects and delivers securities and retrieves them the following day over the term of the transaction.

24.1.2   Primary market

Primary dealers in government securities markets are specialist intermediaries between the authorities and the market. They are known as Gilt-edged Market Makers (GEMMs) in the UK, of which there are currently sixteen left. Their role is to ensure the efficiency of the primary market and the depth and liquidity of the secondary market. Their obligations usually consist of supporting auctions and guaranteeing liquidity in the secondary market. They are required to make continuous two-way prices at which they stand committed to deal. Unusually, they are required to make prices for the whole range of government securities, not just for leading stocks. The privileges of GEMMs are:

- ◆ the ability to put in late bids at auctions and to submit bids by telephone;
- ◆ exclusive rights to bid for certain issues such as tap issues;
- ◆ exemption from the usual requirement to submit payment at the time of bidding;
- ◆ exclusive access to inter-dealer brokers for secondary market trading;
- ◆ the ability to borrow short term from the DMO and to obtain stock on repo.

24.1.2   Calendars

There is a calendar for auctions of issues of gilts. The calendar is announced in advance each year, although it may be subject to revision as the government's funding requirements change. Details of the auction are given one week in advance. Calendars allow for market participants to plan ahead. They allow primary dealers to market issues to their customers and they allow overseas investors, who may not be closely focused on the market, to arrange currency transfers.

24.1.3   Auctions

Sale by auction is the technique used by most governments to sell debt to the non-state sector. The technique is market-oriented and transparent. The sale of securities is announced in advance. Purchasers declare their price on a competitive basis and by the same deadline. Most governments conduct auctions of securities on a sealed bid and bid-price basis. Sealed bid systems, which include bids made by phone or electronically, do not reveal information to bidders during the auction process itself. In a bid-price auction, as in the UK, each successful bidder pays the price he bids.

There are risks in using auctions. There may be insufficient bids to cover the amount the government wishes to sell and the bids may be below the price the government wishes to accept. The market will be aware of any adverse results of auctions.

Fixed rate gilt issues are usually made initially in blocks ranging from £1.5 to £3 billion. To be successful, an issue is expected to be oversubscribed and the 'cover ratio' is carefully monitored by all parties. The 'tail' is also monitored. The tail is the difference in yield between the highest successful bid and the average successful bid. The size of the issue is often increased at later dates by re-openings either through auctions or unscheduled, opportunistic funding (taps or taplets). These techniques help create liquid benchmark issues.

24.1.4   Secondary market

Inter-dealer brokers (IDBs) are wholesale brokers intermediating only between GEMMs for purchases, sales and switches of stocks. They operate screen-based systems, which display firm two-way prices. They execute deals on an anonymous, matched book basis to avoid any distortion of the market.

Prices in the secondary market are quoted in decimals. Dealing spreads will depend on the terms and duration of the particular issue. Settlement is normally for the working day following the trade (T + 1).

24.1.5   Gilt strips

Gilt stripping has been officially allowed since December 1997. It is a technique that can be applied to any bond but is most frequently used for government securities because they are issued in adequate volume to make the process viable. Strip is an acronym for the 'Separate Trading of Registered Interest and Principal'. Stripping is the process of separating a standard coupon-bearing bond into its constituent interest and principal payments. These can then be held or traded as zero-coupon instruments. For example, a five-year bond can be separated into 11 zero coupon bonds, one for the principal amount and ten for the semi-annual coupon payments. Coupon payments due, say six, 12 and 18 months after issue would, if the underlying bond were stripped, become six-, 12- and 18-month zero-coupon bonds. The cashflows on the bundle of zero-coupon strips, which can be traded separately, would be identical to the cashflows on the original unstripped bond. The process can be done in reverse to reconstitute a gilt into its original unstripped bond. Gilt coupon and principal strips created through the official gilts strip facility remain direct obligations of the UK government. They are registered securities in their own right and are held within CREST.

There are no restrictions on who may invest in gilt strips unless investors are subject to their own restrictions on how funds may be invested. Through investing in strips, an investor can in principle achieve a desired pattern of cashflows more easily. Long-term savings institutions may be interested in higher duration assets which stripping will make available, allowing liabilities to be more easily matched without reinvestment risk. The minimum strippable unit permitted is £10,000, which is increased in multiples of £10,000. The minimum displayed bid and offer amount on an IDB screen is £1 million. Each strip is allocated an ISIN. Strips can be used in repo transactions or as collateral in the same way as can unstripped gilts.

24.2 Repo markets

24.2.1 Introduction

Financial institutions continually buy and sell securities of all descriptions, including government bonds, bills and international bonds. Bonds are often purchased before the cash to fund them has been obtained. These institutions frequently seek to borrow cash in the overnight wholesale markets to fund their holdings of securities. Banks and other financial institutions are unwilling to lend the large amounts of money required even overnight because of the credit risk, and they may want to charge commercial rates rather than interbank rates for any funds lent.

If the investments were to be used as security or collateral, a bank would be more willing to lend at market rates. To take this one step further, a lending bank could buy the securities to give it full title to them. It could agree simultaneously to sell them back on the following day. This is how the repo market works. A repo (for repurchase agreement) is an arrangement under which a security is sold with a commitment to repurchase the assets after a stated time or in the event of a particular contingency.

Because of the way central banks operate in the money markets, commercial banks often find, in their daily money market operations, that there is a shortage of funds in the market. The central banks will step into relieve these shortages by providing liquidity. They too have the same concerns over lending unsecured and assistance to the market is frequently provided via repos, or secured lending.

There have long been deep and liquid repo markets in the US. Repo markets are used extensively in Japan, Canada, Australia and European countries but have developed more recently in London. Trading in repos in London is now conducted in a wide range of currencies and securities.

In operational terms the seller transacting a repo usually delivers the securities via a clearing house on a delivery versus payment basis. The cash is provided at a predetermined rate, the repo rate.

Repo

Repo is an arrangement whereby a financial institution *sells* securities to a third party with a commitment to *repurchase* the assets after a stated time or in the event of a particular contingency.

It is an irrevocable commitment. It is the combination of two simultaneous transactions in a single contract: a sale for immediate payment and a commitment to repurchase at a later date.

Classic repo

A classic repo is evidenced under a written agreement, which contractually links the two legs of the transaction. Any coupon on the bonds paid during the term of the repo has to be paid to the seller as soon as it is received. The buyer has the right to mark to market the valuation of the security and to call for variation margin if the value of the security falls. The loan is repaid with interest at maturity against return of the securities.

Reverse repo

This is the same transaction, but from the point of view of the lender of funds. It is a contract under which a holder of cash agrees to *purchase* securities and simultaneously agrees to resell them at an agreed price after a stated time or in the event of a particular contingency.

Specials

All securities are issued in defined quantities. When there are securities which, for any reason, are in short supply and are sought after in the repo market, holders are able to earn extra income by paying lower repo or deposit rates to the repo buyer. The rate can even be negative. If you hear of investment houses 'cornering the market' in an issue of securities, it means that they can dictate the repo rate to houses that are short of the issue.

Sell and buy back

This is the simplest and least common form of repo involving the outright sale of a security for value on the near date with an outright purchase on the forward date. This is in effect two separate transactions. Therefore there is no formal documentation between the counterparties except for the confirmation. This type of transaction is also referred to as buy/sell.

Securities lending

This involves a transfer of securities for a temporary period in exchange for collateral, which may be other securities or cash. It does not involve a sale and repurchase but is used by investment houses that need to acquire ownership of a particular bond or security because of a failed trade or deliberately taken short positions. The borrower of securities is required to deliver collateral to the securities lender and to pay a fee for the use of the borrowed securities. The clearing houses ask holders of securities if they are willing for their holdings to be used for stock lending purposes.

Tri-party repo

A tri-party repo is a repo in which an independent agent (banker or clearing house) oversees a standard two-party repo transaction. The responsibilities of the tri-party agent include ensuring adequate collateral is maintained and keeping adequate records.

24.2.2 Benefits

The benefits of a repo for the holders of securities are as follows.

- ◆ Repo provides a means of borrowing cash to fund securities held.
- ◆ Long positions in bonds and gilts can be financed, whether they are held for investment, risk taking or arbitrage purposes.
- ◆ Because repos are collateralized, often with government securities which are deemed to be 'default risk' free, the cost of finance is reduced. This is particularly the case for institutions without direct access to the interbank deposit markets.
- ◆ With a normal positive yield curve, the return on the holding of the long-term instruments is higher than the cost of short-term repo finance.
- ◆ If a bond provided as collateral is 'special', then the interest payable on the borrowed funds can be substantially lower than normal rates.
- ◆ Because repo involves a temporary exchange, it allows investors access to cash without having to liquidate the securities they are holding.
- ◆ Because the collateral must be issued by creditworthy names, the creditworthiness of the firm pledging the securities may be lower (but it must still be acceptable).

The benefits of reverse repo for the suppliers of cash are as follows.

◆ Reverse repo offers a secure, collateralized use of funds. This reduces credit risks and the use of credit lines significantly.
◆ Capital adequacy costs are reduced as the capital charge under CAD applies only to any shortfall between the mark-to-market value of the collateral and cash loan.
◆ Institutions can go short of securities, which are reversed in and sold outright. This may be done because a dealer feels that prices for the securities are likely to fall.

24.2.3   Documentation

There is an industry standard document for repo or collateral agreements, the ISDA Credit Support Annex (CSA). When negotiating collateral agreements, the following should be considered.

◆ Eligible collateral: Assets that can be used as collateral are specified.
◆ Threshold: A predefined amount of unsecured exposure acceptable to both the lender following marking-to-market (this may be zero, with 100% or more collateral cover being required)
◆ Haircuts: Securities used as collateral are valued as a percentage of their market value to compensate for any fluctuations in the value between collateral calls.
◆ Minimum Transfer amount: Predefined amount of mark-to-market movement before top-up collateral calls are made.
◆ The terms for calling and delivery of collateral. Usually, valuations are made at close of business and calls are made the following day (Value day plus one day or $V + 1$) for delivery of additional assets on $V + 2$.
◆ Interest is payable on cash deposits held as collateral at rates defined in the collateral agreement.

24.3   The gilt repo market

Before January 1996, repo in gilts was restricted to GEMMs. Also repos were not practical because gilts were paid after deduction of withholding tax. These restrictions were lifted in 1996 and now there are no restrictions on counterparties for trading gilt repo.

24.3.1   The gilt repo legal agreement

The key elements of the legal documentation are that it provides for:

◆ the absolute transfer of title to the securities;
◆ the daily marking-to-market of transactions;

◆ re-margining during the life of a repo contract;
◆ events of default and consequential rights and obligations of the parties, eg close out and set-off of all contracts in the event of default;
◆ the rights of parties regarding substitution of collateral.

24.3.2   The gilt repo Code of Best Practice

The Code, dated August 1998, applies to all activities in gilt repo by all participants: market professionals, principals, brokers and end users. The key elements of the Code are as follows.

◆ General market standards should be maintained in respect of:
  ● confidentiality;
  ● being responsible for the actions of staff;
  ● acting with due skill, care and diligence; and
  ● ensuring fair treatment where conflicts of interest cannot be avoided.
◆ Before entering into a gilt repo transaction, and regularly thereafter, participants should review all legal, credit, systems and procedural matters relating to gilt repos to ensure that trading is adequately controlled and understood.
◆ New clients should be made aware of the code.
◆ Participants should be clear whether the capacity in which their counterparty is acting is as principal, agent or broker.
◆ Name-passing brokers are agents paid in the form of brokerage for successfully bringing parties together.
◆ Gilt repo transactions should be subject to a legal agreement between the two participants.
◆ Margin should be called for whenever a counterparty has a mark-to-market exposure which is considered material.
◆ Taking delivery of securities and margin directly or via a third party can reduce potential credit risk. Those leaving securities in the custody of their counterparty (a 'hold in custody' repo) should consider their counterparty's creditworthiness, systems and control procedures.
◆ Before declaring an event of default, counterparties should consider whether the event is real or technical, should close out positions at fair market value and should do so without unnecessarily disrupting the market.
◆ Confirmations should be sent out on the same day and checked on a timely basis. Special consideration should be given to 'stock events', such as ex-dividend dates, arising during the life of the repo.

24.3.3   Calculations

Stock-driven repo

An example of stock-driven gilt repo is:

Amount of securities	£ 10,000,000.00
Type of securities	Treasury 6% 2005 (Coupon date 10 February)
Term	30 days, 5 April (54 days after the coupon date) to 5 May
Clean price	95.00
Repo rate	5.28125%

The all in or dirty price, including accrued interest is:

Nominal x clean price	£10m x 95.00/100	£ 9,500,000.00
Accrued interest	£10m x 54 days x 6/36500	£ 88,767.12
Consideration		£ 9,588,797.12

Dirty price, quoted to two decimal places =95.89 per £100 stock

Stages to the trade are:

- ◆ £10,000,000 of stock transferred (sold) in consideration for   £ 9,589,000.00
- ◆ Repo interest £ 9,589,000.00 x 30 (days) x 5.28125/36500   £ 41,623.48
- ◆ At termination, £10m stock returned (bought) for   £ 9,630,636.48

Cash-driven trades

Where the trade is cash-driven, the cash consideration is likely to be a round amount and the amount of stock to be passed over at the dirty price will be an odd amount. This does not matter since gilts can be delivered to 1p of nominal stock. The amount of stock needed for a cash-driven trade of £10,000,000 where the dirty price is 95.98 is calculated as follows:

£10,000,000.00/95.89 x 100 – Gilts value   =   £10,428,616.12

This may be rounded to £10,430,000.00 of the gilt stock.

Initial margins

Using the dirty price calculated above and a margin call of 2.5%, the calculation gives a lower cash amount that can be lent against the gilt stock available to repo:

£9,588,767.12/ 1.025 = £9,354,897.76.

Twenty five

Securitization

Objectives

This chapter will cover the following topics:

- ◆ purpose and benefits;
- ◆ methods of transfer;
- ◆ origination and structure;
- ◆ credit enhancements;
- ◆ role of servicing agent.

25.1   Introduction

The term securitization relates to:

- ◆ The packaging of designated pools of loans, receivables and financial assets.
- ◆ The sale of these packages to investors in the form of securities, frequently through issues of floating-rate notes and via special purpose vehicles (SPV).
- ◆ The securities are collateralized by the underlying assets and their associated income.

Securitization is a process through which illiquid assets are transformed into a more liquid and manageable form and distributed to a broad range of investors through the capital markets. The packaging typically involves the transfer of the underlying assets to an investment vehicle without recourse to the original owner.

Most securities issued to finance securitizations have been floating-rate notes. This is because FRNs are the best match with the interest rate characteristics of most loan portfolios. This still leaves some liquidity and interest rate risks which need to be addressed.

The securitization markets originated in the US in the early 1970s and have grown rapidly. A wide range of assets is securitized: mortgages, credit card receivables and car loans being the best known.

Pass through securities were the original form of mortgage-backed security in the US. A pool of mortgages is sold to an intermediary, perhaps a trust, with the purchase financed by the sale of securities to investors. During the life of the loans, all payments of principal and interest are 'passed through' the intermediary, with a specified time lag to allow time for administration, to the end investors. The best known pass through securities are those issued by the various US government agencies. Because all cashflows are returned to the investors including unscheduled early repayments, the uncertainty of cashflows is a deterrent to some investors.

Collateralized debt obligations use a variety of structures to enhance the predictability of cashflows for investors. The payment flows are paid to SPVs and the securities issued are split into different tranches with different risk characteristics to satisfy investor preferences.

Securitization techniques are now used in all major markets. The UK market is used principally to finance residential mortgages and property. For specialist mortgage lenders with limited access to other forms of deposits, securitization provides an acceptable form of funding for mortgages arranged by them. A mortgage securitization needs, say, 3,000 mortgages to be viable and credit card receivables 30,000 accounts.

25.2 Purpose, benefits and risks of securitization

25.2.1 Purpose and benefits

The purpose and benefits of securitization for originators are:

- to allow them to free their balance-sheets from these assets and their related capital costs. This can be a deliberate strategy to move away from traditional bank lending in order to concentrate on the business they know best, generating the assets though sales, but not funding them;
- to free capital that can be re-deployed to more profitable areas of the business;
- to generate fee income where the seller retains the service agency role of the assets;
- to actively risk manage by ensuring appropriate diversification of assets;
- to ensure capital adequacy requirements are met and achieve desired capital adequacy ratios (together with the relevant rating).

The benefits of securitization for investors are as follows:

◆ it provides a broader range of investment opportunities. Asset pools are often divided into separate tranches with different maturities and risk characteristics that can be targeted to different investor preferences;
◆ asset-backed securities typically offer a yield premium over other debt instruments with similar ratings;
◆ it offers a greater degree of protection because the risk is spread over many underlying loans;
◆ it provides investors with the opportunity to participate in other markets, especially retail markets that it would be difficult for them to lend to directly.

25.2.2   Risks of securitization

The risks of securitization relate to achieving true sales, conflicts of interest, the sale of the best assets, liquidity and interest rate risk and operational risks.

The main risk that a bank faces in a securitization is that a true sale may not be achieved. The selling bank may then be forced to take losses if the assets cease to perform. A true sale is not achieved if:

◆ There is any obligation for the seller to repurchase or exchange any of the assets.
◆ The seller has to account for any payments of the interest or principal.
◆ Investors have the right to sell back assets (recourse) to the originator.

For a true sale to be achieved, the selling bank must have no ownership or management control of the SPV which owns the pooled assets. There must be no requirement to consolidate the SPV and the SPV must not contain the selling bank's name.

There is a potential conflict of interests if a bank originates, sells, underwrites and services a securitization. A bank that has originated and transferred assets may be exposed to moral pressure to repurchase the securities if the assets cease to perform. Having completed a securitization, the seller does not disappear but usually exercises other functions in the process. Investors are aware of the identity of the originator and could, at least morally, cause pressure to be put on him to support the securitization. Regulatory authorities impose conditions to maintain the segregation of ownership, duties and responsibilities.

Banks may sell their best assets and thereby increase the average risk in their remaining portfolio. Investor demand for high quality assets may encourage this tendency. An ongoing securitization programme needs a growth in new loan business and this may lead to a bank lowering its credit assessment standards in order to generate the necessary loan volume. In practice, banks that have securitized large amounts of loans do not show evidence of lower asset quality. There is always a need to maintain asset quality for reputational and rating agency purposes.

Liquidity and interest rate risks

Because the payment pattern of the assets cannot be predicted exactly at the outset, there will remain some liquidity and interest rate risks which need to be addressed at the outset and during the life of the securitization. A liquidity facility may need to be arranged by the SPV to cover temporary shortfalls in funding. Payments of interest and principal into the pool are held until they are due to be paid out to the investors. If there is a large unexpected inflow, the trustee may be unable to invest these funds at a high enough interest rate to cover interest payable.

Operational risks

The risks for a bank acting as a servicing agent are principally operational, comparable to those of an agent bank in a syndicated loan. However, the number of loans in a portfolio and the different parties involved mean that there are higher risks of error for which the servicing agent might become liable. Servicing agents need adequate personnel, equipment and technology to process these transactions in order to minimize these operational risks.

25.3   Methods of transfer

There are three ways to transfer financial assets: by novation, assignment and sub-participation. The method of transfer determines the risks assumed by buyers and sellers and the treatment for capital adequacy purposes.

25.3.1   Novation

This is the only way of fully transferring both rights and obligations. The existing loans are cancelled and a new agreement substitutes all the original rights and obligations for new ones. The main difficulty with this method is that it requires the consent of all the parties to the original loan.

To cover the practical difficulty of obtaining consent, many loans are now structured to facilitate transfer. Essentially, all the parties agree in advance that all or part of the loan can be transferred. This is the mechanism used in the sale of retail store credit card receivables.

25.3.2   Assignment

In general, under English law, a lender may assign his rights under a loan agreement to a third party, ie his rights to interest and principal payments. A loan agreement may impose restrictions on assignability and in these cases a buyer could have difficulty enforcing an assignment against a seller and/or against the debtor.

A legal assignment passes all the legal and beneficial rights in a loan to the assignee. It must be:

◆ in writing;
◆ cover the whole of the loan; and
◆ be notified in writing to the borrower.

An assignment that does not fulfil these three conditions will be equitable only. An equitable assignment covers only beneficial rights, not legal rights, and in consequence a buyer may not be able to proceed directly against a borrower.

An assignment notified to the borrower can achieve an effective transfer of the seller's rights and the remedies available to him to enforce those rights. These rights may be impaired by any right of set off that exists between the borrower and the seller. When notice is given, the borrower may make payments direct to the buyer. Notice prevents the assignor from varying the terms of the underlying contract. The seller retains any outstanding obligations, for example, to advance further funds.

Silent assignments are those where the borrower is not notified of the assignment. A type of silent assignment is the declaration of trust. There may be additional risks in silent assignments:

◆ for the buyer, because the absence of notice to the borrower removes some of the legal protection he would otherwise have;
◆ for the seller, because as lender of record, he will remain subject to requests to reschedule or renegotiate the loan.

25.3.3 Sub-participations

A sub-participation is a separate legal agreement from the underlying loan, creating a debtor-creditor relationship between the buyer and seller. It does not transfer any of the seller's rights or obligations from the seller to the buyer. It is an entirely separate funding arrangement under which the buyer places funds with the seller, with no recourse to the borrower. The loan itself is not transferred. This is the most common loan sales technique used by banks. The buyer assumes a credit exposure on both the underlying borrower and the seller because it is reliant on the latter to pass through payments received from the borrower.

25.3.4 Conditions for all securitizations and single loan transfers imposed by the FSA

The following conditions must be satisfied for banks to ensure their legal, economic and moral separation of the seller from the assets and their new owners.

◆ The transfer should not contravene the terms and conditions of the underlying loan agreement.
◆ The seller retains no residual beneficial interest in the loan and the buyer has no formal recourse to the seller for losses.
◆ The seller can demonstrate to the FSA that it has given notice that it is under no obligation to repurchase the loan or support any losses suffered by the buyer.
◆ The buyer and not the seller will be subject to any rescheduled or re-negotiated terms.
◆ Where payments are routed through the performer, the performer is under no obligation to transfer the funds to the buyer unless and until they are received from the borrower.

The same methods of transfer can be utilized for the transfer of single loans.

25.4 The origination and structure of securitizations

Packaging asset securitizations is a long and costly business. The first stage will be carried out internally and will include:

◆ creating a securitization committee, which will include members of Treasury, Finance, Loans Administration, Audit and Systems;
◆ reviewing the documentation for all assets it is proposed to securitize. This ensures that no assets are included that do not include transferability clauses. Generally they are included in most asset documentation;
◆ creating the SPV and appointing internal and external auditors;
◆ considering the requirements of the rating agencies;
◆ reviewing the adequacy of data management and management information systems.

SPVs are thinly capitalized and must be independent of the originator and the servicing agent. Where the originator buys subordinated debt in the SPV, the FSA requires that the investment is deducted from the bank's capital.

The SPV will require a liquidity facility to meet any temporary shortfalls and will need the ability to reinvest and short-term surpluses at market rates. This is because FRNs usually pay interest three-monthly but this is unlikely to match precisely the payment flows from the assets. The process of arranging an issue of FRNs is the same as described in the chapter on eurobonds.

The next stage includes:

◆ The preparation of legal documentation.
◆ Selection of a lead manager with the necessary distribution capabilities for the bond or FRN issue.
◆ Consideration of credit enhancements needed for the rating process and the final selection of assets to be securitized.

25.5 Credit enhancements

The securities issued will be rated by one of the rating agencies and will reflect the nature of the underlying assets rather than the credit of the originator. Securitizations may be more highly rated than the originators' own issues.

The level of risk investors assume depends on the strength of the assets in the pool and the level of credit enhancements. To determine the appropriate credit enhancement, the risk of the pooled assets is assessed together with a historic loss profile. The enhancement usually covers the historic default rates of the underlying assets by a multiple of several times. Regulatory authorities require that credit enhancements are undertaken at the initiation of schemes, and are disclosed in any offering circular and are documented separately.

The most common forms of credit enhancement are guarantees or recourse agreements, senior-subordinated debt structures, over-collateralization, spread accounts, cash collateral accounts, irrevocable letters of credit, and guaranteed investment accounts. Different forms of enhancement may be combined in any securitization.

25.5.1 Guarantees

The simplest form of enhancement is a recourse arrangement providing the buyer of the assets with the right to receive payment from a guarantor for the first losses sustained by the scheme. This shifts the credit risk fully to the guarantor. A bank providing this facility will be required to deduct the amount of the guarantee from its capital.

25.5.2 Senior-subordinated structure

Where the enhancement is provided by a senior-subordinated structure, at least two classes of securities are issued. The senior tranche has a prior claim on all cash flows from the underlying assets. Losses will accrue first to the subordinated securities up to the amount of this particular class. If, for example, an issue consists of 90% senior and 10% subordinated securities, the holders of the subordinated securities will carry the first losses up to 10% of the assets of the scheme. Where an originating bank buys subordinated debt in the SPV, this must be deducted from the bank's capital.

25.5.3 Over-collateralization

Over-collateralization means that the value of the underlying assets in the pool must exceed the value of the debt securities issued. If their value declines below the agreed level of credit enhancement, the enhancer must provide additional collateral.

25.5.4   Spread accounts

A spread account is a deposit typically built up from the spread between the interest received from the pooled assets and the lower interest paid on the securities issued. The service agent passes on these funds to the trustee, where they are accumulated up to the level required for the credit enhancement. After reaching this level, all future earnings can be passed back to the originator. To provide for early losses the originator normally has to make an initial deposit of funds in the spread account.

25.5.5   Cash collateral accounts

A cash collateral account is a deposit equal to the credit enhancement, which is held for the benefit of investors in the securities. The balance available will be used if losses occur. Cash collateral may be made available by the originator or a third-party.

25.5.6   Irrevocable letters of credit

An irrevocable letter of credit may be issued by third party banks or insurance companies to cover a first portion of debt default, based on the estimated loss profile.

25.5.7   Guaranteed investment contracts

A guaranteed investment contract may be in place between the trustee and a bank which guarantees, for a fee, to meet the necessary rate of interest on funds deposited before they are paid out to noteholders.

25.6   The role of servicing agent

When assets are securitized, the selling institution often retains the role of service agent to administer the loans. The risks to be considered are:

◆ their continued identification with the loans can mean that their commercial reputation is committed and a complete break is not achieved;
◆ banks in this position can come under pressure to support losses incurred by investors and may be inclined to do so in order to protect their name.

The Financial Services Authority requires that the following conditions be met to ensure that a servicing agent's role is not seen as being more than that of agent:

◆ records must be available to satisfy auditors that the terms of the scheme protect it from any liability to the investors, save where it is proved to be negligent;

◆ any offering circular should contain a highly visible and unequivocal statement that the servicing agent does not stand behind the issue and will not make good any losses in the portfolio;

◆ the servicing agent may not own any share capital in the SPV for the scheme nor have any proprietary interest or control in the company;

◆ the board of the SPV must be independent of the servicing agent, although the latter may have one director representing it;

◆ the name of the SPV must not include the name of the servicing agent or imply any connection with it;

◆ the servicing agent must not bear any of the recurring costs of the scheme. However, at the outset of the scheme, it may make a one-off contribution to enhance the creditworthiness of the issue. It may lend on a long-term subordinated basis to the SPV provided the debt is repayable only on the winding up of the scheme. These factors must be disclosed in the offering circular;

◆ the service agent may not bear any losses arising from the effect of interest rate changes. The servicing agent may enter into interest-rate swaps at market rates with the vehicle company;

◆ a servicing agent may not provide temporary finance to cover shortfalls arising from delayed payments or non-performance of the loans it administers;

◆ a servicing agent may not retain an option to repurchase or refinance loans.

Twenty six

Credit derivatives

Objectives

This chapter will cover the following topics:

- ◆ credit default swaps;
- ◆ total return swaps;
- ◆ credit linked notes.

26.1   Introduction

Credit derivatives are the latest derivative instruments that are shaping the financial markets. Currently only a minority of players are using them in the market but their attraction is slowly spreading. The market is still relatively small, at an estimated value of USD 690 billion in notional amounts, when compared to the more traditional derivatives markets. This also means that there is a restricted number of brokers and participants, but despite these problems the attractions of credit derivatives are significant and use is increasing. The benefit mainly derives from the ability to pro-actively and relatively simply manage credit risk, to an extent that was not previously possible:

- ◆ structuring of new securities, that are not otherwise available;
- ◆ ability to shorten credit risk;
- ◆ improved ability to distil particular risk profiles;
- ◆ ease of rebalancing credit risk portfolio.

Crucial to the working of credit derivatives is the notion of credit spreads. Credit spread is the premium over a benchmark that someone needs to pay to gain exposure to a specific counterparty. Credit risk and maturity will be the key drivers of credit spreads. Thus a credit-spread curve would look very similar to a yield curve. The difference is that yield curves tend to represent yields on government paper, instead of representing company specific risk.

When discussing credit derivative markets a number of features need to be mentioned:

◆ The diversity of credit risk – credit risk comes in all shapes and forms. Even the same issuer may have a different credit risk according to the terms of the paper that has been issued. This means that there is a lack of homogeneity that can make it more complicated to achieve liquidity in the markets.
◆ Only for the largest issues will it be possible to get a view of the spread curve, this will make pricing more difficult.
◆ Because the markets are still relatively small, liquidity remains an issue.
◆ Pricing is complicated by the fact that spreads are driven by the probability of default, the loss given default, as well as the market demand and supply. Some participants price their credit derivatives on the basis that credit risk can be broken down into a series of underlying options. However, in practice, such a methodology is not simple to implement either.
◆ Under adverse conditions the market can dry up very quickly.
◆ Country risk of the issuer is likely to influence pricing.

The credit derivatives market has expanded significantly over the last few years. The Bank for International Settlement reported that at end-June 1998 the market stood at USD 108 billion in notional amounts. This increased to USD 695 billion at end of June 2001. This is thought to be due to the market for credit derivatives diversifying beyond transactions aimed at the restructuring of banks' balance-sheets with the entry of new market participants such as insurance companies. The market has also benefited from a widening in the range of instruments and from improvements in market infrastructure. For example, there is now standardized documentation and rates of return indices exist. A number of brokers now report consistent credit spreads. Nevertheless the size of the credit derivatives market remains fairly small in comparison to other markets, only just having surpassed the market for commodity derivatives.

There are three main types of credit derivatives that have emerged: credit default swaps, total return swaps and credit linked notes.

ISDA documentation has been developed whereby master agreements are negotiated (bi-laterally) between protection buyers and individual trades are evidenced by confirmations. Since June 2003 there is a new version of the ISDA Credit Derivative Definitions in use.

26.2   Credit default swaps

Credit default swaps are the most basic credit derivative. Against the payment of a premium the protection seller of the credit default swap gives protection to the purchaser in case of default. Thus in the event of default the protection seller will pay the protection buyer the loss in value of the underlying reference asset. The premium may be paid up front or on a periodic basis. In the case of periodic payments there is an additional credit risk that the seller, usually a bank, will have to monitor. The loss will depend on how the default is defined in the documentation. This could include insolvency, non-payment, triggering of cross-default clauses or other debt restructuring. In the event of default the swap will terminate once payment or delivery is made. It may consist of either cash or physical settlement.

In the case of cash settlement the buyer of the risk will pay the counterparty a sum of money, which will depend on how much the value of the underlying asset has fallen. Physical delivery would mean that the underlying asset, such as a bond or loan or another pre-agreed asset, will be delivered to the buyer of the risk against the full value of the principal.

The advantages of credit default swaps are many. Previously in order to manage credit risk one would have to physically sell the asset, or obtain guarantees from third parties. The simplicity of credit default swaps, which do not change underlying ownership has allowed a tailor-made approach to credit risk management. It also allows the stripping out of credit risk from instruments, which can be useful if a market participant wants to retain other risk on the book, such as interest rate risk or FX risk.

Reasons for participating in the market would be:

 ◆ Reduce concentration risk, while maintaining confidentiality.
 ◆ Wanting to take on specific credit risk. It is comparable to a synthetic floating rate note with the benefit of flexibility, financial leverage, confidentiality and built-in funding.
 ◆ Ability to shorten credit risk.
 ◆ To take positions, in particular, section of the credit spread curve.

Liquidity in the market may suffer with traders using credit default swaps as one-way bets.

Only credit default swaps are recognized by the FSA as transferring risks out of the balance sheet.

26.3   Total return swaps

In a total return swap the dual nature of a swap comes out more clearly. One side of the swap pays out the total return on a specified instrument. This could be any instrument with a credit dimension, ie loan, convertible, preference share, etc. The second side of the swap would pay the synthetic financing cost as a spread over an agreed benchmark, such as LIBOR. Putting the two together creates a synthetic purchase of a specific underlying asset or index.

Particular uses of total return swaps are:

◆ To structure instrument in credit-linked notes, as they allow a return to be stripped from the underlying instrument;
◆ To overcome regulatory or accounting restriction;
◆ To arbitrage funding costs by taking short positions;
◆ To use as an alternative to repos.

Generally total-return swaps are rarely used on high-quality underlying credits. This is because they require sufficient returns to make the whole transaction worthwhile, a situation which is likely to exist only in the case of high-yielding paper.

26.4 Credit-linked notes

Credit-linked notes (CLNs) can be structured in a variety of ways. The more generic CLNs are a combination of a highly-rated borrower and a credit default swap on a less creditworthy risk. Alternatives would be to combine a note, loan or certificate of deposit with some additional credit risk. This could be, for example, via a total return swap or a credit default swap. An example would be a bank wanting to rid itself of its exposure to an emerging market country. It could then issue a bond linked to that country's default.

With such a bond the bank would reduce its exposure to that country and therefore achieve its aim. Investors would buy the bond because it is different from bonds issued by that country itself. This means that the investor would have to make a decision whether the credit risk on the issuer or the default risk of the country in question is more likely to occur.

26.5 Risks and benefits of credit derivatives

26.5.1 Risks

The risks associated with credit derivatives are summarized as the following.

◆ Counterparty risk – the protection buyer has a risk on the protection seller that the value of the bond is paid on the credit default event. This needs to be quantified with appropriate limits and capital adequacy provisions put in place.
◆ Liquidity risk – the individual nature of most contracts and reference assets

means that protection sellers may find it difficult to hedge exposures in this relatively new market.

◆ Basis risk – there is a basis risk to traders that exact hedges of positions undertaken cannot be achieved.

◆ Operational risk – the issues to be addressed before trading is undertaken can include documentation, trading and settlement infrastructure, trading and hedging limits, accounting treatment, capital adequacy position, modelling of risks for the control of risks and integration into other derivative operations. Complex calculations may need to be made on the dates when payments fall due.

26.5.2   Benefits

Banks, as protection buyers, may use credit derivatives to:

◆ reduce the capital required to support assets on the balance sheet;
◆ reduce credit risk concentrations;
◆ free up credit lines;
◆ manage assets on a portfolio basis.

As protection sellers, they can:

◆ earn fee income using a range of credit strategies;
◆ speculate on market movements without actually purchasing underlying assets;
◆ obtain exposure to non-relationship names where they believe the derivatives are favourably priced, enabling them also to diversify their lending portfolio.

Twenty seven

Forward-rate agreements (FRAs) and FRABBA terms

Objectives

This chapter will cover the following topics:

- ◆ FRABBA and other terms;
- ◆ trading and settlement process;
- ◆ calculations.

27.1   Introduction

While FRAs were one of the earliest of the modern derivatives to go into regular use in the early 1980s, they were preceded by other developments. Forward transactions in currencies had been enacted for decades and where one currency was sold forward and bought back at a later date, the intervening exposure produced the same effect as an FRA. Also, forward-forward deposits had been used, but the disadvantage of the latter is that they involve the whole of a principal amount for the period of exposure. So, for example, if a corporate makes a six-month deposit, six-months ahead, there is still a deposit for six months to be made. The corporate may prefer not to have the funds tied up. FRAs thus provide the solution. The buyer may pay a little more for the flexibility and freedom that FRAs allow, but the principal remains available for other uses. Furthermore, where a hedge takes place, it can be reversed by a compensating transaction if wished, whereas a six-month deposit may be impossible to unwind. Taking a compensating six-month loan may be too expensive. Finally, given that no principal is exchanged the counterparty risk will be much reduced by using an FRA.

FRAs have evolved primarily from the interbank market. It is an agreement, whereby the seller agrees to a fixed rate, from an agreed future date, for an agreed fixed period, on an agreed notional principal. No principal amount passes between the two parties. There may, however, be a fee to the bank for arranging the transaction if this is not incorporated in the margin above LIBOR. At the settlement date (ie the starting date for the notional advance), either the seller compensates the buyer for the difference between the agreed rate and the actual rate for the agreed period. If rates have fallen the buyer compensates the seller and vice versa.

As the centre for the Eurodollar market, London has captured a significant amount of FRA business. Most FRAs are in either pound sterling, US dollars or Euros. Average size is GBP5m or in the case of dollar FRAs USD 10m, although they can reach much bigger notional amounts. They are generally quoted on the basis of LIBOR. According to the Bank of International Settlements there were outstanding contracts for the notional value of USD 8.8 trillion at the end of 2002. About 48% of these were denominated in USD and 24% in Euros. The Yen amounted to 9%, while sterling followed with 5% of the total.

An example of an FRA is given below:

1 January	*1 October*	*1 January*
FRA deal date	Settlement of FRA	Maturity of loan and FRA

The example would fit a corporate that has a £1 million borrowing need at a variable rate on 1 October for three months. To protect against the cost of funds rising from the current rate of 5% between now and the start date of the loan, the company buys a 9-12 FRA. If after nine months the three-month rate has risen to 6%, the corporate has suffered an unplanned increase in borrowing costs for the subsequent three months. Under the FRA, the bank, which sold the FRA, will compensate the corporate for this. The payment made is determined by the following formula:

$$\text{Payment made} = \frac{(S\text{-}F) \times (M/365) \times P}{1 + S\ (M/365)}$$

where:

S = spot or settlement interest rate;
F = interest rate agreed at the time the FRA is taken out;
P = notional principal involved;
M = term to maturity of the FRA in days.

The formula in effect discounts the amount paid to the settlement date at the spot rate of interest. If the spot rate exceeds the agreed rate the seller will need to pay the buyer and vice versa.

FRAs are generally used for one of the following three purposes:

◆ to hedge known or anticipated risks;
◆ to manipulate a principal's funding or investment needs; or
◆ to trade for profit.

27.2   FRABBA and other terms

Standard terms have been published by the BBA in its booklet Forward Rate Agreements, which is generally referred to as FRABBA terms. It is also possible to use the ISDA terms and conditions, although these were originally written for interest-rate swaps.

The standard periods ahead for which FRAs are fixed are 1, 2, 3, 6, 9 and 12 months. The standard contract periods are 3, 6, 9 and 12 months. Deals can be done at terms other than this, but will generally cost more.

The parties will need to exchange the following information:

◆ the name of the counterparty;
◆ purchase or sale;
◆ currency, amount, fixing date, settlement date and maturity date;
◆ price or rate agreed;
◆ variations to Frabba terms where agreed;
◆ payment instructions for future settlement.

Under FRABBA terms, a legally binding contract exists as soon as two parties agree an FRA, either by telephone, fax or electronic communication. While both parties may exchange confirmations afterwards, by that time the contract exists. All the standard terms and conditions which might otherwise be specified are included in the FRABBA terms by which the deal is bound unless both parties specifically agree otherwise.

The recommended terms and conditions include:

◆ Settlement
◆ Broken dates (where no BBA interest settlement rate is available)
◆ Subsequent declaration of non-business day
◆ Payment
◆ Cancellation/compensation
◆ Events of default and notice to that effect
◆ Indemnity by the defaulting party
◆ Rights and remedies
◆ Governing law (English)

Where a corporate is the counterparty to an FRA, the FRABBA terms may be augmented or modified according to the specific legal and operating constraints of that company.

27.3   The trading and settlement process

27.3.1   Trading

When completing a transaction, the dealer should check to see whether there is a credit limit in place in respect of the counterparty in question. If so, he will determine whether the deal is a purchase or sale; and agree the following, keying the relevant information into a dealing system or recording it on his dealing ticket.

- ◆ the currency, the amount, fixing date, settlement date and maturity date;
- ◆ the contract interest rate;
- ◆ the broker involved, if any;
- ◆ the legal basis of the deal: Is this FRABBA terms? Will any special conditions apply?
- ◆ payment instructions for any settlement amount due on the settlement date.

Having quoted and traded, the dealer has the option of covering this exposure by transacting an opposite FRA in the market. He may use other markets, such as financial futures or hedge the position in the forward exchange market (since forward exchange rates are determined by interest rates). Or he may deliberately leave the exposure open because of his expectations on interest rate movements.

27.3.2   Settlement

The settlements office will record the deal and send a confirmation. On the rate fixing date, the procedure is as follows: the settlement officers will wait for the rate fixings on the screens. Comparing the contract and the settlement rates, they will calculate the amount receivable or payable and will advise the counterparty of the result. The amount will be positioned. Where payments are due to be made, instructions will be given to the payments section. Where payments are due to be received, receipt can be monitored for sterling (same day value) but monitoring receipt of currency will need to wait until after the spot settlement date.

The rate fixing will use the 11 am BBA fixings (BBAISRs), which are defined in Chapter 20, for FRAs in the currencies where fixings are available. If a deal is transacted in a currency for which there is no BBA fixing, an acceptable screen rate or formula will have been agreed for setting the settlement rate when the deal was struck.

27.3.3   Documentation

FRAs may be traded under ISDA terms or 'FRABBA' terms, which were published by the British Bankers' Association in 1985 and contain standard formats for confirmations as well as the legal basis of FRAs (in particular, representations and warranties, events of default and payments).

27.4   Calculations

The settlement sum may be calculated in two ways. Using the example above, where there is a movement of 0.5% over three months (92 days) on US dollars 10mn. The sum payable before discounting to NPV is:

$$\text{USD } 10,000,000 \times \frac{0.5 \times 92}{36000} = \text{USD } 12,777.78$$

$$\text{Discounted to NPV: USD } 12,777.78 \times \frac{1}{1 + \frac{(5.5 \times 92)}{(36000)}} = \text{USD } 12,600.67$$

The formula achieves the same result. Where the settlement rate S (LIBOR) is higher than the contract rate (F):

$$\frac{(S - F) \times \text{days in the contract period (M)} \times \text{contract amount (P)}}{36500 \text{ or } 36000 + (S \times M)}$$

Where F is higher than S: $\dfrac{(F - S) \times M \times P}{36500 \text{ or } 36000 + (S \times M)}$

Using the figures in our example:

$$\frac{(5.5 - 5.0) \times 92 \times 10,000,000}{36000 + (5.5 \times 92)} = \frac{460,000,000}{36506} = \text{USD } 12,600.67$$

Twenty eight

Interest rate and currency swaps, including ISDA documentation

Objectives

This chapter will cover the following topics:

- ◆ interest rate swaps;
- ◆ currency swaps;
- ◆ documentation: ISDA terms;
- ◆ risk of swaps;
- ◆ managing a swap portfolio.

28.1   Introduction

The currency swap market developed from the back-to-back or parallel loans markets that were used to manage currency assets and liabilities in the 1960s. Counterparties used their relative advantages in their own markets to derive cost benefits, which were then shared, and to restructure their liabilities and assets. Banks would act as intermediaries.

The market remained small until the late 1970s/early 1980s. At this time the interest-rate swaps market emerged as banks learned to arbitrage issuers' and investors' preferences. The amount of interest rate swaps outstanding at the end of 2002 was USD 79 trillion (notional principal amounts). 40% of these were denominated in Euros, followed by the USD with 30%. There is also a market in Yen (16%) and sterling (8%). The Swiss franc market only amounts to 2% of the total notional outstanding amounts.

The swap market today is a commodity-type market in the major currencies with a large number of market makers quoting prices for a wide range of maturities. The markets have developed to the extent that any stream of cashflows can be transformed into virtually any other stream of cash, no matter what basis or currency is required or used, with banks acting as principals. Banks are involved in these markets as market makers, in selling swaps to their clients and also for managing their own balance-sheets.

Interest rate and currency swaps are over-the-counter, off-balance-sheet products separate from contractual balance sheet obligations or liabilities.

Interest rate swaps are contracts which commit two counterparties to exchange streams of payments in the same currency, over an agreed period, each calculated on a different type of interest rate, but based on the same notional principal amount. The payments are usually netted, with there being no transfer of principal.

Currency swaps are contracts that commit two counterparties to exchange two streams of payments in different currencies, over an agreed period, each calculated using a different interest rate. There is an exchange of the principal amounts at the end of the period, at an exchange rate agreed at the outset. There is usually, but need not be, an exchange of principal at the start of the swap.

The terms 'asset swaps' and 'liability swaps' are sometimes used. If an investor is restructuring his portfolio using swaps, these will be 'asset swaps'. This term also refers to the purchase of existing bonds by investment houses. These bonds are transformed using swaps to make them more suitable to investors' requirements. 'Liability swaps' are where borrowers use swaps with bond or other debt issues to create their desired funding obligations.

28.2 Interest rate swaps

In interest rate swap contracts, the principal amount of the contract does not change hands. The contract is based on a notional principal amount. The most common interest rate swap is the *fixed-floating* swap.

In this type of swap, one party agrees to pay interest calculated on a fixed-rate basis, often annually, over the life of the deal, and the counterparty agrees to pay interest on a floating rate basis. The floating interest rate is re-fixed, usually, every three or six months for the life of the deal.

Interest rate swaps can be portrayed as follows, with the fixed flows being shown by a straight line and floating rate flows by a jagged line.

Figure 28.1: Interest rate swaps

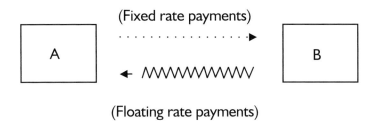

(Fixed rate payments)

A → B

(Floating rate payments)

The parties are identified primarily in terms of who pays or receives the fixed rate: A is the fixed rate payer and B is the fixed rate receiver at the end. Many diagrams show a bank as intermediary between the two parties and earning a fee. That was the way the market started when counterparties were brought together for matched deals, before banks were confident enough to run portfolios of swaps business. It is normal nowadays for swaps to be bilateral deals between a bank and a counterparty.

Features of interest-rate swaps are as follows.

◆ Currencies: Swaps can be arranged in most major currencies.
◆ Amounts: Market amounts are from GBP1 million to GBP100 million or more notional principal amounts. The larger swaps are related to the size of bond issues that are swapped.
◆ Term: They are usually agreed from one year up to 10 years with longer periods being possible for US dollars, Euro and sterling.
◆ Value dates: In the London market, fixings for sterling deals are for same day value but, for currencies, rate fixings are for spot value.

28.2.1 Types of interest rate swaps

Among the variations to basic fixed/floating interest-rate swaps are the following.

◆ '*Basis swaps*' are swaps where interest on one floating-rate basis is exchanged for interest on another floating-rate basis. Examples are US dollar prime rate versus three month LIBOR or LIBOR swapped against a commercial paper rate.
◆ *Forward start swaps* are swaps that start at a future date but with the fixed rate set now. To protect their return, dealers may buy or sell government bond futures to cover the time to the start date. Any net cost of hedging the position until the start date will be reflected in the fixed rate.
◆ *Cashflow swaps* allow the notional principal amount of the swap to be varied during the life of the swap. This is usually by way of an amortising programme.
◆ *Zero coupon swaps*: The fixed-rate payer does not pay interim interest but pays an amount at maturity representing the future value of the payments.

◆ *Index linked swaps*: The fixed leg of the swap is linked to, say, the Retail Price Index.
◆ *Callable, puttable and extendable swaps*: One or other party has the right to terminate the swap before its maturity date, or to extend that date, on terms agreed at the outset.
◆ *Swaptions*: For payment of a premium, banks will write options on swaps where the buyer has the right but not the obligation to assume a position in a swap at a future date at a rate agreed now.

28.2.2   Pricing interest rate swaps

The fixed-rate leg of a swap is usually priced as a spread over the most recent government bond yield for the respective period. Short-dated swaps are priced off short-term interest rate futures. Bid and offered rates are displayed on screens: prices may be quoted as 'all in' rates, which is usual for sterling (including the spread over gilts) or may split out the spread, as is usual for US dollar swaps. An example of the latter is:

Offer-Bid

Term	US T Bond	Swap spread	(All in Swap rates offer/bid)
2 year	3.00	32 – 30	3.32 – 3.30
3 year	3.12	33 – 31	3.45 – 3.43
4 year	3.19	36 – 34	3.55 – 3.53
5 year	3.31	37 – 35	3.68 – 3.66
10 year	3.53	42 – 38	3.95 – 3.91

The offered price is the price at which traders are willing to receive fixed-rate funds. The bid is the price at which traders are willing to pay fixed-rate funds. The swap spread is the only element of the pricing that is quoted firm by the dealer. Once this is agreed, the respective bond yield is established and the all-in rate set.

The swap spread over the bond yield fluctuates in line with supply and demand. If there are a large number of fixed-rate payers in the market, eg commercial companies wishing to pay fixed-rates but unable to issue bonds, the swap spread will increase.

The screen rates are for interbank deals and commercial clients will receive lower bid rates and pay higher offer rates and receive lower bid rates, with an all-in fixed-rate being quoted to the customer. The extra margin reflects the counterparty credit risk or intermediation premium.

Floating-rate payments will usually be based on flat or unadjusted reference rates such as LIBOR. The basis of the LIBOR fixings to be used must be agreed. BBA Interest Settlement Rates (BBAISRs) or ISDA fixings are usually used.

Where rates are quoted 'semi-semi' both the fixed-rate and floating-rate payments are on a semi-annual basis. Quarterly/quarterly implies quarterly fixed and floating payments.

Cashflows can be established at the outset for the fixed-rate leg of the swap. The LIBOR rate for the first period will be set by reference to LIBORs at the time the trade is agreed.

28.2.3   Negotiating interest rate swaps

In negotiating swaps, the key financial details are agreed orally between dealers. Key details are then confirmed in writing. The legally binding contract is established when the traders agree terms. The contract documentation for that swap is exchanged subsequently.

Dealers should:

- ◆ identify themselves and the capacity in which they are acting, ie as principal or as broker;
- ◆ identify which side of the swap they are on in terms of what they wish to pay and receive as cashflows throughout the life of the swap, eg payer of fixed-rate dollars against floating-rate dollars;
- ◆ specify the maturity of the proposed transaction, giving details of any date matching requirements and how any 'stump' periods will be handled;
- ◆ identify the principal amount(s) and currency in which they are to deal;
- ◆ specify, in respect of pricing:
  - ● the fixed-rate at which they pay/receive and the basis on which the rate is calculated, ie actual/360; actual/365; actual/actual; 360/360 (bond basis); paid annually/semi annually/quarterly;
  - ● the floating interest rate periods, frequency of reset and frequency of payment;
  - ● the extent of the commitment, ie whether 'indicative' or 'firm' and, if a firm price is being shown, the period during which it is open for acceptance. If a party is to place reliance on a firm price as a basis for proceeding with an associated transaction, this should be stated. It is always advisable to re-confirm that a price is firm before entering into related deals;
  - ● whether rates quoted in respect of a brokered deal are gross or net of any commission payable;
- ◆ specify in whose name the contract will be concluded and whether a guarantee or any form of collateral will be given/is required;
- ◆ state clearly the conditions to which the swap is subject prior to being agreed, eg:
  - ● obtaining credit approval;
  - ● ability to execute an associated transaction;
- ◆ specify any terms that are not in accordance with BBAIRS or ISDA terms.

The business day convention for the floating interest rate periods must be agreed. This may be 'end-end', 'IMM' basis, or 'modified following business day'.

In 'end-end' contracts, the interest payment dates are always on the last business day of the calendar month. 'IMM' swaps have interest payments on the third Wednesday of March, June, September and December to match the maturities of futures contracts. The 'modified following business day' convention means that interest payments will be on the following business day if they would otherwise fall on a weekend or holidays, but will revert (be modified) to the original date in the month for subsequent payments. The money market convention is for transactions to continue to go to the next succeeding business day, except at month ends.

28.2.1   The uses of interest rate swaps and new issue arbitrage

Uses of swaps

Swaps enable financial institutions and commercial customers to:

- ◆ obtain the lowest funding costs possible;
- ◆ obtain access to fixed-term debt;
- ◆ restructure debt or investment portfolios;
- ◆ take views on interest rates without restructuring their balance-sheets.

It is not always possible or desirable for financial institutions and companies to access debt markets directly or continuously to achieve these objectives. Bond markets may be closed to issuers for a variety of reasons and using swaps overcomes the following barriers.

- ◆ *Credit and country risk*: Names that are readily acceptable in the short-term money markets may not be so attractive to the longer-term capital and debt markets. Where a particular name or group of names from the same country taps an international market too frequently, the market's appetite for that issuer or country may quickly dry up and premiums be placed on future issues.
- ◆ *Anomalies in the ability to raise funds in different financial centres*: A 'Triple A' rated US corporation may have little difficulty raising funds from the US capital markets but may not be able to raise funds in other capital markets where its name is not as well known.
- ◆ *Liquidity:* A lack of liquidity within a particular sector of the market may mean that there is no scope to make new issues.
- ◆ *Differentials between pricing of bank lending and capital debt:* Floating-rate funds from banks may be raised at lower rate differentials than longer-term fixed-rate capital because of the higher risks perceived in long-term lending. This is illustrated in the next paragraphs on new issue arbitrage.

New issue arbitrage

New issue arbitrage is the term used to describe how interest-rate swaps can be used to create cheaper floating-rate funds for one party and allow access to fixed-rate funds to another. Fixed-rate issues have bigger differences in coupons than floating-rate loans, which are less risky in interest rate terms.

As an example, company A (rated Aaa) can raise five-year fixed-rate funds at 6% and floating-rate funds at LIBOR plus 10 basis points (bp). Company B (rated Baa) would have to pay 6.75% pa for fixed-rate funds but may not be able to make an issue because it would not be investment grade. Company B pays LIBOR plus 50 bp for floating-rate funds.

Company A will issue a fixed-rate bond because this is its market of comparative advantage. It can issue 75 bp cheaper than company B. Company B will raise floating-rate funds and will suffer a 'loss' of 40 bp compared to the rate at which company A could do the same. The saving of 35 bp might be shared: 30 bp, to company A and 5 bp to company B. The information can be set out as follows:

	A pays	*B pays*	*Difference*
Fixed-rate	6%	6.75%	0.75%
Floating-rate	LIBOR + .10%	LIBOR +.50%	0.40%
Net benefit to be shared:			0.35%

Figure 28.2: Interest-rate swap

* The fixed-rate for the swap can be calculated as follows: since you know that Company A will reduce its costs by 30 bp the 10bp on the LIBOR loans will not be paid and the remainder, 20 bp, will be obtained from the swap. This can be summarized as follows:

Cost of funds to A	%	Cost of funds to B	%
Pays fixed coupon	6	Pays floating debt	LIBOR + 0.50
Receives from swap	6.2	Receives from swap	LIBOR
Net gain	0.20	Net cost	0.50
Pays swap floating	LIBOR	Pays swap fixed	6.2
Cost of floating	LIBOR − 0.20	Cost of fixed	6.70
(normal cost LIBOR+10 bp)		(normal cost	6.75, saving 0.05)

28.3   Currency swaps

Interest payments on the two currencies may be on the basis of:

- ◆ fixed-rate basis for both currencies (fixed-fixed);
- ◆ floating-rate basis for each currency (floating-floating);
- ◆ fixed-rate for one currency and floating for the other (fixed-floating).

An example of how and when currency swaps are used is as follows. When Disney wanted to finance a project in Japan, it required long-term yen, but its name was not well enough known to obtain the best terms in a yen issue. However, it could access the Swiss franc market on favourable terms. A Japanese counterparty was found that could issue yen and could make use of Swiss francs. In this case, the principal amounts were exchanged at the outset. Disney made the interest and principal payments in yen.

Currency swaps are akin to long-dated forward exchange transactions. Long-dated forward exchange rates are determined by the premiums or discounts applied, which reflect the interest rates of the two currencies. In a currency swap, the rate of exchange at the maturity of the deal is the current spot rate. Interest payments are made on an ongoing basis rather than being built into the forward rate.

28.4   Documentation: ISDA terms

The British Bankers' Association (BBA) issued its terms and conditions for London interbank interest-rate swaps in August 1985. Development of the market had been inhibited because of the lack of standard documentation, a need which BBAIRS terms were designed to meet. Previously, deals had been documented individually, a process which often took months of negotiation for each deal.

BBAIRS terms did not, however, become the industry standard. The standard documentation used in the market is produced by ISDA, the International Swaps and Derivatives Association (formerly the International Swaps Dealers' Association). It covers a wide range of derivatives products including swaps, options, caps, floors and FRAs.

An ISDA Master Agreement, once in place between two parties, covers all subsequent swaps through the process of novation whereby individual contracts are cancelled. This means that there is a single contract in place between the parties, which allows netting of payments on the same date in the same currency. The aim of netting is:

◆ to reduce settlement risk; and
◆ to give legal force against 'cherry picking' in the event of the liquidation of one of the parties. This is where a liquidator might seek to honour profitable contracts and disclaim unprofitable ones.

The ISDA documentation falls into three main parts: The Master Agreement, the Schedule and Confirmations. The *ISDA Master Agreement* includes the following.

◆ *Local and cross border* versions, covering the situation if both counterparties are governed by the same or different jurisdictions. This relates mainly to taxation issues.
◆ *Interpretation* clarifies the position where the document is inconsistent.
◆ *Obligations* of counterparties; the clause includes netting and settlement definitions.
◆ *Representations* require that each party is legally formed and that the officers have authority to contract.
◆ *Agreements* require each party to supply the appropriate documentation as requested, for example, lists of authorized signatures.
◆ *Default/termination* covers the failure to pay, bankruptcy and similar events.
◆ *Early termination* details the procedures required by both parties.
◆ *Transfer*. This limits the ability of each party to transfer its obligations without the other's agreement.
◆ *Payment*. This sets out that payments will be made free of withholding tax.
◆ *Expenses* covers the obligations of each party for expenses.
◆ *Notices*. This sets out the procedures for serving notices.
◆ *Governing law* and jurisdiction.
◆ *Definitions* of the major terms in the agreement but supplemented by the other booklets of definitions.

The *Schedule* is designed to enable parties to alter or amend the provisions of the standard master agreement as they wish through specification of additional or alternative provisions.

Confirmations: A standard confirmation is defined for each type of instrument, including swaps, options, caps, floors and FRAs.

28.5   Risks of swaps

The risks of swaps and other derivatives business are market, credit, liquidity, legal and operational.

28.5.1   Market or dealing risk

A dealer who has not matched a swap in his book and is paying a fixed-rate risks a loss if rates fall before a matching deal can be put in place. The trader would be committed to paying out more fixed-rate interest than he would receive.

To hedge this position, he may buy Treasury stock or Treasury futures for a similar amount and maturity to obtain an asset with a fixed-rate income stream. Any loss, if rates fall, will be compensated by an increase in the capital value of the Treasury stock. If the Treasury stock were purchased, how would the purchase be funded? Almost certainly using repo, which demonstrates how these markets are inter-related. If the dealer was due to receive fixed-rate, Treasury stock would be sold, with the stock being obtained by reverse repo, if needed, or Treasury futures would be sold.

This type of hedging may be used with any currency where there is a suitable government bond market. There are associated risks and costs that must be quantified. The main criterion is that the hedging instrument must be as 'default-risk free'.

Market liquidity risk is where an institution will be unable to unwind or offset a particular position at or near the previous market price because of inadequate market depth or disruption in the marketplace. Provisions should be in place to access alternative markets (for example, cash and futures markets) for hedging positions.

28.2.2   Credit risk

Although 'credit' is not extended in a swap transaction, there is the risk that the counterparty might default during the life of the swap. The risk relates to the cost of replacing the cashflows of the deal.

This cost can be calculated as follows. A swap for $10m with a five-year term is written with the bank being a fixed-rate receiver at 9%. The counterparty defaults after one-year and four-year swap rates are 8 – 8.05%. The bank can replace the swap with one where it receives a fixed-rate of 8%. The loss is 1% over four years, ie, $400,000, discounted to present value, with a further adjustment if the default does not fall on a LIBOR fixing date.

The amount of credit or counterparty limit to be used for a deal will be a percentage of the notional principal amount and will take account of:

◆ whether fixed or floating-rate interest is to be received;
◆ whether foreign exchange exposure needs to be included;
◆ the term or maturity of the swap;
◆ the level of volatility of interest rates in the currency/currencies of the deal. For example, swaps in high interest rate currencies are more risky then those in low interest rate currencies;
◆ current risk – the loss that would be suffered in the event of immediate default;
◆ future risk – a risk element is added for potential future losses.

28.5.3   Liquidity risk

The periodic cashflows require transaction banking accounts to be open for receiving and making interest payments. The treasury function will finance shortfalls or invest any surplus in each relevant currency of payment.

28.5.4   Legal risk

The first major default on swap contracts was by the UK Local Authority, Hammersmith and Fulham Borough Councils. It was ruled by the House of Lords that local authorities had no power to enter into swap contracts. The swaps had been used for speculative purposes and were simply a bet on interest rates. The underlying authority of counterparties to make valid and binding contracts has been subject to scrutiny ever since.

28.5.5   Operational risk

The administration of swaps by the back office must take into account:

◆ the complexity and diversity of the products in use;
◆ the volumes of swap transactions and the required speed of response;
◆ the need for speedy confirmation and documenting of transactions;
◆ the number and size of cashflows and rate fixings involved.

Over the life of a typical swap, one or both sets of payment flows may be variable and require interest rates to be set on pre-determined dates. Counterparties will need to:

◆ determine the relevant rate fixing on the given date;
◆ calculate and advise the settlement amounts payable. Depending on interest rate levels, net payment flow directions may be reversed from one payment date to another;

◆ advise the other party of the rate and settlement amount(s) for the next period;
◆ make or monitor receipt of amounts to be paid/received.

28.6　Managing a swap portfolio

When transacting an individual swap, an active swap trader will rarely seek to find an exactly matching counterparty immediately. Instead, the swap book will be managed on a portfolio basis with the aggregate interest and currency exposure being calculated and hedged as a whole. This increases the dealer's ability to quote two-way prices in varying sizes and for most dates while covering his position in standard market periods and amounts.

The principle underlying portfolio management of a swaps book is that of discounted cashflow, giving a present value of cashflows that have been marked-to-market. The sensitivity of this present value to movements in interest rates or to the shape of the yield curve can then be estimated. There are a variety of other products that can be used to provide a hedge for this sensitivity, eg futures or FRAs. Relative costs and credit limits must be taken into account.

28.6.1　The secondary market and cancelling swaps

Exposures on swaps can be controlled by trading out positions in the secondary market. The methods of selling or cancelling swaps are:

◆ *Swap Sale or novation*. It is possible under swap documentation to assign a deal to another counterparty. This will be for a cash consideration paid or received representing the difference in fixed-rates for the remaining term, discounted to present-day value. The original counterparty will need to be satisfied with the credit of the new counterparty before giving its permission for the assignment;
◆ *Cancellation* by the original parties for cash settlement.

Twenty nine

Financial futures markets

Objectives

This chapter will cover the following topics:

- ◆ definitions;
- ◆ futures exchanges;
- ◆ function of clearing house;
- ◆ margin requirements;
- ◆ treasury considerations;
- ◆ calculations.

29.1   Introduction

A financial futures is a legally binding contract to buy or sell a fixed amount of a financial commodity at an agreed price on a specified day in the future. What is actually being bought is a defined contract and the details of this purchase or sale are clearly specified in the contract. While it may appear to be similar in nature to other hedging instruments, there is one fundamentally important consideration for a future. Whereas with an option, for example, the risk of loss is limited to the price actually paid for that option, in the case of a future, the risk or potential gain is almost unlimited.

While derivatives in general can seriously damage corporate health, financial futures are potentially the most dangerous. They offer huge potential gains and losses. They are ideally used to manage risk, rather than to create them. Most futures do not run to maturity, the transaction usually being reversed before the specified delivery day. In the case of those that do run to maturity, either the underlying goods can be delivered, or a cash settlement can be made for the determined value. Because futures are traded in order to avoid the need to trade the underlying commodity, it is not surprising they are settled for cash, rather than physical delivery.

The basic function that a future performs is to offer protection to individuals or institutions that are exposed to the potential consequences of adverse movements in interest rates, equities or currencies. A future can be used to transfer that risk to someone else, although the key characteristic of a future (as opposed to other forms of hedging) is that, if markets move in the opposite direction to the risk which is hedged, the costs of owning it can increase, sometimes alarmingly.

29.2   Financial futures contracts

There is a standard terminology for all the contracts dealt on LIFFE, which this section will focus on. All contracts are designed such that a price increase reflects a positive move in the underlying commodity. So for bond currency futures an increase in the contract price means that the underlying commodity is improving in value. When it comes to interest futures this is done by creating a reference price of 100. To represent a beneficial change in the cost of money, the absolute value of the interest rate is deducted from 100 (eg 5% produces a price of 100-5 = 95.00).

The unit of trading is chosen to reflect a representative amount of the underlying commodity for normal market trading purposes, eg £500,000 for the short sterling interest rate future. The delivery months are always three months apart, stretching out as far as will be supported by reasonable liquidity in the futures market. The last trading day is the third Wednesday of the delivery month. This can lead to market distortions, especially in the US, as contracts expire on 'witching day'. Positions are almost invariably closed out before the last trading day. Delivery day is the first business day following the last trading day. The minimum price movement determines the value of 'one tick', ie the incremental cash value of a minimum price movement of one unit. Other information such as the trading hours and contract standards for each future are predefined.

29.3   Futures exchanges

The futures exchanges themselves have a number of responsibilities and roles to perform. Firstly, they need to administer and control the orderly operation of the markets, in conjunction with the regulatory remit of the FSA. Secondly, they have a vested interest in ensuring that their markets are successful and popular, to the benefit of all participants. Market makers benefit from higher turnover, leading to greater rewards. Users benefit from active and successful markets, through greater liquidity at competitive prices in a wide range of contracts.

The exchanges themselves are responsible for the membership, organization and trading rules, with the purpose being to maintain financially sound, orderly, competitive and well-supervised markets. Because of the enormous potential impact on the overall markets of which they are a part and the possible economic and monetary effects of failure, exchanges are themselves subject to supervision by the FSA.

LIFFE, being the largest futures exchange in the UK, provides a good example of how future exchanges are organized. Through its committees, LIFFE has broad powers to ensure that free and open markets exist for the trading of futures contracts. With overall responsibility for the rules of the exchange, they have the power to take immediate action to deal with anything that may threaten the maintenance of orderly trading. Although separate, an integral function of the successful operations of LIFFE is the clearing house. In the case of LIFFE this service is provided by the London Clearing House (LCH). Sudden changes in market circumstances, such as a devaluation of a currency, the failure of a major entity, or the announcement of a rights issue, could threaten the orderly trading of one or a number of instruments. In such cases LCH has the power to vary margin requirements widely. One of the most important tools available to LIFFE is the ability to restrict trades to 'liquidation only'. This means that no new positions can be opened. The exchange can also change the limits within which the price of a contract can trade in a day before a halt is called. However, these tools are used sparingly, as their use can undermine confidence in the market itself.

Thus the functions of an exchange include the following.

- ◆ Establishing trading, accounting, recording, procedures and practices.
- ◆ Regular review of the financial standing and integrity of all its members.
- ◆ Maintenance of audit, investigation and other supervisory process in relation to member activities and records.
- ◆ Disciplinary procedures, including suspension, expulsion and withdrawal of membership of market makers who abuse their special position in any way that might undermine the stability or reputation of the Exchange.
- ◆ The same powers where members threaten the orderly conduct of the markets or fail to meet the accounting requirements, financial criteria or rules of the exchange, or its clearing house or supervisory authority.
- ◆ Establishing confirmation procedures.
- ◆ Supervision of the process to protect customers in the event of failure of a clearing house member.

29.4   Functions of the clearing house

The previous section touched on the role of the clearing house. It plays a crucial role in the whole process in a number of ways.

- ◆ It clears all trades on the exchange every day. Assuming all bargains have been matched there is also the matter of margin to be calculated and collected. Before each trading day starts, the clearing house will clear all accounts with clearing members. Often there will be a balance owed by the clearing member, which must be accounted for, split separately between margin required for clients' positions and that required for the clearing member's own positions. Sometimes the net position will be a credit to the clearing member to be paid away. This will be covered by margin, which is the largest estimated variation expected in a single day's market movement. This limits the risk for the clearing house.
- ◆ It guarantees all cleared trades.
- ◆ It provides a common automated processing system for all its members, allowing the up-to-date statement of account for each member to be produced after the end of each trading day and giving an audit trail which can be followed by members' back-office settlement functions.
- ◆ It provides a real-time information service, available across the market with up-to-date prices.

While members of the exchange may also be members of the clearing house, they must make separate application to do so. Nevertheless, the clearing house will deal direct or transact only with its own members. For trading and clearing purposes, members may either trade and clear for customer or their own account; or delegate trading and clearing or assume delegated responsibility on behalf of other members. The roles performed are based on the specific category of membership, as authorized by the clearing house.

29.5   Margin

The nature of financial futures makes them potentially highly risky. Accordingly, and to protect the market, clearing members are required to put up margins to protect the underlying risk of contracts. The clearing members will in turn require margin from their clients, at least sufficient to cover those positions. Commission brokers may require more margin from their customers than the clearing members would have to put up. This is simply because of the double risk of transactions one step removed and the potentially higher credit risk of a client who may be either a hedger or a speculator or both, and who is not directly involved in the futures market itself. There are various types of margin.

Initial margin is that margin required to ensure performance of all outstanding contracts. Its value is proportional to the notional principal value of the contracts. It will vary, based on a calculation of the likely maximum movement in the market prices expected in any one day. It is a relatively small percentage for short-term interest rate contracts, varying out to five or ten times as much of a long-bond contract. This is due to the greater volatility. The clearing house can vary the initial margin. The examples of compensating positions in requirement at any time, based on its judgement as to changes in volatility. This margin variation will change the amount that has to be settled daily on the calls and repayments of members' net outstanding positions on their accounts.

Where a futures client opens a position one way in the contracts for a particular future and a contrary position in the same group of contracts, this is known as spread or straddle. For example, if a trader buys a long position in, say the May three-month sterling interest rate contracts and simultaneously sells short the August delivery of the same contract, he has created a spread. For margin purposes, his net requirement is reduced as a result, because the risk in one position is outweighed to some extent by the risk in the other position. The examples of compensating positions that the clearing house will recognize include: inter-delivery month spreads; inter-commodity spreads; and hedge margin, where someone is registered as a hedger with the clearing house. All these are examples of spread margins.

At the end of each trading day on the futures' markets, all contracts are marked-to-market with the closing prices. They must then be settled to market before the following day's dealing begins. The initial margin is a basic level of security, but in addition, contract holders must put up or receive variation margin, based on the closing price. Where anyone defaults on daily settlement of margin in Liffe, his position will be liquidated and any net shortfall will be made up from the total net margin available. Where prices of underlying commodities are volatile, positions on contracts and associated margin requirements can fluctuate daily. At any time, a trader should be prepared to use his judgement and therefore exercise his choice between putting up more margin as the position deteriorates or closing out the position with a compensating transaction.

29.6   Treasury considerations

Treasury considerations should primarily be based on the use of futures for hedging purposes and the circumstances in which different tactics might be used. There are many different hedging possibilities and futures, not all of which can be discussed in this text.

29.6.1   To hedge the cost of borrowing

A treasurer may have a loan needing to be renewed in three months. Rather than borrowing the funds now or taking the risk of a possible interest rate movement, the company could, by using a futures contract, lock in today's cost of borrowing for three months, without the need to take out a loan, by using a futures contract. This can be achieved by shorting the three-month sterling interest rate futures and buying back (closing out) the position in three months time when the borrowing need crystallizes. If during the intervening period rates have in fact increased, the gain on the futures contract will offset the increased cost of borrowing. If rates have fallen, the loss incurred on the futures contract will be offset by the cheaper cost of borrowing at that time. If the treasurer changes his opinion in the meantime, or the anticipated rate increase occurs before the borrowing date, there is nothing to stop him closing out the position early and leaving himself unhedged.

29.6.2 To protect against a change in the shape of the yield curve

The shape of the yield curve represents the interplay between the current interest rate experience and longer-term interest rate expectations. Suppose that interest rates are expected to fall next week, but the market is likely to take the view that this will represent the bottom of the interest rate cycle and the next move after that is expected to be a rise. The short end of the yield curve will fall and the longer end will steepen as a result of this scenario.

The treasurer can protect against the consequences of this by simultaneously going long of a short delivery month in the sterling three-month futures and selling (going short of) a later delivery month. This is known as buying the spread. If rates fall as expected, the earliest delivery contract will change in value by more than the later delivery contract. Consequently the profit on the short month will outweigh any possible loss on the later day. The treasurer can then book the profit by closing out both positions. If instead, short-term interest rates rise unexpectedly, the loss on the short delivery contract will be offset by a gain on the longer position.

29.6.3 Overview

At first sight the apparently limited range of futures contracts may appear to restrict the capability of treasurers to hedge all possible risks, it is usually possible using computer simulation tools to put together a number of different hedges to make up the overall position to be achieved. With high liquidity and so many players in the markets worldwide, futures have become a very important tool in portfolio risk management.

The following are some of the many possible benefits of futures for hedging purposes.

◆ They allow treasurers to manage the forward consequences of known and seasonal cashflows.

- The trading levels for futures contracts give a fair indication of market expectations of future interest and currency rates for planning and treasury purposes.
- For many, futures are an 'off-balance-sheet' activity, although banks will have to report them.
- Futures are competitively priced for everyone, due to the depth and liquidity of the market, the nature of the market processes and the quality of regulation. The dealing and margin costs are also reasonable, allowing highly leveraged positions to be taken up for relatively little capital. Nevertheless traders need to remain aware of volatility and ensuing margin requirements.
- The credit risk is far lower than for the cash market, not only because smaller sums are involved, but also because the clearing system takes on much of the risk.

29.7   Calculations

Let us take an example from the three-month sterling interest rate. For the sake of simplicity we will ignore the cost of margin requirements in this example.

Suppose that a corporate treasurer has a £500,000 six-month borrowing requirement from 12 September. In the Spring, the cashflow normally surges after a lean winter, allowing the borrowing to be repaid and spare funds invested. The treasurer is concerned about interest rate volatility in the short term and therefore sells the September contract and buys into the March contract.

Transactions are as follows.

a) Sell two September contracts at 94.29 and buy two March contracts at 93.91. The two contracts counter each other in risk terms. This limits the exposure and therefore the necessary margin. Although the underlying unit is £500,000 and the borrowing and investment will be for the same amount, the borrowing is for six months, rather than three months for the sterling contract. So the treasurer has decided to double the cover on both transactions.

b) The treasurer was right and on 1 September base rates rise from 5.75% to 6%, which is echoed by the three month LIBOR rate. The six-month LIBOR rate, however, rises further from 5.75% to 6.25% as a result of the fears of further changes in interest rates. The September contracts have now fallen from 94.29 to 94.00 (representing a move in discounted rates from 5.71% to 6%) and the March contracts have fallen from 93.91 to 93.40 (6.09% to 6.6%).

c) The treasurer decides to close the September position on 12 September, the day the loan starts. He takes the profit by buying two contracts to close but decides also to run the March position, feeling that markets have overreacted and being confident that an investment rate of 6% pa is more likely by then. In the meantime, by running the position he has effectively bought the contract at an equivalent rate of 6.6% pa by not selling. On 1 March, three month rates are indeed 6% pa and the March contract is trading at 94.00. The position is then closed out though a closing sale of two contracts.

The minimum price movement on the three-month sterling contract is 0.01 and therefore the value of one tick is £12.50. (£500,000/100 x 3/12 x 0.01)

The gain on the sale and repurchase of the September contract is 29 tick (94.29 – 94.00) = £362.50 x 2 (2 contracts) = £725.00. The funds are borrowed at 6.25% pa for six months at a total interest cost of £15,496.58 (£500,000 x 0.0625 x 181/ 365). The offsetting gain on the futures transactions closed in September was £725.00. This reduces the interest cost of the borrowings to £14,771.58, equivalent to a rate of 5.96%.

The gain on the purchase and resale of the March contracts is nine tick (94.00-93.91), although in opportunity cost terms, from the time in September when the treasurer decided to run the purchase, the increase is 60 ticks. Nine tick on two contracts is 9 x 12.5 x 2 = £225.00. The interest return on the three-month investment of £500,000 on 12 March at 6% is £7,561.64 (£500,000 x 0.06 x 92/ 365). The gain on the March contracts was £225. This increases the effective return on the investment of £7,786.64, equivalent to a rate of 6.18% pa.

From 12 July to 12 September, the treasurer was hedged both ways, through compensating transactions in different delivery contracts. The exposure was therefore very limited. From 12 September, when the treasurer decided to run the contract, the maximum cash at risk would probably have been no more than £10,000 for margin purposes. Savings were made on the loan and the return was increased on the investment. Without using futures, either of these would have been foregone, or £1,000,000 cash would have had to be borrowed from 12 July to 12 September and £1,000,000 invested (with the attendant credit risk) from 12 September to 12 March to achieve a much worse result in opportunity cost terms.

Thirty

Financial options

Objectives

This chapter will cover the following topics:

- ◆ definitions;
- ◆ pricing;
- ◆ ICOM terms;
- ◆ OTC and exchange traded options.

30.1   Introduction

Although highly flexible, options are easily misunderstood and while currency options may be regarded as relatively straightforward by some, interest rate options can be highly complex. The notion of an option is fairly straightforward: you can buy or sell the right to buy or sell something in the future and if things do not work out as you hope, you can abandon that right, having lost only the price you paid for it. Three important attractions are that:

- ◆ you can buy or sell an option and also have the commodity on which it is based, thus getting the best results of both worlds;
- ◆ you can, for example, protect yourself against the risk of rising interest rates while not excluding the gains from falling rates if they occur; and
- ◆ finally you can use options to speculate from a limited capital base, without having to tie up large amounts of principal and with certainty of your maximum loss.

An option is a binding agreement between two parties which confers on one the right, but not the obligation, to buy or sell a defined amount of a commodity or financial instrument (including other hedging instruments) at a known price, up to an agreed future expiry date. This means that the holder of an option is not contracted to deliver or accept delivery, but may choose to do so only if the circumstances suits him.

30.2   Terminology

A call option confers the right to buy, a put option confers the right to sell. The person who buys is the holder, buyer or purchaser; the seller is often known as the writer. The price at which the holder has the right to call or put is known as the strike price or exercise price. When the market price of the underlying commodity or instrument is the same as the strike price, the option is said to be 'at the money'. When the option is standing at a loss, it is 'out of the money' and when at a profit, it is 'in the money'.

Exercise of 'American' options may take place on any business day up to and including the expiry date and up to the expiry time stated in the option. 'European' options must wait until the last day of the period specified in the contract. According to market practice, it is now commonplace for an option standing 'in the money' at expiry to be exercised automatically on behalf of holders. Otherwise, the onus lies with the holder to exercise the option, failing which it is regarded as abandoned and the duty of delivery on the writer lapses.

The buyer of an option, whether a call or a put, pays a premium to the writer for the rights he acquires. This premium is usually payable immediately, together with any fees or commissions. The premium for a put tends to be smaller than for a call. This is because a price can only fall as far as its absolute value, whereas it can in theory rise without limit. The premium represents the value the writer of the option places on the risk he is taking. This risk can be substantial or unlimited unless it is immediately or later hedged in some way.

Two possibilities would be to hold or acquire the underlying commodity or instrument, or to enter into a matching transaction in another option or hedging instrument to hedge all or part of the risk. It is thus possible to use options alone or in combination to create or neutralize known or finite risks. The hedger can consequently completely insulate his portfolio against risk and the speculator can define his expected gain in a given set of circumstances, while being able to lock in a gain or change stance rapidly if necessary.

Intrinsic value is the amount the option would be 'in the money' if exercised immediately. The time value is the part of the premium that does not represent intrinsic value.

Implied volatility is very important in the option markets. Volatility is one of the key factors for determining an option's price. As a result it is possible to calculate the implied volatility of an option if all the other factors are known. This is important because volatility, or expected future movements, are by definition unknown and traders may use different volatilities to price their options. Knowing the implied volatility can thus help compare options with each other.

Since options came into being, they have proliferated in number and type. An option is not the same as a warrant. There are now options on equities, currencies, interest rates and bonds. In combination they can provide caps, floors, collars, swaptions (options on swaps), convertibles and many other combinations with other hedging instruments. Although warrants are very similar to options they are different instruments. Unlike an option only the issuer of the underlying stock can deliver on a warrant.

30.3   Pricing

The pricing of options is one of the more challenging areas of option trading. It is based on the assumption of a Random Walk. In other words, at any point in time, a market can move in either direction, or stand still, irrespective of what has happened in the past. The most frequently used pricing models are based on the Black-Scholes model. The premium, ie the price of the option, represents an approximate mathematical estimate of the amount necessary to 'insure' the writer against likelihood of loss. Whether a premium is expensive will depend on the probability and possible size of any payment to the holder. The main factors involved in determining the premium are as follows.

♦ The relationship of the strike price to the current market price. The higher the strike price, the less likely it is that the market price will exceed it in the option period, and therefore the lower the premium.
♦ The option period. The longer it is, the higher the premium is likely to be. The price of the option should increase in proportion to the square root of the option period. A change of one day has a greater proportional effect with just a few days to run than at the start of the option period. This curve of time value decay is also a square root curve.
♦ The expected volatility of the market price. The greater the volatility, the higher the premium. This is the most important factor, because it is the most sensitive and the hardest to predict. Historical data is not necessarily a reliable predictor of the future, but it is often used as a basis for the calculation. It is possible to structure deals so that speculators can take advantage of volatility alone.
♦ The level of interest rates. The premium is paid up front and therefore there is a loss of income for the holder and an immediate earning potential for the writer. If interest rates are relatively high, the earnings potential is increased and this may help to reduce the premium.

◆ The current levels of supply and demand in the market. Premiums will be higher in thin markets and lower in more liquid markets.

30.4   ICOM terms

In 1992, in conjunction with appropriate authorities in New York and Tokyo, the BBA issued the International Currency Options Market Terms (ICOM Terms). ICOM terms incorporate a model Master Agreement, which, together with appropriate confirmations, will constitute a single agreement between two parties to an option deal. The Master Agreement is a comprehensive document covering all likely common clauses for such agreements. As with other model agreements in the money markets, this saves immeasurably in terms of time and money. Without it, the options markets were unlikely to have become as successful as they are. The agreement is a document by exception, in the sense that it carries standard terms and a bank must indicate by exception where it proposes to depart from such terms. The key elements fundamental to normal market practice relate to price quotations, expiry dates and the exercise and settlement of options.

Prices are quoted on either premiums or volatility. In addition, the counterparts need to agree:

◆ the option style (American or European);
◆ the amount and currency;
◆ the time and date of expiry;
◆ the dates for paying the premium and settlement;
◆ strike price.

Options may also involve a contemporaneous foreign exchange transaction ('delta hedge'), which needs to be incorporated in addition to the Master Agreement. ICOM terms do, however, provide for the automatic netting of premium payments due on the same day and in the same currency. Where a price is quoted as a premium, the counterparties will agree the terms and how the premium will be expressed, together with a spot rate of exchange for a delta hedge agreed. An option based on volatility pricing is not legally binding until the premium has been agreed. It will be based on a number of factors, as agreed between the parties:

◆ a percentage per annum;
◆ the spot rate;
◆ interest factors in the pair of currencies used;
◆ the strike price; and
◆ the expiry day.

Expiry dates may be quoted on straight dates or by calendar months and allow for the foreign exchange market practice of spot settlement (ie two days). Accordingly, calendar month options expire two days before the third Wednesday of the month, to coincide with exchange-traded options. Straight date options expire after an exact number of calendar days.

An option may be exercised any time up to the expiry time on the expiry date. For settlement to be effected two business days after exercise, it must be before 15.00 hrs, otherwise it will be deferred by another day. Settlement between parties may be made by gross payments as for foreign exchange contracts. ICOM terms provide for automatic exercise of options, which are in the money and at least 1% outside the strike price. They may be settled by calling for delivery of the commodity or instrument, or on a net cash basis. The BBA provides daily settlement prices for the major currencies used, by reference to eight interbank spot foreign exchange prices at 15.00 hrs on the exercise date.

30.5   OTC and exchange traded options

Options have developed down two parallel routes to provide an extraordinary array of choices for the sophisticated hedger or speculator: exchange traded or over-the-counter (OTC). The variety of traded options is enough for many purposes, but while these may provide deep liquidity, they may not give sufficient flexibility for every user. OTC options fill the gap and between the two every need can be catered for. OTC options have evolved in many varieties and it is proposed to mention here only the main varieties, some of which have transformed the choice of financial services produces for consumers in the High Street. For example, a capped mortgage may be obtained either by the individual buying a cap in the market, or the building society or bank entering into a substantial capped deal and using the size available to hedge a limited capped mortgage issue. Equally, investment products with a minimum guaranteed return could be arranged by buying a floor on interest rate, or even on equities. In the main, however, the more exotic options are used by banks, corporate and building society treasurers and fund managers to hedge specific risks or create specific products to be marketed to customers.

Exchange-traded options, often referred to simply as traded options, are dealt on either open outcry or electronic exchanges. The relative concentration of options into a limited number of instruments and maturities with the widest possible appeal helps to ensure optimum liquidity. Contracts can be used to build portfolios with good hedging ability at relatively low costs. Furthermore, the flexibility and liquidity are combined with almost no credit risk because the clearing house guarantees performance.

OTCs are much more flexible in currency, type and size, with market makers often able to tailor them to individual requirements.

◆ Premiums, initial and maintenance margins are more flexible and can sometimes be absorbed within the contracts. Commissions and brokerage, front end, exercise and delivery fees are not normally charged.

♦ Quotations, strike prices and transactions are not limited by exchange routines.
♦ Business is often done principal-to-principal by banks, allowing an individual service and pricing based on the bank's needs or opportunities and an understanding of the clients' needs and circumstances.
♦ OTCs may not be so liquid but they are tailor-made, especially in unusual currencies or maturities where liquidity is poor.

A major benefit of traded options and futures is their efficiency in providing high visibility and liquidity. Lack of liquidity could outweigh some of the benefits of tailor-made options, especially in terms of overall cost.

♦ Traded options also provide options on futures, stock market indices and individual stocks that are rarely available over the counter. Thus OTC options are mainly in interest rate and currency or related instruments.
♦ Exercising and closing out traded options is straightforward. Repurchase of OTC options may prove impossible or costly.
♦ The risks inherent in traded options are no greater than for OTCs and the associated risks (counterparty risk, settlement risk, negotiation and misunderstanding) are far less.

List of abbreviations

ALCO	Asset and Liability Management Committee
AMA	Advanced Measurement Approaches
APACS	Association for Payment Clearing Services
ARROW	Advanced Risk-Responsive Operating Framework
AUD	Australian dollar
AVC	Additional Voluntary Contribution
BBA	British Bankers' Association
BBAISR	British Bankers' Association Interest Settlement Rates
CAC	Collective Action Clauses
CAD	Canadian dollar
CCP	Central Counterparty
CD	Certificate of Deposit
CEA	Credit risk Equivalent Amount
CHAPS	Clearing House Automated Payment System
CHF	Swiss franc
CHIPS	Clearing House Interbank Payment System
CLN	Credit-linked Notes
CMO	Central Moneymarkets Office
CPSS	Committee on Payment and Settlement Systems
CSA	ISDA Credit Support Annex
DbV	Delivery by Value
DMO	Debt Mangement Office
DvP	Delivery versus Payment
DvV	Delivery versus Value
EAD	Exposure at Default
EC	European Community
ECB	European Central Bank

ECP	Eurocurrency commercial paper
ECU	European Currency Unit
EDS	Eligible Debt Securities
EEA	European Economic Area
EONIA	Euro Overnight Index Average
ERM	European Exchange Rate Mechanism
EU	European Union
EUR	Euro
EURIBOR	European Interbank Offered Rate
FATF	Financial Asset Task Force
FDIC	Federal Deposit Insurance Corporation
Forex	Foreign exchange
FRA	Forward Rate Agreement
FRABBA	Forward Rate Agreement British Bankers' Association market guidelines
FRCD	Floating Rate CD
FRN	Floating Rate Note
FRS	Federal Reserve System
FSA	Financial Services Authority
FSAct	Financial Services Act 1986
FSAP	Financial Services Action Plan
FSAP	Financial Sector Assessment Program
FSMA	Financial Services and Markets Act 2000
FX	Foreign exchange
GBP	Pound sterling
GEMM	Gilt Edged Market Maker
HKMA	Hong Kong Monetary Authority
IAIS	International Association of Insurance Supervisors
IBF	International Banking Facilities
ICOM	International Currency Options Market Guidelines
IDB	Inter-Broker Dealer
IMF	International Monetary Fund
IMRO	Investment Management Regulatory Organisation
IOSCO	International Organization of Securities Commissioners
IOU	I owe you
IPA	Issuing and Paying Agent
IPC	Interprofessional Code
IPMA	International Primary Market Association
ISA	Individual Savings Account
ISD	Investment Services Directive
ISDA	International Swaps and Derivatives Association
ISIN	International Securities Identification Number
ISMA	International Securities Markets Association
JPY	Japanese yen
LCH	London Clearing House

LGD	Loss Given Default
LIBID	London Interbank Bid Rate
LIBOR	London Interbank Offered Rate
LIFFE	London International Financial Futures and Options Exchange
MAS	Monetary Authority of Singapore
MLRO	Money Laundering Reporting Officer
MMI	Money Market Instrument
MTN	Medium Term Note
NCB	National Central Bank
NCIS	National Criminal Intelligence Service
NDF	Non-deliverable Forward
NOK	Norwegian Krone
OCC	Office of the Comptroller of the Currency
OFC	Offshore Financial Centre
OMO	Open market operations
OTC	Over the counter
PD	Probability of Default
PEP	Personal Equity Plan
PIA	Personal Investment Authority
PvP	Payment versus Payment
RCH	Recognised Clearing House
RIE	Recognised Investment Exchange
RTGS	Real Time Gross Settlement
SAFE	Synthetic Agreements for Forward Exchange
SCP	Sterling Commercial Paper
SDRCD	Special Drawing Rights CD
SDRM	Sovereign Debt Restructuring Mechanism
SEDOL	Stock Exchange Daily Official List
SFA	Securities and Futures Authority
SIB	Securities and Investment Board
SIBOR	Singapore Interbank Offered Rate
SPV	Special Purpose Vehicle
SRO	Self Regulatory Organisation
SSI	Standard Settlement Instructions
STP	Straight Through Processing
SWIFT	Society for Worldwide Interbank Financial Telecommunications
TARGET	Trans-European Automated Real-Time Gross Settlement Express Transfer system
UCITS	Undertakings for Collective Investment in Transferable Securities
UKLA	UK Listing Authority
USCP	US Commercial Paper
USD	US Dollar
VaR	Value at Risk
ZAR	South African Rand

Index

market, development of, 323, 324
market or dealing risk, 332
meaning, 324
nature of transaction, 324
operational risk, 333
trading purposes, use for, 242

D

Dealing
front-office activities, 193, 194
operations, internal controls over, 16-18
Deposits
certificates of, 29
long-term basis, on, 8
retail, 28, 29
source of funding, as, 42
source of, 7
wholesale, 137
Discount houses
implementation of monetary policy, use
for, 139

E

EU law
banking business, conduct of, 145
banking Directives-
Banking Consolidation Directive, 146,
149
First, 148
post-BCCI, 149
Second, 148, 149
Second Banking Co-ordination
Directive, 146
capital adequacy Directives, 149, 186,
187
credit institutions, for, 146
financial services-
Financial Services Action Plan, 147
further work, 147
Investment Services Directive, 146
single market, ensuring, 145
summary of Directives, 146, 147
Money Laundering Directive, 225
Eurobonds
calculations, 282, 283
characteristics of, 274

closing, 278
currencies, 275
current yield, 282
denominations, 275
distribution, 277
documentation, 280, 281
fixed-rate issues, 279
floating-rate notes, 279, 280
interest on, 275
lead manager, 276
listing, 282
meaning, 274
origination, 275, 276
primary markets, 275-278
repayment types, 280
secondary markets, 278, 279
proceeds of sale, 284
size of issue, 275
syndication, 276
term, 275
European Union
law. *See* EU law
role of, 145
Eurozone
payment systems, 198, 199
Exchange rates
arbitrage, 242, 243
Bretton Woods system, 3
cycles of, 3
European Exchange Rate Mechanism, 3
floating, 232
fluctuation in, 3
foreign exchange market. *See* Foreign
exchange market
risk management, 3
swaps, 242, 243
volatility, 3
Exchanges
dealing costs, 204
financial markets, intermediaries in, 190,
204

F

Financial futures
basic function, 336
calculations, 341, 342
change in shape of yield curve,
protection against, 340
clearing house, functions, 338

U

W